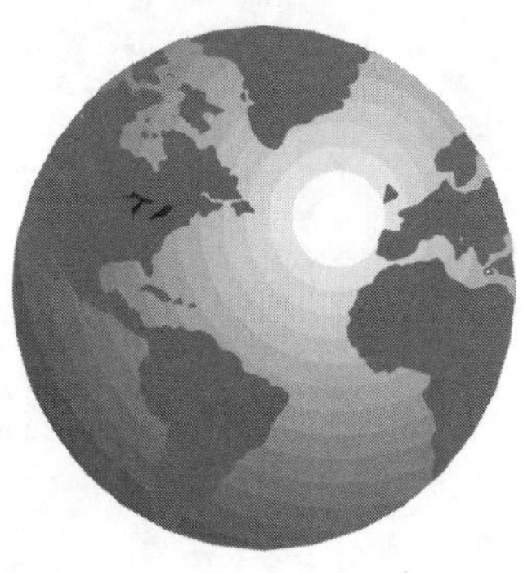

LETTERS FROM HOME

Loving messages from the Family

Kryon

Book VII

International Kryon Books

See [www.kryon.com] for more info

Spanish
Kryon Books
One and Two

Chinese
Kryon Books
One and Two

Hebrew – Kryon Books One, Two, and Three

International Kryon Books

See [www.kryon.com] for more info

French
Kryon Books
One, Two,
Three, Five,
and Six
(shown on this page)

Coming:
German
Italian
Greek

Danish – Kryon Book One

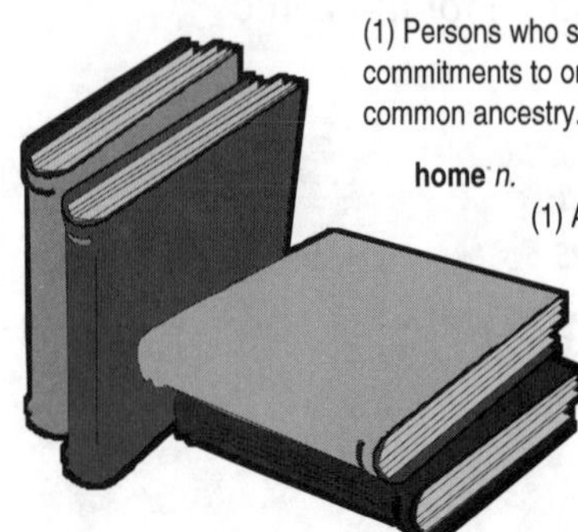

fam•i•ly *n.*

(1) Persons who share goals and values, and have long-term commitments to one another. (2) A group of persons sharing common ancestry. (3) Lineage, especially distinguished lineage.

home *n.*

(1) An environment offering security and happiness. (2) A valued place regarded as a refuge or place of origin. (3) The place where something is discovered, founded, developed, or promoted; a source.

LETTERS FROM HOME

Loving Messages from the Family

Kryon Book VII

Publisher: The Kryon Writings, Inc.

PMB 422
1155 Camino Del Mar
Del Mar, California 92014
[www.kryonqtly.com]

Kryon books and tapes can be purchased in retail stores, or by phone. Credit cards welcome.
(800) 352-6657 or EMAIL <kryonbooks@aol.com>

Written by Lee Carroll
Editing by Jill Kramer

Printed in the United States of America
First Edition—First Printing—June 1999
Second Printing—August 1999

ISBN# 1-888053-12-7 : $14.00

Table of Contents

continued...

Table of Contents... continued

Thanks!

Again my thanks to those who are part of the Kryon work, who give so freely of their talents and their energy, and who have helped me greatly in these past two years.

Garret Annofsky
Linda Benyo
Zehra Boccia
Jennifer Borchers
Robert Coxon
Norma Delaney
Peggy & Steve Dubro
Trisha & Winston Ellis
Janie Emerson
Jean Flores
Patricia Gleason
Louise Hay
Barbara & Rob Harris
Geoffrey Hoppe
Ann K. Hudec
Jill Kramer
Gary Liljegren
Jan Liljegren
Sarah Rosman
John Stahler
Marc Valleé
Martine Valleé

And, of course to **Jan Tober**, who has been at my side presenting the Kryon work from the beginning.

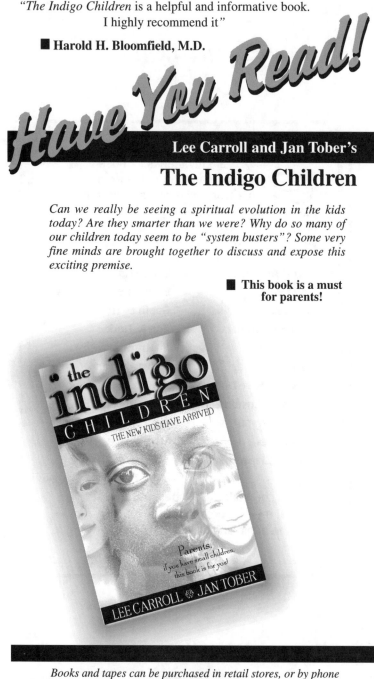

Preface

From the Writer

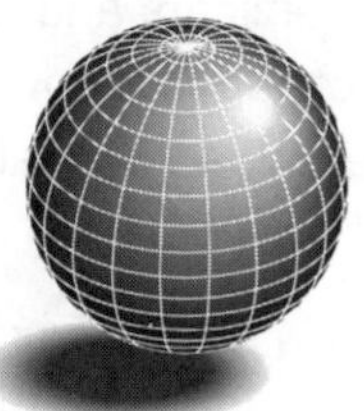

Kryon

Letters From Home
Kryon Book VII

From the writer...

Welcome to Kryon Book Seven, the largest of them all. I appreciate you! You probably think I say that to everyone, huh? Well, I guess I do, but it truly does not diminish my gratitude and excitement that you are opening a new Kryon book. I am pleased to have your eyes meet these pages, for it's the way I get to communicate personally with you.

As of this writing (5/99), it has been a year and a half since the release of Kryon Book Six, *Partnering with God.* I know I am speaking to many who have read all the Kryon works, and I wish there was time to stop life and meet each one of you. Many of you have attended the Kryon seminars and have personally met Jan and me, as well as the Kryon team. I know that you understand that I mean this sincerely. We indeed care about who is reading this material!

If you are completely new to the Kryon series, this book will still stand on its own. You don't have to go back and find Kryon Book One to understand what is taking place. I guess an author's favorite book is always the last one, but for those of you who are newly discovering the Kryon work and want some direction as to which books to read in what order, here is my recommendation. After you read this book, read Kryon Book Five, *The Journey Home*; and then Kryon Book Six, *Partnering with God.* After that (if you are not "Kryon'ed-out"), you can read the remaining ones, starting with Kryon Book One, *The End Times.* Although Kryon Book One is the oldest (channelled in 1989), it is still the overall best-seller of all of them, and indeed represents the beginning of the new energy messages.

Kryon Book Six, however, was probably better received than any Kryon-channelled book so far, when you measure the popularity within the first year of its release. With a demand that kept us scrambling for reprints (we printed it four times in the first year), it outsold any Kryon book for that time period.

Within these pages, I have decided to keep the format of Kryon Book Six. If you read and enjoyed that book, then this will seem to be an extension—keeping the flow of love and information growing right into the year 2000.

It was the end of 1997 when I promised myself that I would never again release two books at once. Kryon Book Five had just been released simultaneously with Kryon Book Six. Why did I do that to myself? Was I dumb or what? I thought back on all of it and said, "Hey, I'm in control of my life. I will spread out my work and not exhaust myself ever again doing two books at the same time."

Yeah, sure.

This book is being released simultaneously with the Hay House book, *The Indigo Children*. Good grief! I've done it to myself again [sigh]. Two books at once. How could this have happened? I teach synchronicity, so I "went with the flow," but I'm going to have to talk to my guides soon about what "flow" means.

Chapter 7 of Kryon Book Six was called "The Indigo Children." Never have we received so much mail or comment on any subject in any Kryon book. Jan and I were flooded with letters from parents, day-care workers, and educators saying, "Finally someone has noticed! What can we do?"

I tell you about this since many of you expected to find an expanded section on the Indigo Children in this new book. Instead, Jan and I set out in 1998 to research the subject, and we came with an entirely separate book about the Indigo Children. We were not specialists in kids, nor did we have any academic credentials, yet we seemed to be in the driver's seat in the discovery portion of the subject.

We called upon educators, Ph.D.'s, children's specialists, M.D.'s, authors, and regular parents to give us a "heads-up" on all aspects of the Indigo Children subject. We received what we needed right away. Not only were we able to qualify the existence of these new children through experiential testimony of the day-care workers and parents, but we were also able to get answers on what to do and how to do it. We even got some wonderful health advice regarding the Indigo/Attention Deficit Disorder (ADD) issue (many Indigos are being diagnosed with ADD...but are not). As I mentioned, the results of our efforts are now available in bookstores as part of the Hay House book called *The Indigo Children.*

The Indigo book is not a Kryon work. Okay, so you folks reading this know that the Indigo Children information came partially from Kryon channelling, the work of Nancy Tappe, and some other intuitives who had prophecied it. But we wanted the Indigo Children book to be as mainstream as possible. We wanted parents to be helped by the information and not be frightened by the fact that it might be a spiritual book—or, (gasp), a New Age book. So we are not calling it a "Kryon numbered book." If you are a parent of a young child, look for it. I think you will relate! (see page 8)

What's in these pages...

Again, most of this book was transcribed from live channellings all over the world. We let the most recent transcriptions of these meetings be the subject matter for the books. The most amazing, energetic crowds that Jan and I have ever seen were in Europe. Although we also went to Australia and Asia since our last book was published, our experiences in France topped them all. With thousands in attendance, the toning (intuitive singing) blew our socks off! When we tried to dismiss a huge group in Périgueux, they just sat there. Then they started singing to us! Perhaps someday it would be fun to present a chapter in a Kryon book just on our experiences.

Some of you are subscribers to *The Kryon Quarterly* Magazine. Again, we promised you that you would receive channellings months before anyone else would see them. Therefore, you might recognize some of the material in this book as having been published in the magazine (aren't you glad you subscribed?). Geoff Hoppe, our volunteer editor of the magazine, again gets kudos for his ability to publish a full-color international quarterly magazine—without any advertising.

Also, as before, I wish to mention Kryon's style. He often gives a loving congratulatory message in the first ten minutes of every channelling. It's quite powerful. Some of these messages are for new ears each time, but will be redundant if repeated over and over in these pages. I removed some of the similar comments, as the channellings are presented in this book to conserve your time. Sometimes core information is reiterated from city to city. I left in some of that duplication since we need to hear it presented over and over.

This book is the last Kryon work before the new millennium. Wow! Are you aware of the marketing related to the upcoming change? "They" are talking about everything from the end of the world to the end of technology to the end of the end—you name it! The entire subject of this book is *change*! I almost called it "Becoming Spiritually Y2K Compliant," but decided not to (aren't you glad?). Here is what is in this book:

Chapter 1 is very special. First, it's a short message from me (just seven pages) about what the New Age is. Do you have any friends who are worried about you, wondering if you have "gone off the deep end"? Ask them to read the first seven pages in the next chapter. It won't hurt them, and it doesn't evangelize the New Age. It's just an explanation to help them understand who we are. Here is a hint: They may not wish to hold this weird, spooky book, so just copy the seven pages and give it to them (I give you permission to right here). Read it yourself first, so you are comfortable with the fact that I am indeed speaking for you.

Next, did you ever wonder what Kryon's message is with respect to religion? Here it is. It might surprise you. The channelling is called "The Integrity of God." It's a plea to use spiritual logic to see the difference between what belongs to God and what belongs to Human Beings.

Chapter 2 contains the five-part series of channellings called "Letters from Home," which is what this book is named after. They not only explain who *we* are, but Part 5 explains the big picture. Very lovingly, Kryon gives us the channelling called "The Meaning of Life."

Chapter 3 is the power chapter. It speaks of transition. Not that all of them don't, but here are some specific subjects that will really hit home.

Chapter 4 is about the Earth. Can it really have consciousness? What did the indigenous people know that we can learn for the coming millennium? What is "shadow termination," and "the crystalline grid?"

Chapter 5 is the story of the 1998 United Nations channelling. Hold on to your socks! This one is perhaps one of the shortest, yet most potent, of any Kryon channelling ever given—and Kryon elected to give it in front of United Nations delegates.

Chapter 6 is tough. Here are some issues that some people would rather not hear about. Not only does it contain a channelling about some of the things that may be difficult for us, but also a testimonial from an individual who has lived it. I wanted you to have a balance regarding these issues—from both sides of the veil.

Chapter 7 is the science chapter for this book. We have a very special Kryon validation regarding nuclear waste, and after that, there are two very profound physics channellings regarding the energy of the universe called "The Cosmic Lattice."

So that this scientific information doesn't just "sit there," with everyone wondering what to do with it, we have included a revealing article from those who have discovered how to use this very energy to help us right now! The "EMF Balancing Technique" by Peggy and Steve Dubro is the first profound application of the Cosmic Lattice energy that we have seen. It's energy work at the highest level. We know that there will be more very soon, for Kryon has said so. This one is unique, however. It is so potent that even NASA wanted to know more about it!

Chapter 8 is an interview with an Israeli magazine called Haim Acherim (Different Life). I wish to honor all our Jewish readers with some specific information about their spiritual lineage. This interview gives me that opportunity, so I included it.

Chapter 9 is a section originaly presented in Kryon Book Six. This format represents direct Kryon answers to the most-asked questions that we have received through the mail and at seminars since the last Kryon book.

Chapter 10 is a compilation of some of the Kryon news, ways to get on-line with us, and a very special report regarding the miracle of Kryon on-line. The Kryon on-line internet web-site experience has reached tens of thousands of people. Our WebMaster, Gary Lilgegrin, has a "show and tell" message that may surprise you in its scope.

Thanks again for reading this. As you read what follows, I hope you will be able to feel some of the "love wash" that I felt as I sat before precious family members in many cities around the world when Kryon delivered those now-famous words:

Greetings dear ones, I am Kryon of magnetic service...

June 1999

"The Journey Home is the latest work from one of this reviewers favorite authors. It is also his best. Lee Carroll has given us a well-written book that flows like a mighty river. And that river takes us to places like truth, hope, destiny, awareness, and home!"

■ **Richard Fuller, Senior Editor**
Metaphysical Reviews

Books and tapes can be purchased in retail stores, or by phone
~ Credit cards welcome ~

1-800-352-6657

The New Age

Chapter One

The New Age

From Lee Carroll...

It's no accident that this chapter is first. I wanted this message to be the initial one in the book, and it's from me. You will be hearing from Kryon soon enough, but this is a very human communication. It's a long-overdue discussion of the New Age, and it is presented here mostly for those who are curious (as I used to be).

Perhaps one of your friends has asked you to read this portion of the book—to help you understand what they are "into" these days. Perhaps you are worried that they have joined a cult of some kind? You won't have to read any other part of this spooky, channelled book to understand your friend, and this information isn't presented to make you change your religion. Its purpose is only to inform you, and perhaps along the way, to eventually change your tolerance level.

So who is writing this? Okay, I'm the channel, and author of this book, but before I got "weird," I was a very logical 20-year audio engineer and "straight thinker." I still feel that I'm a straight thinker—just a weird one. Being an engineer does not automatically exempt me from free spiritual thought, and my intuition regarding spiritual matters finally won out over what I was taught from birth about God. It became very logical to me, even more than the myths of history.

Many hear the words "New Age" and have a whole bunch of predetermined, market-driven perceptions of what it's all about. Some immediately think of flying saucers, cults, astrology, tarot, alien autopsies, past lives, and hordes of people lined up to go to their psychic. I won't deny that many of these things play a part in the overall picture of the New Age, because they do. But first, let me give you some other perspectives.

Please identify the belief attached to the following: Jonestown; Waco Branch Dividians; Heaven's Gate (suicide cult that, in death, went to join up with a flying saucer behind the Hale Bopp comet); and a Denver cult that is in Israel right now (5/99) waiting for the millennium change so that their leader can die in the streets of Jerusalem and come back from the dead three days later.

Strange and head-shaking stuff, huh? The belief associated with all of these? Christianity. What? That wasn't your perception? The Jonestown and the Waco group were originally followers of Christian gospel preachers. The Denver cult in Israel right now is called "Concerned Christians." The Heaven's Gate folks were not New Age, even though it was reported that they were by all the news networks and national magazines. I guess when you commit suicide in order to board an invisible flying saucer behind a comet, you automatically become New Age! The facts show that the Heaven's Gate cult was a self-professed Christian group! Their web-site said as much, and on it they quoted the Bible, and Jesus. It was available for all to see for about a week after they left.

Why tell you this? Because obviously mainstream Christianity **isn't** at all like these isolated, dramatic groups. Mainstream Christianity has integrity, does not promote cults, and presents a very loving invitation to join a family-oriented, love-based religion. But the kooks are indeed there—big time.

The New Age belief isn't about cults and weirdos either, but since we also have our share—okay, more than our share—that's often the only press we receive. There is a reason why this happens, and why there isn't much resistance to this kind of reporting.

First of all, we are not evangelistic. So, if you are the skeptical person who has been asked to read this by a friend, know this: When you're finished, your friend isn't going to ask you to join anything, make a life decision, kneel down and meditate, go to a channelled meeting, get a reading, or even finish the rest of this book! They would probably just be happy if you told them that now you understand them a bit better—and love them more.

The New Age is not a religion, and there is no accompanying doctrine for you to study. It is, instead, a world philosophy. There is no central building that New Age folks have built with common contributions. In fact, there is no centralized control or headquarters of any kind. That's why we have no political clout to bring to bear against those who would ridicule us. We don't have an organization! We have no lobby in Congress.

There is no priesthood or ministerial program—no approved schools or even courses that graduate ordained New Age pastors. There are no elders or deacons, and no programs for teachers to be trained in the church. Oh, by the way, did I tell you that there is no church? That means we don't have any New Age parochial schools for children, with New Age teacher influences. We have no single person whom we call "leader," whom we can turn to for advice when things get tough. We have no sacred shaman, present or past.

There is nothing to join, nobody to follow, and no central book that explains what we believe! There are no regular meetings, no syndicated television programs, no ministries to support, and no rules to follow. Some cult, huh?

Oh yes—and there is no place to send our money.

Well, you might say, it sounds pretty wishy-washy. Yep. It did to me, too, until I realized what was happening. The New Age philosophy pulls upon an intuitive knowledge that we believe every Human alive possesses. And within this knowledge there is incredible singularity!

No matter where Jan and I travel on this globe, thousands of people come to our seminars who fully understand this "wishy-washy" philosophy as though all the centralized buildings and teachers were there! There seems to be wisdom at the cellular level that understands even some of our weirdest concepts. No matter what language is spoken, or what culture, or how many there are, the people somehow intuitively "know" what we teach. They "own" it, too. Almost item by item, our belief system has a group understanding as though it was all written down somewhere—inside.

You might say, "Okay, you just gave me a laundry list of what you are **not**. Then, what **are** you?"

We are a group of Humans with a philosophy that teaches that all of us go through life cycles. Indeed, this means past lives. We believe that there are no accidents, but rather challenges or lessons that we actually help create at some spiritual level. That means that we believe in **taking responsibility** for everything in our lives. A mainstream New Age believer would never join a cult, never follow a leader in a suicide, and never sit around blaming others for who they are. A New Age believer is aware that there is tremendous power within the Human Being. Self-Worth is taught, as well as how to work through fear and uncertainty. Human enablement is the key, and "intent to create positive change in our lives" is our mantra.

We believe that there are forces at work that can balance Humans using energy. We regularly use hands-on healing and energy work to balance others in order to help them heal. We pray for others, meditate for world peace, and strive toward attaining wisdom that will allow us to love one another no matter what.

Hey...what about the flying saucers? Even Shirley Maclaine talked about UFOs.

It's not a big deal. If they are there, then so be it. Following flying saucers and being abducted is not a staple of the New Age philosophy; in fact, most abductees are *not* New Age believers. Many of us believe that there is other life in the universe, and that there is a great chance that we even have some of their biological evolution. Pretty weird, huh? (By the way, scientists are beginning to believe that there is a good chance of "life exchange" from planet to planet through the visits from one astral body to another of comets, asteroids, and even meteors). We can't prove this any more than Christians can prove heaven and hell, or prove that the Pope is divine. I mention this as a comparison, not to pass judgment on another belief.

We believe that today's weirdness is tomorrow's science—perhaps even tomorrow's religious doctrine if someone finds out how to build a church around it. A decade ago, science said that God is dead and that there was no evidence of other life in the universe. Today (according to *Newsweek* magazine[see page 340]), science has "found" God! There is positive evidence that life could exist, and as of this writing, astronomers have discovered 12 planets outside our solar system! Yesterday's (1980) New Age weirdness has become mainstream science (1999). We believe that there is much of our "intuitive" teaching that will be validated over time, since it is happening all around us even as I write this.

We do not pass judgment. We believe that to "love one another" means tolerance of belief. We celebrate another's miracle within their belief system. We honor the pure search for God, no matter what course it takes or what the "name is on the door" of the building. Many New Age believers attend church regularly. To be in the New Age belief does not mean that you have to throw away your love for Jesus or Elijah or any other master, either (just in case anyone told you that). We are joyful when things are in balance, and we willingly join together with anyone in any religious belief system who will pray with us for a common humanitarian goal. We don't make others "wrong." We don't tell our believers that God smiles only on us. We encourage the search for the true essence of God!

We believe in taking care of our own personal spirituality as the catalyst to changing the planet. We do not believe that our work is to change others. Each individual will decide that for him or herself. Many who briefly look into our beliefs find it difficult to grasp, since there is no structure, no rules, and no doctrine. Some have called us the "church of what's happening now," a comical critique indicating that we float a lot.

Our "floating" attribute is that there is no man-made structure around God in our belief. It's not boxed into compartments that are easily followed. We feel that Humans are empowered to make grand spiritual decisions on their own. That is not like the religions of today, where there has to be a system. By the way, Jesus taught the same thing. According to the scholars studying the Dead Sea scrolls, Jesus was called "the wicked priest" by the Jewish priests of his time. This is because He told common folks that they were empowered (all by themselves, without all the religious ceremony of the day). He told them that they could be just like Him (Sons of God). That's what the New Age believers think, too—no big buildings or restrictive doctrines—only responsibility at the cellular level for all that is.

We believed in guides and angels long before the explosion of angel shops on the planet. Our channelling (the weird part) agrees with most of the predictions of the indigenous peoples of the planet. Ten years ago, our intuitive information spoke of the weather patterns that we are seeing out our window today. For decades we have given you unsubstantiated healing techniques. Suddenly, in this last year, many of them were validated through scientific study, as reported in the November 11, 1998, issue of the Journal of the American Medical Association (see page 373).

We also have a belief in the future of humanity that is far different from Armageddon, or the doom-and-gloom predictions of Nostradamus. We believe that what you are seeing in the world today is far closer to what we told you would happen than what others have presented in their fear-based scenarios. We invite examination of all this, but not to win you over—rather, to help you understand that perhaps there is a far grander and bigger picture of God than you thought. Perhaps Humans are grander than you thought. Perhaps we are more grounded than you thought.

Do you believe in an after-life? So does 85 percent of the world's population (according to an article in Time Magazine in 1998). So do we. That means that most people on the planet believe that Humans are eternal somehow. The New Age believer thinks that, too. We also believe that an eternal being is created in the *image* of God, and that perhaps this means we are *part* of God. We also believe that Jesus taught just that—that all humanity shares the equal image of God—divine, with choice, and very eternal.

So we celebrate you! We don't care if you join us—really! We teach that there is no heaven or hell, and that when we die, we pass over to our original spiritual state. We go home. We believe that we are all *family*. If you read the rest of this book, you will find that that's what the channelled information is about—*family*.

What do we want from you? To think like us? No. We ask you for your tolerance and understanding. New Age people who group together to meet and take spiritual responsibility for themselves and practice self-worth and forgiveness are not the weird, spooky folks that are "out of touch" with reality. We are not "off the deep end" or brainwashed. We are a spiritually unstructured group of gentle people, and we don't care if you believe what we believe. We are disappointed, however, if you fear us. Is your fear coming from your heart, or from what others told you? Without doctrinal judgment, we covet your love, and in return, we will have a bond that surpasses all doctrines, yet frees us both to have our own.

Let me close this discussion with an example that millions of people around the world saw in the form of the most popular film ever made. I don't know if director James Cameron knew of the metaphor that he created in the last scene of *Titanic.* I just about fell off my chair in the theater when I realized what he was doing. For those of you who didn't see the movie, I won't spoil it for you—but I have to tell you, the ship sinks (sorry).

Many who saw the film remembered that the last scene had something to do with an older woman standing at the stern of a modern research ship, about to throw something off. They forgot. Instead, the last scene is a metaphysical statement that ***we are all eternal!*** It shouts to all of us that after death there is a realization that "the play is over," and even the villains are standing there next to the heroes with smiles, welcoming home the one final member of the *family.* The entire cast was there—young, vibrant, and applauding the last one to come back home. What a statement! What love!

Thank you, James Cameron. Your cellular intuition gave us the ultimate visualization of what the New Age is really about. It's about loving each other. It's about being spiritually equal. It's about *family.*

That's what we are about.

Thank you for reading this!

In Love,

"The Integrity of God"

Channelled in
Salt Lake City, Utah

The Kryon Writings, Inc.

PMB 422
1155 Camino Del Mar
Del Mar, California 92014
[www.kryonqtly.com]

About what's on the next page...

The writing of this book is the ten-year anniversary of Kryon. He started channelling with me in 1989. I was timid (to say the least), and didn't publish the writings until 1993. By now, this is an old story.

It took me four years to "put it all together" and to have proof after proof that it was real. Such is the process of my brain, and even my spiritual logic. Part of what I had to do was justify what was happening to me with what I had been taught about God from birth. I had to "unlearn" and start over. All through it, Kryon only asked me to keep an open mind and an open heart. He told me that "truth will seek its highest level." Many times, when I could have gone either way in my torment over religious issues, Kryon would tell me that God is not religious! He would encourage me to "follow the love" when I asked him who was right. I only fully realized what he meant a few years later. Man is religious. God is Love.

Kryon has never before spoken of religion in a channelling. He has left much of that to me (as in chapter 6 of Kryon Book One, entitled "Jesus Christ"). Then he admonished me not to get into it. Leave it alone. Then he said, "Be still, and let the scrolls do the work." Evidently, the timing is about right for release of information in that area, and in conjunction, Kryon has given us his first message on what I will call "the problems and puzzles of the spiritual differences on Earth."

What follows, then, is Kryon's message about "The Integrity of God," given in a live seminar in Salt Lake City, Utah. That's a funny name for a channelling about world religion, isn't it? The word *Integrity* was used as a plea for us to start looking at the overview of who God is, what God is, and how we can deal with the differences. As I said in the preface, it's a plea to use spiritual logic to see the difference between what belongs to God, and what belongs to Human Beings.

This book does not proselytize. It does not call for you to change religions. Instead, it explains the precious integrity of God and asks you to "look around," understand, use your wisdom, and begin to really love each other.

"The Integrity of God"
Live Channelling
Salt Lake City, Utah

This live channelling has been edited with additional words and thoughts to allow clarification and better understanding of the written word.

Greetings, dear ones, I am Kryon of Magnetic Service. Let it go on record that this evening and this time together is a reunion! For as in the past family channels, this is a time when the *family* from this side of the veil flows to the *family* on your side. There are entities this very afternoon who are pouring into this place who know you by name—names that are sacred—ones that have always been. These names are etched, literally, upon the crystals in the cave of creation. They have the sacredness of contract. They belong only to Humans, and they represent *family*!

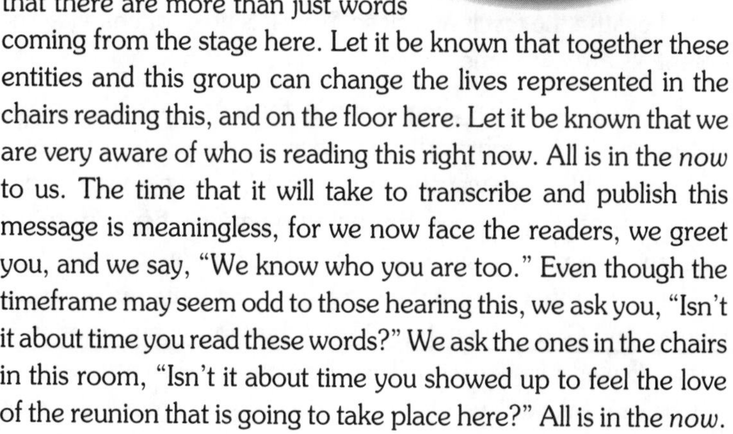

It's a sacred time, this reunion. The energy that pours forth into this place, and around those reading this, shows you the spiritual power of the Human Being. Let it show you that there are more than just words coming from the stage here. Let it be known that together these entities and this group can change the lives represented in the chairs reading this, and on the floor here. Let it be known that we are very aware of who is reading this right now. All is in the *now* to us. The time that it will take to transcribe and publish this message is meaningless, for we now face the readers, we greet you, and we say, "We know who you are too." Even though the timeframe may seem odd to those hearing this, we ask you, "Isn't it about time you read these words?" We ask the ones in the chairs in this room, "Isn't it about time you showed up to feel the love of the reunion that is going to take place here?" All is in the *now*.

Oh, the information will be special this afternoon—never presented before. Some subjects today have never been broached before, because it is time that *family* talks to *family* about sensitive things.

First, we want to tell you what is going on right *now*. We'd like to tell some of you why you feel the pressures you do (physically sitting in the chair), and the love that you do (emotionally), as the foot washing is beginning. You know that's why we come, don't you? We've said it every single time this reunion has taken place. All of these years that the entourage has come to honor and present itself before humanity, one of the things we have done is to bow before you and wash your feet. We have done it because you are the ones who do the work. Our entourage represents helpers—supporters—perhaps even past loved ones. For those of you who are feeling that now, it's real. We're here to figuratively walk between the chairs—to sit, perhaps, upon your laps. Some will hold you from behind, pushing upon the shoulders—because we miss you!

We talk to family now. We talk to those of you who know at an intuitive level that this is the last time that you, as a result of your contracts, have a passion to be here. The requirement is of your own making. Perhaps this is the last time. Here you sit, mostly Lemurians, knowing full well that you wouldn't miss it—this ending of the plan. No matter what happens, you wouldn't miss it. It's because the test is at a close. Now it is time for change. The potentials are awesome.

Let the foot washing begin, and let the message of the energy of this day be brought forth in a sacred way—in a way that is understandable—in a way that is balanced. We are going to broach issues that have never been brought up before—never from the chair that my partner sits in. For it is time for you to understand a relationship that we call the "awareness and integrity between Human and God." We define God as the *family*, but so often in this particular message we will use the word God in a way we have not before. We will use it in the way it is commonly used by Humans on the planet.

We speak now about the integrity of the relationship between God and Human. We're going to tell you what that means. It's time that humanity begins to understand what God *is*. That's a tall order, isn't it? Some Humans feel that they are in a "special" spiritual group—one that God smiles upon exclusively. Did any of you think that the true understanding and wisdom of the family aspects of Earth and the spiritualness of God would be sequestered to one group alone? Of course not. There is no sequestering of Spirit any more than there would be a sequestering of family love. Love is universal, and it is part of all of humanity. Every single Human who walks the earth is *family* and is known to us. Every single Human is loved beyond measure.

Humanity lives in a timeline that almost demands that it compartmentalize the aspects of spiritual work. This is because it does not work for men and women to put their perception of God in the *now*. You are working with historical value systems and cultural differences on this planet, where literally billions of Humans put together spiritual information and place it into systems that work for all of them. This is what has happened through the ages, and it is no surprise to God. Perhaps we have not said this before: Each system that has high integrity and searches for the "God within" is greatly honored. There is nothing grander than the search for the higher self. This search is all over the world, and it's *family* wishing to know more about family.

In this searching process, however, and within the scope of what has happened in history, Humans have decided to put God in boxes, usually with high walls. It is the linearity of thought that takes the interdimensionality and grandness of God and compartmentalizes it—and there are many compartments, you know. Within each box, there often is membership—acknowledgment of belonging; and within each box there is belief—acknowledgment of sacredness. Within each box, there is leadership and priesthood—acknowledgment of shaman-ship. Many times there are also rules to observe, created by Humans to help other Humans focus their spiritual quest. Sometimes there is high integrity, and sometimes there is not, but the boxes exist, and it no surprise to

God. The fact is that within the duality that exists within humanity, the interface between spiritual and humanity has come to this balance. That's appropriate.

But within those boxes, however, an interesting attribute takes place that is totally and completely created by men (humanity). Often within each *box* (spiritual or religious belief), there is a system that states, "*God smiles on us and only us. The thousands of other boxes on Earth are meaningless. Only pay attention to this box, because God smiles only on this box.*" In addition, to make it even more interesting, there are some boxes that also say, "*Don't look around! The other boxes are not for you! They are evil or deceptive and do not represent the 'true' God.*"

The Joy and Passion of Birth
Metaphor of Earth Arrival

There is a woman who gives birth to twins. One is a boy, the other a girl. It's an awesome thing, Human birth. At the cellular level the woman truly understands what is taking place. Even those who watch her tend to weep with the joy of the event. There is nothing like the mother who takes an infant to her breast and looks in its eyes for the first time. At the cellular level, there is an awakening of information. She not only feels the preciousness of the event, she knows who she is holding. It often becomes a spiritual reunion. She knows who they used to be. She looks into the eyes of a wise old soul as if to say, "*Welcome to the planet again.*" Oh, there is so much celebration when a mother holds her child for the first time. I know that many of you remember.

If you've ever been part of this situation, you almost can't help but weep with joy, because birth is joyful. It represents new beginnings—repeated lives—purpose—freshness—purity—innocence—contract—sacredness—pure joy! Indeed, it is a time for celebration.

Selective Love?

There is a woman who gives birth to twins. One is a boy, the other a girl.

Now, which one, do you think, will be her favorite, and which one is she going to cast off? "*Kryon*," you might say, "*she's not going to cast either of them off! These are precious souls. They are loved equally—beyond measure. They are her children—precious. They are family.*"

And you are right! The Mother/Father God does not smile only on one *box*, eliminating or frowning on the others. Humanity is humanity, and it's all family, loved equally and universally and unconditionally.

"*Why is it*," you might say, "*that many Humans would be so preposterous to think that God would smile only on their spiritual box*?"

This is where it gets good. Because, dear ones, they have had miracles in their *box*. They felt the love of Spirit in their *box*, and they absolutely have felt the validation of the "thickness of love" that has visited them. Therefore, God has smiled on them. Indeed, they are right! Family has loved them, and they have felt it!

I wish to tell you, however, that if they were to look with open integrity within some of the other boxes, they would find the same miracles! They would find the same integrity, and they would find the same "thickness of love." The process of Spirit is universal, because everyone is family. Naturally, the assumption by the leaders of many *boxes* is that because they received validation, it somehow devalues the others. Actually, the opposite is true. Each time Spirit validates a family member with a miracle from within, it actually validates the individual—not a religion.

What do you think Spirit thinks about the ones who sequester their belief in God and they say, "Only God smiles upon this one *box*?" What do you think Spirit thinks of them? I'll tell you. Spirit loves them without measure because they are family!

Do not misinterpret this message. This is not one of judgment. This is a message of information and a plea for tolerance and understanding about the way things work. The love of family is absolute. Which twin do you think is going to be favored, and which twin is going to be cast away? The answer is that both of them are going to be loved without measure. *That is the relationship of integrity between humanity and Spirit.* And that, dear ones, is the goal of the relationship between Human and Human—between box and box. This integrity of spiritual relationship is going to have to change in order for you to move into what we call *the New Jerusalem*.

This exact relationship was exemplified in the parable of the Prodigal Son, which was given to you so long ago. Look at it again. The son who "didn't get it right" was honored exactly like the son who did! The gifts of the father were squandered by the one boy. They were not used properly, and they didn't enhance the goal of the task, yet the son was welcomed back with open arms. This is what we mean when we tell you that the family is honored equally, no matter what *box* they claim to be in or what they tell their own about your *box*. It's the journey and the quest that is honored—not just if they "got it right."

It's time for humanity to emulate this parable. It is going to be necessary if you wish to move forward into a graduate Earth.

Spiritual Logic—What Do You Think?

Let me tell you about some of the *boxes* on this continent (the North American continent). This is given for you to examine in order to apply "integrity of Spirit" to the situation. Use your discernment about the family—then be your own judge of how much of what you are seeing is God in this presentation that follows, and how much is man.

There will be those who will tell you that God is love—and they're right. God loves every single Human Being. They are totally correct about the love of Spirit. God is the absolute "perfectness" of love. In the next breath, however, they tell you that every single Human Being—man, woman, little child (even the ones who are too young to speak the language) will be judged at the end of their lives. And each one is going to be sent to a horrible place and tormented by this loving God forever. They are going to be tortured for eternity because they didn't happen to find one key or one book or one information segment on one continent! If they happened to find it, then they are going to a wonderful place of love where they will be safe. It is because of this fact that the one box validates its evangelistic posture—to save as many as they can from eternal damnation from God.

Does that sound like Spirit to you? Is this the God who loves you beyond measure and Whose very name is *love*? Does that sound like home? Does it sound like the family who loves you like a newborn?

Humans create "boxes of spiritual isolation" to protect their culture. This is common, and it was a staple of the old energy. There is no judgment around what men (and women) have made from the core spiritual information, which is the love of God. This has been caused by the many years of men and women protecting their culture, and, dear ones, it has very little to do with God. It has a great deal to do with Humans. It's time to use your "integrity discernment." If it doesn't "ring true," then it isn't. If it doesn't sound like the way of the *family*, then it isn't. If it sounds and feels like a Human attribute instead, then it is.

Here is some validation that these boxes were created for cultural protection, for the next item does not make intelligent spiritual sense. Some in those *boxes*, who decided the rules, will tell you not to look at any other *boxes*, because the other *boxes* are evil! Again, they will tell you that somehow God only smiles upon them! Looking into the other *boxes* will get you in trouble. With billions of Humans on the planet, all created by God, they will tell you that only <u>they</u> are spiritually "correct." Does this sound like *family* to you? If God is the "Father," then why would He throw away most of His children and smile only on a few?

There is more, which shows you how fragmented your perception is of the family. Even within the main belief system in your continent, there are over three to four hundred boxes that we will call sub-boxes. Each one of them has their own set of rules—all unique to them, and supposedly the "way of Spirit."

Here is the biggest proof of all that cultural protection in the old energy was the process that created spiritual differences: The wars of this planet, especially the early ones, were often about God. Did you know that? It was about forcing the Humans in the other *box* to "think like yours." Which one was being smiled on, and which one wasn't? In the name of the love of God, Humans were slaughtered by the tens of thousands. Those who would not join the "correct" *box* were killed. Populations who were thought to be in an "evil" *box* were eliminated by those who belonged to the more powerful *box*. Does that really sound like the incredible love of God?

There is a woman who gives birth to twins. One is a boy, the other a girl. They are wrapped up, kept warm, and are precious. She looks at the two of them closely. Which one do you think she is going to throw in the trash because it doesn't believe a certain way? I'll tell you: Naturally she's not going to do that. Instead, she's going to love them equally, beyond measure, because they are created equal in her sight. Both have a spiritual essence. Both are angels! Both are on the planet with equality—with choice—members of the family.

Love One Another!

How can Humans develop this kind of equality of love? We have a set of instructions for you, something that you're going to walk away understanding. This is the key, and I hope you are ready: three words, and it's about time you heard them, "**Love one another**." With those instructions, and with pure intent, I'm going to tell you what's going to happen.

"Kryon, are you telling us that the cultural r planet are going to have to be wiped out of the religions of the world going to have to disappec order!"

We are not saying that at all. We understand the cultures of Earth. It is why there are nine main Kryon channels. One, on this continent, speaks to you with a lineage of your culture because he grew up here. The others have the same attributes on the other continents, speaking other languages. That's why there are nine. We understand culture. We understand that to be born in some cultures is also to be born into a belief system. That is not the way it is for you. This should show you that God (Spirit) understands what is happening at each cultural level. This is why there are miracles within each box! We honor and respect each independent "search for the truth." The fact is that this is your test! This is why you are here (as we have explained). Your searches are anointed.

The Need for Tolerance

Here's what we are saying can happen. There can come a day when the priests, wizards, gurus, monks, rabbis, shamans, ministers, and other religious leaders in **all** the *boxes* get together—not to form a coalition of faith, not to study each other's doctrines, not to alter their own beliefs, but to look each other in the eye and raise their hands together to God and say, "We are all family. We give the other family members permission to believe as they choose! Together, we choose love! Together, we choose tolerance."

That's what's going to have to happen as you move into, and pass, 2012—permission from one another to worship as you wish—never making the other box incorrect—never evangelizing the one who wants nothing to do with what you believe. It will require respect for the other's culture—respect for the other's interpretations—an overlay of spiritual growth and wisdom whose actions shout that you are loving one another!

"*Kryon*," you might ask, "*where is this predicted in Scripture...that of getting together like this?*"

It isn't. Scripture stops at 2012. Did you know that? You are about to write the next spiritual chapters of Earth, chapters written by new evolved Humans with a deep blue spiritual color.

"*Kryon, is this really possible? There are some cultures and belief systems whose doctrines are based on the fact that the others are unGodly. What are they supposed to do?*"

Look at your history. We just told you that men make the rules. All of those rules came from the writings of men. That means that new spiritual Humans can change them with the authority of the membership, and the changes can be looked upon as improvement on the individual doctrine. This is not new. Some of your religions have changed the "rules of God" within your very lifetimes.

As for it being possible? Yes! We expect it to happen, because that is where you are headed within your energy potential. Not all at once, but over time. It's like the energy of peace. When the benefits are seen, intuition knows what to do to expand it.

Other Items That Require Work

There's more—items that we have not spoken of before that are important for you to hear. Let us talk about the integrity of gender. There is a joke in this room and for those reading this: Every single Human Being is pretending to be a gender. You come in with the attributes of the gender, and you own that gender. You cannot even fathom being the other. Yet all of you have been! When you came in as the other gender, you owned that one, too. All of you participated in all of the energies that are precious, and the attributes that are known about each gender. It is on purpose, you know, that we have genderized humanity. It is one of the attributes that creates the cauldron of karma. It is often what creates the lessons and tests. Think about it. The gender gap is a play, and the joke is that you've been both, over and over and over.

Some Human Beings in certain *boxes* will say that one gender can only be priests. They will site historic precedent for this, and they will tell you that the other gender does not have what it takes. Even though God has no gender, and the family takes turns, they will tell you that one gender has more spiritual enlightenment potential than the other. Does this sound like Spirit to you?

There is a woman who gives birth to twins. One is a boy, the other a girl. Of course when she saw the girl, she threw it away! She knew that only a boy could be enlightened. Does this sound correct? Believe me, this is not from Spirit! For the boy and the girl are seen together as equal, and they are precious in the sight of the mother. And if you're understanding the metaphor in this particular case, the mother is on the other side of the veil. It's the entourage—the *family* that visits you now, who looks upon you as a genderless family—adored equally, each one. Of course the mother does not throw away the other gender! Who do you think made those rules? Use your new energy spiritual discernment. Was it from the *family*? Was it from God? Does it have integrity?

So we say to you that it is time that through the love and wisdom of Spirit, and the understanding of the integrity of a relationship that has spiritual integrity, you begin to understand how to **love one another**! Those who reach this plateau first will find that they will have energy given to them that is pure. They will have longer lives. They will have higher vibrations. They'll step into an energy where there is no thought given to any gender being anything but equal *family*.

But, there's more.

Some of you who are living with the gender you were born with seem to have come in with a passion only to destroy the other one! That's called "lesson." Let me tell you this: It takes both of you to create the lesson. Daughters, are you listening to me? It takes the abuser and the abusee to create the energy of karmic lesson! What are you going to do with the one you hated? The new energy is about solving this gender-specific issue. It's about completion. It's about love. The instructions?: **love one another**. Do you understand that it takes two to create the test? Perhaps that will give you an alternate meaning of "being in the right place at the right time."

It's important that you understand: There is no gender gap when it comes to God. God is both! What you may be feeling toward the other one is simply part of your lesson. It's why you came in with that feeling. By the way, one gender is actually designed to irritate the other regularly—but then, I don't think I had to tell you that.

Different Challenges

Here is something that you might have wondered about. We're going to call it "those who come in with high and low challenge." You planned to come in like you are, just exactly like you are. That is the contract. Some of you have come in with challenges at the cellular level that are profound. You come in with actual chemistry, predisposed, perhaps, to certain fears—predisposed, perhaps, to certain attributes of psychology. Some of you fear easily. Some of you depress easily. Some of you have come in to be with those who will actually enhance the test, aggravating it to make it worse. Some of you were born into areas that do nothing but aggravate your lesson. That is called a "cellular predisposition," and it has to do with challenge. Remember: You planned it!

There is a woman who gives birth to twins. One is a boy, the other a girl. She looked in the eyes of these two, and she was very, very wise. She could "see" that one had a challenge greater than the other, so she decided the one with the greater challenge must be hated and evil, and so she threw it away. Does this sound correct?

Blessed are those who come in with the gender of one physical type, but who have the consciousness of another. For they are indeed loved beyond measure, just like you. They are family! They have chosen a difficult challenge, and *you* are part of it!

God does not hate. All are *family* members, and it's time you understood, dear ones, that there are cellular challenges given to some of you that are great, indeed. Some have to do with those who have one physical gender and another gender of consciousness, and that's a profound challenge, right on schedule. Some in your own culture have decided that God does not smile on these individuals. They actually have told you that God deplores and hates them. Does this sound like the Mother/Father God? Does this sound like *family*? Who do you think made those rules long ago—and for what reason?

Here are our instructions to you—family—three words: **Love one another**. Understand what *family* is. Understand what challenge is, and understand that Spirit never gave you those things. These are manufactured by the rules of men and women in their own *boxes*—boxes with high walls of fear and distrust, high walls of cultural protection. It's time for them to understand the overview and to **love one another**.

Abundance

Here's a subject that you may not think fits into this discussion, but it does. Oh, it does. It's called the abundance issue, and we have not dealt with this much. We're going to define *abundance* for you. Abundance is sustenance. We've already described to you the bird that awakens in the morning that has no stash of abundance. It depends daily upon finding the food, and indeed, the small bird finds the small worm. It is sustenance. Therefore, it is abundance because it happens every day. It sustains each day. If you suddenly won a contest that provided you with daily sustenance for life, would you turn it down because it was not enough? No! It's a fortune! It's true abundance.

The hawk? Now, it has a bigger challenge. Rather than a worm, the hawk must find a rat. It, therefore, has a bigger sustenance bucket to fill. It seemingly has to have more abundance because it is larger. Yet, it is still sustenance, and even though one bird is small and one bird is large, the sustenance is totally relative to the bird. Both challenges take the same amount of spiritual energy, even though one seems to be far larger. Each effort is seen as the same because it is about the creation of energy through synchronicity. In truth, both birds use the same amount of effort relative to their sustenance challenge.

We give you this example for two reasons: The first is so you might understand that sustenance is abundance. The second is so you can fully grasp the concept that there is no difference between sustenance for one person or a family. The *amount* is not a consideration in the energy of creating sustenance.

It is the culture around you that places energy around your currency. Some of you have felt failure, depression, and fear over this sustenance issue. It is only sustenance, and when you learn how to work with energy, the abundance energy will also be learned. It's synchronicity for the day. How many of you work with energy? Oh, you say, *"I can heal people. I can create an energy here, and I can create it there. But I can't quite seem to make a living."* In effect, you've stopped yourself. You've decided that money is difficult, and the other is not. Some of you have decided that in order to be enlightened, you cannot have money! You cannot, therefore, have sustenance. It somehow isn't spiritual. What do you think God wants for you?

There is a woman who gives birth to twins. One is a boy, the other a girl. She looks at them with all the love that she can, and she says, "I hope for you, dear precious twins who are loved dearly, that you both will grovel forever on the dirt of the earth—that you will have nothing physical to call your own. I hope you go hungry, live in rags, worry a lot, and have a really hard time with money."

Does this sound like Mother/Father God—the love of family? No!

I want to talk to the lightworkers who have decided that they don't want to charge for their work. In your mind, perhaps, some of you have decided, "*This is the honorable thing to do.*" Let me ask you something: Do you remember being the monk? Do you remember the groveling in the dirt—the past lives where you gave away things? In those times, it was the spiritual thing to do. It fit your culture. Back then, you just gave and gave and gave. Now, that past-life residue has you thinking it's honorable again, but the energy of the planet will no longer support your past-life residue.

What you are really doing from a metaphysical standpoint is sending a strong message. You are going to "honor" yourself right into poverty, where you will be able to help no one! By deciding not to charge for your work, you just established the worth of what you do! Your body has heard it, and those around you have heard it, and the spiritual aspects of *you* heard it. You will indeed glean what you have put out, for you have just *told* everyone that what you do is worthless! Therefore, the intent is set, and sustenance will be difficult, for you have asked for that.

Here is what you should know: Sustenance is yours! It is abundance, and there is balance connected to it. In so-called high spiritual places, there's a saying that an abundant Human can never be enlightened—any more than you can put a camel through the eye of a needle. Here's a challenge for those of you who are academic. Go back and find that phrase at its original source. You'll find it in the scrolls, and you will find that the language of the time never said that! The phrase refers instead to energies of those times, whose meanings are far different. But, oh, how convenient it is for those in the *boxes*, is it not, to keep you poor? For it puts them in control, literally, of the abundance. Does this sound like family? Does this sound like God to you? Does this sound like a relationship of integrity from Spirit to Human? This is not a judgment. It is simply information for your examination—so that you might find the truth of where the love is.

Abundance, and all the things around the sustenance issue of living within your culture, will clear up when you really understand that you are worth it! When you *own* it and *allow* it, then *expect* it. It's when you also understand that those things that you came in with—which are precious, spiritual, and meaningful—can actually be used to help other people. Ask for an exchange if you feel there is value. If what you have is worthless, then don't. Remember, there can be barter, and there can be energy swaps as well. It doesn't matter if you charge for it in the traditional sense or not, but no longer feel you have to give it away. Establish the fact that you are worth something and that there is value. Then watch the others line up to exchange their value for yours. This is called energy balance.

There is synchronicity in abundance and in value exchange. We have spoken of it in the past—the movement of chi itself is designed to bring balance in all areas, including sustenance and abundance. It is time you understand that this new kind of "abundance thinking" is honored by God. It is all part of the integrity of Spirit—the balance in all things that you do.

There is a woman who gives birth to twins. One is a boy, the other a girl. The woman looks at her children, and of course, says, "I want for you rich, abundant lives. I never want you to be hungry. Each day will bring sustenance. I'll be at your side as long as you live. As long as I live, I'm here to help. I'll do anything I can, I'm your parent." This, dear ones, is your family. The integrity of Spirit looks at you in the same way.

Let it not be lost on anyone here, what the guides are for, and what the family is for. Because we stand beside you and we walk with you through your life, we help create the synchronicity. When you take self-worth and finally put it upon yourself—when you say into the mirror, "I AM THAT I AM"—when you start to place value on yourself, then abundance will start flowing into your life.

Competition—an Old Energy Concept

There's one final item that we would like to discuss. One lightworker meets another. They realize much to their horror that they're working on the same thing. What they thought was "their" energy or their project only is suddenly being seen in the other as well. So what happens, do you suppose? One decides to get ahead of the other. After all, they can't work together—one has to go.

Plans are made to make it difficult for the other, perhaps even to discredit the other. "*Oh, I'll know what we'll do. We'll call the other one evil. That'll do it. That will create fear, and many will run the other way. Then we can have our work and our ideas to ourselves.*"

Does this sound harsh? It is a fact. It is an old energy concept that remains ingrained in the old cellular structure. It says to you that there must be a winner and a loser in all things. The thought that both could win is not a consideration—and this odd assumption is with you today, even among lightworkers.

There is a woman who gives birth to twins. One is a boy, the other a girl. They are precious, loved beyond measure. She watches their lives and sees that they are both developing something artistic. Indeed, they are fighting over the crayons and brushes. So, of course, the mother decides that only one can be an artist, and she denies the other access.

Again, does this sound reasonable within the scope of the love of family? No. What you just heard (and read) is not the reaction of a loving family. Instead, it represents what a competitive rule of humanity used to do in a competitive energy. It represents an old energy way of thinking—as though the other lightworker might somehow diminish the work of the first—simply because he is doing the same thing. It shouts that there is fear about not having enough of something—or that there is a limit. It assumes that two cannot have the same thing—and it does not celebrate the true consciousness of the love of family for family.

When the mother saw that the children were both interested in the same thing and fighting over the same tools, do you know what she did? She went out and got another set of tools! She let them grow together, and the two children together created five times the energy that one alone would have done. Lightworkers, are you listening? When you find the one who seems to be in competition with you, let it be known that there's synchronicity around this. What do you have to give them? What do they have to give you? Together, perhaps—existing together on the planet doing the same thing—you might have five times the energy created because of the integrity of Spirit that allowed them to also have what you had. Again, this has to do with balance and the movement of energy. Watch what happens when you share with them what you have, and you both exit to your respective lives—both with a balance that neither had before. It's this wisdom of a new paradigm of working that will create additional synchronicity and abundance for both. **Both win! Both are enhanced. Both are family**.

This exact situation also has to do with the new paradigm of working with the portion of the world that is Islam, that is Christian, that is Jewish, that is Buddhist, that is Hindu—and all the systems in between, including the indigenous of the earth. What are they all about? They represent the individual search for the Love of God. They represent a cultural quest to find the God within. They are all about family! What are we asking of you? That someday there can be a new consciousness that has all systems coming together in one room, and raising their hands together proclaiming: "We love one another!" We have our own ways, but the other is no threat. We honor the other, and we honor ourselves. It's time for the walls of the boxes to be lowered. We are family.

Let me tell you who else is in that room. It's the one who calls himself/herself, "New Age." It's the one that calls himself/herself "metaphysical." For they are not in judgment, either. They are right alongside all the others, letting each belief exist, not in competition, but in celebration. All join together saying, "Isn't it great, finally, that the family has the option to love another—to bring down the walls of the boxes?" Impossible, you say? The actual grid of the planet has now changed enough for all of this to be manifest through the cellular shift of humanity—but it will take conscious intent. Perhaps those of you hearing and reading this will help it along? What is your intent?

There is a new wisdom on the planet, even though you might wonder sometimes when you watch the old and new energies battle it out in these last years before 2012. The balance between the old and the new is profound, and there will indeed be sparks as it settles the differences and decides where the balance should be. Do you remember when we told you in 1989 about the potentials for chaos in 1999 regarding unbalanced world leaders? Look for it in past transcriptions. [See page 303]

Potentially, the dictators will slowly die out and be replaced by the potentials of choice for their countries—but they will go down "swinging." The old energy will not die easily. The walls are thick. The tribes that fight between themselves now will have the opportunity to draw new borders right through existing lands that haven't changed for hundreds of years, and they will begin a mending process instead of one of annihilation. These are the potentials—not certainties. These are your challenges, for unlike any other time, right now the time is ripe with your ability to make a profound difference. Your intent is the key.

You know what could happen? It's called Peace on Earth. Nothing can get in the way of a planet whose Humans have learned to love one another! It's an old message, is it not? You can find it in Scripture, and you can find it in the sacred writings that are very, very old on many continents. Because that particular message was given to you, dear ones, thousands and thousands of years ago in many places at once. It has not changed. It will not change. That is because your family does not change. The love is absolute. The difference between then and now is that the "family on Earth" *has* changed. You now have the power to create something that was always elusive before—true tolerance, the ability to tear down the walls of cultural protection, and the beginning of world peace.

There is a woman who gives birth to twins. One is a boy, the other a girl. They are both loved beyond measure. They are a piece of the whole of the Mother/Father. They are family. That's who you are—a piece of God. There are no favorites, and the family does not smile on one and not another. For all are equal in our eyes—all with great gifts waiting to be manifest into abundance and peace. Like the mother at birth, we hold you in our arms and say, "*Welcome to the planet again.*"

It will take the wisdom of a shaman to sort out the overview of what is really happening on the planet in the months to come and the years to follow. Many will follow a path of "shadow termination" [a concept of cellular memory of the former end of the Planet—one that leads many to "go with the old"—See page 276]. Many will never see the potentials that we speak of, and will only see the way things were. That's what choice is all about on Earth.

Remember the new mantra of the times: "Things are not always as they seem." Today's seeming setback is tomorrow's learning. Today's hurt is tomorrow's healing. The fact is that today's potential is far grander than anything you every have seen as Humans. This house called Earth is in renovation—and much will have to be torn out to allow for the new to begin.

To get you through this?

"Love one another."

And the walls will come tumbling down.

And so it is.

Kryon

Letters From Home

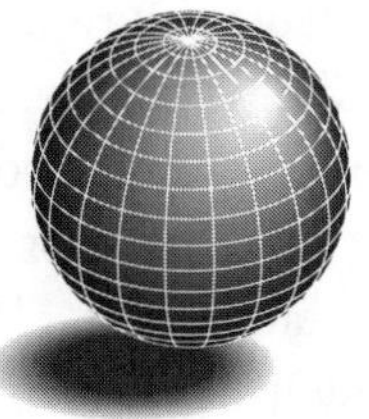

Chapter Two

Love

"Love is the most powerful force in the universe. You'll find it in the smallest particles of matter—in the space between the nucleus and the electron haze where it's thick with divinity! It is the stuff that you're made of. It has power! And when you release that power, there is *nothing* that can touch you. There is no evil or darkness on this planet that can get close to you, because you've claimed the energy of who you are. The angel that sits in that golden chair in your life, the one that has your image, is activated when you give intent for this love to permeate your being and create peace. The "I AM" begins to show itself, and meld with the Human."

Kryon

From Kryon Book Six
Chapter Three
"*Peace and Power in the New Age*"

"Attributes of the Family"

The Family, Part One

Channelled in
Idaho Falls, Idaho
and
Sydney, Australia

The Kryon Writings, Inc.

PMB 422
1155 Camino Del Mar
Del Mar, California 92014
[www.kryonqtly.com]

"Attributes of the Family"
The Family, Part One

Live Channelling
Idaho Falls, ID & Sydney, Australia

The live Channeling that follows is part one of five sessions concerning "The Family" as Spirit sees us. It is a transcribed combination of two events on two different continents...with the same message...given live, two months apart.

Greetings, dear ones, I am Kryon of Magnetic Service. For the next few minutes there are some of you who must get used to the sound of my partner's voice, as the meld takes place, and some of you will actively wonder how it is that such a thing could be—that the consciousness and the message from the other side of the veil could come through a Human Being. I'll tell you where the proof of that is: Those of you who wish will receive change during this time, and the energy in this room and in those reading and understanding this will change. Some of you will feel the heat that is generated from the energy in this room, and some of you will feel the pressure of love as we come in and walk, literally, between the chairs and even around the space where you are reading from. For this is as real as it gets, and we tell you that this experience that you have given intent for (permission for this visit), creates energy around you. All it takes is the *intent* or the Human Being.

Your *intent* allows for a visitation of the "family" in an area that is precious and special. And when we tell you, dear ones, that you are loved beyond measure, there's never, ever been a time where that was more profound. For we are speaking now of the "family" that comes into this place by your chair and visits you now. We're talking now about the entities on the other side of the veil, whose names perhaps you've forgotten because it's been a while since you were in that place. This is a visitation from Home! The information that comes about during this time comes from family, *family*! For in this room, and for those reading this message now, not only do we have the entourage and the consciousness of those who love you and have messages for you, but we also bring with us the consciousness of those who lived here before and then removed themselves by choice—to be here and have their energy available to visit you — and you know what I'm talking about.

We're going to speak about the attributes of the family as we see them in just a moment. But before that, we wish to tell you why it is that we know this room so well, and even the place where you have chosen to read this. You think you came to see us, didn't you? You think that you sat down to read this at a chance moment? Maybe you wanted some wisdom, or maybe some knowledge? Well, we are going to tell you that this "meeting" of ours has a huge potential energy around it. You had an *appointment* to be here! I'll tell you why you had this appointment. You see, we knew you were coming! This has nothing to do with predestination. It has to do with potentials and possibilities and energy within your consciousness that brought you here. We know the synchronicity that allowed for you to know of this meeting, or to be reading these words. We expected your presence where you sit and where you stand, or where you lay. We absolutely know *who* you are, and we know your name. We know your name because *you are family!* We are filled with honor for your name, no matter who you are—reading in belief—in disbelief—it doesn't matter.

We are here to tell you that you are loved beyond measure—that there is a purpose for your life — and that your very existence on the planet was known, planned for, and is precious and sacred! Long after this meeting between us is over, you may think about these things: "*Is it even remotely possible that there is more to life than just being and doing?*" We say to you that with intent to discover more, you're going to find out about the spiritual seed that sits inside, which is grand and huge. You're going to find tools that are practical—that are going to give you value for day-to-day existence. You'll find peace where there seemingly has been none—understanding and wisdom for intolerable situations that exist in your life—solutions to the unsolvable, and an overview of Human life that allows you to finally relax, for all is in proper order. You may create an inner knowing that says, "*I belong here. There is a reason and an overview that is far greater than I ever realized before. I'm a piece of the family.*" That's the realization that you can have.

And, of course, that means that along the way there will be solutions...solutions as my partner says, that may come "through the back door," but they're there, since you created them. What is the secret that you carry that you have not told anyone about? The secret that gnaws at you, or that you fear. You see, we know what that is. That's why we love you so much. You think you have to carry that burden alone? You're never alone! *You are never alone*! You have the power to vaporize any problem! Take the negative of what's in there and balance it with the positive of the divinity inside, and together those elements are going to make an energy that is called "solution through love." There is no problem in the lives reading this and hearing this that is not solvable! It only requires pure intent to let it be solved. Pure intent releases great power, and this is the enabling of the Human spirit, and that's what we speak of in this series of messages.

Oh, dear ones, let the energy that is open and flowing, released through the crack in the veil of this day, provide awareness that this is a real energy that is being dispensed to this group of readers and listeners. We are going to wash your feet, and for those who will allow it, it will be a slow process that starts now and lasts until we're done—one foot at a time. The significance of the washing of the feet is honor for the Human Being. Over and over we have told you this, as the family comes to see you. Perhaps you wish to know why we knew you were coming? Because you gave *intent* or it sometime ago. Guess who has been here, waiting on the other side of the veil for the potential of your seat to be filled, the one with your name on it? Oh, not the name you think you have, but the name you *really* have—the one I know as *family*! I'll tell you. Do you know what it means to us to visit you? You think you've come to see us, but you're wrong! You're wrong. Our honor is that we could visit you for the brief moments that we come to hug you, to communicate with your guides, and to give you the seeds of understanding and the gifts you've asked for. We will honor your intent to change a life, perhaps with your potential. It's time. That's why you're here, you know. We've been waiting for you. This is a special place, where you are sitting. We've been here, waiting for you.

These "Letters from Home" will be given in five parts, across two continents. The "family" is the family of Earth! It represents the family of Humans…not of countries. Many of you hearing and reading this now will hear and read the other information in the other parts later. "Later" and "tomorrow" are interesting concepts to us. Your linear time makes you "wait," but we are experiencing it "now." Dear ones, there are those right now reading this information in what you call your future, who are experiencing life changes. We know the potentials—and we know what is happening, because they are discovering this information for the first time. We know their names, too, because they are also *family*! That's what the "now" is about. We also see something else: We see profound changes in those in this room and in those reading this, who are going to affect other lives. This is why we face you off and say, "You have no idea of your power as Humans. You create a consciousness shift—countries changing—Earth shifts, others responding to your consciousness, and the alteration of physics. These changes are all around the Human Being, for the Human is the center. The Human has always been the center, and we want to tell you some of the attributes of the center. We want to talk about the *family* right now.

Part one of this series is going to be called "The Attributes of the Family." We're going to present four other concepts later, and they will be: "The Tasks of the Family," "The Awareness Power of The Family," "The Renovation of The Family," and "The Meaning of the Family." Some of the information will be similar and repeated for emphasis as we go.

Created Equal

Here are some of the attributes of the family members we wish to speak of. We have spoken of this before, and it's important that you hear it again: All Humans are created *equal*. Now some of you will say, "*That is not so, Kryon. All I have to do is look around! Obviously we're not equal.*" If that's your answer, then you're not looking at things correctly. You are not seeing *family* members like we are. Oh, the biological exterior is far different, so that's not the equality we speak of. You've heard this before, and we're here to tell you again, that there is no class society here in *our* family. Look at who speaks to you now from his chair. This energy, which we call Kryon, is a brother/sister energy. There is no hierarchy, gender, and there is no class structure. I'm telling you that the equality is the *spiritual center* of who you are. Every Human Being born into this planet has an angel inside. This angel has the same splendor, and it has the same color identification light-body as the highest of the high. It's from the same place—it has the same purpose—it is equal with all the others, and it has your name. It's part of *you*! Think about it. For those who feel a lack of self-worth, or feel that there is nothing one person can do, or feel "less than," it's time for your revelation!

If you will allow it at this sitting, we're going to pass you a gift. The gift is the overview that you *belong here*! The gift is the overview that you are equal to the highest spiritual being that you can imagine. Here is something I have told you before in channel after channel: You and I have seen each other before! Your brother/sister (Lee) sits before you now and speaks to you again in the same kind of love as when I saw you last time in the Hall of Honor. The voice that is his says, "It is so good to see you again." Ours is an interim visit, a visit accomplished while you are doing the work in duality. Oh, I know it is a stretch of the belief of the intellect to think for a moment that this could really be happening, but we're telling you that the proof is in the energy being developed here, and the proof is in the aftermath—the change in your life. For the shift of energy is at hand even now for those giving intent as they sit in their chairs...some hearing... some reading...some feeling. The family is created equal! And if you're prone to worship, then you better start looking in the mirror. For we say in the most loving sense, "Look inward, and find the sanctuary that some of you have been looking outward for all your lives." There is nothing more sacred then what's inside the Human. If you could see yourself as I do, you would be astounded at the beauty.

There's more. Although difficult for you to conceive of, you are part of an interlacing wholeness that is incomplete without you. This is an interdimensional concept. It says that Spirit is made up of a vast number of parts, and that each part is critical to the whole. When combined, the individual parts make the whole complete. Each part is equal, and is known by all the other parts. The parts cannot exist alone, and they belong to the whole. For you, this is *family*. It's a kind of family that is far beyond your idea of Earthly family. Your "real" family is awesome! It is a multitude of angels who know you, and you know them. I am one, and therefore I am just like you. I am family, and I am one of many...just like you. The difference, which is impossible to make you understand, is that your energy makes Spirit complete! Without the one, the whole is not whole. This concept is the actual meaning of the "I AM." The I is the one, and the AM is the whole. Claiming the "I AM" affirmation is saying to the Universe, "My existence *is* God. God *is* my existence. God, the collective, is my *family*! That's attribute number one: You indeed are all equal.

No Central Control on Earth No Center in Your Dimension

Another attribute of the family on Earth is that you are all from the same "place." This family we talk about is the family of Spirit. It's me and it's you, and it's all of those from a place, if you can call it a place, called the "Great Central Source." It's not a place at all. You have no word that could possibly come close to what it is. It transcends time. The word place would indicate a three-dimensional thought. Place would indicate a height, a breadth, a width, even a moment in time—it is none of those. Oh, a better word is home. You see, there is a "feeling" in connection to home. That's where family exists, you see. That's the "place." It has no coordinates in 3D or even in 4D. It has energy. It has feeling. It even has color. But it is not what you think. It is a consciousness with construct.

There is something else, something my partner speaks of in your 3D: The New Age has no central Earthly control. There is no building, no priests, not even a central book—and no "place" to contribute your money to! The belief system you have on Earth relates to *family*! It does not need a hierarchy of authority or a center. Its source is an energy string (or lattice) between each Human Being—making up the whole. Therefore, the whole is also the center!

Spirit works the same way. There is no central portal. There is no place on or within the planet that you could say is the source for all spiritual power. Again, this is inter-dimensional, and it's difficult for my partner to explain. The Human desires structure on a 3D level. You wish to see a hierarchy of levels in everything. Many times you "see" things from the inside out. Sometimes you envision spiraling circles, or circles within circles, indicating perhaps, levels of emanation of control, authority, and importance. Every Earth organizational structure demands something on this order, but for the *family*, none of that exists. None of it exists. You are part of a consciousness that existst only as an entirety (a whole) with all the parts active. Therefore you are a "piece of the center," and you are always active as part of the family. And that is why we can say to you that the center is always available by going inside. We are going to explain more about this "center" in the fourth attribute.

Awareness Creates Power

The first attribute was about being created equal. The second one was that there is no center, and the third one is about personal central awareness. Let's talk about your attribute as a family member, and as a Human Being.

Some of you might ask, "*Kryon, where is this spiritual seed in my body? What part is it? Top? Bottom? Where should I point when I want to indicate the Golden Angel that sits inside?*"

I'll tell you where it is. It exists as an awareness that is the basis of the very molecules in every single cell of your body. Your biology is special. The spiritual part of you is married to the biological part of you physically. Many are beginning to discover where it is, and it should be no magic to you or revelation to you that it is in the code that you call DNA. What this means, dear ones, is that your spiritual blueprint of existence is in every single cell—equally. Part of the code of your DNA is the special meld that combines your spiritualness with your biology. This is the essence of your duality. It creates the duality, which hides who you are. It is by design—your design, and it is active and working in everyone hearing and reading this.

Here is the news we give you about your biology: Every single cell has the entire spiritual picture imprinted upon it. In other words, there is full awareness and knowledge stored in every cell. This goes far beyond the old ways of thinking where you were "ignorant until enlightened," or that somehow energy came from above, flooded you with wisdom, and you walked away a better creature. The center (as you wish to see it) is within your cells. Every single secret—the full blueprint of spirituality of who you are, what your colors are, what your name is, what you "look" like, and why you're here—is in every cell of the body. Every cell of the body! So it's exactly opposite of what some of you have believed. As the revelation occurs to you, and you claim the new gifts with intent, you become more spiritually aware. What is taking place is that this "secret" information is being slowly released for you, by you. Is it any wonder that we tell you that in the "ascension status," you must "take the biology along"? That's where the secrets are!

This may give you an entirely different concept about miracles and healing. There is no outside source that comes in and visits you when you heal yourself, or when you receive a miracle—did you know that? No outside source. Instead, there is revelation through

balance and awareness—a true wholeness that heals you miraculously. All healing and miracles come right out of the middle of you! They come from the very essence of your cellular level, as if by "magic." Let me define that "magic": It's the sacred inner self—that higher part of you that deals with interdimensional concepts, which knows the highest parts of physics and biology. It's the part that can create matter and knows the greatest secrets of love. This is the part that is able to perform miracles within your body—through your intent—through your complete knowledge, and it's the part that has always been there. So often your quest for God to grant you a miracle is actually *you* asking your own cellular structure to create one.

"*So, Kryon, where do healers come into this picture? I'll bet healers don't like this new concept about our own internal power doing all the work*," some have asked.

This is not a new concept. Every wise healer will tell you that *healers don't heal—they balance*. The job of every healer on the planet is to help Human Beings balance themselves in order to create health. Health is then created *by the Human*, from the internal spiritual power of the Human's higher self. The healer's job is to give the Human processes, facilities, equipment, substances, and information that enables balance. Think about this the next time you sit in front of a facilitator. Healing takes two! Healers create the "push" to help you balance. You give permission to let this balance take place, then *you* create the actual healing yourself! This is the power of a Human's pure *intent*. How's that for a revelation? That's awareness. Did you ever consider giving ceremony around the healing process? Perhaps you might entertain the thought. It will enhance the healing. The love you create through the ceremony of celebration of the healing as it is being created is a catalyst for great energetic healing!

You want to know how awareness manifests power for the planet? Let me give you an example—one that is happening right now. Awareness at the cellular level is released automatically with spiritual, pure intent, and that should be no surprise. When a

Human Being says, in all honesty, "*I want to know more about who I am and why I'm here*," some of you should be able to hear a great fluttering of wings! There is no quest like that. There is none like that! Many of you are aware of how this happens. It's facilitated in many ways. Some of you do it automatically because you're there in that brilliant spiritual light, and your karma (past-life potential carried into this life) is clear. Some of you only do it after you are spiritually and physically beat down to your lowest ebb—sometimes by circumstances around you and sometimes—by another specific Human. In either case, it is by design and with your permission. In the next set of teachings ("The Tasks of the Family"), we will examine more closely the "gifts" given to you in precious love by other Humans in their actions, and many times in their deaths. It's one of the greatest gifts there is.

When Human Beings give permission to become more aware of who they are, they are using *pure intent*. This intent is a catalyst for an energy shift. You might think this energy is only about *you*, and those entities around you, as we have channeled before. Actually, this energy is released in several ways, but one of them flows to the planet itself. We have spoken of the energy balance before, and how the actual act of becoming enlightened creates energy transfer. Guess why your planet is suddenly more active and less predictable than usual? Guess why the magnetics are moving around? Guess why the potentials I have given you as far as eight years ago are now upon you. *You have changed Earth!*

Your simple awareness of your spiritual selves has actually begun the planetary shift necessary to complete this picture of an enlightened Earth. Have you seen any changes in your politics lately? Didn't we tell you to look for it? Didn't we tell you that an aspect of Human consciousness change was that there could be *no secrets*? How about your economy, and the efforts to "pull together" to facilitate worldwide balance? We spoke of every one of these things, and now they are here! This is *you* releasing your energy to the planet.

There is awesome power in the realization of awareness by Humanity! We will speak more about this in a separate channeling (the third part).

Your Star Seed Lineage

I want to tell you an attribute of the family that's sacred. You are *all* from the same source. In the second attribute in this channelling, we were quick to tell you where the source *was not.* We told you to look inside, and told you that the source isn't a place in your reality, yet it *is* in ours. If you could identify it, you would name it "The Central Source." Each of you has this sacred lineage—one that identifies you as family. I can face you and tell you, dear ones, that there was no beginning of your entity, and that there will be no end, and you will not understand or believe me. The energy of your origin is far larger than Earth, and carries with it tremendous cellular awareness. That's why we are calling these communications "Letters from Home." There's a reason for you to be here—a reason that hides very, very well. It hides to enable you to do the job you have come to do.

I want to tell you more about this sacred lineage. Here is something we have told very few others: Your planet is populated *only* with entities from this place we call the Great Central Source. That is a metaphor, there are no words that would be grand enough to tell you what or where this is. As we also indicated within the second attribute, the word central is wrong. Source is also wrong in your language. Actually, the only English word that is accurate is great! "Great Central Source" would indicate to you that there is a center, but the "center" is as big as the whole. Here is what we want you to know about yourselves: As grand as it sounds and as odd as it may be, the sense and the logic of it is that

the Earth is the *only* place in the universe where this attribute exists.

"*Kryon do you mean that there are no other planets with life in the universe?*" No, that's not what I'm saying at all. Life is abundant in the universe—absolutely abundant. Hopefully, even before you leave this planet, whenever that is, your science will indeed prove it. It is now even being shown to you. The proof of it resides in the files and on the photographic and electronic records of the astronomers, should they choose to look. It's there now—waiting. And when they finally tell you about it (in the next pages, and again later in this book), remember that I told you where they should look. This Earth planet is special. It is the only one that is populated by beings that are from the Great Central Source, uniquely and specifically. It is also where no others are allowed. You have a purpose that is unique to the universe, which some of you are aware of and some of you are not.

"*Wait a minute, Kryon,*" some might say. "*I happen to know intuitively that I actually came from another planet and that I have starseed memories of an entirely different type of life. What about that?*"

I ask you to take a look at the logic of Earth population. With each passing day, many of your family is being gathered from all over the universe to populate this planet. "The elect are being gathered from the skies." Although you might be from the same origin, you indeed work in many places. Some of the work is in biology on other planets, and some is providing simple energy placeholding for portals in the universe that need it. None of this is important to the real message here. It only shows that we have more family members on this planet now than ever before, and that all Humans who have ever lived on the planet are indeed back living here now. Wherever you were called from, you are *here* now, and you are family from the same original source. You, as all the others, know the purpose—and that is why you came with glee.

This purpose is known to your cellular structure, but it is the hidden test for you to discover, and we'll tell you more now, though it may seem cryptic to you. I will give it to you slowly, so it will be accurate and complete—because it is splendorous. What is taking place that you call a challenging experiment in energy here, is to find out where the dark and the light will balance itself. What happens here, dear ones, and the result of what you do here, dear ones, is going to create the pattern and the mold for a much grander thing that is currently taking place in the universe over 12 billion light years away. Your astronomers are noting it and talking about it. Did you know that? The stamp of the energy of humanity is visiting, so to speak, another area of the universe by design, and that's why you're here. I have to leave it at that right now, but will explain it fully in *family*, part five. (see page 132)

Some of you object to the word experiment. It makes you sound like so many animals in a labyrinth. Let me tell you, dear ones, that *you* are the experimenters—the angelic scientists. The actual experiment run by you is about *energy*. That is why we say to you, "Each of you, as family members and experimenters are equal in the sight of Spirit and are honored for your visit, and what it means here." It isn't about what you do here. It's about what happens to the energy here—more precisely, what has *already* happened to the energy here.

This may sound like a dichotomy, so take a look at the parable of the Prodigal Son again. It is the story of the family. In the parable, the father held a celebration for the returning member—no matter what he had done with the family's resources. It was about *family*, and not about works. We celebrate you and the *family* work you are doing while much is hidden from you. You are from a source in the Universe that is unique. Not all entities are from this place, but all the ones living on the planet in biology are. You are my own lineage, and I know each of you.

Although this is not the subject of this channel (and may not ever be given by Kryon), you should know that **not** all biological planets have the energy of a unique purpose or are populated with only one kind of entity. Perhaps you thought that all planets were as yours? No. Someday you will discover just how unique you are. Here is a hint: Most planets with biological life are located around dual sun systems. The astronomical development of planets with life is most common around **dual suns**. This is why Earth "hides" so well. Even those who have found you cannot and will not land en masse. They are not of your family, and although they don't totally understand it, they see your power (the joke is that you don't). We have mentioned this many times before—that logic will make you ask why a race of biological extraterrestrial beings who seem to be technically advanced, have visited here for more than 60 years and have even interfaced with Humans—yet have never officially landed and introduced themselves. Why? They can't. Those of you occupying your lives waiting for this event will be disappointed. The ones who continue to predict it will also be disappointed. Perhaps you should change your quest and start looking for the ET within? (Kryon humor). There is an off-world entity inside *you* that is grander than anything that will ever come from the sky and land on your lawn!

All of you are equally loved, equally celebrated, equally grand.

Eternal

Needless to say, you are also eternal. Your biology isn't, but you are. This fact is well hidden from you, but true. This attribute is an important one, and is the way we see you. Can you really accept this? Here is something to ask yourselves in the quietest moments of your existence: When you breathe your last breath, is there even one of you that really believes that you will stop existing? There is a "spark of intuitive truth" in *all* Humans that somehow knows better. Look around at your Earth's religions and the overall search for God. Isn't it so that almost all of them feature a "life beyond" for some part of your consciousness? Yes. Why would this be perceived so strongly if it were not the truth?

All of you are pieces of a divinity that always was, and always will be. Some Humans have a profound feeling of this on their death beds, and are extremely peaceful at their transition. Some fight the idea until the last minute, then they begin to "feel" a familiar feeling and are somehow afraid of it. It is the approach of the family, and all the activity and celebration of *home*. Remember the original parable of "The Story of Wo"? He feared the approach of "family" while alive, and he was told by others that it was evil. Such is the duality of Humanism—that your real family is often seen as the devil.

We mention this only to reinforce the fact that you will never die. The biology may crumble, but *you* are forever. The next time you are feeling unloved or unimportant, think of this: **You are eternal!** It is an attribute that in your mind is reserved only for God. That should tell you a bit about who you really are!

Dual Citizenship With The Others

Here is an attribute that you might not have thought of. You are part of a number of entities that support you on this planet. Therefore, you have an entourage. Some of the entourage follow you and are assigned for life. You call them angels and guides (neither name is totally correct, by the way). The name does not exist in your language for what they actually are. They're more than just "attached" to you—they are part of your "signature," did you know that? They exist within your biology—they're a part of you—they're not attached through friendship or even by love. Some are with you forever, and some change as you change. As you change your enlightenment, and one leaves, another one is assigned. You actually feel it in your innermost being, and there is mourning and loss, and you know about it. It's part of the biology—part of who you are—part of the sacredness of the pieces that you call "cells." And that description fits only part of the entourage. You have only one word, *entity*, which begins to describe them, yet there are gradations of that life force that exist within the planet that actually have your name! Therefore, there is far more of "you" than you realize—something that we have been telling you for years. Some of you have seen these kinds of life forms in the sky (not ET's)—and, by the way, this curiosity may be discovered soon. A puzzle will be offered to your science that broaches the issue of another kind of "life" on your planet. It will cause you to examine the definition of "life"—and it will be discovered in the atmosphere. This is all part of the support of Humans.

Remember that you are the experimenter. Can you walk on this planet and discover these other "parts of you," or not? What will you do with it if you discover it? Which way will you let the energy flow? To the dark? To the light? What will you do? The result of the energy experiment is profound to the universe, and that's why I'm here. This visit from Kryon would not be here in this room for you to hear and read had it not been for the Harmonic Convergence measurement of these, the end times. These are still the end times, dear ones, but they are no longer the kind of end that was prophesized. No, it's the end of the *old energy*. That's *the end* are speaking of. It's also the *beginning* of a new kind of Human Being. There will be another measurement in 2012, and we still tell you this: The grandest attribute of the family on this planet where you sit—the grandest—is that you are *not alone*! You are loved beyond measure—by the ones who have flooded through this crack in the veil right now to be with you and sit with you wherever you are!

Therefore even though you exist in biology, there is part of you that does not—and that is what we call your dual citizenship. You are a creature of the universe, sacred and loved—and a biological citizen of your planet as well. This is one of the most special attributes of all, and as we have said, it is *not* common among life forms in the universe.

Return

The last attribute isn't really last at all, for it pervades all the rest and is part of all the rest. It is the one that is most obvious to us, yet still hides from us. To exemplify, it we're going to be quiet for a minute and just love you—and we're going to finish washing your feet. We want you to feel love as it pours, literally, over your head and onto your shoulders. We want you to *know* that you're not alone. See, this is about energy that we're not going to "take back" when we leave your chair. It's about energy that can stay with you as you eventually get up from your chair—energy you can call on—a family energy from Home that you can "paste on" yourselves for life—like your skin. It will serve you in a new way, increasing the synchronicity within your life through your intent, and reveal at the cellular level a bit more about who you really are. It will let that sacred light shine a little more—until you come back. This last attribute is that no matter how long you are on this planet—no matter what you accomplish in this playing field—no matter what you discover or not—you will be coming Home! The return to the family is absolute, and you have done it over and over even though you don't remember.

This attribute is hidden from you, but to us it is primary...you see, we miss you. *We miss you*! Again we wish remind you of the story of the Prodigal Son/Daughter. My energy is not masculine or feminine. It's just like yours, which has the essence of both. When you return, you will be welcomed with open arms. Celebrations will erupt, and not one entity will be giving you a tally sheet about what you did with your formerly Human resources. You are loved for your family membership, and that is why we know *who* you are—because you are part of the whole, part of *our* family—and we watch over your place with us, keeping it fresh for your eventual return.

There is nothing that will deter this attribute—and that is what we look forward to.

My partner is filled with emotion because of what we see about the potentials of the "now" that are here. We don't view things in your time frame. Instead, we see the potentials and manifestations because of what you're doing in what you call your future. We see the lifechange possibilities—the potential for such a grand healing event that is here now. We see extended life. We see potentials of joy, where there is none now. And we see love, and the realization of a greater plan for those of you who are finally going to release the worry and stand from your place in that chair and proclaim out loud "I AM!" And because I allow my partner to share in the joy, there is often the reaction of his weeping. That's what the meld creates, dear ones, when you step into that space where Spirit can partner with you. You see, that's when you really understand *family*.

And so it is that we retreat from this sacred place around your chair—the one you have created with us. So it is that we remove those bowls that we've been using to wash your feet that are filled with the tears of our joy. As we retreat back into the crack in the veil, we say to you, This is not our last meeting. We know you, and you know us. You and I are *family*. There'll come a time when you will remember this meeting, and we will, again, figuratively and metaphorically, hug one another. And when that grand time comes when we intermingle our energy again, I will be able to say to you face to face,

"Welcome Home."

And so it is.

Kryon

Kryon at The United Nations!

In November 1995, November 1996, and again in November 1998, Kryon spoke at the S.E.A.T. (Society for Enlightenment and Transformation) at the United Nations in New York City. By invitation Jan and Lee brought a time of lecture, toning, meditation and channelling to an elite group of UN delegates and guests.

Kryon Book 6, *Partnering With God* carried the first two entire transcripts of what Kryon had to say ... some of which has now been validated by the scientific community. Kryon Book 7, *Letters From Home* carries the meeting in 1998 (page 289). All three of these transcripts are on the Kryon web site [www.kryon.com].

Our sincere thanks to Mohamad Ramadan in 1995, Cristine Arismendy in 1996, and Jennifer Borchers in 1998 who were presidents of that bright spot at the United Nations, for the invitation and for their work to enlighten our planet.

"Tasks of the Family"

The Family, Part Two

Channelled in
Idaho Falls, Idaho
and
Melbourne, Australia

The Kryon Writings, Inc.

PMB 422
1155 Camino Del Mar
Del Mar, California 92014
[www.kryonqtly.com]

"Tasks of the Family"
The Family, Part Two

Live Channelling
Idaho Falls, ID & Melbourne, Australia

The live Channeling that follows is part two of five sessions concerning "The Family" as Spirit sees us. It is a transcribed combination of two events on two different continents...with the same message...given live, two months apart.

Greetings, dear ones, I am Kryon of Magnetic Service. Sorry for jumping in so quickly, my partner, but the time is right for the message that is at hand. [Spoken after Kryon came in immediately after the mediation, much before his usual entrance]. Many of you realize that the message is no longer my partner's message, but rather a message from Spirit—that which you call God—that which is eternal, but which is also of *you*. It's going to take a few minutes while you get used to this event and understand that the energy in this very room, and even where you are reading this, is changing. It is changing with intent from those who are here, and from your intent to read this information.

We are aware of those hearing this information "now," and of those reading this information "later." Both cases are in our "now," and we know of the potentials involved in the energy contained here—for all of you. Some have given permission to receive a certain gift this day. Although knowledge and information will be passed between us, I'm here to tell you that this family member (Kryon) has a task, as this room is filled to the brim with love. I want to tell you that the task is way beyond the information that is going to be developed for you. As we have said before, the real task right now is to wash your feet—to let the entourage I have brought with me walk between the chairs, both here and as you read, and to stop and recognize, honor and hug, every single Human who is "here."

The bodies that you find yourselves in right now are all part of the design you have allowed, and they are all perfect. The design is perfect. Even though you know without a shadow of a doubt that they are temporary, we say that they are perfect. But when Kryon and the entourage come forward to greet family, we tell you that we know every single one of you. It has not been that long since we have seen you before, or that we will see you again. You are the forerunners of the ones expected to change the very fabric of the consciousness of this planet!

By agreement you are here. By intent you sit in the chairs now, both hearing and reading. Do you know how long we've known you might be here absorbing this energy? Days ago, in your linear time, the potential of this was known. How does it make you feel to know that there is an entourage, a spiritual work group, that has your energy, knows your name, and has arrived to simply celebrate the event (the event of your intent to find out more about the *family*)? These are interesting days, dear ones, which find an attribute that allows this kind of an interim visit. It wasn't always this way, you know.

Today you carry with you problems, concerns, challenges, secrets, worries, and fears. There is nothing that is unknown to us. The thing that you have shared with no one is like a beacon to your spiritual *family*. We know who you are, and we know what you've been through, and we see all. We tell you this in the most loving manner, because the energy of solution sits like a hat upon the fears of the challenge, waiting to manifest itself through your intent. There are different degrees of challenge represented here. Some of you are at a junction—a null point—and that's why you're here—that's really what brings your eyes to this page. Some of you are on a long quest, begun years ago, culminating in this year, dear ones.

The last time we were together, we spoke of the attributes of Humans (the attributes of *family*), and again we will say this: The additional information that will be presented about the family this night continues to be called "Letters from Home." It is to be transcribed for those who are not here, but who really are! After all, aren't you reading this *now*? For we are speaking *now* of the ones at this moment in your future who are reading the very words you are hearing. And through their intent to pick up the transcription and read it now, life changes will occur. The energy they allow to come in *now* has the potential to create episodes in their Human lives that will finally help them to recognize and realize who they are and what they contribute.

This all may sound cryptic to those of you who are used to the linear time frame, but we tell you that there is potential within the words of the energy of the Humans here that goes far beyond this room. There are life decisions and changes, even potential healings, that sit in the chairs receiving this message. I am aware of them, and so is my partner (Lee). Sometimes it is difficult for him to keep from welling up, since in this state he "sees" the absolute profundity of potential that can occur from those who will later rise from the chairs in this room (and who are reading this) and who take out *more* energy than they came in with. That energy is called "love," and it is being dispensed to you with intent.

I want to tell you how that translates. It translates to **power** for humanity, and that's a shift in the balance of dark and light. You might say, "*What difference does that make, really?*" The last time we were together we told you, but we'll tell you again—and it may sound unbelievable, but all of your cells know it. It's about a measurement—an energy posturing—that God cannot

make. This must come from a concentrated energy place we call the Great Central Source. It is not a place at all, but rather a concept with substance. It's an interdimensional concept that does not fit within the paradigm of your consciousness, but if you could imagine such an attribute of pure love where you live (when you are not here), you would call it *Home*. That's what I'm talking about. And I'm telling you that the universe that you look out upon is not finished, and never will be. I'm telling you that this universe that you look out upon, the very physics of it, has an energy overlay that is not predetermined by the collective of love you call

God—for that would bias it entirely. Much like your planet is free to set its energy balance, the universe has much the same feature, only in a far different and slower way.

We have told you in the past that we have known of the potentials of your being in the chair where you are, and that we often "wait" for you to arrive there. "*Why,*" you might say, "*would Spirit be here before we were?*" You think you came to see us, you see, or that you picked up the transcription by accident—and that's funny! Spirit has a sense of humor, too, you know. This beautiful emotional state is passed to you in its purity as Humans. At the very center and seed of humorous celebration is joy. It's there. You are the only living creature on the planet that can laugh at concepts, did you know that? It ought to tell you something about who you are. We've been here for days expecting you, since you are *family*! You do it, too, you know. You travel far distances to be with a loved one because you haven't seen them in a long time. And when you see them, your eyes light up, and you run across the room and hug them. Deep within your heart, some of you will wonder how often you can do that, and how long they'll be there, since Humans are only on the planet a brief time. That's what happens with families, and that's what's happening here. Although the divine "real you" is eternal, "you" have been gone for a long time from your Spirit family (on our side). You can't remember it like we do, so it doesn't affect you like it does us. The truth is that, indeed, our eyes light up as well, and love wells up when we recognize who we are speaking to now. No matter who you think you are, you are *family*! All of you. Each of you. Each one seeing these words.

The Family — Part II

Here is the *family* information today. At the last meeting, we gave you some family postulates—attributes of who the *family* is. We talked about how you are created equal. We talked about the fact that there is no central source—and that the real "central source" is within. We talked about the awareness that is in every single cell of your body. We talked about the fact that the cells are perfect. We talked about the fact that the divine plan for you does not come from without, but comes from within. We talked about some of the Earth changes, and we talked about your spiritual lineage. We spoke of the fact that Earth is populated with angelic Humans in duality—the only planet in the universe with creatures totally of divinity from the Central Source. It's the only planet with this purpose—and we spoke about that.

We also talked about another attribute of eternalness—that you are dearly loved, and as we always do, we washed your feet. Now we want to talk about just a few more items regarding *family*. We're going to call them "The Tasks of Family." This information will be presented two times. The transcription shall be a combination of both sessions, thereby enhancing the message from two energies of the planet. Then it is to be combined with the other sections and presented in the transcriptions called "Letters from Home." [The book you are now reading]

Tasks

Tasks are potentials—potential manifestations and realizations of Human Beings on the planet as they take what you call "the ascension status." To our way of thinking, this status is simply that of creating a vibratory level that is closer to *home* than it was before—one that lets the Human seemingly have one foot in the "now" and one foot in 3D linear time. It's a status that features the Human creating peace no matter what happens around them, with full knowledge that the future can create a win/win situation for them and the planet. Dear ones, when we say "winning situation," sometimes it is not exactly what the Human considers "winning" to be. To fully understand, you must put on your "interdimensional hat." You have to put on your mantle of wisdom for the following knowledge, for some of it gets difficult to comprehend. I want to tell you about the tasks of the family—why Humans are here in general. These tasks do not necessarily apply specifically to those in the room or those reading this. These tasks represent information for **all** Humans in general on the planet. These items are not "have to's," but rather they are potentials.

Change

The first task of all Humans, should they reach that place where they are aware, is to change who they are. When we say "who they are," we mean it! If you could see the attributes within the very cells of your body, you would see that even your spiritual guides are part of your actual biology (as we told you before). That's why your biology hurts so much when they leave. All the things you consider spiritual about yourselves have the essence of their origin within the structure that you call your DNA. It has to be this way. It is the marriage and the meld that creates your balanced duality. You could not have a sacred Human Being walking in biology without this kind of sacred structure. Some of you are actually finding the sacredness of it in the numbers and shapes, as you discover the smallest parts thereof.

The first task, therefore, is to change the structure. The structure is changed with desire and intent, and the intent must be pure. We know the difference, and so do you. You wonder how Spirit works? "*Oh, Kryon, how can we have a winning situation around death and problems? The kinds of things we're going through seem to have no win/win solution!*" I tell you that anything that makes a Human go to his or her knees and inspect his or her spirituality is a winning situation. A winning situation, because that's why you're here! Some of you in this new vibration had a contract that you have voided with intent, and you've decided to walk a new one. This is your new ability in the New Age, as we have spoken of many times. Because of this, some of you are passing "markers" of the old energy along your new path—days in your life when you may not feel well, and you might wonder "what's up." Here's what's up: You just passed an old marker—one that you actively chose to dodge—one that may have brought you to your knees—but you didn't need it because you actively gave intent to pass it up. Did you know that? By choosing a new path, you have given intent to void the Human karma carried in your DNA that you came in with. When you did that, your very cells "knew" it, and they reacted.

Some of you who did this have said, "*I have given intent to clear my karma and step off the old path. My life is okay, but I am not aware of any great change.*" You, as Humans, see half a picture, you know. You look at what *is happening* to you. You have no idea what *hasn't* happened to you! You have no idea what the old path contained—the one you left behind. That old contract—it's gone, you see. But you still expect great things to happen, perhaps. I'll tell you that great things *have* happened by way of the absence of the effect that didn't! Maybe it's time to sit down and celebrate that if it's the first time you have become aware of it. Because **you** still exist—and maybe you wouldn't otherwise! You're here because you've recognized the gift at the appropriate time and have taken it. That's a miracle. Change! That's the first task of the Human. Don't be surprised when you ask for spiritual change, and it's your biology that reacts first.

Hold The Light!

Here's another one, and I'm talking now to lightworkers. This is a task of Humans after they have given intent to leave the old energy path. To "hold the light" might sound trite to you, but we have told you before that all Human Beings at the cellular level contain the entire blueprint of why they're here (personal spiritual information), and it's very well-hidden information. They go an entire lifetime with it active and working, but without it being revealed consciously. We told you that it is revealed, however, with your pure spiritual *intent* to have it so. We told you that your very physiology changes with that intent at the cellular level because you have given permission for the cells to have the information expanded (which is exactly what happens).

My partner (Lee) told you earlier that this creates a situation of energy where your light is held, and you carry it in a profound way. The energy "pushes out" from you everywhere you go. Like the parable of the tar pit (a published Kryon parable given at the United Nations), you end up walking around as a beacon to others. Eventually they notice your improved countenance and benefit by your knowledge. Therefore, you are indeed "holding the light," and it helps others. We have also told you that to "hold the light" actually brings energy to the planet—and *you* become part of the catalyst for planetary change because of this. It's a profound task!

I give you a challenge: As you go into areas on Earth you've never gone before, I want you to look at what happens. People look at you differently. For a moment—just a moment—when you walk into a room, they will turn to look at you. You'll wonder if something's wrong. I'll tell you what's happening: There is an instant, brief recognition that even surpasses the duality. Like a little greeting from one divine Human to another, it says, "I know who you are and what you've done" (speaking of the intent to hold the light), and then the glance turns away. After that, there is no remembrance or recognition. Lightworker, watch for it. Those glances mean something. You're "pushing energy," and the cellular structure of every other Human around you "knows" it.

When you come together as lightworkers, you feel a sense of family from the light that you radiate. It marries to the light the others radiate, and you know you're in the right place. It feels like Home. I'll tell you, that's no accident. It's what you came here for! That's why we encourage you to assemble more often—that you may discuss with one another what it's like to know that you're not alone and that there are others just like you. Each of you has an extremely unique print—a potential that belongs to no one else, and some of you are actually voiding old potentials and creating new ones as you go. That's being in the Now! That's co-creation! Holding the light. (More in Part three.)

Anchoring The Energy

The next task is similar, but different. It goes to another level, and we wish to be careful as we present this. I want this to be succinct and clear. As we enumerate these tasks of the family, we are talking in general, and it is not about you specifically. Each Human is called to what they must do, if they choose to do it. The **choice** is *always* there. Do you realize, even those of you who are vibrating at a high level, that you have a choice not to? We have discussed this in the past, but we'll say it again. You have active choice to move backwards if you choose. But we want to tell you an axiom—a postulate—a rule of Human biology that we have not really discussed much before: We have just told you that it is the cellular level of the Human that reacts to a vibrational shift in spiritual consciousness. Therefore, what do you think happens when a Human goes backwards by choice into a lower energy? They go into imbalance, that's what happens. You ought to know that before you embark on any spiritual path. You always have the choice to do as you wish—but be aware that your cells will know it, too. Your biology knows spiritually what is happening!

An entire informational discourse, which you call a channelling, was given to you some time ago about "anchoring the energy." In that channelling, we told you that there are some *called* to be at certain areas. This is their chosen contract in the new energy, and they find themselves living in areas where they are *needed* by the planet. Figuratively and metaphorically, they send down a shaft of light energy into the planet, which is the partner of the Human—a real family member. There, this shaft anchors and holds an energy that is divine—which is you. And if this is you, you are anchoring the energy on the planet where you live. *You* change the area around you. Some of you know exactly what I'm talking about, because you know who you are. Some of you hearing and reading this may be called to certain areas that seem odd. There, you will live for a while with the knowledge that you're there to anchor energy until you move on to another area. Some family members are actually what we would call "spiritual nomads," and their whole task is to be gypsy spirits moving and anchoring, moving and anchoring, moving and anchoring.

Others of you might resound to an area of your birth so completely that nothing will ever pull you away. You will tell your friends, "*No matter what I do, I won't leave this town.*" That's anchoring, too! That's because you **know** you belong and you have wisdom about removing yourself, because you know who you are—and that you belong to a certain land. You know what you're doing, and there is some part of you that says, "*If I leave, it's going to change.*" If you have that intuition, dear ones, I want to tell you that you are *anchored*. In a subsequent channelling, I will further discuss what an "anchor" is able to do—a very powerful concept! That's the third task.

Completion

The fourth and fifth tasks are difficult to relate. There's a reason why we give you five at this sitting. If you do the numerology and examine the energy of what you call the "five," it's about **change** (the first task). There are no accidents in the presentation methods that Spirit gives you—the numbers of attributes and tasks that are presented—the way they are presented—they all mean something else, if you haven't noticed. Spirit often presents a multilayered message for those who wish to search for the other meanings—which are *always* about love and Human enablement. Sometimes the hidden meanings are simply there for you to find so you can know how much we celebrate you. That's why Spirit gives you information at all!

The final two tasks are difficult to present and difficult to understand as Humans. Before we present them, we want to tell you that this is the time we have chosen to wash your feet. We haven't brought it up yet, as we have in other channels, because this is what you need to have during this message. We speak now, within these next tasks, about death. It's an abhorrent subject to every Human Being who vibrates at a high level of consciousness—to think of the sorrow, suffering, and death of another Human Being—or groups of Humans. Yet I want to tell you that some of the tasks of humanity fall into those very categories! That's why we're going to take a moment to wash each foot, one at a time—figuratively—so you will be surrounded with a love bubble—the mantle of Spirit, the wisdom of God, so you'll understand better what is going to be presented to a group that has given intent for interdimensional information. It is difficult even for my partner to present this.

There are some Humans who come to the planet just to "finish." It's the energy of this finishing that must be accomplished, and they know it at the cellular level when they come in. How does it make you feel, dear one, to know that right now on other parts of this great planet there are *family* members with the same spiritual cellular structure as you—with the potential of being lightworkers like you—with the potential of high vibration, or wonderful lives of healing and longevity—who have actively chosen by their own design to instead come and finish—often as a group. They knew before they came that there would be attributes of suffering and death in large groups—presented upon them so they could close out an energy for the land that they exist upon—so that Earth could move forward into a new era that we have called "The New Jerusalem."

And at some level, you know their names, since they are *family*! And you will celebrate what they have done with them when you return—and some will have the wisdom of God to even celebrate spiritually during Human grieving. What I want you to remember is **who they are**, for they know you, too. It's about closure, balance, and it's necessary and voluntary. I want you to think about it—what a gift that is for you! It's a gift for your culture—a gift for your very divinity. It's the essence of love from a spiritual *family*. You have a name for it, but it's not really the correct one. It cannot possibly convey the real energy of what these family members are doing for you and the planet, but it's the closest word. The word is *sacrifice*. But that is not the essence of what they're doing, really. It's in love, and they are simply performing the task of completion. Remember nine years ago when we told you of their group task? Look for it.

Service

If you felt that the last task was difficult to celebrate, let me give you the fifth one—*service*. This one is going to touch your heart. We've spoken of this many times before, because you've got to understand how it really works. I speak now to the *family* in this room, and to those reading this. It's about the seemingly inappropriate deaths of those around you, and again, we speak of family. We speak of the kind of departure that leaves you empty and in sorrow, broken and asking God, "*How could you do this?*" We've explained it before: It's not about what happens, it's about the journey. It's about the contract. That's why, dear ones, as we wash your feet, we want you to know something that is so critical and so important about these, the small ones who come in and die in a family—or the grown ones who come in and do the same thing.

They place upon you a burden for life, which you call great sorrow. They come in with an overlay that is great, divine, and extremely anointed—a task that is called a "gift" for you. Hiding within the seemingly horrible event is a gift that is surrounded not by what *they* did, but by what *you* do in response. You see, it's not about their death; they did it for *you*. You call it sacrifice, but it isn't. That's the wrong word. It's called *love*. It's an appropriately designed contract—a manifestation of a gift on this planet for you. And I'll tell you what the gift is: If the event didn't bring you to your knees, it should have, because that's where you decided to give intent to examine who you were. That's where the process starts that is often the catalyst for enlightenment. And if it didn't do that, I want to tell you it's about time it did. Because if it didn't, they wasted the gift! Perhaps this is a new twist on how you feel, and perhaps you do not wish us to be so direct—but it's absolutely true! This seemingly heartwrenching event did not happen to them—it happened to **you**. If you doubt that, look around: Where are they, and where are you? Realize that all the energy around it was for **you**. What have you done with it? Have you been consumed with anger? Guilt? Perpetual grief?

We challenge you to look at this event with clearer eyes and start the celebration! I challenge you, as a Human Being, to have the wisdom to celebrate their birthday, and the gift that it was. Know that this special Human Being came down in uniqueness, with a contract to give you something grand—and that's called **service**. What a task!

This service doesn't simply stop at the event of their passing, dear ones. The potential around the energy created by this special service is awesome! It promotes self-examination. It promotes the search for truth. Within the broken hearts of Humans are the seeds of greatness. Within the sorrow and grief of Humans is a purity that simply cannot be generated in any other way. Many of you understand and can trace your enlightenment to these kind of events—where you finally were able to clear away what mattered and what didn't—and find out about the divinity inside. Is it any wonder we love you as we do?

We're going to finish washing your feet. We move between your chairs and fill this room with an energy that we invite you to take *home*. Home is where your inner being is, and that is often what you call the heart. Stand from this place where you are seeing this, and take energy from this session. That's really why we are here.

The only reason we visit in this way is because we love you. You are *family* in the first order. You are a piece of the whole, and you're the ones doing the work. For a few moments, the crack in the veil opens so that you can experience our presence, and in a few moments it will snap shut—and all you will have is the remembrance of the reality that it was indeed here, and was indeed precious.

We invite you to walk from this place in peace. We even use the word *protection*. You know what the protection is? It comes from inside you and radiates with the light you carry. It is there as you hold the light and as you anchor the energy. That's where the protection is. Perhaps you felt that it was generated from us? No. It's through your connection to the family. It's from the attributes of who you are. No darkness can penetrate light that is eternal, sacred, and generated by the highest angels on the planet—the Human. ***You***.

The withdrawal is complete, and again we take away the bowls of our tears of joy, with which we've washed your feet. The washing of the feet, metaphorically, means one thing: We **shout** it to you again, and that is "***honor***." Honor.

There will come a time later when we will be able to intermingle our energies, when you revert and return to the grandness of who you really are. This is a promise—that we will see each other again. Eternal, each one of you. Loved beyond measure, each one of you. *Family*, each one of you.

My brother and sister, this entity retreats from this room but leaves the energy of *family* radiating with an eternal flame of remembrance and love.

And so it is.

Kryon

The End Times

"The simple manner in which the material is presented makes this a highly accessible work for newcomers to Metaphysics"

■ **Connecting Link Magazine - Michigan**

Books and tapes can be purchased in retail stores, or by phone
~ Credit cards welcome ~

1-800-352-6657

"Power of Awareness"
The Family, Part Three

Channelled in
Portland, OR
and
Adelaide, Australia

The Kryon Writings, Inc.

PMB 422
1155 Camino Del Mar
Del Mar, California 92014
[www.kryonqtly.com]

"Power of Awareness"
The Family, Part Three

Live Channelling
Portland, OR & Adelaide, Australia

The live Channeling that follows is part three of five sessions concerning "The Family" as Spirit sees us. It is a transcribed combination of two events on two different continents...with the same message...given live, two months apart.

Greetings dear ones, I am Kryon of Magnetic Service. It is again time, my partner, for the meld that you call the love wash to not only creep over your very essence as you elevate your being, but to also have the potential of doing the same for each who is here, listening and reading. We speak now also of a situation we have described in the past, which you are going to get used to me saying to you. The words that are falling upon the ears of the precious one who sit in the chairs are also being delivered to the eyes of the precious ones who are reading this right now. For to us, it is all the same, and the potential of the hearer and the reader are the same. The time frame that might be somewhat different for you, however, is identical to us. And so we speak *now* not only to what you perceive to be who you are here, but also to the ones reading this who perceive they are here. And if you are one of those reading this now, know this: This is for you as much as it is for the one hearing with the ears.

This is a transmittal of love—a journey from my side to yours of an incredible love that can pour into you if you wish. It can fill you to the brim. It allows you to sit in a chair with a peace you may not have felt for months—peace over situations that seem to have no answer—over situations that seem to have no possible solution.

In all love we say to you: There is no situation here where *you* sit that cannot be solved. We are here to tell you again, as we have told you over and over, that the solutions are the ones designed perfectly by you. Ah, there are some of you who still don't understand. You are family, you know—each one. Kryon comes in to a group such as this to talk to *you*, not to a group—to *you*. This is a brother/sister whose voice you are hearing and feeling—one that knows you well because you are family! Let the feeling of *home* spill into you now as you hear and read these words—as I transmit to you the energy of peace. Let the peace of God fill you with understanding. Let the disbelief you might have transmute to acceptance so that the seeds of truth can finally be planted after all this time. You know that's why you're here, don't you—reading these words?

Part of the message that is going to be transmitted in English to you today, not the third language but in English, is more of our information "from Home" for you. We are calling these messages "Letters from Home." A letter is something that arrives in a system that you have designed yourself, you know. There is expectation, as you make an appointment through intent to open the envelope. And when you do so, if the letter is from a loved one—one of the family—someone you're missing at the heart level, you are warmed by its arrival and message. Many times the words will make you weep with joy, not sadness, at the communication that is there. This is why we call what we have here "Letters from Home." Dear ones, please understand that the situation here is not that much different. There you sit in a chair ready to accept a spiritual letter from home—through a delivery system of your own design. Lest you think this channelling is some form of energy totally beyond your reach—which some of you would call magical—we're here to say, "This is the system that *you* designed." There you sit in your chair, pretending to be Human Beings! [Kryon humor] This energy transfer can be a two-way letter, you know, There's the writer (Spirit), and the intended receiver (you), the one who opens the envelope as you're about to do now. Perhaps you will weep with joy at the message as it flows into your space.

The letter is about awakening the angel inside. There's a beautiful entity beyond description inside the "pretend" Human. If I could show it to you now—if I could bend the rules that you have set up for this place and just show it to you now—you would draw back in awe. You would be astounded perhaps by what it looks like—the energy of it—the light that comes from it. Yet I'm here to tell you that all of you would have an instant and totally complete remembrance. You would know what I speak of when I say the word *family*. There has never been a time in all of the energy of these messages where I could look at you and more fully say, "You are family!" For you stand with me in the *now*, and some of you are experiencing tremendous change. That's why we're all here for this, the third message about the *family*.

In previous messages, we have given you some understanding about family, and we're talking about the Human Being on Earth, and the spiritual being that I see in each of you. Even in this time, in this energy, in each of you I see this entity. Part of the reason my partner keeps his eyes closed during this communication process is that it is distracting for him not to. My eyes are open, and I see who you are.

This is the part where we start the foot washing. This is the beginning of the message, you know. Why should we do such a thing, you might ask? Why does Kryon wash the feet of Human Beings? What is happening here? Metaphorically, when we say we're about ready to take one foot at a time and wash your feet, we want you to look at what that means. It means *honor*. Each one who washes your feet from the other side of this veil is poured into this space by appointment.

Oh, some of you feel that you come to these kinds of meetings or read these kinds of words, so that you'll get a message "from beyond." After that you'll get up and go do something else—perhaps an errand. This time we invite this experience to be different. We want you to understand that the energy that flows into this space is for you today—by appointment. There may not be another time when you can make this kind of appointment, dear ones. This is the time, and this is why you are reading these words. When you arise, try celebrating with us for a moment that the family loves you enough to communicate with you and know your potentials. Just take a moment before you arise and say, "I love you" back to the family. Feel the energy when you do. We **will** hear it, you know.

So the outpouring of those who come to sit at your feet and walk between the chairs and wash each foot are because of honor. Why is it, you might ask, that the honor is so great? We'll tell you what we always tell you: This entourage, including the Kryon energy, and those of the family of Lord Michael, have never, ever been Human. This entourage has something in common tonight. These are your family members from the other side who support you. They don't have to do what you have to do. They don't live in duality, as you do. They have nothing hidden from them, as you do. They don't walk around in weak biology on purpose in order to affect another part of the universe. These family members look at you and see the grandness of what you're doing. They see the love it has taken for you to return and return and return, and they weep with joy that such a thing could happen. And there you sit, some of you, still in disbelief about any of it! That's why we love you, you know. It's because you're in the process of working this energy experiment through to the end—an end that is very close to being measured. And we'll say it again: The one who gets up from their chair completely and totally unconvinced of anything that has happened within this transmission is one whom we love as much as any other. It's not about what you do, it's just about being here.

Let me tell you of a potential. Someday there my come a child who's going to point at you, and they're going to tell you who you are, because they will know. The new breed—they know. You'll do better with them if you know, also. So claim the gift now. They're going to need this from you. They want to look at you and see the same spark of understanding that they have. Parents, are you listening? Walk from this space and know about the "angel inside" and feel the purpose you came for. The children will wonder what's happened to you. I hope you're ready for them. They're going to change everything. You talk about the hope of the planet? That's where it is—in the new ones with the Indigo energy [speaking of the Indigo Children, spoken of in Kryon Book 6]. They come in with tools you never had. When they're grown up, they're going to change this planet dramatically.

Oh, it's all about choice, and they can do what they wish with it, but they have brand new tools: purpose, self-esteem, self-worth—they are not going to let this planet drag itself down, and neither are you. I know that because you're my family, and I know what's in your heart, I know why you sit here. It's no mystery. We're not in a vacuum, you know. When this "message from beyond" is finished and you leave this place, do you think we're not with you? Oh, there are so many who go with you! We've spoken about the family in the past during the other "Letters from Home." And in this lineage of information we have given you, some attributes and tasks of the family indicated that you were created equal, and that of course refers to the angel inside. We spoke to you about your lineage and who you are. We told you of the duality. We told you of the remarkable lineage of your ancestry—all from the Central Source. We've talked to you about where that is, and at the same time we told you it is not a place. We told you that you are unique. We have told you that this is the *only* planet of free choice, and it is. [See part V of this series, for more information on this.] We've told you what the "joke" is, which you all know at the cellular level—that you know how special this Earth really is—yet you "pretend" through the duality not to know.

Let us say again, that you Humans show it to us constantly through your postulates and your scientific logic. The scientists believing the Earth is alone—the only life in the universe—with everything revolving around it! Even with overwhelming odds that you are not, your science still tells you that you are the only life. Let me tell you, in some ways they are right! You have the only planet that is inhabited purely and completely with creatures like you—with the angel inside. It had to be that way. It could not be a hybrid world like so many are. The universe is teeming with life, but you're the only planet that is pure, and the only one that can raise itself by choice and intent alone. Those that try to come in and destroy the purity can't even land here because you're very powerful. And if they do, they don't stay very long. We have mentioned this before, and that's the way it will remain until the time is different—a time when you will give permission for it to be so. It's the family that makes the choice, you know, and *you* are the *family*.

The Power of Awareness

In past communications, we have told you a remarkable thing: At the cellular level of each Human body, there is a code system that represents everything. And when we say "everything," we mean it. Everything! We spoke of the power of awareness, and now we are going to expand upon "awareness at the cellular level of the Human body," and we're going to give you a number of attributes regarding this awareness. Some of them are going to sound odd indeed to the disbeliever—it will be fodder for ridicule. And if that is you, we love you. It doesn't matter. The truth remains the truth, whatever you choose to believe, and we're going to give it to you here. Let the energy of truth show itself within the proof that it develops through manifestation. In other words, let the reality and truth of the information be developed through your use of it.

You're a changing species. When you talk about evolution, there is also spiritual evolution, and you're sitting right in the middle of it. Things that you could not do ten years ago—even a half a decade ago, are now in your grasp. Your cells have an awareness that is astonishing. As I said in the *family* part I, all of the power of the miraculous happens from the *inside* out. Most Human Beings stand in awe, raising their hands, thanking God that it happened from the outside in! It didn't. It didn't. It's the cellular awareness that changed, and a miracle developed. Didn't you ever wonder if that angel inside *did* anything? (more Kryon humor) Now for those of you who sit in dis-ease, in imbalance, in fear, even in hatred, we're going to tell you that all the solutions are already inside you. Healing is not going to come through some flash in the sky. It's going to come from a flash inside—through awareness—through realization—revelation of the secrets—of the energy that is within. We want to walk you through some new attributes that you might not even know you have. Again, we're going to tell you that some of them sound miraculous.

Now this is a "laundry list," as my partner calls it. I don't know why he objects to lists, but this isn't really a list. It's a circle. Unfortunately, it has to be presented in a linear time frame for you, so you get it one item at a time. I'll tell you the kind of communication that you and I are used to when we are in a place that is not here: That's when all the information is instantaneous, at the same time. When it's presented in that manner, it interrelates with itself, and you understand the interactivity of it. Then you have a full understanding of its true meaning. We can't do that here, so it must be presented in a list. There are seven, but the first one represents them all (there's that circle again).

First, we are going to speak of the miracle of cellular awareness. That is the subject of this "letter." And for the communication of *now*, it breaks into seven revelations. When you as a Human Being decide to take the status that we call "ascension," you are asking for the ascension (or raising) of the vibration within your cells. Through your pure intent, the awareness of your cellular structure begins to build. Each cell of your body holds with it the entire blueprint of all that is. It is carried within the code that you call DNA, and another around the DNA [see "The Cosmic Lattice," in this book, page 341]. This code was named after the chemistry in two of the strands. Therefore, the code is misnamed, because there is a great deal more of it than you are aware of. We're not going to give you a name, but we will tell you that eventually someone will, and it will reflect all of the parts that you can't see, as well as the chemical one you can. It will mean "life code."

The contract that you came in with—the knowledge of who you are—your magnetic imprint—all of it is located in the code. This might interest you: You want to know what's different about the new kids? If you had the ability to examine the parts of the DNA that are nonchemical, you would find that it has alterations, and that is called *evolution*! Spiritual evolution, by permission of Humans on the planet, These new children are the next logical spiritual consciousness that you're allowing for. And if you could go in there (to their code) and look, you would find that the awareness (a part of the nonchemical DNA) has been altered. It's the spiritual part, but a physical part, nonetheless.

All that ever was, the record that exists in the Akashic records—the record of your existence as a Human on Earth—all of your lifetimes—it is all there in the code. The blueprint of your conscious decisions of contract are there, too. This should be no revelation to those of you born into this world with fears and anxieties that make no sense from your own experience. Where did these attributes of your makeup come from? It should be obvious: They came as a blueprint from real-life experiences that happened the last time you were here, and the time before that.

Now, some will walk from this place, perhaps in fear of spiritual change. Some will arise from reading this in disbelief. Both are exercising, very much, the seeds that have been planted in the cellular awareness level. That's the duality that is also sewn in there very carefully, as it should be. You see, it's *all* there, and when it comes time for a miraculous healing, the cells are informed—especially the ones that have disease—that it is time "to go," and they do! Let me tell you, that even the kinds of miraculous healing where there is manifestation of bone and tissue and flesh that was never there before—happens from within! Sometimes congenital problems are corrected, conditions are healed and changed, and the doctors stand in awe and want to know what happened. I'll tell you what happened: The cells that have all of the knowledge about rejuvenation of tissue—what is appropriate and inappropriate, and what is the proper energy—

are awakened. Then you get a miracle. It happens from the inside out. You want to see this in your science? Look for evidence of "cell suicide." This is the destruction from within the nucleus of cells who somehow "know" that they are out of balance—and your science will tell you that the cells explode from the inside out—as though they were "aware." You know what? That's the divinity in *you*. It shows the awareness in you. You want to thank God for that? Then you better look inward instead of outward for God, because that's where it came from—inside.

There are seven miracles of awareness that you carry within you.

Connection to The Cosmic Lattice

The first miracle is also *all* of them, and it is the connection you have to the Cosmic Lattice. We've defined the Cosmic Lattice for you before, and again we say it's the energy of the universe. It's an energy so real that someday you'll understand it and tap its potential. It's more than physics. It's also esoteric. It is the energy of the transmission of information from here to the farthest parts of the universe that you can even imagine—instantly—because the Lattice is alive, in a way you do not recognize yet. It does not take any "time" to get from here to there, because it's all one consciousness that thinks together. It's hooked to the family, and you're part of the family! Your connection with the Lattice allows for the next six attributes to occur.

So you might say that you are awakening the parts of your cellular level that are connecting to the Lattice. Some ask, "*How can I do that? How can I do that?*" When this channel is over, you're going to say, "There are some things I've read here, and I would love to do those things. How can I do that?" There are multiple ways of connecting and awakening the cells. Some are energetic, using the newly given energy facilitation that you already know of [speaking of the Dubro EMF Balancing Technique that uses the Lattice]. Some are physics [speaking of the work of

Dr. Todd Ovokaitys, who has discovered some rejuvenation communication at the cellular level], and some are totally within you [speaking of your own power of *intent*].

Connection with the Cosmic Lattice is first in this case because it is the most important. It will now facilitate the other six as I give them to you.

You have some new abilities that come directly from the Lattice connection. After their examination, some will say, "*I knew that. I've been doing that.*" Others will say, "*This is very different!*" It all depends upon the ones that you grasped and used and understood. Let me tell you about some of these, and let's starts with the most obvious.

Health

Oh, you turn to so many things for health. There's part of you that's been trained, in this culture, especially, to release all responsibility for your cellular structure. You literally wander from healer to healer, hoping that in the process someone will be able to *fix* you. That's why we love you so much, dear ones. The duality hides your power! That holy grail, as you call it—that elixir of healing—that rejuvenation to youth—it's already in every single cell, and it's waiting for you to wake it up.

You can control your health in several ways, and I'm not giving you any information that some of you don't already know. First, you can control your health through facilitation—with emerging chemistry and physics. Even this last year, your scientists gave you wonderful hints on how to keep the rejuvenating process cleaner than it's ever been before. Information is being given worldwide for your increased life span.

You can control your health personally, however, far beyond what you might expect. Even the automatic systems can be controlled. The real power of control comes from the *inside out*. It's time for the meetings to begin, and the meetings we're talking about are the ones between You and You—the ones between the cells of your body that are longing to communicate with the part of you called consciousness. Let me tell you, there is spiritual awareness in every cell of your body, and as we've said before, it's time to stop saying, "*My toe hurts*" and instead say, "*We hurt.*" It's time to stop saying, "*I'm going to cure this or that*," and starting saying, "*We're going to cure the whole.*" It's time to start thinking about the collective cells as *one cell*—one which you can speak to *as one cell*, and have good spiritual meetings. Have those meetings together, where you become one and where you interrogate and speak to your personal spiritual structure at the cellular level. Start to clean up what's inside, and then don't be shocked when healing occurs.

This takes spiritual "muscles" that you have not used lately. You must visualize yourself as "one with your biology." The ancient yogis did it. Now you have the ability, also. Ask your body daily: "Is this what *we* want? (with respect to pain and disease) Your consciousness will trigger the spiritual portion of each cell, and things will begin to change. This is a profound ability and power that we cannot underestimate. If you are going to extend your life span on this planet, you *must* learn how this feels, and how this works. Can you imagine a body that will respond in this manner? Can you imagine your biology "knowing" what you know? Can you imagine your toe as enlightened as your mind? It is. Now, bring it along, too.

Substance Intent

Then next miracle is remarkable, yet difficult to describe. It has to do with the intent of the Human Being around the substances of healing. You have an awesome power! The Cosmic Lattice allows for your spiritual pure intent to carry far beyond your cellular structure. Intent is like a radio beacon, not a light. A radio transmission beacon in your science is specifically tuned *to* something; it only stimulates the thing it is tuned to. Your intent is the same way. It doesn't affect those around you unless they're tuned to it by synchronicity—unless they've also asked to be tuned to it. The same thing happens in physics, with the elements of the planet. You have the ability to hold in your hand some of the greatest medicines that have been developed on this planet, and take from them the very essence of the intent from which they were created, simply by the very holding of them in your hand. The healing attributes will pass into your body without ever injecting them or ingesting them. This is called "substance intent."

Science, you know, is part of the whole scheme of life on Earth. Your medical discoveries are part of the plan. Don't ever look at medical science and turn up your nose because you don't think it's spiritual. It's absolutely part of the whole puzzle. Some won't be able to heal themselves with energy since they are not yet vibrating at a level that would support that ability. Chemistry and medical science is then what God has provided on this planet to help them. Sometimes it is a wise combination of physics and spiritual energy that brings about the finest healings for a light-worker! Remember that the next time you shun a substance that was provided to cure an ailment.

However, some of you have said, "*I would like to take this or that substance for healing, but it has other effects that I react to.*" Spirit is not in a vacuum. We have asked you to vibrate higher in what you call the ascension status. This higher vibration sets you apart from much of the chemistry that has been developed for healing. It makes you sensitive and reactive to many things that would not otherwise affect you in the lower energy you used to be in. Does that mean you can't enjoy your modern scientific chemistry? No. There is another way. It's called "substance intent."

We challenge you to try something: Grasp your hand around the actual healing substance, whatever form it's in, and give meditative intent for it to surge through your body. Use the attributes of the second awareness power we just gave you—with the "*we*" of your biology. You are giving permission for a physics miracle: The substance's healing properties will pass into you!

There are those of you who will rise from your chairs in a few moments and have this happen because you intend it. It will be the beginning of a very new awareness ability of yours. There are also those of you who will laugh this off and say, "*It isn't possible, it isn't possible. Kryon's really gone too far now!*" You see, intent is consciousness over physics. *Intent* is what has provided for miracles within the body for centuries. The most miraculous things you have ever seen had to do with pure intent, and the healing came *from the inside*! Intent travels into molecules. Intent has the power of a spiritual delivery system that flows into and sticks and manifests itself and blossoms. Remember when we said, "Watch for the live essence medicines?" Now you know why. Because the intent that was created in them—in the essences—in the chemistry, stays and sticks because it's *tuned* to your "intent to have them work."

Recently we channelled information to you that was about five chasms of the New Age [Chapter Six], and one of the chasms was about substances you will be able to cooperate with that will heal your body. We told you that those who do not understand about vibratory shifting will take the same substances you do, but nothing will happen. You may be cured, but they will not be. This is because of the intent that I'm now discussing as a power of awareness within your cells. And that's because of the Cosmic Lattice, and your ability to tune into it.

You see, you're a very powerful person! Every physical element on this planet understands and "knows" about the angel inside you. Did you know that? There are those of you walking around saying, "*I'm in a despicable life! Things happen to me that I have nothing to do with. What am I gonna do about it? I'm a victim of Earth!*" That's that duality working overtime, dear ones. It's actually just the opposite! Earth responds to *you*. How else could a lightworker anchor the energy to hold down an earthquake or keep the weather less severe or keep the mountain from exploding? They do, you know. We have told you of that very fact. The actual physical Earth "knows" who you are.

Purification of Ingested Food

Some of you have practiced this for some time, and some of you haven't a clue about this ability. You live in a society where you have problems that you call "the processing" or "overprocessing" of the food that is prepared for you. Many of you have little choice about this unless you grow all your own food. Some of you fear the chemistry that is added to your food and your water. You're not alone. The other cultures have their problems also, but it's not the same. They have just the opposite—food that is completely unprocessed, fed to the masses with the impurities therein, and diseases therein.

We're here to tell you that every single thing you put into your mouth as ingestion for the purpose of sustenance can be purified with your intent. Believe it! At your next meal, address the plate, and speak to the food in some way—silently, perhaps—or with your hand. "*I bring you to my vibration.*" The angel inside that carries the miracle of control over physics purifies the molecules so that only the sustenance attributes will be applied to your biology and nothing else.

You can take food that has potentially poor nutritional value and make it work for you in a way that's miraculous! Again we will tell you that there will be those who eat the same foods you do, where you will be sustained but they will get sick. This is due to your awareness, and the power you will have over actual physics. For over eight years I have spoken of the physics of love—now you may start to understand why the Kryon work is both mechanical and spiritual. Physics is spiritual!

Do you know what is going to eventually happen when a whole group of people is able to eat food that another group cannot? Or perhaps take medicine that will cure them whereas the other group will remain ill? It won't be long before there is a rift that develops between you and them. Do you think that they will turn to you and ask you what you have that they don't? No. The majority will go into fear, and they will brand you as different. As odd as it may seem, and as illogical as it might be from a spiritual standpoint, they will call you "dark" because you can do it and they cannot. And when you lose those friends, continue loving them! For in you is the seed of light, and they will always have the choice to stand in it! Do not throw anybody away! No family member deserves that. Throw no one away in your mind. Each one is known to your cellular structure as a member of the *family*.

Holding The Light (again)

We've talked about the energetic area around you before (in part two of this series). We told you that it is something you can affect. This process also speaks of the connection to the Cosmic Lattice, and it also gives you indications of knowledge at the cellular level that you have. You have the ability to affect the physics around you, and I'm not talking about bending spoons, dear ones, I'm talking about changing Human hearts.

By holding the light, a term that means "your choice to vibrate at a higher level, and to have an awakening awareness at the cellular level," you alone **push** energy wherever you go. And that energy, dear one, is tuned energy. Tuned energy is that which is "specific with intent." If I could explain the Lattice to you, I would explain about multiple Lattice energy ports, specific energy receptors waiting for the arrival of matching energy tunings. Because this is not a lesson about the Lattice, we will wait for another time, but the Cosmic Lattice is an energy maze that is alive and aware and recognizes *family*! (See Chapter Seven.)

This "tuning" is why one person, literally, can change a room's energy. Each intent and vibratory level is like a complex instruction set to the Lattice. Each high vibrating Human can tune to the Lattice in a different way. The Human cellular structure understands the tuning of the Lattice, and as you walk on this planet, these gifts of the "push of energy" will be different for each of you. Some of you will be able to walk into a room and everyone will turn—you call it charisma. It isn't. It's a "tuning of the Lattice," with the energy being changed by one but felt by all. Some of you will be able to place hands on others, and they will feel that you're helping them. You are then called "an energy worker." You become a facilitator. Many of you will understand that the hands actually work better without any touching at all. You are actually affecting the area around yourself and around them. The "tuning" of healing is one that actually changes the energy of the Lattice, allowing for the communication with strands of the DNA within the healee, awakening not only permission to heal—but also of the power to heal, using information that has always been there. It also promotes great communication from within the cells of the healee—where everything that is, is known.

This is a gift that you have known for some time, but expect it to be enhanced. For those of you in energy work who are used to this already, who know absolutely that the area around you can be changed, look for enhancement of this energy. Test it—take notes—find out the "hows and whys"—it's science, you know—energy science. It has attributes that you can feel, thus helping you to know how to tune it better.

We have told you before: This goes far beyond energy healing work. This push of energy has to do with dropping what you have called in the past "your protective shields." You now can drop all of them. There is no dark entity that is going to get through it—not with the energy level you have! Instead you create a bubble of energy **push** around you that is absolute. It's divinity, and nothing will get through it that is of a lower vibration—nothing! This is also simple physics. Can water run uphill? Can the weak energy of a battery go up against lightning? Can dark exist in the light? No. Its very definition [dark] is voided by the presence of light.

Listen to this, dear ones—this is for those of you who fear the dark side. Please listen, for this isn't just physics, it's also spiritual logic. There are many powerful magicians who work in the dark, who have discovered that there's energy in the dark They are right. It's all part of the balance of the universe. And they can attack you with their spells (their powerful dark intent), seemingly to poke you, metaphorically, with the energy they've got. The first thing that happens is that your cells acknowledge the energy (because it's real), and sends your mind a message to go into *fear*. Fear enhances the effect, and soon your physiological makeup and demeanor is actually cooperating with the energy of the spell. That's the way it works. Many of you have been "energetically aware" for years and have protected yourselves with your own "shields." This is no longer necessary.

Suddenly we are telling you that your new vibratory level, plus *intent*, is producing a gift that is a **push** of energy wherever you walk. [Kryon readers, remember the Parable of the Tar Pit?] This energy is like a beacon of light within a dark place. No dark energy can exist. Shields are an old concept, dear warrior of the *light*. Finally, you get to stand tall without any shield, since the arrows of darkness evaporate with the light—and your **push** *is* the light. Here is a fun attribute. The shield was always a defense against the dark. Light is an offensive energy against the dark.. think of it as a "dark destroyer." I want to tell you what's going to happen when you meet a person who is trying to use dark energy: You're going to end up affecting them! That's what's going to happen. This active gift of yours to "hold the light" is a precious, precious gift of the Lattice, dear ones. None of you with the wisdom of the mantle of God will abuse it, because you can't. It simply comes with the territory. God is biased in love. The wisdom of the use of light comes with the gifts of being able to hold it. And the **push** you have is that of love, and it's divine.

Control Over Emotion

The sixth miracle is your ability, through your connection with the Lattice and your attunement to it, to create peace in a situation that, in your duality, would never, ever let you do it before. Now we're talking about the emotional Human Being. Emotion, number six, is with a big "E." I'm speaking now about things that are very close to you. I'm talking about the transmutation of hate, jealousy, drama, and fear. I'm talking about the elimination of sorrow!

We stood before a group like this, with our entourage among you, holding your hands and hugging you, when we talked about the sorrow of Human death and the tasks of the Humans that have come here to give you that gift of sorrow (in *family* part II). We have spoken of the overview of what it is really about, and how a seemingly inappropriate and horrible tragedy is often laced with spiritual learning and purpose—therefore, an intentional gift from the one (or those) who left. We've talked about that, and we've pleaded with you to understand that through the Lattice and through the awareness of the cells, you can change the emotion of your sorrow into wisdom—wisdom to understand that the gift was for your enlightenment. It's not about the ones who left. They are gone! It's about you, and that's why they went through it. What a tragedy it would be for the death of one around you—a gift given to you by them, with your permission— for you to mourn it all your life instead of celebrating the intent and the love that went into its implementation. What a tragedy it would be! For the gift was for you, and it helps to open the awareness of the Lattice in yourselves, and that's what the gift is for—the one or ones who passed helping the other or others, who remain.

It's transmutation of sorrow—transmutation of hate—any emotional state that keeps you imprisoned. Let me give you the big one: transmutation of **worry**—fear's brother. Gone! That is the gift. Your cellular level will not let it fester and remain. Some might say, "*What has worry got to do with my cells?*" I'll tell you: When you worry, are you aware of the cellular change? Some of you stop eating, that's a clue. Your cells know! They know about worry or fear. Dear ones, listen: If your cells know about worry and fear, proven to you over and over, then do you understand that your cells also know about joy and enlightenment?

The transmutation of worry into peace—it's one of the greatest gifts of the wise Human who holds the light. For some of you sitting there—this is the best miracle. And I want to tell you from a family member: It's real!

Change

Number seven: You may not call this miracle a gift, but it has to do with cellular structure and awareness, and it's called change. Just when you get used to feeling spiritually different, it'll change. There are those of you walking the planet, in the process of "waking up," understanding your spiritual essence. One of your interesting attributes is that in the midst of your awakening to spiritual things, you are anxious!

Many of you are "waiting for the other shoe to drop," as my partner says. There's a level of anxiety because nothing is staying the same. And you're feeling it at the cellular level, of course. That's where the change is. It's time for you to grasp the theory of *a constantly changing cellular structure* being the normal status for the spiritual evolving Human Being. The evolution will not stop from now forward. It is called *ascension* because there is a rise involved, a constant, continual evolvement. This indicates that it is always changing, which is the way of things for you now.

What you couldn't do today, you'll do tomorrow. What you did today *okay*, you'll do tomorrow *great*. There will be discoveries in your life about why you're here on the planet. Great honor goes out to those who will feel the urge to leave one place and go to another, feeling "called" to do it. That's change! It's about holding your light, and holding the energy in other areas—and some of you will respond to that task. That's why we call it "work." Because there's always the duality that will talk to you at night in those strange hours about three o'clock in the morning and say, "You're a fool." And as long as you live, I'm here to tell you that the darker parts of your duality will be there too, usually presenting their arguments to you in half-awake moments, when you are most vulnerable. But there's part of you that knows better, that puts it to rest and says, "I'll be okay." That part is the new and peaceful wise part that carries the light now. It knows the truth—that now you're wearing the mantle of Spirit. You are now aware of the angel inside, and nothing will ever be able to take that awareness away.

Change is number seven, for it is, dear ones, the real miracle. It's the evolution of the spiritual Human Being—the ones we call *family*, who sit here hearing and reading this message. Family are the ones whose feet we've been washing for the last few minutes. If you haven't felt it, maybe it's about time you did, because we're not going to be here much longer giving this message. But not all are leaving. The entourage that is here, that has delivered these seven points of awareness for you, have a specific energetic sum. The sum that goes back through the veil will be different. It will be less! This is because some of the energies have poured in here with the potential of leaving with you when you get up from your chair! This is about *intent*, and about energetic delivery, which is spiritual. Now you know why you are reading this. Did you "feel it"? Did you respond to truth? Did you give intent? If you did, there will be some you call "friends" around your chair who will stay with you to enhance your spiritual evolutionary process. And make no mistake—for those who might not understand this and think it's too spooky or weird—the process is because you have called them. You have been in the right place at the right time, and we knew of the potential of your understanding and of your "feeling" that family is here with you now.

Awesome—all of you! We celebrate the ability to call you sister and brother—to visit you at a time in your Human lives, like this. That's another miracle! A decade ago, this communication wouldn't have been possible because the evolution that is here now to accept it was not here then. It speaks of how you have changed the energy around you. It speaks of how you are holding the light!

So it is, that figuratively we remove the bowls of the tears of our joy, which we've been using to wash each foot—each foot of every single individual in this place has been touched. Each foot of every single individual who has been reading these words has been touched. Not one has been left out. The little ones, the wise ones, the ones who have come in disbelief, are all loved without measure.

All of you are known by name. All of you are family. This is not about joining anything, since we are already joined as family. It's not about promising to do anything, since you are already here—fulfilling your promise to the family to walk the test of humanity. It's not about giving us anything—since you have already given of your entire entity the eons of time and energy to walk this planet by your choice. It all comes down to love. Will you allow us to finally love you? Will you let the awareness of the family of God enter your consciousness? Will you give intent to discover your *real* self?

And so we go from this place, having known that this has been a special time of hearing and of reading. It was more than that. It was our time to be with you again and to love you. Regardless of what you feel happened in your chair, we know that we got the opportunity to hug you. That was important to us. We are your *family*.

You are *never* alone.

And so it is.

Kryon

"Renovation of the Family"

The Family, Part Four

Channelled in
Breckinridge, CO
and
Perth, Australia

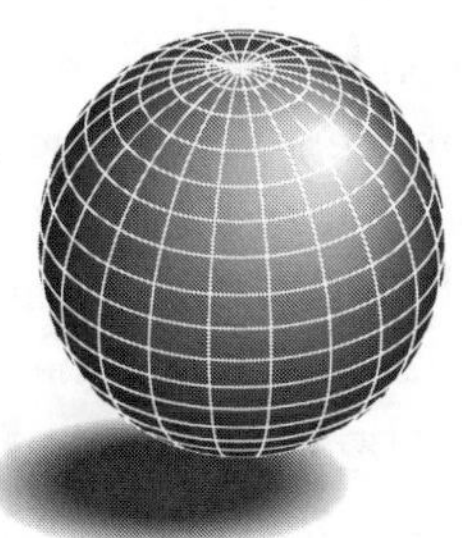

The Kryon Writings, Inc.

PMB 422
1155 Camino Del Mar
Del Mar, California 92014
[www.kryonqtly.com]

"Renovation of the Family"
The Family, Part Four

Live Channelling
Breckinridge, CO & Perth, Australia

The live Channeling that follows is part four of five sessions concerning "The Family" as Spirit sees us. It is a transcribed combination of two events on two different continents...with the same message...given live, two months apart.

Greetings, dear ones, I am Kryon of magnetic service. Indeed, this place is a precious area! Dear ones, we will now take a moment to allow the entourage that is Kryon—all of those entities who have been waiting for you to arrive here—to flow through this crack in the veil. And what this is about is the energy of "family", for the ones that come this night into this place are known to you. And many of you will feel and recognize the energy of some of those who used to be called "Human" and have recently passed over. Their energy will flow into this group along with the other angelic entities that I bring with me. By their very presence, they shout this to you, "We are eternal and so are you!" They bring an energy into this place that is love and that is also precious—to match the energy that you have created—even the one who is reading this *now*.

We say to you right now: Let this energy that now comes through, move between the seats, between the aisles, between the Human Beings, and let it allow you to feel the presence and light pressure of your spiritual family. Let the love in this room press upon you and become thick with its presence and reality. For we are meeting you at this time as family, one-on-one. Believe it! You see, we know your name. Doesn't that shock you that we would know of your invitation and the potential, and the fact who you were going to fill that chair or read this? Oh, the potential was strong, even to the ones that are here who only found out about it yesterday, or the ones reading this who have never read a Kryon channelling before. We can say to you that your name was known and the potential was known.

Dear ones, we miss you! We're slowly beginning to let you know about how this interaction between Spirit and Human really works. This family connection you have—this "home" energy that flows in here, should tell you a lot about who we are on the other side of the veil. My partner (Lee) has told you about partnership. My partner has told you about the enabling of the Human spirit. Now perhaps you'll start to get the picture, and that is this: You and the family are partners in all things! Dear ones, you cannot hide the light that comes from you. We told the other groups in this fine land about an interesting thing. We told them that there was an entourage that comes in with you at birth and stays with you—that there are far more of them than there are of you to support you on this planet, energetically. And so many of them are brought into action when you give spiritual intent. You can feel them around you, and some of you know of what I speak. Some of them become your maps and your intuition and help create the feelings you get to know and recognize. These are the intuitions that help you know whether to turn right or left, or to move forward or back, or to just sit still. These are what you would call the angels—the guides—those who love you beyond measure and are with you for life—and they are here, too.

We wish to fill this room where you sit with the presence of love in a way that's never been done before in this place or any other place where you've been. As you sit reading or listening, we want you to be aware that we're here. And let me tell you, if you're giving intent for what you came for, you are going to receive energy, for the solution! Perhaps it's only information you need—perhaps it's an actual healing! But that's why you came, or picked up this book. You think we don't know that? Don't you think we know, in addition to your names, everything about your life? That's family, you know. That's the love of family.

The tests that you face, much like the ones that my partner has described this night (in seminar earlier), all have solutions. You can't be shocked, can you, if I tell you that the solution was created by you? Ah, Humans think they come and walk in this plan called Earth, and are tested to find out where the energy balance is going to go. They accept this. They think that all their lives they're going to have tests and tests and tests. And those who are wise among you say, "*We understand that these tests are the ones we've created for ourselves. We understand how things work. We'll walk through them in this new partnership.*"

I want to tell you why you're going to walk through them—because you don't just have tests and tests and tests. Dear ones, there is a balance for you on Earth that we have described before (See "The Golden Tray," Chapter three). The message is given here in such love because we want you to have a revelation tonight. The revelation is this: With each test there is a solution of your own making! These energies come in as a matched set. Even though we've spoken before about this to many, there is still confusion. Know this: As you walk through this life, there are also solutions, solutions, solutions. This balance of test and solution creates a win/win scenario, one that you often can't even imagine on your own.

We wanted to emphasize this because there are so many of you who need the realization of this now. And we say in all love, "Don't you think we know what you've been through?" There is something you should know: You are never alone. Oh, you might try your best to think you are not, and there may be times when you're convinced of it, but I'm telling you, "It's not so!" There is never a time when you are without protection—even during a guide change, even during a shift. There's that word again: protection. It's new in this age, you know. It has to do with what we described one meeting ago when we talked about the power of your awareness. We spoke about what happens when you hold your light—all the activity of the angelic realm around you responds. We talked about this because there is protection there—

protection from making an error. It is so. It is part of the new energy—a part of the new gifts and tools. It's part of the map that Michael Thomas had in the story that we gave you (from the Kryon book *The Journey Home*). It is the gift of wisdom given to you by those who surround you called family!

You wonder why Kryon and the entourage become excited? You wonder why there is emotion—why sometimes my partner will actually weep with joy during a time like this? I'll tell you. We haven't just come to deliver messages of information. We have also come to give you the feeling of home—to make you aware again of who you are. There is also another reason—one that is common to each of these meetings: We're going to take this time to wash your feet. Let this process not be wasted on any of you, and as we've said to the other groups, and those individuals reading this—the potentials that are resting here for Human awareness and power are awesome! We speak not just of the Humans who sit in what your linear time frame says is your now, but also the ones who are reading these words now.

Let me address the ones in this room [the seminar in Perth]: There are many beyond this building who will hear and read this message. They may feel what you may feel on this day. They will know of the energy that can flow into a space like this and surround you in the love of God, for it may do the same for the space around them as they read. And as this love surrounds you, dear ones, and the vortex moves it between the chairs, we wish to remind you that this is given to both you and the reader. So as you sit here and listen, know that there are also family members on other continents who are "seeing" this at their "now." This event, therefore, is actually interdimensional since it speaks to you in a linear timeline, yet all at the same time.

[For all] We want you all to recognize this feeling, because you've felt it before. This feeling is the energy of "home" that comes here to your chair, dear ones, and it ought to remind you of who you really are. It ought to make you stand up and say, "I AM," because there is an angelic energy in every one of you that hides convincingly. The duality wants to beat you up and tell you you're nothing—but your family is here to let you know the opposite. For in this room, we greet those exactly like us. The only difference between you and those who have poured in here to congratulate and honor and celebrate the sacredness and preciousness of this moment is that you have agreed to come to this planet and have your magnificence hidden. There you sit, some of you, even wondering if this can be so. Oh, the duality does a good job, does it not? To hide such grandness—and it does. Each of you has a color spectrum that is awesome.

The energy of the room is precious so that you will be able to get a gift this day—a gift that I'm going to put on your laps right now, in a metaphoric way. It is a small box with a lid on it, and before the end of this time between us, I will give you the option to open that box. At that point, we're going to tell you what's in it. It's going to be a help for you because this crowd, and yes—even the reader, has asked for it. Ah, we don't speak to crowds, dear ones; we speak to individual Human hearts, and we know who you are—and we're speaking to you now. The box that is on your lap, which will be opened later, is for all of you. It's needed and necessary for your energy. It's going to enhance your vibratory rate. And the ones who choose to go from this place and not open the box, are honored and loved every bit as much as those who do. You are all loved as family. If you look at the story of the prodigal son, you will know what I mean, because the celebration in the parable was not based on what the son did. Rather, it's about celebrating the return from his journey. It's about just having gone the distance and returned!

There will come a time when we see each other again in a place that is far grander than this, when there will be a space for you to expand [indicating there is no space for that where you sit]. If all of you were to spin your energies at once, it would be far too crowded here. [Kryon humor]. But we're spinning energy right now, and we're filling this room, and we're filling the spaces between the chairs with the thickness of our love for you. Even as you might sit alone reading this, we are here. We'll speak more of this in a moment, but it's time for the teaching to begin.

We have said that this meeting is going to be about the future of Humans. Indeed, let us speak about this future. Right now, we're going to tell you something that may seem odd and strange. It goes like this: Gone are the days when Spirit can predict what you are going to do, or what is going to happen on the planet. Gone are the days when there is an overlay of strong potential that can lead a prophet to a conclusion based on energy. Gone are those days when any prophet can stand up in front of you and say, "This is going to happen," or "That is going to happen." And I'll tell you why. Humans are in what we will call "renovation." And as you renovate the very core of your existence, you are going to co-create a new energy that even we cannot predict. Renovation! And so right now, your future is one that is in renovation.

We want to give you several items to think about in the following list (which again, unfortunately, we have to give to you in a linear fashion). In this list of items there will be a message for you. That's why you came. That's why you're here. For when we are done, many of you will think that it is tailored exactly for you. We know this, because we know why you are reading and hearing this information. You think it's an accident?

Family Renovation

The Human Being in this New Age is in renovation! Since this is so, you must understand that you are not finished yet! And in the state of being unfinished, there are some attributes that you should recognize. Get used to it. Celebrate, and consider this the next time you're frustrated. Now I'm talking to lightworkers here—I'm talking to the ones who have given intent to move forward in their lives, who are sitting here saying, "*I accept this love from the other side. I recognize family, and I'm ready to go.*" But there will be some of those who will say, "*I've been ready for a long time. What's going on?*"

You've got another thirteen to fourteen months of renovation before some of you are going to really feel what it's about [spoken in September '98]. That renovation is due to the fact that things are changing far faster and quicker than your consciousness can catch up with them. We are speaking of Spiritual consciousness at the cellular level. Some are having difficulty every day—waking up and feeling different than they did the day before. There's no time to stop and relax, and get used to the feeling before another one comes along. Things seem to be moving very fast!

Cellular Shift

So, let's talk about what's happening at the cellular level first. This is number one, for it's the one you are feeling the most right now. We've told you before that this list must be given to you in a linear fashion. It really ought to be given to you in a clump—a circle—all at once. Some of you who understand what the third language is will get this information in that fashion—all at once. In this room some of you will believe you went to sleep when this is over. If this happened to you, then you have received the information in a far better way! For the transcription, we give this information to you in a linear fashion, but we tell you again that one element is no more important than the other. There is still a reason why we give these energetically in the order we do, but it has nothing to do with importance. It has to do, indeed, with the interdimensional aspect of energy.

Some of you are waking up feeling odd at the cellular level. Things are changing in your body, and you know it. There is a vibratory shift going on, and it's uncomfortable. I want to give you a metaphor related to that discomfort. How many of you ever had a situation in your homes where you've decided to renovate and at the same time live there? Some of you will say, "*Yes, I remember. It's awful, and we'll never do it again.*" Well, guess where you are right now? You sit in the biological house, and it's being renovated around you. You go to reach for things at the cellular level that were always there before, and you find they've moved! It's disconcerting—it throws you off balance. You're used to a certain feeling, and you don't have that feeling. This renovation is "cellular," and "cellular" means DNA.

"Kryon, are you saying that Humans are changing their DNA?"

"Yes."

"Kryon, how does my body's DNA relate to being spiritual?

That is what the magnetic shift is about [the reason for Kryon's work]. We have told you this before, even in the enablement meeting [one of the past "family" channellings]. Your enlightenment is related to your biology! Every cell knows of this and is as enlightened as the next cell. They all respond to magnetics. That is why the magnetics are shifting so grandly—now even in a way you can measure yourself. Do you understand that some of the Earth changes and situations you are fearing are happening on schedule, with your permission, for your DNA? It's happening so that the cellular level can shift—be enhanced—and increase in its awareness.

I'm going to tell you something about the cellular DNA of Human Beings. You've got a lot of children being born right now with a different DNA than you have. We speak of the whole DNA, not just the two biological strands. It is an evolvement—an evolution of Spiritual cellular enablement. The children are different from you, and the magnetics (Earth's grid system that is changing) will affect them differently than it did you. They will have equipment that you don't, that you will have to develop—one of the reasons why you are reading this. Did you know that? It is no accident that those dark blue children [the life force color], which you call the "Indigo," are being born in such abundance. The average age right now (1998) of the Indigo is between three and twelve, and there's a good reason. Carefully timed, it is, and planned around Earth spiritual measurements. You think the Indigos are special? Watch what happens with their children! Their children are going to start being born on or about 2012, and you better get ready for it because they are going to be startling—very different, even from the Indigos of today.

It will be the next obvious evolutionary step, should you choose to allow it. When we say that, we mean that you have every opportunity to stop this evolution or to advance it. It's up to you. You have free choice over the energy of this planet—free choice. We are only giving you the potentials—the ones we see based upon what is happening now, and what has happened that has indeed been awesome in these last years. The children of the children are going to be special. They're going to have attributes that even the Indigos do not have, and you're going to look at them and say, "*If this is what one generation has done, what will the next be like after that?*" Talk about the future of Humanity! As we run down this list, you're going to understand a lot more when we get to the bottom of it. We are also going to give you a far better overview of the *why* of this entire timeline when we present Part Five of this series—before the end of 1998.

So, what should you do if you are feeling these uneasy feelings? Do you find yourselves unable to "connect" like you used to? Cellular shift causes sleep changes and different eating desires. It gives you an odd feeling of "health anxiety." Honor these feelings—stop and be still. Celebrate them and understand what is going on. Understand that in any renovating, there's always the time when it's complete. Look for it. Expect it. But while there is any renovation, there is also change. The end result is worth it.

Consciousness

The next one is what we would call consciousness. The consciousness of Human Beings for millennia has been one of group following. In the cellular structure house that is being built (a metaphor), no longer are you **observers**, because you've become the **builders**. The renovations that are going on, therefore, are of your own making. You are the designer and the builder.

Many of you have traveled your lives [meaning all of your past lives], following, following, following. You've said that this is what you should do—it's expected and spiritually correct, and so you do it. Someone will come along with something new and say, "*This is what you should do now*," and then you do it. And some of you have a long string of disappointments in that "following" process. Now, we're telling you something amazing: We're informing you that the consciousness of following is now changing, and now we're asking you to be the shepherd and not the sheep. We're sitting here together as family, discussing something profound. You lightworkers are the leading edge of the front line of what is to come. Each of you considers yourself a worker in the Light—holding the Light—anchoring the Light. Each one can raise from your chair today with the potential of a shepherd, and never as a sheep again. It's part of the new awakening of "who you are."

Let me tell you what the consciousness does and what is happening. As you make this shift, the change is one that is uncomfortable. You may awaken unsettled. It's the same feeling as the renovation at the cellular structure except that consciousness is also emotions. It's how you think, and some of you generate uncenteredness, and even fear is created from being unsettled. In the past, these emotional feelings of being unsettled meant that something was wrong. This time, something is very right! The feeling of being unsettled should actually be celebrated! Be still, and know that *you* are God! Be still. Know that the I AM presence belongs in that renovated Human Being. It is the transformation of followers to leaders, of ones looking for knowledge, having the equipment slowly given to find it. It is part of realizing that you can ask for it and have it granted. This is new, and it's going to take some getting used to. You're renovating your consciousness, together with your biological cells, in a spiritual manner.

"*Kryon, I feel so emotionally uneasy*," some are saying. "*I wake up in the morning and don't know what's going to happen. Things seem okay, but I still feel uneasy. I'm not certain about my life. I don't really have clear direction. I don't know where I'm going. My emotions, well, they're often disturbed. I guess I'm having a consciousness shift, but I don't know what to do. Sometimes it makes me depressed, and sometimes I'm just tired. It isn't the real me.*"

I'll tell you, dear ones: Don't you think we know how that feels for you? We do. The renovation of the consciousness is going to take awhile, and we're asking you for patience, for stillness, and for celebration. There is time. You feel a sense of urgency, but there is time! Some of you are vibrating at a higher level, and the very vibration is making you feel uneasy. Almost with a sense of urgency, you feel you've got to do this, or you've got to do that, and you've got to do it quickly. This is not so. There is time. So we ask you to celebrate the feeling. Know that when the renovation reaches a stage where synchronicity can apply itself as you've asked, you will also have the answers you asked for. They will have been deserved, created by your awareness, and therefore designed by you. And until that time, be peaceful. Recognize the renovation, and greet it as a friend. I invite you in the morning when you feel odd, to say to yourselves: "*Hello, depression. Hello, uneasiness. I recognize you, I'm changing because I gave intent for it. During this change, I'm going to celebrate right through it until it's complete.*"

Your Spiritual Path

Here's number three. Some have said, "*I don't know anything about my path. Oh, Kryon, you've talked about this grand map we have. Well guess what? I'm in the dark! I don't know where I'm going. I have too many options! It's confusing.*" Some of you have said, "*I have no choices at all. I'm stuck. What am I supposed to do? Kryon, you come in here with this grand message, and I feel the love and I know this is real. I've given intent to be on my path, but I'm not seeing anything happening.*" Here's a metaphor, regarding the path, dear ones. Some of you will also realize that it's the metaphor we also gave you regarding how to "partner" with your higher selves.

Again we say, for years you have been passengers in a lifeboat—tossed about, seemingly in the ocean of life. And so many of you have reached up and asked God to put his hands on the tiller of that lifeboat and steer you into a safe harbor. Some of you actually live from episode to episode, storm to storm, believing that's the way life works. You figure that's what your path is. Some of you feel that you've got to flounder around and bump into walls until God comes down and helps you.

There is a new paradigm, and you are invited to get used to it. Dear ones, many of you are used to riding, and now it's time to drive. Instead of a lifeboat that God comes and steers, it's time for you to get directions from God, and then put out the outboard motor and pilot it yourself! And in this process of transformation from rider to driver, there is shift, and also the uncertainty of change. The path often looks like it doesn't have definition. For as many of you that say, "*I have no options*," there are as many who say, "*I have too many!*" Indeed, it must look confusing. Which is the correct way?

Have you ever been driven somewhere? Perhaps you are in a strange place, but there is a driver who knows the area. The driver is responsible, and all you do is ride. You arrive at the destination, but you really don't know much about how you got there since the driver took care of it. Therefore, what happens in life is that when you were not driving, you really didn't pay much attention to how the driver got you to the destination you asked for. Suddenly we are telling you that the driver is going to be *you*! Now you are really worried! You don't know where anything is! You never paid attention!

"*Kryon, what am I supposed to do with my job, my relationship? What am I supposed to do about my health? What's my path? I've never had to be in the spiritual driver's seat before!*"

First: Learn to use the map that Michael Thomas was given in the story *The Journey Home*. Oh, there's so much energy around this! So much! If you have not driven before, you are going to need the map! The map, which is a metaphor for intuition and discernment, will give you peace to "drive" in unfamiliar territory. What you simply trusted in the past will now be your responsibility. It will feel uncertain at first, but very rewarding as you get used to it. Remember, the road is seen clearly by your God partner. The communication to your map is through discernment and intuition.

Second: Whatever energy you're in, create your way out of the fear that surrounds it. Transform it through the I AM presence into celebration! Remember, it's possible to celebrate even in uncertainty. Celebrate the uncertainty! Then start asking for direct guidance that will be obvious so that you don't feel you're guessing. Now it's your hand on the tiller of that boat, with divine guidance as your partner!

For those of you who enjoy the vision and metaphor of being in that lifeboat, I want to tell you what your new vision can be. I want you to wrap your hands around that tiller yourself. The instant you do, give intent for guidance. Say out loud to Spirit, "*I'm going to use my partnership with my divinity to steer myself into those safe harbors of life.*"

I'll tell you what's going to happen when you say that: Those giant hands of Spirit are going to come and wrap themselves right around yours, and the two of you together, as family, are going to guide that boat to safety. As the driver on your path of your life, you can expect there to be another set of hands right there with yours. That kind of partnering is new, and it's going to take some getting used to. You're used to so many things being handed to you, and now with this new power you have, you're going to have to take action yourself. With the action comes awareness, and your *intent* will create solution with the guidance of a very loving familiar energy called family.

I hope you're getting the picture. It is one where we honor you for being in this place of uncertainty. Do you know the honor that goes into washing your feet? We know what you're going through, and we know the difficulty of the changes before you.

Energy

Let's talk about energy for a moment. So many of you work with energy. You've gone through protocols and spiritual disciplines that use energy, and you are comfortable with how it works. You are accustomed to what it feels like, where it goes, how it flows, and the results of it on others. And suddenly, it all changes! Here is something we have told others recently, but that you need to hear as well concerning spiritual energy: Yesterday's energy solutions are not necessarily tomorrow's. And what you feel right now—what works right now—may not work tomorrow. This may frustrate so many of you who are workers in energy, and I want to tell you why the rules are changing regarding energy. There are pieces and parts of the energy puzzle that are moving into new areas around you to complement the new power of Human enablement. These familiar tools have not left you. Instead, they're waiting for you to take new action to discover how they have renovated themselves for a better "fit" to your new renovated biology and consciousness. Dear ones, the master carpenter gets better tools than the beginner. The master chef receives a new kitchen with all the facilities for his craft. The spiritually renovated Human receives newly tooled energy to enhance the work he is doing on the planet!

For those of you who are working with energy, I'm telling you that it might feel different, but the tools are sharper now. Again we say, celebrate the fact that your power is increasing. You're going to have more profound results in your work than you ever had in your life! Pay attention to some of the new energies that are coming in and the intuitive information being given to you, because it will "marry" to what you already have and know. Dear ones, some of you meditate with certain kinds of energy and you expect certain feelings and certain ways of knowing you're in tune with Spirit. These very communicative energies have to be shifted to allow better intuition and discernment, and some of you will feel suddenly that you're out of tune. "*What happened with the meditation stream? What happened to the feelings I always felt?*" you might ask. When communication changes, do not be afraid. Stop and celebrate the fact that you've moved beyond the fear, and now you're searching for the next way to better use the renovated tools. Ask Spirit for guidance—which way to turn in your energy work, in your meditation, in your approach to your communication. Don't be shocked or surprised when intuitive ideas pop into your mind, much like the process of my partner channelling now.

There is never a situation where a puzzlement is beyond the energy of the solution. Let me rephrase that: You will never be given a puzzle that is too hard. The answers are there waiting to be found, and in the energy department, the changes are spectacular. The new energy is going to play a large part in renovating the very way you live.

And so we review the energy subject for a moment more so that you will be clearer. Whoever is using energy for whatever reason, know that it's going to shift and it's going to change. I'm talking even to the facilitators with seemingly new information. Look for the shifts. Look for the change. Change the protocol of the teaching to reflect the new information as it lands upon your intuitive self. Bring your students up to date as you have revelations regarding these energetic disciplines. Then learn the new ways of "feeling" when it comes to communication. Even the oldest spiritual systems on the planet are going to be enhanced. The energy of the spiritual part of humanity will change, and change more, and then it will change again.

Finally, we wish to give you another kind of energy "hint" regarding communication with Spirit. Take a moment every day to sit and be quiet. Don't meditate during this time. Just sit and be quiet. This is new. We wish you to sit quietly and simply be loved. Find out what it's like to be hugged by Spirit simply for being you. Don't ask anything or make noises or interrupt the flow. Do nothing but feel the arms of the family around you. Then go ahead with what you normally do. We invite you to become more aware of the whole. Be still, and let us love you! And that was number four.

Purpose

Next, we want to talk about purpose. What is the purpose of Humans here? In the old paradigm—the old days—the purpose was always about lessons, and perhaps you've heard that all your life. Those of you who have been part of this spiritual philosophy, who have understood who you are, and the grandness of the changes, have understood that this life is about learning, learning, learning. Now, suddenly, we are telling you that even this is changing. Whereas, you have always felt your place among humanity as students, we're telling you now that you're starting to feel like graduates. Oh, it goes beyond graduates; you are now the teachers.

So the metaphor of your existence is moving from student to teacher. And the renovative attributes that we are discussing are actually changing your purpose on the planet. Oh, you're still here to walk through tests, dear ones, but some of the reasons you're going to walk through them is so that you can teach others. So teachers, we invite you to pay attention to this—this new way of being as the purpose of humanity itself shifts. Ask the new children what the purpose is of their lives. They're going to give you some alarming answers. Why are you here? Go ahead, ask them. They're going to give you answers that are so wise and so profound that it redefines purpose. Don't be surprised if they also tell you about the love that they're here with!

You know, Spirit does not exist in a vacuum. We understand how disconcerting shift and change can be. We're asking you not to allow shift to knock you off the path. Remain focused on the work even during a shift at the cellular level, at the consciousness level, at the energy level. If you understand renovation, then you know about change. Even during confusion or apparent disconnection, we invite you to laugh and know that it will eventually settle with even a simple effort and intent to find out where the new "center" is. Celebrate the change, since it would never be happening unless you were indeed the worthy one being changed!

Interaction

Let me tell you about number six. This relates to number one, which also relates to number four, for it's about the cellular and it's also about the energy. It refers to the future of interaction with Human Beings to other Human Beings. This is an arena in which you have already started to see dramatic change. If you want to see consciousness shift, it is going to show itself first between Human and Human. This is the area where it is most dramatic. How many of you are feeling a change in passion? It is going to be part of the shift of consciousness and purpose. Do you see how these are interrelated? There is a renovation going on regarding the interrelationship between Human and Human—and the way they "see" each other. We are not speaking of just lightworkers now, for this is taking place on a planetary level. It is the kind of shift that the magnetic grid adjustment is giving all humanity. Let me give you some attributes of that shift, dear ones, for the lightworkers reading and listening as they hold their light high.

Some of you in these last few years have been given a change of passion. Many of you are aware of other Human Beings on the planet in a new way—far more than you ever were before. Oh, you cared, but never to the point you do now. Perhaps something energetic will happen on the planet that is far away, but you feel the Human reaction from it. This is new for you. You are "tuning in" to the family.

There might be gifts delivered in a spiritual way from one Human to another, which normally you would translate as a tragedy, but there will be an overview of wisdom regarding the whole event. And although you will weep for them, you will realize that your emotions are different from the way they used to be. For with the magnetic grid shift comes an interaction between humanity, which is far more humanitarian, as you call it, than it ever has been before. It has to do with a shift in family. Family is beginning to see itself as family. No matter how far away the event on the planet, no matter what language the participants speak, and no matter what they believe, many times the passion will well up in your heart and go out to them. And you'll say a prayer and give them energy, and you will say, "*This is different for me, for I never used to do that.*" You are beginning to care about the family.

I'll tell you what's happening to Human Beings, and you can see it now in the children. I want to tell you what the children do in the families. Watch for this. The children in the family try to make peace. If there is dissension between mother and father or brother and sister, you can expect the children to be right in the middle of it, playing the part as peacemakers. Dear ones, Humans are moving from observers to peace makers. There is so much hope and so much potential even as you look at the Earth and you say, "*There are too many Humans here, and there is so much potential for strife, disagreement, and war.*" That's the paradigm using the old Human in charge.

We spoke of the children of the children: The attribute of the Human beings that are going to be born from the Indigo children is one of peacemaker! It is the peacemaker that has the potential to arrive around the year 2012. In a way that you have never seen before, all of them can understand the wisdom of living together in peace. They will also have improved immune systems. They will have tolerance for things that you don't, and it will amaze you. Watch for it. The potential for this is profound. Peacemakers, each one. That is the Human potential. That's the future of the power of the seventh one, which we are going to tell you now as we wrap up the teaching.

Awareness

From the first moment the teaching began in this series called "Letters from the Family," the attributes of humanity were given. One of the chief attributes of the new Human was awareness. And this subject of Human awareness was expounded upon, and the powers that awareness brings to you were listed, one through seven.

Now, here it is, the seventh in the list, and it's also called *awareness*. We list it again because it is an important one. If there was a hierarchy to be assigned, this is the one that threads its way through all of the messages. Awareness is action, and it is manifested with intent. Another word for *awareness* is *enlightenment*. Awareness brings power. Awareness activates the Cosmic Lattice (the energy of the Universe). Did you know that? Look at the energy of awareness. Analyze how it responds to intent, and you're going to have a key if you want to plug into the Lattice. Number four was energy, and now we're again talking about that, too. The energy of communication with Spirit is all about contact with the Lattice.

"*Why so much talk about the energy now, Kryon? Didn't we always have the Lattice?*"

Yes, you did. But it is only within the last few years that Human Beings had the power, through awareness, to reach up and grab it spiritually. It's the presence of the I AM that allows such a thing to take place (the enhanced awareness of the sacredness inside you). That's the partnering we have spoken about. That's the spark of divinity inside you speaking. That's the I AM presence that is taking hold. Awareness!

There's a box in your lap that we gave you earlier. Oh, I know it's metaphoric, but some of you can feel it. Some of you know of its vibration. It's been there for some time, and for some of you it's getting hot because it has potential. And I want to tell you what's in it: In that box is the catalyst to awareness. It's the thing that you're going to have to face in order to find out who you really are. It's the thing you're going to have to *own* for your awareness level to start building—in order for all of these things to work that we've discussed here today. And the box is closed.

Inside that box there's something that has your energy on it. It has been brought to you in this time as a gift, a fast track for manifestation. Because there will be some who will walk from this place who don't understand the box, who don't want the box, who don't see the box. Others will welcome it gleefully. For those of you who wish to open that box, you can do so now, and I want to tell you what is going to come flooding out—flowing into you. It's something that you've needed for some time. It is the ultimate catalyst for awareness, and it is called "self-worth." It is finally yours for the taking, and you can stand from the place where you sit and feel taller than you ever have before because this gift is yours—with your very essence on it. And this gift of self-worth is going to finally let you receive the things that you've given intent for! Perhaps you wondered what the missing piece was to get spiritual action in your life. Some have said to Spirit, "*I want to stop worrying. I want to understand healing. I want some direction.*" The key is self-worth! It is going to give all those things a jumpstart, for it allows for the awareness process.

Oh, it's time, isn't it? It's time you felt this. And I'm going to tell you what self-worth is all about. Self-worth is the knowingness that you are part of this family. Self-worth is going to let you feel, in some way, the love that goes into the foot washing that is still in progress. Self-worth is going to let you understand and finally feel that "you are not alone." You have protection. You have energy around you that is so specialized, as you "push" your light to those around you.

There is nothing inappropriate that will ever be able to penetrate that "light push" of yours. What we're saying is that the energy of your spiritual countenance—of your light that is fueled by your connection with the lattice, is so strong that there is no need anymore for shields. You *are* the light as you walk into and around your space and your family and your work and your life. Newly established and powerful self-worth is going to amplify that light you carry to a degree that you are going to do the active pushing of sacred energy from now on. Wherever you go, that light is going to be sufficient to push out, push out, push out. And there will never be an energy that can get through it that is inappropriate. You can walk among the darkest energies you can imagine with a smile on your face and celebration in your heart, knowing that it cannot touch you. You have the self-worth that is the catalyst for awareness, which creates the power of the connection to the lattice.

Oh, some of this may seem interdimensional and odd to you, we talk, perhaps, in riddles. For as many who feel that way, there are also as many who are right now starting to truly understand why they decided to receive this message!

[pause]

It is for the healing now being received that we give celebration as your family! Because there are some hearing and reading this who are finally in full understanding. It is for the remarkable changes that are going to take place in some Human lives that hear this message, that we give celebration as the family congratulates you. And isn't it about time? That's why you are reading and hearing this!

I want to give you another vision, dear ones, and it's about your duality. It's about those fears that like to chase you down the street—telling you that none of this is real. It's about that consciousness that wakes you up in the middle of the night, usually about three A.M., and says, "*What are we going to worry about now?*" I'll give you a vision. You're in the driver's seat with your self worth. You've got the light. The part of your duality that creates fear is very real and belongs here. It's part of the balance you agreed to. But now it's going to take a back seat! It's time for

fear to be the passenger, not the driver. You see, you're the driver now. So, next time that fear rears itself in your life in all its ugliness and energy, we want you to face off with it and say, "*Hello, old friend, I know who you are! It's time for you to get in the back seat now, because I'm driving. Get behind me now, because you're never going to lead me around again, never!*" That's what fear does, you know. It leads you. It takes you here, takes you there, disappoints you, throws you on the ground, makes you sorrowful, and changes your countenance and makes you sick.

"*Fear, get in the back seat now. I don't want anything to do with you anymore.*"

That's your vision. You know how you can do that? It's the thing you took out of the box that lets you do that. And I invite you to celebrate the fact that you now claim it. Feel the I AM presence as it flows into you. Celebrate the guides that have been activated because there is so much love here for you. Feel the family as it hugs you, before it removes itself—as we collect the bowls of the tears of our joy, as we finish washing your feet. Feel the family touch you, as it says, "It's about time that you came to a meeting such as this." There's so much family here—those whom you've known, that you've spent eons with. Yet, you may walk from this room not even recognizing they were here! Such is the duality. That's why we love you the way we do. What a task you've chosen for yourselves! What a challenge you've chosen for yourselves.

I'll tell you what we've chosen to do: We've chosen to love you through it. With every passing month on this Earth, this "crack in the veil" is easily opened—more often, and with greater opportunity each time. This kind of transmission you're hearing and reading now is going to enhance itself. And each time it happens, we ask you to look for the verification that it's real. The real verification? It's the love that goes into it. It's thick, and you can feel it.

And now it's time to withdraw. Dear ones, there will never be another time exactly like this one. This family in the room here, and the ones who have come to be with you even as you read, will never occur exactly like this again. Oh, there will be other meetings, other reading times, but this is a profound time. This is a precious time for this family. Even as you rise from your chairs and leave the room and go back to your work, we want you to feel and understand the preciousness of this moment. This is indeed a precious moment—when Spirit can come in and family can touch you—because you gave intent for it. And the feeling? It's the feeling of *home*! It's an energy you know well, but which you only capture occasionally during times like these when you are surrounded by the family.

And so it is, dear ones, that we retreat from this energy. As we've said to the others, there is something extra for some of you: We are aware of the ones through this teaching time who have given pure intent to receive information who have awareness and understanding, and who have made shifts even in this short time together. And so it is, dear ones, that the number and amount of entities who pass through this crack in the veil will be fewer as they return than when they came. What we're saying is that there are some of them who are going to stay with you—ones whom you've given permission to stay. The guide changes have taken place, right here, right now—the verification of the colors that have been seen. That's because you needed it, dear onesss, and you know who I'm talking to.

Isn't it about time you recognized yourself? You've spent a long time waiting for this time. Could this really be so? A family reunion right here? Yes, it is real, and so is the love that visited you here—and so is the feeling we have as we miss you in our retreat from here. We know full well that there will come a time when we will see each other again, dear ones. Oh yes! And you'll recognize me by the colors I have, and I'll recognize you by the colors you have. And you will say to me, "Greetings! Wasn't it a grand time when we saw each other for those few moments when I was a Human, in that year when so much was happening, when you reminded me of who I was?"

And I will say to you, "Who are you?"

And you will say, "I AM that I AM!"

And then I will welcome you *home*.

And so it is.

Kryon

"The Meaning of Life"
The Family, Part Five

Channelled in
Laguna Hills, CA

The Kryon Writings, Inc.

PMB 422
1155 Camino Del Mar
Del Mar, California 92014
[www.kryonqtly.com]

Before you read the next section.... Read This!

Many of the readers of the Kryon series of books know that the gamma ray mystery activity that is now fresh in our local news was foretold by Kryon in Kryon Book Three, "Don't Think Like a Human," page 67. This information was channelled in August of 1993. At that time, he told us to expect this discovery and look for it. Kryon Book Three, "Alchemy of the Human Spirit," also discussed it on pages 236 and 242; and Kryon Book Six, "Partnering With God," mentioned on page 367.

Many recall that in a meeting in Sedona, Arizona, in March of 1995, Kryon told us that the "Big Bang" never happened. In a surprising scientific channelling (published in Kryon Book Three), he gave us another explanation about how the universe creates itself, and invited scientists to find it for themselves. In Kryon Book Three, he states, "The truth is that there were many expanding events (many bangs) over a great amount of time. The truth is that your planet sits among one of many overlapping creative events, some of which were earlier than your own." In 1995, this information was unacceptable to mainstream science, which was becoming more convinced all the time that the entire universe started with one genesis "bang."

Finally, the idea that perhaps the "Big Bang" is suspect is starting to be realized and postulated by a few scientists and astronomers. In a new magazine published by *Scientific American* called the *Magnificent Cosmos,* there was an article by Andrei Linde, a Russian-trained professor of physics now at Stanford. He championed a theory of a "self-reproducing" cosmos, which is now being studied for its merits. The universe started (he postulates) with one small creative event, which then over time led to another, then another—explaining what we are actually seeing as we look out with our telescopes, and also the paradox of age that was reported last year when the Hubble telescope discovered stars at the edge of our known universe that were younger than we were! (If the Big Bang theory was correct, they should have been the oldest.)

According to Dr. Linde, "If my colleagues and I are right, we may soon be saying good-bye to the idea that our universe was a single fireball created in the Big Bang. The evolution of inflationary theory (multiple bangs) has given rise to a completely new cosmological paradigm, which differs considerably from the first version."[1]

I report this because the next section of channelled information informs us that the gamma activity that astronomers are seeing almost 12 billion light years away is indeed another universal creative event (another bang).

What are they seeing? Here is a report from *Science News*, Volume 153: "Astronomers are calling this gamma ray burst 'the most powerful explosion since the Big Bang.' — 'This burst was as luminous as all the rest of the entire universe,' says George Djorgovski of the California Institute of Technology in Pasadena."[2]

I just wanted you to hear it from science before you read what Kryon has to say in "The Meaning of Life."

[1] *Magnificent Cosmos* Magazine; Andrei Linde; "The Self-Reproducing Cosmos"; Scientific American Presents; (ISSN 1048-0943); Volume 9, Number 1, 1998; Published quarterly by Scientific American, Inc.; Madison Avenue, New York, N.Y.; Copyright © 1998 by Scientific American, Inc.; All rights reserved. [www.sciam.com/specialissues/0398cosmos/0398quicksummary]

[2] *Science News* Magazine; R. Cowen; "Gamma-Ray Burst Makes Quite a Bang"; Volume 153, Number 19, May 9,1998, page 292; (ISSN 0036-8423); Published weekly by Science Service, Washington, DC. [www.sciserv.org]

"The Meaning of Life"
The Family, Part Five

Live Channelling
Laguna Hills, CA

The live Channeling that follows is part five of five sessions concerning "The Family" as Spirit sees us. It contains additional words and thoughts to allow clarification and better understanding of the written word.

Greetings, dear ones, I am Kryon of Magnetic Service. Oh, and you thought you came to see me? We are here to tell you this very night that there is a spiritual entourage pouring in to this place. And they pour in because of the intent in this room, and because of those who have chosen to read this transcription. Every single one of you is known to us. Every single one who sits in a chair reading or hearing is known. For we are speaking now to those we would call our "family"—a family that is well known to each of us.

This particular information on this particular evening is indeed going to be about family. It's going to be about *you*, and let me tell you what's happening right now, before we get into the teaching. For this is a time, dear ones, where the energy of the entourage that has been brought this evening pours in, and it walks between the seats. It walks down the aisles. It presents itself to the lone reader, and it knows who you are because it is family. It knows of the message to come and the profundity of it. It knows that perhaps you are going to "hear" it for the first time—but you will absolutely remember it!

There are those of you hearing and reading this who will indeed feel and know the touch of Spirit before this is over. You will know it because you have given intent for it. Even the ones who come unprepared for the energy, if they have given intent, will feel and will know. Let the proof that this is real be in the experience of those of you who wish to feel it. Every name is known. There is an energy of every single earth creature here. This is a sacred place! We have told you about this before: You come and sit in these chairs pretending to be Human—all of you. You don't know how it all works because it's not obvious. The duality hides the fact that you come as grand family members—each one of you—yet you are just like me.

There are those of you who say, "*Well, I have come to feel the energy, and I've come to listen to Kryon*," or "*I just like to read the messages*." I want to tell you that there is an entourage that has been here a very long time, knowing of the appointment in the chair that you sit in, knowing of the potentials that you would be hearing and reading, ready to flow forward and meet you. We know of the message tonight. We know of the new information that it represents. You think it's an accident that you are reading these words? We speak now about love. We speak now about those in this entourage who wish to "hook up" again with you, and all they want to do right now is hug you and prepare you for a message that is different indeed—and filled with revelation.

Feel the love pressures—placing their hands gently onto your shoulders, onto your legs, onto your arms. There are those here who wish to do nothing more than hug you through this message. That's all. There's nothing profound that they wish to do besides sit a moment with the family. It's the only chance they're going to get for a while, and it is by your intent that you have allowed such a thing. In the process of this evening, there's also a whole bunch of them who have come for one reason, and that is to wash your feet. What we have for you tonight is a story of who you are. Finally, we have the ability to tell you, in a succinct fashion, who you are and why we love you so much.

This message has been a long time coming. We told you that we would give it, and some of you have been expecting it, since we told you when it would be. Now we can speak so freely—so powerfully to the family that is here! We have something in common, you and I. It's more than you know. Oh, this is a channelling, yes, and the entity who is Kryon comes to work with the magnetic grid system—and to love humanity—to give you information. That is the task of Kryon. But in the process, I want to tell you that truly, there is no distance between us. For the voice you hear, literally from the other side of the veil, is one of you. There's a spark of divinity inside each of you, which we call the angel inside, and it has the attribute of family.

Let the foot washing begin! Let the entourage pour in here now and celebrate humanity! We know who is here—hearing and reading this. We know of the desires of your hearts. We know of the struggles that you have gone through, and we're here again to say that there are those of you who will leave with more spiritual essence than you came in with. There is going to be less energy leaving with us than came in, because there is intent here—marvelous, sacred intent.

Be still for a moment. Quiet. The information that follows is sacred.

This is a precious place. If you haven't started to feel the family, you're going to. If you give intent for it, you will know we're here. This precious, precious family sits in these chairs...hearing, reading...each one with an angel inside. And the one who has come wishing for a sign to know what to do, let it be given now. The one who has come with the expectation of a healing, from pure intent, let it be given now, because that's your Human miracle, created by you, for you, and with your power. The Human is an incredibly powerful instrument—an entity that is awakening spiritual power on Earth—an entity who is unique in the universe. That is what tonight is about.

Let it be known that this is the fifth in the series of the **letters from the family**—the **letters from home**. This is number five. For those of you who study numerology, you know that there are no accidents within any of the numbers. Five is about change, and it's appropriate that number five be the explanation about the change in humanity. And finally, finally, we have some answers as to why you're here. When we tell you what the title is of number five, there will be some of you who will be taken aback. The title of number five in the series, the one you are hearing and reading, is: *The Meaning of Life.*

"Kryon, do you mean to tell me in the next few moments you're going to us the meaning of life?"

"Yes, I am."

This is why I say, "Be still." Quiet. There has never been a disclosure like this before. It is sacred information, and it drips with truth, with closure, with purpose, with remembrance.

When we are finished, you are going to know why you're here. You're going to understand what the timetable is, and you're going to know more fully what's happening—what has been hidden from you—and where you are going. So much information we have for you right now—we cannot move into this without celebrating. We are quiet and reverent. My partner wells up with this experience, now knowing what is coming. There's nothing more sacred, dear ones, than when one on this side of the veil gets to come and speak to you. Do you know who's in this room and who is reading these words? Family! You don't come home very often, you know.

Review

We've been talking about the family, literally, for months. All the family channellings were scheduled to be delivered in 1998, and this is the last one [Dec. '98]. We've talked about the attributes of that Human who is really an angel. We've talked about your power. We've talked about what's happening at the cellular level to your body. We've talked about the fact that each of you knows, at your cellular level, the entire story. I told you that the family misses you. We gave you information that was startling to some when we told you that there is no other planet like this one, and we're going to expand on that.

We've told you that every single one in the chair right now hearing and reading this is a frontrunner—drawn to this energy by something they remember. It's no accident that you're sitting here, even the new ones. No accident. You are drawn to be here, or you would not be sitting here reading and hearing this. The intent you have agreed on to sit in the chair is seen by Spirit right now. [Child makes a noise.] We're going to talk about you also, little ones, very soon.

And so it is that through these months, we have discussed some of the attributes of the family—some of the responsibilities, some of the purposes, some of the powers. But nothing like this has ever been given to you. It's time to tell you why you're here—the whole story—from beginning to end. We're going to reveal what is taking place right now, and some of you will go away in disbelief, for the duality is strong here, as it should be.

My partner continues, before he starts this, to well up with what is coming. He sees our appreciation and love in honoring what goes into why you are here. I'm talking about *you*, those of you sitting or reading here right now, as this entourages moves through here. You are not hearing or reading about others. *You* are the subject.

Let the foot washing begin.

Let the truth unfold, and resound at a cellular level.

Before we can begin, we have to take a trip, metaphorically, to a very faraway place so that you will understand how you fit in. Angels, each one, listen up! Much of this will resound at the heart level as I tell you the story of what you've agreed to do and what the lineage is for humankind—the reason and the purpose. It will resound at the heart level. It has to, because you know it already. I'm just here to awaken it within your existing knowledge.

I want to take you to a physical place in the universe that is 12 billion light years away. I want to tell you about an event that is transpiring there right now, in that place where there is very little matter. It is an unfathomable distance from you. You cannot even imagine how far away it is, yet from that place there is emanating, in real time, energy that is actually striking Earth right now and causing you to pay attention.

It's important that you understand that this event is *current*. It is not 12 billion years old as you may think. It's in real time. We spoke sometime ago about how the speed of light is slow, but the speed of energy is not. All is related to that, but for now it's important for you to realize that what is being "shown" to you is indeed in your time frame...expected...planned.

Do your scientists see it? Yes. Let me tell you what your best scientists are saying about the event that is happening now, 12 billion light years distant. For years we have told you [published in Kryon books] that the gamma ray activity you would discover striking your planet was significant—even that it had a spiritual meaning. Indeed, the scientists are finally seeing the energy, and the gamma ray activity riding upon the energy. They're reeling from what they're seeing, and they're trying to understand the reasons for it. They have said that there is a giant explosion taking place in that far region of space—very large, indeed. Your astronomers are saying that the explosion taking place 12 billion light years away contains the greatest amount of energy ever seen in the known universe! They have reported to you within their journals that it is equivalent to all the light in the known and seeable universe—all at once—in one event. That's what they say. It's real. It's happening. This is not something that is only metaphysical—only seen by those who believe, "known" only by shamans or prophets. NO! This is something that any Human can look at and see for themselves. (see page 133)

Why would I take you there—to this event so far away? Why would I want you, dear angels, to see that? Humans, as you sit in your chairs, why does this family member called Kryon take you there? Because there is something happening in that vastness that has the energy of your humanity stamped all over it. I'm going to leave you there for just a moment because I want to tell you why this is important.

Why is it, do you suppose, that things are happening the way they are here in this millennium shift? What are you feeling that you've felt before? Your meteorologists tell you that this is a unique time, that there has never been one like it—at least not one they've measured in Human history. They're right.

Did any of you ever wonder why you are receiving the gifts of Spirit right now? Why is channelled information increasing at this time? Why is there so much fear around termination right now? Some of you have postulated that perhaps it's just time for it. Some feel that it is simply where the Human race has taken you at this point in history—that these things would have happened anyway.

I am here to give you information that there is purpose—there is planning—there is a timeline here; there is consciousness behind the events as they unfold. It is no accident that right now, health facilitators are seeing an increase in their powers. It is no accident that right now that those dealing in science are having an increase in what is being given them in specific areas—in physics and also biology. It is no accident that the Human Beings and finally being understood biologically so that they can live longer. It is no accident that the consciousness of the planet is changing dramatically. Something's up, and many are feeling it. Something's up, and many are starting to celebrate. Some are beginning to fear, but in all this, we tell you that the timeline is indeed coming to an end. We're going to tell you about all of it.

The Cosmic Timeline

Let me tell you about the cosmic timeline, which is something that is ingrained in every cell of your body. I know it's ingrained in every cell here because I know whom I speak to. I know who the family is. We sit around a living room, so to speak, in a very loving circle where the family can talk to the family. That's what's happening right now as you read this. We want you to *feel* this family chat that we're having right now, because you're going to recognize why you're here. Even if this is new information, there's going to be a point where you recognize why you're here. You can't help it, because everything in you will resound when you find out.

The cosmic timeline reveals a purpose behind why you're here—a purpose behind spiritual history itself. Some have called it "the grand five billion-year experiment." Do you know whom I sit in front of? Again, I will tell you: I sit in front of Lemurians—almost all of you. That's what brings you here today, to hear and read this. This time in history calls to you and brings you here because you're feeling the Lemurian energy again. That's how long you've been here. That's who the *family* is who sits in the room and reads these pages—old souls each one. You come and go so fast! You don't spend much time at home—my home, your home. And we see you for a brief moment, where you pick up a stripe of color—where you have an honoring and a loving—then from the depths of your wisdom, you return to do it again and again and again.

Some of you have been through a thousand or more of these experiences called incarnations, and you know it. Here you sit, facilitator, are you listening? Here you sit on the edge of the very point of, perhaps, potential termination, or potential emancipation. Most of you hearing and reading this are of an age that when you were born this time, Earth's energy was predicted to bring you a violent end—yet every single one of you came in on purpose anyway. You came in willingly and lovingly, because you knew why you were here. We have told you that you figuratively "stood in line" to be here! What kind of an entity would do such a thing when the prophecies gave you such a bleak potential? Why would you willingly come back, raise families, and desire to be here? It's because you knew that this was the end of the journey. You were not going to miss the outcome, no matter what. It's everything you have worked for. It's what the Family is all about.

The termination of Atlantis, the great flood—these were the things that postured the energy of your duality in order for a grand test to take place. Most of those hearing and reading this were there for most of it. You were also the ones who programmed the crystaline markers. Listen, family, we're going to tell you about the grand plan. We're going to tell you about the test, and we're going to give you the timeline.

It was all on purpose, this Earth. Humanity was not an accident. Grand spiritual entities who disguise themselves as Humans did not just "happen" on this planet. The timeline and the test were known to you before you came—all lovingly appropriate in Spirit. And here you sit on the only planet of free choice—and that is the key. You didn't hear it here first, the phrase, "The only planet of Free Choice." It was given to you eons ago. Now the meaning will be clearer to you when we're done. But now we're going to review for you the trilogy of energy that has taken place around your lives. We've spoken of these things before, but this is going to be an expanded review, with more information about the three things that took place not too long ago which changed the outcome of this known time line.

Dear ones, you've lived for eons [baby cries in audience]. Even the "little one" who comes back does so, knowing full well the energy he brings in. And he comes back again, this time, knowing full well that this indeed is the end of the timeline.

The Harmonic Convergence - The Next-to-the-last Measurement

It was in August 1987 when some of you first understood, during the Harmonic Convergence, that there was a measurement going on. Those of you who were intuitive and metaphysical understood that Spirit was measuring the planet. And we have spoken of this before, because the product of that measure was higher than the potential from the measurement that preceded it. Earth's vibration was not going down; it was going up! It was considerably higher than the measurement that was taken the time before.

Some of you will ask, "*What measurement that was taken the time before?*"

Here is information that some of you have known, but which has not been transcribed from this entity, ever. There has been a measurement of this planet's energy and vibrational rate every 25 years, from the first point of time when spiritual humanity came to Earth. That's right—every 25 years from the beginning of humanity, there has been a measurement. Twenty-five years, to Spirit, is a Human generation—the average amount of time for the Human to grow up and have children of their own. Twenty-five years. If you do the numerology on 25, you will get the sacred energy of 7; that explains the 25 year period.

This means that the immediate measurement before 1987 was taken in 1962. 1962 was a "9 year," and the 9 has the energy of "completion." The last three measurements, getting to the end of humanity's timeline, would indeed determine the outcome of the test you have been part of. The energy of the 3 is about "action." The 1962 measurement, the first of the last three, indicated what the completion of humanity, and the test, could potentially be.

In 1987, most of you were alive to experience the Harmonic Convergence. This was to be the next-to-the-last measurement. That was a "7 year" (1987)—sacredness. Its measurement would be indicative of your spiritual energy. The last measurement is 25 years from 1987, and that's going to be your year 2012, the end of the test—indeed, the end of some Human calendars. 2012 is a "5 year," carrying the energy of "change."

Those three events, 1962, 1987, and 2012, are a trilogy of energy and potential, which are extremely important to both the universe and humanity. Together, they represent the energy of 3 and that is the action number again. If you will add the "9 year" (1962) and the "7 year" (1987) and the "5 year" (2012), you will again get the 3, which is action. This trilogy, the action trilogy, dear ones, is the end of the test—the end of everything you came for. We all knew it on this side of the veil, and you knew it, too. That's why you couldn't wait to return. Some of you even died early so you could be here at the very age you are now—all poised for the end.

Most of you have lived for eons, lifetime after lifetime after lifetime, and you've gone through so much! Yet, you couldn't wait to get back, because this was it—the culmination of all your work. The timeline is a set one. That is, all have known of the duration of the test, and the potentials. Yet, in you came—and here you sit.

When the next-to-the-last measurement was taken at the Harmonic Convergence in 1987, a revelation was upon all. Earth was found to be raising its frequency. Human consciousness had shifted far, far beyond what was expected for only 25 years. What happened due to the high measurement in 1987 was the creation of still another series of events, which was given to you to prepare you for a heretofore unrealized potential!

The "permission poll" and the "passing of the torch" were to be events unscheduled in 1962, but now very appropriate in 1987 and beyond. The "permission poll" was called the 11:11 window of permission [January 11, 1992]. It would never have taken place had the Harmonic Convergence not showed Earth to be at an accelerated level. Some of you have studied the 11:11, and you think you know what it was. I wonder if you really understand what it was. The numerology of (1)+(11)+(21) = 33. [In dates, add the whole energy number of the month, day and year separately]. This is a master number of great significance.

11:11 Revisited

For some of you, this is going to be a stretch, because this is interdimensional information. Every Human Being on the planet—all of you—were polled as a group of angels (which you are), and asked if it was appropriate to move to the next level. The reason that permission was needed is because your biology was about to evolve past what the past potential was, and a meeting was necessary for you to give permission for it. It would be the first time for the allowance of a biological, spiritual evolvement of humanity, and you said "yes." Within that polling, there were a large group of Humans (everyone on the planet). This poll was done at a cellular level, and a high spiritual one. You probably can't remember ever being asked, but you were—all of you were. Needless to say, there was excitement at hand, and the excitement was universal—that is to say, you all shared it, and you all felt it. That higher part of each of you, who knows all things, really knew it. The planet was about to change in a profound way.

Some have asked, "*If we are indeed all pieces of God, and angelic-like beings with the duality of humanism, why did we have to be asked? Isn't it understood that we would indeed say yes, and isn't that what the energy of Spirit is?*" The answer should show you how much we honor the Human, for this is indeed a planet of free choice. Free choice got you where you are, and because you are still Human, there was part of this process of spiritual evolution that had to have permission from the Human who was alive doing the work within duality.

Here is something else that is important: How many of you are aware that on the 11:11, there were many groups that agreed to terminate over the next generation? Indeed, groups of Human Beings, family that you know and that I know, agreed that the "fast track" to the critical mass of a high vibrational Earth was termination (to allow their quick return as Indigo children). Some realized that if the planet was going to move into an accelerated vibration, their tribe would have to be slaughtered. How's that for the love of God? I told you this would be difficult. This is not new news, for you can find it in many Scriptures. You can also find it in the ten-year-old channellings of Kryon, and you can find it in ancient prophecy. Potentials were there for some to give away their life force so that the others could raise the vibration of the planet faster. And that is exactly what is happening. That is why the 11:11 has so much potent energy around it.

Stop for a moment, and be still. Do you understand the significance of all this? When you heard and read of genocide, and horrible atrocity within other parts of the planet, that you call the "third world," what was your reaction? Most of you were appalled. Most were greatly saddened, and you mourned. Let me ask you this: How many of you celebrated and said "thank you" to the family who decided to do this? Not to celebrate their deaths, not to celebrate the horrible way many of them died—but to celebrate the fact that they gave permission to help the planet! This is *family*! This is how *family* sees the planet. This part of the family, so far away from you, is connected in a profound way to your work! Celebrate *them,* not their deaths. Celebrate the fact that *you* will benefit spiritually from what they decided was appropriate in the wisdom of God. Then celebrate the children that are here now, many of whom represent the soul extension and reincarnation of these precious souls who left early. I hope this gives you a wiser perspective of some events that perhaps were considered inappropriate, or "not of God." Things are not always as they seem.

12:12 Revisited

The 12:12 event (December 12, 1994) was also far grander than you knew. Again, the numerology of this date is (12)+(12)+(23), the sum being 11. Eleven, as you might know, is another "master number," and is also the known Kryon energy. There are no accidents in the numbers.

The "Passing of the Torch" is what we call that event on 12:12. First, there was the measurement (1987 Harmonic Convergence), then there was the permission (11:11 in 1992), and then there was the action (12:12 in 1994). With your current vibration and potentials, there have been entities on this planet, who have been here holding the balance of energy for you until now. They have been here since the beginning of humanity, and all the measured potentials indicated that they would probably remain. The spiritual energy balance of the planet (as previously channelled) must remain constant. As humanity increases, the entities holding some of that energy leave. But even with eight or nine billion Humans potentially on Earth in the future, there would still have to remain many of these "balancing entities" for spiritual purposes.

Upon the 12:12, they left. They all left. Some of you felt it. Some of them left from the secret areas of the forests; some were the guardians of the canyons where the red rocks are. They are no longer there. If you go there today, you will find that the energy that used to be there has changed. Perhaps some of you felt that this was a negative thing? It actually changed some areas of nature, and those areas don't "feel" as sacred. Understand, however, what happened, for this is the time when these entities passed the torch to humanity, on time and on schedule, with appropriateness caused from both the Harmonic Convergence measurement and the 11:11 permission.

It is important that you understand *why* the entities specifically balancing the planet were given permission to leave. Within the 11:11, you gave permission to take on the spiritual power that they had been keeping for you. As previously channelled, this passing of the torch was not just metaphoric, for 144,000 Humans actually received an increase in their spiritual awareness. Also, as previously channeled, most of them were not on the American continent.

The 12:12 event, unbelievably, was known by the entire spiritual Universal community (not the seen, physical universe, but the spiritual Universe). It was a celebration because we knew what the next step had to be. We knew what the potentials were. Dear ones, the things that could have happened on this planet, didn't. The prophecies from long ago, which represented the known timeline and targeted certain potentials at the end of the timeline, are now incorrect because of what you've done. Ah, but there is more, and we're getting to it.

Things That go Bang

Along the journey of the Kryon channelling, there have been some big hints given to you as to what is currently happening. In March 1995, my partner took the Kryon work to Sedona, Arizona, where a scientific channel was given. This is not the first time we gave you hints of science before your scientists actually got to see it, but this time was important regarding the physical universe. At a cellular level, there was actually a lot of winking going on from all who attended, for as we have stated many times, the Human cellular structure knows everything.

At that time, we told you that what you call the "Big Bang," wasn't. There actually is no such thing as the "Big Bang." We continue to invite your scientists to have a three-dimensional look (measurements from other platforms, along with Earth) of the energy of the universe. Within that channelling, we invited them to release their bias. There is far more going on as they look into the heavens than a simple unified paradigm created from one creative event. Scientists also believe that there is only one kind of physics—their kind, the local kind—which they see around them. Therefore, because of assumptions that there is only one kind *seen*, then there must be only one kind everywhere. This is the common biased belief. Even though one of your most three-dimensional thinkers explained the physics of time, scientists also believe that "local" time applies everywhere. They also look at life, and they feel that because they can only see one paradigm (Earth life), no other might exist.

Finally, they see only one creative event. All of their instruments in the area of space measurement tell them that there was one creative event. They see a telltale "residue" of "bang" energy, and even though they can only measure from one point of view, they have decided that the residue is everywhere...equally. Therefore, they say that everything they can possibly see everywhere was indeed made from one creative event—the local one—the one whose energy they can measure and seemingly find everywhere.

Dear ones, what if you were able to biologically query the cells in your body and ask them to look around the billions of other cells. Ask them what the beginning was: They will tell you that it was the birth of the Human Being. They will tell you that there was one birth—and only one birth—and that it is responsible for everything they see. This is due to the fact that they are part of a closed system—a system that is profoundly complex, working together with billions of parts—all from one birth. The one cell does not relate biologically to any other cell outside its own system.

Therefore that cell would be shocked to know that there are other Human systems! The truth would be revealed only if you could find other cells from other Human systems and query them together with your own. Then you and they would know that perhaps the evidence would indicate at least two births. You get the idea?

It is time for science to "unbias" itself away from the singularity of matter creation, and understand that there are dual and triple and quadruple creative events even among the universe that you can now see and measure. There are variables with all of the things you see as you look out—variable physics, variable time-frames, even variable matter ages—which will eventually prove to you that all matter did not come from your local creative event. It is time for science to drop the biased premise that if they cannot *see* it, it must not exist. Develop instead what it might be. Postulate beyond what is, and go to what could be. What does the physics of what can be seen tell them it could be? For already there are dichotomous observations with the new instruments of astronomy—giving hints that indeed there might be indications of a series of "multiple bangs"—multiple creative events in your own observable physical universe.

Some of you are saying, "*So, Kryon, that's nice science. What does that have to do with a grand Human plan?*" You will see, for I'm now going to tell you what the plan is.

The Grand Plan

Let me tell you of the "Grand Plan." It is a five-million-year plan, of which you have participated only in the last portion. I want to tell you about the physical universe and a little bit about balance. We have told you that you are angels from the Great Central Sun—that's everyone here, and those who are reading this. The word angel is not exactly right, but it indicates the sacredness of who you are. We have told you that Earth is pure and that every single one of you is from the Great Central Sun. We have told you that we hid you as Humans in a system with one sun. Those of you who remember this information will now realize that these messages were hints. What does it mean when we say, "We hid you"? Hints? We gave you one sun. Most life forms in the universe have dual suns. When you find it, you'll know why. We hid you because you had a task to do.

Dear ones, the universe—the physical universe—is not where the Great Central Sun is. The Great Central Sun is representative of "home." It is yours and mine. It is the place where I will again see you someday—the place where we will have a grand party someday. And we will look back, even at this time, and on this night, and remember the spirit of the preciousness in this room. We will say, "That's the night Kryon told us who we are and why we are here. That's the night it resounded in our hearts."

The physical universe, much like your own planet, must have balance, and this balance is represented in many shades of energy. The shades of energy we speak of are different shades of love—just like on Earth. Some of you will call certain shades negative energy, but it isn't. All balance is simply shades of love. Some of you have read stories about the struggles of those who are not Human, perhaps on other worlds or on other planets. Seers and intuitives have told stories and have written about marvelous and dramatic things that have taken place apart from your world. The lineage of those other entities has actually been channelled off and on through the ages. It's a hint, you know. It's a hint that there is balance in the physical universe. There is pushing and pulling regarding the different shades of love in the universe—just like on Earth. Those channellings prove it.

There's another creative event happening, dear ones—another "bang" twelve billion light years away, and it was scheduled for "now." It was always scheduled for now. As we indicated at the beginning of this channelling, what astronomers are seeing is indeed the evidence of another "bang." It's another creative event, in the process of making another part of the universe! It will be added to your universe, just like all the other creative events were.

Tens of thousands of years ago, you agreed to come to this planet and disguise yourself with duality—an energy posturing of the Human Being, which would keep you from seeing who you really are. It has worked well, for it has presented you with an even, unbiased playing field that is neutral in its energy potential. And the challenge is this, the test is this: If left alone in this test without any spiritual interference, dear ones, where would the energy go on Earth? Perhaps you are asking, "*Why? Why go through this—these thousands of years? Why come and go? Why the duality? Why the struggle? What's it for?*"

Some of you have said to Kryon, "*I feel like I'm a lab rat for God. I'm pushed and pulled around in my life. Oh, I'm a good, spiritual person, and I'll go through my struggles. I'll face my fear. I know I planned it, and I'll take responsibility, but I hate it. I don't know why I have to do this.*"

Here is something we have told you before but that is now germane to this subject like never before. Let me tell you something, my dear family, my dear angels, the ones from the Great Central Source who sit in these chairs, who read these words, who know who they are at the cellular level: *You* are not the experiment. *You* are not the test. *Energy* is the test. *You* are, wearing the white coats. *You* are therefore, the experimenters, facilitating the work of the test.

The energy of the creative event, twelve billion light years away, is incomplete. The birth of matter and of billions of life forms that will develop in that portion of space is incomplete. There is something missing. What spiritual energy is that new universe going to have? What kind of "shade of love" is that new universe going to have? Who's going to decide that?

Some will say, "*Well, let's just let the family decide that. The family represents love and is spiritually attuned. Our family, by definition, is God! Just paste the highest energy possible on that universal birth. Make it high!*"

Isn't that a bit biased? You see, the family is biased in love! God cannot make that decision. The universe must have balance, and to simply paste a high love energy on the new creative event is a biased decision. Some have said, *"You mean there are some things that God cannot do?"* Yes. God cannot lie. God cannot hate. God cannot make that unbiased decision.

So it was agreed that a planet would be created with life designed in neutrality and hidden appropriately, so that the angels from the Great Central Sun could populate it over tens of thousands of years to achieve a test of spiritual unbias. They would come to Earth to have hidden from them who they were. Part of their core biology would be given by others in the physical universe along the way to help balance their spiritual evolution. They would walk in Human form, die in Human form, and be reborn—die and be reborn. There would be a quick turnover of life. Biological bodies designed to last for 950 years would only receive 30 at first, then over time, 70 or 80. Preprogrammed spiritual information within Human DNA would create death and disease and aging. Residues from one life would follow to the next, creating tests that would be either resolved or unresolved with the energy that was being tested. The resolution of the tests would create additional energy that would change the planetary vibrational rate.

The end of the test was set for approximately your year 2012, the end of the calendar of some of the ancient ones of the Earth who intuitively presented that information. The final measurement, plus the end of the test, would come then. All agreed.

Other entities finding the Earth, even though it was well hidden, would not be allowed to interfere. They would recognize the great power of the spiritual attributes of Humans, even though the Humans oddly, could not (due to duality). Many of these visitors would only be able to "get close," to investigate humanity Human by Human—but never without the Human's permission. They would use fear to disable a Human's consent, thereby tricking permission at the subconscious level. A fearless Human could easily say no, and the entities would have to depart. They would be interested in the spiritual power, the choice, the ability to change—all of which they do not have. They would even try to breed with humanity to discover this and try to capture it. All of that was to poke and prod and find the essence of the Human's "angel inside." Humanity's hidden power would keep them from landing en mass.

All of what has just been described has indeed happened.

What has just been written is a description of *you*. *You* have done it all. Indeed you are the *family* that we speak of from the Great Central Sun. Earth is the testing field. It's one of a kind. There is no other planet like this in the physical universe. What finally happens here, dear ones, will be the energy applied to the new creative event, twelve billion light years away! What happens with the energy of the year 2012, when the last measurement of the spiritual calendar is taken, will be the energy of the new universe, as yet unnamed. Your energy is going to be supplied to that new universe—then it will have a signature. It's going to have the stamp of humanity upon it—your names upon it. Many of you may even eventually live within it.

Earth has been called "the only planet of free choice," and of course, that is a metaphor. It's time for you to know what that means: It means that there is no other planet—no other life force or form in this physical universe—that has the ability, by it's own consciousness and intent, to raise it's spiritual attributes. No others have it! But you do. Other life requires an evolutionary process for spiritual change, and intent has no power. That is the "free choice" that is spoken of. You are the only one! How does that make you feel? Historically, spiritualists and scholars intuitively knew that Earth was very, very special. It is! It was no accident that Galileo, who agreed with Copernicus, had to go up against such religious fervor that insisted that the entire universe revolved around Earth. Well, guess what? Metaphorically, it does! It does! That's who you are. You are *family*.

The plan is almost over, you know. The timeline is finishing, and what's happening is a miracle of your own making. It's why you've come back over and over, and it's why you're here again. Human consciousness and world events are not turning out like you thought. The prophecies that were developed from eons of consistent potentials are now failing to come about, and it's because of what you did from 1962 to the present. What kind of entity would metaphorically "stand in line" to come back, with the high potential of being destroyed horribly in the prophesied end times along with their precious earthly families? Who would do such a thing? You. You were not about to miss the last chapter of your work. Representing the incredible wisdom of the mind of God, you are here again, dear family, to witness something that no family member could have predicted.

The energy that has been developed, which has the potential to be placed upon that new universe being created, is a very high shade of love—very high. Your family on my side of the veil is biased in love. Your family is, therefore, celebrating what you have done. Your family is also standing in line...to have you back!

The future: What now? The Test is Over.

Some have asked, "*Since there is now no Earth termination, and the test is almost over, will we vaporize in 2012? What is going to happen now?*"

I want to tell you the kind of Humans who are on the planet and who are coming. It will help you understand what is before you if you wish.

In the parable of *The Journey Home* (Kryon Book 5), there is information about the "House of Gifts and Tools," which we channelled right here [in Laguna Hills, CA]. In that story, Michael Thomas (the main character of the parable) saw many, many crates in a huge chamber. He understood that they were the gifts and tools of the ascension status. Indeed, there was a crate for every man, woman, and child on the planet. But nothing was going to happen until the Humans who belonged to the crates realized that they could open them.

Almost all of you here, and those reading this, are of a Human that we will call, "Type A," for lack of a better designation. You represent *biological birth within old energy*. You have come through the stretch of eons of time, and here you sit with DNA and spiritual attributes as it always has been. But now there is one change in your potential. Because of what you've done, there are now gifts being given to you, by permission from the 11:11. As "Type A" Humans from the old energy, you have earned the ability to go beyond your imprint and move to a new cellular vibration. The tools are here, and pure intent is the key. Next, connection to the energy of what we have called "the Cosmic Lattice" is what some of you have discovered, for it is the way you will go far beyond the energy you came in with. It's powerful, and it's time for this. [There have been two channellings exactly one year apart, regarding the scientific attributes of the Cosmic Lattice. Both are presented in Chapter Seven of this book].

Cells are being reawakened by the science that is being presented in the new energy. Your biology is being reawakened in a way that is appropriate, with your permission. In other words, those in this room, and those eading this, have the ability through your study and your intent, to find ways to live longer lives, to move into ascension status, to have fears drop away, and to find life passions you never knew were there before. You have permission to have the old contracted lessons in your lives taken away—to have peace over the things that seemed impossible to have peace over, and to live a life that is far different than ever imagined. That's what you are being given.

Do you think that this would happen if you were just going to vaporize?

Earth will take on a new task. Like millions of life forms within your physical universe, this planet will eventually join with many of the others. The potential is great, and I now speak of a new plan that is not immediate, but you have the ability to move toward. This new plan will eventually bring you into an energy, that we are calling the "New Jerusalem." It is what some of you have been waiting for all along, and it's within your grasp. This is also the time when you will eventually "officially" meet other life forms.

You have the hard part, dear ones. You're the "old guard." You're the ones who will have to change your biology to match the coming energy. You're going to have to do things for yourself that the new children are not. That's why we gave you the other four parts of this message and waited until now to give you the fifth. The new children represent the kind of Humans who are of pure "Indigo" status, born after 1987. They come in with equipment that you never had, and although they may seem like misfits now, as time goes on, you are going to be aware of whom the misfits are going to be. For when there are more of them than of you, it will be obvious that unless *you* have changed, you will be the odd ones.

The Indigos come in with a purity you never had. It is a spiritual overlay you never had, and the reason is that they have raised themselves with permission. Remember the ones who gave permission on the 11:11 for their tribes and their countries to be visited and scourged with great death? Do you know who they are? They're the Indigos! They had the fast "turnarounds," coming right back to participate in spiritual evolution. They're the *family*! Look into their eyes. Do you know what they've been through? These are old souls. Watch for them. Before they're of the age of six, some of them will tell you all about who they've been. That's how clear they are as they arrive. We will call the Indigos, "Type B."

Ah, but there's another kind of Human on the way—"Type C." Do you really think that spiritual evolution is going to stop here? This is still the only planet of free choice. This planet has the ability to raise itself spiritually, and that's just the beginning. The first test is over; now Earth is moving into a role that will actually have the ability to change the parts of the universe that it is *in*! In 2012, you're going to see the beginnings of the next generation—that is, the children of the Indigos, and that's when it really begins. That's when the true Human spiritual evolution will really be seen clearly. These children of the children will be far different than even their parents. They will represent a generation of spiritual evolution that has the ability and potential to change Earth completely—and we're going to name them. We're going to call them the "Peacemakers"—with a DNA change you can actually see!

Not all of them will be spiritual giants. No. This is, and will remain, a planet of free choice, with Humans in a form of reduced duality. These children, however, will have a predisposition to create a peaceful planet—and will have the wisdom and self-worth to make it happen.

That's what you've got in front of you, dear ones, if you choose it. You sit here in front of *family* as you hear and read this. This has been precious family-to-family talk as we have washed your feet. Some might ask, "*Was the five-million-year test worth it? We're reaching the end. Was it worth it?*"

Yes.

As we told you at the beginning of this series, every single Human who has ever been alive is alive again now. The others joining you have been gathered all over from *family*, from the Great Central Sun, and also other parts of the physical universe. Some of you come in with astonishing star karma from other places, but you're Human now, and you're here for the duration. And that's why we love you so much.

Some of the old guard, who began it all, will not come back. Many of you are finished after your current lives, and we will welcome you with open arms because we miss you! It means that this is your last lifetime on Earth—and some of you know it. Many of the others, non-Lemurians, will indeed come back, for their challenge, like yours was, is to now create a new Earth.

What can you personally do right now? Perhaps it's time for you to fully understand at the conscious level who you are. The first thing you can do this night, when you're alone, is to look at yourself in the mirror. I challenge you to say something to the mirror, three times. I want you to look into your own eyes. Stand tall, and say these words: "I AM, THAT I AM." Perhaps then, when your biology hears it with your own voice through the air, and sees it in your eyes, it will be easier to **own** the concept that there is more to you than what you thought.

Each family member receives an "energy stripe" when he/she leaves this place called Earth. It's a stripe of color that applies to you in your dimension. Wherever you go in the universe, other entities will realize that you were part of the great energy experiment of the planet Earth—the test that's wrapping up right about now. That's why there's so much fear right about now within humanity, for at the cellular level, Humans know that the end of the test is at hand. [More about this fear in Chapter Four, "Shadow Termination."]

Blessed are those who do not hear this message, for even though they will fear the coming of the end, when it does not happen as scheduled, they will be ready to receive increased knowledge from those who have been joyful throughout all of it. Many will turn to *you* and ask why. Now you know.

Celebrate the end of the test!

Celebrate the new universe whose energy is that of humanity!

This is the hard part, where we gather the bowls of our tears of joy and start to leave this place. You've finally allowed the information to pass to you. Is it any wonder why we're so excited here? This is the end of a massive project that you planned so well. Some will get up from their chairs in disbelief. It's not important. The truth remains the truth no matter what is accepted or not. Some will only remember when they get "home." Some know now. Some are about to change themselves dramatically. We celebrate the types of healing that are beginning due to your acceptance of this loving time.

I'm speaking to *family* whom I have known personally—forever. We have no beginning and no end. Each of you is eternal in both time directions—like a circle, like the "now." We are all eternal. We are all *family*.

The entourage slowly retreats from this area. Those who have been hugging you for this time begin to come back through the crack in the veil, a crack that was opened through your intent to sit and hear and read. But the love remains. It remains in your heart should you intend for it to be so. Remember, guides are activated with loving, pure intent. Indeed, you are never alone, and it does not take a Kryon meeting or a Kryon message for you to feel the energy of a loving family. It is within you constantly. We know what you're going through, and we know who you are by name, each and every one—because you're our family.

So what is the meaning of life?

Go outside and look at the stars. They are yours.

The meaning of life on Earth is that there was a design that you have put together, implemented, and lived through. You did it appropriately, successfully, responsibly. Now there comes a time when some of the family will come home.

And I want to tell you: I'm going to be there when you arrive.

I'm going to be there.

And so it is.

Kryon

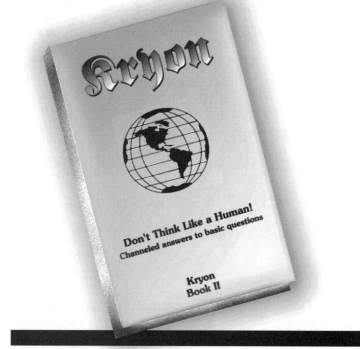

Transition Knowledge for the New Millennium

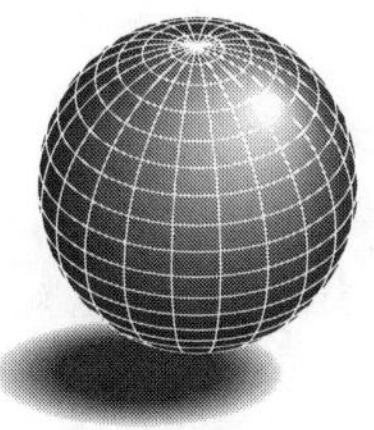

Chapter Three

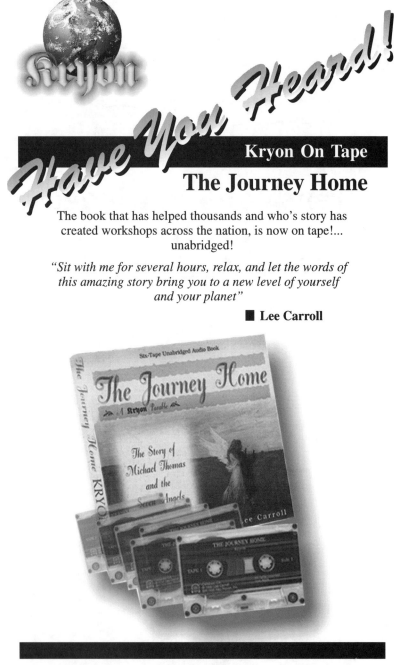

"The Absolute Power of Love"

Channelled in
Detroit, MI

The Kryon Writings, Inc.

PMB 422
1155 Camino Del Mar
Del Mar, California 92014
[www.kryonqtly.com]

"The Absolute Power of Love"
Live Channelling
Detroit, MI

This live channelling has been edited with additional words and thoughts to allow clarification and better understanding of the written word.

Greetings, dear ones, I am Kryon of Magnetic Service. It's an anointed time—a sacred time, for there is a crack in the veil that is opening, literally, right now. As my partner comes to you with the love that is felt this afternoon, we want you to feel the energy as the entourage presents itself to you. This is an entourage from "**home**," and we say something to you that we've said before: "We know who you are, each and every one of you hearing and reading this."

There is a tendril from our hearts to yours, which we call the Cosmic Lattice. It is the connection to home. It is the spark of divinity that is in all of you, and that is in all of us as well, and it is a communication which that is always there—currently hidden and suppressed by the design of the duality in each of you. There is a preciousness here, a preciousness of love and it's going to flow like a soft blanket through this group. These entities that you can call brother and sister will come and sit between you. Some will stand beside you, and some will stand behind you. They will flood themselves into this great assemblage in this room and also where you sit reading, and make themselves known to some of you who wish to feel their presence. For it is an anointed time, by appointment, that you sit in these chairs with the intent to know more about who you are.

I am Kryon, and I am in the *now*. When you are not on this planet, so are you. There is no grander entity in this room or where you sit reading, than any other anywhere. I come to you now as your sister and as your brother—even to some of you as the mother/father figure. For all that is "family." We come in a posturing that perhaps you're not familiar with that is of total and complete unconditional love for you. We're not here to tell you that you've done this or that incorrectly, or even correctly. We're just here to love you. That is the entire reason for these events. As long as my partner (Lee Carroll) has put himself in this space—for the linear time you have designed for this planet—as long as he is going to do it, that is what will happen in a meeting such as this...the emphasis of love.

We have known for days the potentials of your sitting here, and even of those who are reading this seemingly by "accident." As we have said before to so many—especially those of you for the first time who are hearing this voice and beginning to feel this energy—we want you to know that we knew of your arrival—of your sitting in your chair reading these words. We know of the chair you sit on or the floor you lie on—it's the energy we expected here because you are of our family. Perhaps you think we didn't know you'd be here? We speak to those of you who only discovered this particular gathering days ago. Don't you find it interesting how things melded together that let you sit here and feel this energy? You think that was unplanned? You created your own synchronicity—and now here you are at the right time at the right place.

So we tell you that this is much like a reunion—a precious time where all of us can meld our energies temporarily, and you can remember and you can feel. The things we wish you to remember and wish you to feel are as follows: In each and every Human in this room, there is a divinity that is awesome. It matches everything that you think of when you think of an angel. It matches everything you could think of when you think of any divine being. Before we end this afternoon, we're going to revisit a little bit of that angelicness and speak of that again.

As we come into an assemblage like this and flow through this group—as we press upon you an attribute of the thickness of love—we are again here to wash your feet. And so it is that this spiritual assemblage comes before you and kneels! These brothers and sisters from the other side of the veil, one by one, will honor you through these moments, metaphorically, with the tears of our joy, and will wash each foot one by one. That's our joy! You wonder about the joy and the love that we have from the other side? You are our joy! This is because we're talking to family. Each and every one of you—all of you—are eternal.

Over these last months, we have presented messages that are linear for you. These messages have been about the family. Although we are not going to call this another "family" message, in effect, *all* these messages are for the family. Before we continue, we wish to review some of the previous messages: We spoke a great deal about the power of awareness. That was one of the attributes that we presented the first time—the essence of awareness that you have as a sacred family member on the planet. In the second session, we talked about the tasks of the family, and we mentioned again the power of your awareness—your intent and what it does. In the third session, we zeroed in on the power of that awareness and the changes that occur when you give pure intent. In the fourth message, we spoke of the rejuvenating Human. We spoke of the renovation going on within your bodies. We spoke of an absolute physical, mental, and spiritual change happening on the planet right now, which you are the focus of.

Now here we are again speaking to the family about your *power*. Can we use the word *pride* as our reaction to your work? Perhaps it is not the perfect word, dear ones. You don't have a word in any language that can express our love and honor for our family here! For those of you who have come to your chairs and know you are sons and daughters of the family—for those who know exactly what the feeling is to stand up and say, "I AM"—you are the ones we are really addressing when we say we are proud to have a family that has done what you have done. There are more of you all the time, but we sit always, before the frontrunners. We always sit before those who have been here many times, for that is what has brought you to this energy, you see. That is what you related to when you heard my voice, metaphorically, through the words of the transcriptions that were responsible for bringing some of you to these chairs. What you felt as you read those words was not simply interesting new information. It was indeed a message from *home*! That is why it resounded as it did. So here you sit, on schedule, on target, for a reason—and that is to feel this energy—the reunion energy of a family gathering.

You are the **family on Earth**. There is purpose for your life, and a grand plan for you, which we revealed before ("The Meaning of Life," Chapter Two). So many of you continue to say: "*I wish there could be obvious solutions for me. There are problems in my life, and I feel so anxious. I need help.*"

Don't you think we know this? Do you know how many entities surround each of you? There are far more of us than there are of you! You have a support group around you that you never see. They're here for energy balance. They're here for love. Some of them are here to be activated by your *intent*. We have discussed this before. Even with that kind of support, many of you still stand there in the darkness, thinking you're absolutely alone and nobody cares—thinking that nothing is going to happen that is good for you.

There is literally a huge working entourage around you that loves you. There are family members standing there waiting for you to take action, to give intent, to stand up and say, "I AM," and to say to God, "I recognize that angel inside of me."

That's the reason I'm here. How many of you really, really believe that when you lie on that final bed, that you would call the bed of passage—the death bed—that it's the end of life? I'll bet if I could poll this group and present the results so they could be seen, there would be none of you who really believed that. You see, there's a "spark" inside of each Human. It's a spark inside that says, "*I know there's more after Human death. I don't know what it is, but I absolutely know there is more.*" That feeling is by design, dear ones. It separates you from every other living being on this planet.

You are eternal, and you're here only temporarily. In this temporary form, you have chosen to come at an auspicious time. Ah, there are so many of you who decided to come here with full spiritual knowledge that perhaps you might leave in a difficult way. Once again, the planet might go through a termination stage because your work is finished. Simple as that! It has *nothing* to do with judgment. Instead, it has to do with appropriateness. It has to do with a far larger scheme that you directed and planned, and that by being here, you are also fulfilling and facilitating. But instead of termination, here you sit today with a brand new future! Dear ones, there are some of you sitting here "now," and reading this—and I think you know who you are—that under the old energy would not have made it. With your pure intent to Spirit, you have thrown away the karmic map you came in with and have begun to create another...day by day. You have voided out some of the challenges you might have faced, and instead you are sitting here now...some confused or anxious...waiting to see what it all means. Dear ones, stop for a moment, release all your worries and fears—enjoy this reunion with us. This is a time to celebrate you and family, for you're still here! Did you ever consider that?

It is the duality consciousness of the Human Being on this planet that restricts spiritual sight. The Human only sees half of reality—the half that's in the Human dimension. You don't see the other half. You don't see the overview that we and your guides know. You don't know what *hasn't happened to you* due to your pure intent to find the "sacred inner self." We want you to think about that. It really is time to celebrate! And in the celebration, your body will indeed feel a vibrational shift. It can't help it. It responds to your spiritual awareness, and the awareness of celebration in the face of uncertainty and fear brings about tremendous wisdom and enlightenment. That's a simple spiritual axiom about the way things work.

You are in a position to co-create a brand new life. Michael Thomas in the story *The Journey Home* (Kryon Book Five) discovered that although there was a path laid out for him—one he could have followed from one spiritual place to the other—there was far more honor and joy when he left the path—when he got off of it and found his way with his new spiritual map. Think of the support group that goes with that map! He learned an important thing about his new map—he might see a problem looming in the future, and he knew the map would take him through it—but only when he stood in the problem itself. He understood the new attributes of his new spiritual path—the fact that energy matches energy and that the match of the solution needs to match the challenge, but only at the point where a real marriage can take place—at the focus of the challenge! And that, dear ones, is a new paradigm of existence for humanity. You know what it requires? It requires an emotional adjustment. Some of you have called it "faith," and it also requires self-worth—an absolute "knowing" that when you get to the focus of the challenge, there will be a solution—a "knowing" that no one can sway you from that belief! The more times you do that, the more you are trusting what my partner called "the Mantle of Spirit," which is the same as trusting your higher self.

It is our joy to pass on more information this very afternoon, but we cannot help but tell you that in this energy posturing that some of you have allowed, the family visits you, perhaps, in a way that is unique for you. You've never felt this energy in this fashion, in this way. Some of you are going to walk out of this room far different from how you came in. This is not a suggestion. I'm telling you the actual facts, because some of you are feeling this energy pour into you now. Even as you read, you might be feeling the touch of Spirit, and you know that this is real. You are beginning to understand that this message is not simply some Human you don't know who has come to speak from a chair to have the words transcribed so you could read them. Soon you may begin to understand that what is in this room is far beyond that—that the transcription you are reading has an energy for you on it—that we actually knew of the potential for your reading this. It's the family visiting you in a way you may have never expected, and as they love you, they touch you on the shoulders, on the head, and along the arms. This family of yours is saying, "We know who you are. We know why you came. We have expected you."

The Absolute Power of Love

We're going to talk about the absolute power of love, perhaps in a way you hadn't thought of before. You are getting down to a time when you're close to a date that was given to all of you long ago, in many of the prophecies that tell you that *it is the end*. You came in with a stamp—literally an imprint at the cellular "knowledge" level, which told you what was going to happen. It is intermingled with other imprints that you came in with. It's all there. It's all stored in your DNA. It's part of the strands that are not biological or chemical. Spiritual storage is part of DNA, as we have told you in past channellings. It is contained in the strands you cannot see—the ones that are wrapped around the magnetic ones, which are wrapped around the chemical ones. It's all in there.

You may wonder sometimes when you get a reading of a past life—a process that lets you know what the energy was around the lessons learned in an incarnation before the current one—and you think; *Isn't this wonderful that Spirit delivered that past life information to me when I needed it most?* You have no concept that the pastlife information came right out of your own cellular structure! You see, past lives, spiritual contracts, and karmic lessons are a process of cellular memory. It's all in there—all of it. That's the way you're designed. That is how the lessons and the karmic attributes are delivered to the Human Being. They have to be within you.

So you cannot be shocked or surprised to know that the power to undo all of that is also within you. The duality tells you something else, however. It tells you that you come in with all the potentials for trouble. It tells you that if for whatever reason you get anything good, it must have come from "up above," you see, somewhere outside of you. What a duality you've chosen!

Then comes a time when you make a transition from Earth and briefly come "home." That's what we call a "return." You and I meet each other again, and the entourage is there to celebrate your grandness. We celebrate your essence, and we celebrate the beauty of the plan. Then back you go to Earth. Naturally this is all hidden from you while you are on the planet—and disguised on purpose.

Here are the eight Absolute Powers of Love, brought to you, perhaps, in a way that is different than before.

Power Over Basic Seed Fear

We would like to talk about the power of love over fear. Now, wait a minute before you say, "Kryon, this is old news. There have been transcriptions and transcriptions about that. You told us long ago that we could walk into fear and pop the 'black bubble' that it represents." That's not the fear we're talking about. You see, we're talking now to the spiritual family here, and we're talking to those who have felt this energy coming. The "new" New Age is approaching. We like to call it the "Now Age." We're talking to those of you—some of whom are sitting in the chairs—some of whom who are reading this—who have felt this before. It's actually what brings you here. I would like to tell you that there is an internal fear that is connected with what is going on right now on this planet. We've discussed it in the past as the "seed fear," indicating that it was "planted" early on.

The seed fear is this: As you transmute pieces and parts of your duality, you are moving into a stage of awareness that has never been broached before...except one other time on your planet. At that time, the planet was out of balance—and you chose to terminate it. What we're telling you is that I sit in front of a family of *Lemurians*, almost exclusively! These are the ones who come and sit in these chairs and are interested enough in their internal spiritual engine to read these words. Did you ever feel like a wise old soul? Did you ever think you knew things that other people didn't know? It's all in there, you know, within your DNA.

And I tell you, there is a seed fear as you broach this "new" New Age that can only be overcome through love, and a full disclosure to your duality that you have felt this before.

Questions have been asked, even this very afternoon, "*How can I have more belief? There's something blocking my belief. I want to grasp it all. I want to stand up and claim the 'I AM,' but there's something holding me back.*"

I'm telling you what that is. It's the seed fear of enlightenment. You have all the tools, and all the gifts are in line. You sit in your chair calling yourself a "lightworker," and yet there's still a little bit left to do, isn't there? Many of you wish to broach that last step that seems to be so difficult. I tell you, the solution to this is the real power of love. You can walk from this place, or where you sit, finally breathing the essence of real belief—owning the "I AM" within you. This ability is long overdue, and it's going to come from the love source because you have given intent for it. The new energy of the planet really "belongs" to you, and we're here to support in it—and that's why you're here. That's why you are having this "awakening."

So when we say the power of love over fear, we're talking about the one fear that is prevalent in every single lightworker who is reading or hearing these words right *now*, and who is also struggling with full awareness.

Know this: Your trip into spiritual remembrance is anointed. It is not going to end the same way as before. You are the catalyst for planetary change. You are the old souls who will awaken first, and lead the others by your example. You are the lightworkers! Fear not, for the past is the past, and what is before you now is of high vibration—waiting for you to claim it!

Power Over Grief

Let's discuss number two, and it may seem out of place here. We'd like to talk about the power of love over Human emotion. One of the most powerful Human emotions there is, except for love, is grief. It's brought here now because some of you need to hear this. The power of love, with intent of the new Human Being walking in the light, can completely transform grief. Some of you have grief over the loss of loved ones. Some of you have grief over the loss of love. It affects you the same way because it is the same kind of grief. Some of you hold secrets of grief from your past that you think are kept from everyone—but not from us—not from family. Some of you walk through this life with a false exterior, saying to all, "*Oh, I'm okay now. I'm okay.*" But you're not. And guess who knows that? *Family* knows that. That's why you're here.

Listen, dear ones: Listen, dear ones: Challenges are issues given to you to solve—not to *endure*. God does not receive joy and pleasure from Human challenge that remains unsolved! Spirit does not delight, nor does the planet benefit from *family* members who elect to stay in challenge! Lack of closure and unresolved energy *never* benefits God! Perfect solutions found through the process of love and wisdom are what we all celebrate together!

Oh, it's time to reconcile these feelings, isn't it? I want to tell you that everything that has caused that grief in your life—absolutely everything—is by your design. Do you wish to ultimately do something wise with it? Do you wish to know what Spirit asks you to do with it? Celebrate it! Tough to do, isn't it? There is spiritual purpose behind it. There is sacredness behind it. Therefore, there is an energy of joy behind it. It's time you started thinking about that. Start celebrating the event that caused the grief. Start seeing the situation with an overall wisdom, which only comes from the Mantle of Spirit that you, as lightworkers, wear.

There are some who will tell you that grief can only subside over time, and that's the only thing that will work. They're wrong. They haven't realized or experienced the new tools of your new planetary enablement energy. They haven't experienced the love of family coming into your life to transmute it with you! You can stand and walk from this place, or from where you sit reading, and have this burden cut in half—cut in half! And when you walk away, I want you to understand that *you are never alone*. Never! It is part of your duality that wishes to convince you that you are, however. It's part of your duality that tells you that you have to carry the burden alone, and nobody will ever understand you. I tell you, there is an entourage that understands! Don't you really think that Spirit knows you? There's a family beside you. There are arms that wrap around you in your darkest moments and love you, and they're here visiting you right now—no matter where you are hearing or reading this. Indeed, you are dearly loved!

That was number two.

Power Over Matter

In this "new" New Age, love has absolute power over matter. Here we are again, year after year, discussing the subject of the assumptions from Humans. This is a subject that we have dealt with before. The assumptions we are speaking of are defined as "what Humans are used to, and therefore what they project." The new energy voids "what to expect"!

What do you think miracles are? First of all, let's establish the fact that they are real. We often talk about healing—healing of the mind, the body, and the spirit. All of those things have to do with matter. Some of you have witnessed, as my partner has, the creation of matter where it did not exist before in healing—bones that will snap back into place—cartilage created when there was none before—chemistry altered—the miracle of matter—"divine intervention," you call it. I want to tell you something: This is a power that each one of you has through the divine angel that sits in the golden chair within you. It comes from inside, dear ones—not from "on high." This great miraculous energy is generated from the spectacular spiritual essence that each of you carries. When awakened, it is awesome!

Do you want to know why some are healed and some are not? It's a complex question, and one that Humans ask constantly.

Some of it has to do with the contract you made with respect to your plans on the planet, and where you fit in with what helps those around you—did you know that? Do you ever wonder if you are in a situation that seems inappropriate for you, or that is designed to facilitate a lesson for those around you? Who, then, is helping whom? Do you have an affliction that remains and remains, even though you have asked repeatedly for it to be removed? Back up and see the overview. Is it possible that somehow your affliction is actually helping others around you? Is it a challenge for them? Does it somehow bring them closer to Spirit? If so then, dear one, know who you are! Understand what being a "lightworker" means. Things are not always as they seem.

Then there are others of you, seemingly born to be healed. I want to tell you, there is power over matter, and it isn't only seen in healing the Human Being. We'll tell you more about that in a moment, when we get to the next item.

We'd like to tell you about the power over matter that you can see within the planet. Did you ever wonder what it meant when you heard the message from us to "anchor the energy"? We have told you that there will come a time in this age when the Earth will spit pieces of itself upon you. What we mean by that is that there will be volcanoes erupting. Listen to this: You have heard the expression, "You have the power to move mountains." In this new energy, "you have the power to keep the mountains from moving!" And when you're called to go places where you know there is potential for trouble—where the earth shakes or the mountains are unstable—there are reasons for it.

I'm here to tell you that when enough lightworkers move into those areas and anchor those unstable spots, there is power over matter! When the earth decides to move in a certain way, it's not going to move as much when there are lightworkers present, anchoring it. This has already happened. You've already seen it, and you don't even know it. We've spoken in other messages about those of you called to certain areas to anchor the energy.

That is exactly what we're talking about now, and that is the power of love over matter.

Remember when we defined matter for you, and we couldn't even say the words of the definition without including the word "love"? Remember when we defined love as the soup of energy that was between the nucleus and the electron haze of the atom? Both matter and love had similar definitions—and included each other! It's physics. Therefore, is there any question in your mind that love would have power over matter? Many of you feel that you are helpless. You think you walk on this planet and you are a product of the elements—pushed to and fro—dancing from place to place as the Earth pushes you around.

Did you know that there are lightworkers who are actually keeping weather patterns away, keeping the earth from shaking, and keeping the mountains still? This is part of the power we are giving you in this new energy.

[For Detroit] Some of you who find yourselves in this very area are actually anchoring a spot. There are places all over this land that need your help, and there are even prophecies about this very area. Lightworkers *need* to be here! Because even though you do not understand why you are here holding the energy, you will put down your anchors, and that is why so many of you are here. That may sound cryptic, but it has to do with potentials. It has to do with earth changes. It has to do with why you find yourself in this area—why there is a resonance with this area for you—and that's why we have dwelled upon this attribute of "power over matter." We want you to hear us very carefully: The very elements of the planet will respond to you. The very building blocks of matter are variable and respond to love.

Power Over Biology

The power of love over biology is absolute. We spoke before about the healing power you have—the power within that you have. You might say that we have said just about everything we can say. Dear ones, we will never, ever leave this subject alone! It's because you've only begun to understand the reawakening of certain energies that have been latent in your body, waiting and dwelling there for this very time. In their awakening there will be a quality given to you that slows down your aging. It has to do with intent. It has to do with being circumspect and looking around at what energy balances are available. It has to do with the power of love, and with claiming the "I AM" of the mantle of Spirit.

Perhaps some of you reading this, or those who have come here this afternoon, are saying, "*I'm tired of my affliction. It's getting in my way. I can't seem to get rid of it. I've tried so, I've tried that.*" For some of you, the affliction was given so that you could come here today and have it removed! Such is the way of Spirit. In doing this, you will have a life change—and your life change will affect those around you in a loving manner.

The power of love is actually connected permanently to your cellular structure. It is part of the sacred source and can change matter within the cells. Cells respond to spiritual intent, and as we have told you before, it is time for you to start looking at the body as one enlightened cell. Before the healing can be complete, you've got to look at the body as one vessel—one vase—one cell that is enlightened throughout. There is no part of your structure that is expendable. When a certain part of it has pain, all of it has pain. When a certain part all of it is enlightened and is joyful, it all is enlightened and joyful.

So again we bring you this fourth power, and we say this is an absolute: You can change your chemistry. You can create healing within you. There are those taking in this group of information who can sense energy, and they know what is taking place right now. We have a gift for the healers—those who have spent years doing energy work for other Human Beings. The gift is enhanced awareness, and it is yours for the asking—with pure intent. Look for it, for each of you who wishes to have it now may have it. It is a fast track—a catalyst for healing—and that's why you're here, or sitting in the chair as a healer reading this.

Didn't you expect it? The ability to sense energetics in a Human Being has just been enhanced, should you choose to accept this. When you have an entourage of this size, visiting a room of this size and a readership of this size, there is a great deal of intent from the gathered humanity—and that's when these kinds of things take place. There are gifts dispensed because the intent is strong—because the belief is pure—and the "mantle" is in place (speaking of the mantle of Spirit, as discussed earlier in the seminar). There are those of you in this room and reading this who can now stand up and claim the "I AM" and mean it, where you could not before. We know this, and that's why we are having this reunion! And that was number four.

Power Over Anxiety

Number five is one that has been given piecemeal here before. It's about anxiety.

Dear ones, so many of you are going through a process now that you would describe as anxiety, and you want to know what to do about it. First, let's describe why it's there, and maybe it will give you a different impression about how to handle it.

Do you know what happens when, biologically, you are allowed to evolve while alive? It goes against the very fabric of your past Human existence. It's a new paradigm of Human development, and it's part of the ascension process created from your pure intent.

It's the power of love that gives you this ability, and it's the power of love that will also settle the feelings around it. Go back to number four. The power of love allows you to evolve biologically while remaining here. It's a physical change—a chemical change—a life force change. It may shock and surprise you to know this. Never before in the history of humanity on this planet have you been allowed to make these kinds of evolutionary changes at the cellular level while remaining alive and living here. In the past, it has always been through the death and birth process, dear ones, always. This new paradigm often creates a mental condition called anxiety.

Some of you wake up in the morning and say, "I keep waiting for the other shoe to drop. Something is going to happen. What is it I feel? My life is okay, but I'm really anxious."

Understand that much of the anxiety and uneasiness you feel has to do with the evolution that is going on inside. For those of you who have anxiety, fear, and uncertainty about the things you see around you, again we tell you that the power of love can transform those feelings just as it did with grief. If the intent is there and you stand up and claim the angel inside, the link will be there of transformation. It's absolute. It has to be, you know. You are the powerful one. It is you who we are here to enable through your intent—intent that will transform the anxiety and give you peace. That's what it's about, is it not? The transformation—the alchemy of the Human spirit into joy and peace in situations that would not normally seem to be conducive to that attribute? That's how you know when you are starting to become enlightened. Your body starts to change. Did you know that? When you are able to become peaceful situations which used to be very dramatic and unsettling to you, you have just crossed an important bridge—the one which honors pure intent and that is the catalyst for enlightenment. It represents the power of love at the highest level because it changes Human consciousness in a dramatic way.

And that was number five.

You know, we present these attributes in a linear fashion because we have no choice. As some of you list them, you might think that some must be more important than others. This is unfortunate, and it's because we have no way of giving them to you in a circle! Your time frame is the means of communication for you, and so it is. The train of time never stops for you. It's always moving. It can't go in a circle like ours does.

So this next one is number six. It's not the least or the most important—it just *is*. Let me tell you that in a circular presentation, there is always one attribute in the middle—try delivering that concept in a linear fashion! And in that circle (which we cannot easily present), the one in the middle is always swapping with the other ones. This is an interdimensional attribute of these love powers.

Power Over Duality

Love has the power to transmute duality. I want to tell you what that means, for this is a very powerful quality. Duality is that which keeps you from seeing the angel inside. It's that simple. You have created a situation where you have allowed a portion of yourself to be at a lower vibration than some others—to keeps things balanced in a neutrality of spiritual awareness—as you yourself designed the system. Seemingly, it keeps you in the dark, and that's as it should be. This neutrality, or duality, is the only way the tests can be delivered, to eventually see where the energy balance will go.

Even some of the most enlightened of you have said, "*I'm pushed and pulled around, and it feels like an experiment, and God is the one pushing and pulling.*"

Ah, dear ones, we have news for you. You're in charge, you see—totally in charge, and the duality hides that very clearly. We have told you this before, but you should hear this again in a different way. You cannot hear or read this too many times, for it deals with the new tools of your duality. So many of you again feel like you are tossed around in life, seemingly in a storm beyond your control. We told you in the last "family channelling" that your spirituality is accustomed to a "hands off" approach to life. You "let go and let God," and God totally takes care of things. Now we are telling you that God is a partner with you. You're being given the permission, the tools, and the power to reach within and say, "Let's change things, the **two** of us." Then you take the first action of intent and start to celebrate and visualize your own answers. As soon as you take that action with your pure intent intact, guess what happens? Your sacred God partner comes and wraps his/

her arms around you, and **together** you co-create your life intent. What's the difference? It's *intent*. That is your new power. The partnership is stronger than the "let go and let God" approach. This is new, and you have earned it!

We also told you last time regarding fear itself, that the new magnetic energy that is being given to you, dear ones, puts you in the driver's seat when it comes to duality. No longer is this duality balanced in a neutral way. For the adjustments of the grids have altered your duality potential. There was another magnetic alignment, also—one that we have not spoken of. Nine years before the Harmonic Convergence you agreed to allow an event 20 light-years away to blast you with a large dose of magnetics which would arrive in the year 1998. This additional grid alignment is potent, and it arrived right on time. The numerological energy of this blast is that of "completion." Since it was scheduled considerably before the 1987 measurement, it should tell you something about what you allowed for yourselves. Without the current grid status, this blast would have been troublesome. With the current grid alignment, however, it has actually enhanced your potentials. I'm not going to say any more at this time regarding this subject.

This posturing of your duality is no longer balanced to zero, you see. You now have the upper edge. I'm going to tell you what that means. It means that you're driving your future in a way that you never have before. Those of you who wish to begin driving practice are going to be amazed at how much you can change yourselves.

Let's again speak to those of you who are feeling fearful. I speak now to those of you who are feeling anxiety, concern, or worry about the events in your life. It seems like a series of hills and valleys, does it not? Things get good, then there is a challenge. Then there is resolution, and often another challenge! Some of you think to yourselves, *God, when am I going to get it right?* This reveals a Human assumption that you are in some kind of judgment—and that the challenges of life are beset upon you due to something you did wrong. If you only knew! The challenges for lightworkers are often given specifically to those who **hold the light**! Did you ever think of that?

For those of you who are wise, indeed, you will understand this—that in order to create the energy necessary to lift the planet, those most able are going to go through the tests. There is never going to come a time when you reach some final magic plateau where there are no more challenges—not while you are Human. Some of you feel that you are climbing a ladder of tests to get to a place of bliss—where all the challenge will be gone. Listen: Remember the goal that you came in with? It's about raising the vibration of the planet! Lemurians, are you listening? Do you remember? You are here to work, and by climbing the ladder of challenge, you raise the planet's energy. What the magnetic alignment does, along with all the other tools of this New Age, is to give you the ability and power to *solve the challenges*—not remove them—and who better to climb that ladder than a wise one who has the tools? We are here giving you information on how to make challenge a part of your life, which will become regular, and not catastrophic like it has been. We are here to give you information regarding the power of love to transmute the aspects that have made challenge so difficult! That's the entire purpose of this message. That's what all these attributes have been about.

In a "family" channelling series (The Family Part IV, Chapter Two), we gave you an exercise over fear. Again we say, you have absolute power over fear! The next time fear comes to you, try greeting it out loud (as in the exercise). You can even do it right now where you sit if you are in fear of any kind. Greet it! I want you to look at its arrival as a love situation—given to you, designed by you. It's here again—right on schedule. As we discussed, greeting fear disarms it.

When you disarm it in this fashion and show fear that you're in control, everything changes. This is because your duality is being transformed. The balance of dark and light is changing. It's a higher balance now, and you have far more control over these potent, controlling things in your life than you've ever had before. Fear will let you know it's there. It will tell you that you are handling things poorly. It will whisper in your ear that you don't know what you are doing, and that all this verbalizing is silly. Meanwhile, you are solving challenge—co-creating win-win situations—using the wisdom of love without the interference of the destablizing emotional response of fear. Some of you won't believe you can do this until it is upon you. Let the seeds of this potential power be planted in your mind so that you can remember the words. Then combine it with *intent*. It may redefine the word *miracle* for you.

Protection

Number seven may seem odd to you if you've given intent to walk the path, dear ones. We promise you **protection**. This attribute is filled with the power of love, since it directly concerns your path, and the honor we have for it.

Some have said, "*Kryon, I'm concerned as I learn to use my new gifts of guidance and power. What if I fail, especially in the synchronicity department? I have a vision of somehow missing the synchronicity you mentioned, and I see myself being shuttled off my straight path into another scenario that might make me miss my spiritual goals altogether! What if I make a mistake while I'm learning to use all these new gifts?*"

Here's where the word *protection* comes in, for when you have given intent to walk a new spiritual path, that path in your vision is no longer a straight one. Instead, it is one that surrounds a middlepoint—call it a target, if you wish. The target is your spiritual goal—the result of your co-creation, and it's a potential in your future waiting to be manifested. Therefore, it's interdimensional. To get there, you must travel a puzzle you are creating as you go, one with many avenues of travel, all leading to the eventual center. Think of it as a hedge-maze, where no matter which way you turn, there is always another passage that will move you to the center.

Whereas you had a vision of being shuttled off to "nowhere" if you missed a synchronistic encounter, now we show you that if, indeed, you miss an event due to your learning, you will travel not into "nowhere," but onto a path that still surrounds your goal. It might take you longer, but more synchronicity will be presented, and you are *protected* along the way. The protection is that your path *never* reverses itself, and you are constantly moving inward toward the goal you made with your intent. This is the *now*! This is living in the circle that we have called a suspension of the paradigm of what you call a linear life. It's part of the ascending Human!

Do not fear, therefore, stepping up to the challenge of learning what synchronicity feels like. Do not fear making an error that might send you into "nowhere." Go ahead and begin to understand what it feels like to walk the *now*. We are right with you, walking in that circle, moving slowly towards the goal.

Power to Change – Real Change

Finally, comes the eighth one, and it's the easiest one. It has been in every single session regarding Human renovation and spiritual evolvement. Human Beings now have the power to change. Some of you changed the worst thing you could have imagined. In the series where we talked about the renovating Human Being, we established a picture for you to see—where you decided to renovate your house, yet live within it at the same time. Some of you know exactly what I'm talking about. There are inconveniences, aren't there? And there are anxieties. Things don't seem to go well. The schedule is always changing! You wish it would be over. That's real change, and many of you hearing and reading this are right in the middle of the renovation, dear ones, and that is why we are here to honor you so. That is why we are here with the entourage that loves you as they do. You see, we are not going through what you are. We are here to support your incredible work. Some of you have shown up today, or have picked up these words, thinking that you were going to sit in front of a grand entity called Kryon. Instead, you find out that this sister or brother of yours called Kryon is speaking—like a letter from home—a message dripping with love, telling you that you are honored for doing the work, and that we're just here to applaud you, wash your feet, and be there for you when your *intent* is given.

The power to change is directly related to the phrase "the only planet of free choice." You are the only entities in biological form right now in this Universe with the ability and permission to actually lift your own vibrational rate with choice and intent. This is due to the grand plan, as we discussed ("The Meaning of Life," Chapter Two).

Dear family, sisters and brothers, you can leave this place and say to yourselves, "*That was interesting. What's next?*" Or you can really feel the truth that is here. Do you want to change? There is a price. It's the one you have known all along. The price is indeed that Spirit will put you through testing—testing of your own design and of your own making. At the same time, you can be joyful and peaceful during the testing, and we are here right now explaining the tools. It's not about torturing Human Beings or putting them through a maze. It's not about God punishing or judging. It's about "lightwork," and that's why you call yourself "lightworkers." It's about our angelic family, who has decided to come to this planet lifetime after lifetime in an effort to actually change the Universe itself. It's about those we love dearly—miss dearly. It's about *you*.

So it is that the entourage that is here, is here solely to love you—to applaud you—to put their arms around you and say, "We know that we will see you again. We know that this Earth is difficult, and we know what you've been through." This is the theme of Kryon, and always has been. As you approach the ominous time where prophecy told you that Human life was going to be over, there will be a buildup of those who oppose love. Some will even tell you that the energy of Kryon is evil and that you should not listen. These are the ones who do not want you to know that you are empowered. What does Kryon ask of you? Let this be the test. Is there something to join? Is there worship involved? Is there a Human who wishes to be powerful? I only bring you information that is powerful and loving and enabling. I bring you the love of the family with no strings attached. I bring you the "Letters from Home" to enhance your life.

There is an energy on this planet of those who still have the old imprints, and who still would like to pull you down. They will use fear. Watch for it. They would like to have all these things take place as the prophecies have said. It will enhance their own power to make you fear. It will give them importance. There will always be those to pull it backwards—to stir it up. The old energy will not give up easily, and the year 1999 will be a grand test of this—the beginning of dark against light. You're going to have to get past it, and when you do, dear ones, you will have a feeling of release. That's when this planet is going to soar! But the task is to get through it. The task is to understand that from now until then, we wish you to hold your light and to anchor it. It will intensify from now through the year 2012.

There is a family that's going to be here with you all through that time, and if you go from this place knowing nothing more than this statement, we'll say it again: *You are never alone*! To even think that you are is preposterous! If you had any concept of the entities that surround you now, you would be amazed. These are the ones we call *family*—the ones who you agree should be here. They are with you all the time. Feel their energy. They will give you a whole new idea of what family is all about. You see, that's the truth, and that's what's going on here.

This is the time when we retreat. There will never be an assemblage like this again—not exactly like this. The family that is in this room knows each other very well, and there is a cosmic joke at hand: You look in each other's eyes, and you think you're strangers? You have spent lifetimes together, with karmic attributes you've given one to another through years of anger, fear, and love! You all "know" each other! The grand Human family is here, yet you don't see them as your own. At the cellular level, we invite you to understand and celebrate this energy at this very moment.

This is the time when the spiritual entourage that has visited you retreats again through that crack in the veil we came through earlier. If you could say that there was ever a time when Spirit grieves, it is now, for we have to leave you. Before we do, however, we are going to tell you something that has happened this session, as it does in so many of the others. If you were to measure the energy that came into this room a few minutes ago when I first started speaking to you, and you could measure it again when it departed, you would find that some of it remained. In other words, some of you have absorbed what has been given. There are entities here that are going to stay and go with you when you exit your chair because they have work to do based upon your intent. There will come a time—I guarantee it absolutely—when we will all see each other again. You are my family.

And so it is.

Kryon

"Dark & Light"
Channelled in Reno, NV

The Kryon Writings, Inc.
PMB 422
1155 Camino Del Mar
Del Mar, California 92014
[www.kryonqtly.com]

"Dark & Light"
Live Channelling
Reno, NV

This live channelling has been edited with additional words and thoughts to allow clarification and better understanding of the written word.

Greetings, dear ones, I am Kryon of magnetic service. Again we sit in the marvelous energy of this area—an energy that is unique to the country [Reno, Nevada]. This is an energy that allows only certain subjects to be discussed easily—as we did before in this very place (two years earlier).

Before we get to the teaching, we are going to put the bookends on this group as we've done previously. The "book-ends" have a great and tremendous intensity, and they're called the "bookends of love." We call them bookends because we begin and end with a message that is universal—one that you are going to hear from every entity that comes to you in love from Spirit. We open with great love and close with the same.

My partner has told you that it is the Human Being who is honored on this planet and that this is the subject of Kryon and has been since I arrived. It will always be so, and as you sit in these chairs, hearing this voice or reading these words, I invite you to feel your Higher Self responding to the entourage that comes with me—the ones who walk these aisles and sit beside you—the ones who poke and prod those beautiful Guides to encircle you with their arms. It is times like these that they wish to love you so!

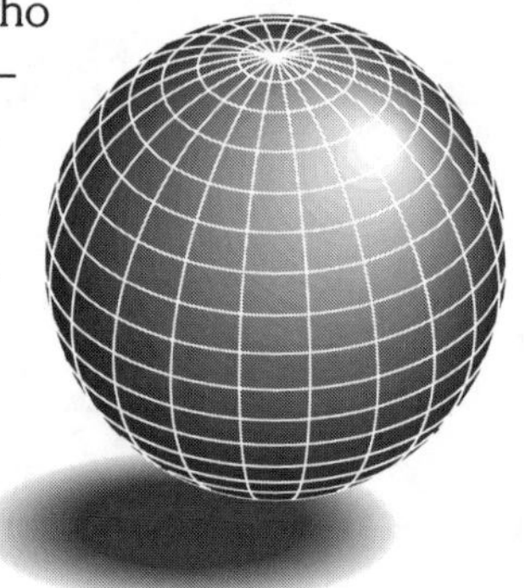

So it is, right now, that the "third language" begins—something that will be transmitted to so many of you this day as you sit in these chairs. This language is just for you—a language that is universal—a language that you may not actually hear, but one that you will feel. For it is the love of God that shakes hands with a remembrance of who you are. These are the few moments that we spend together, as a family reunited, where Spirit comes before you and says, "Oh, I remember you! I remember you! Isn't it grand that we can again communicate like this?"

Again, we figuratively stand before you eyeball to eyeball and ask, "Do you remember the time when we sent you here?" It is because of the honor of your contract that you sit in these chairs at all, allowing us to be in front of you, to wash each foot, one by one. And it is the love and the sacredness of this process that says to you, "You are dearly loved." It says to you, "You are honored without measure." Dear ones, it's acknowledgment that *you* are here to do the work.

So it is that an angel of the New Age sits in front of you, along with the Family of Lord Michael. This angel, which is Kryon, comes to you and says that you are protected and loved. This angel brings truth and wisdom—just like another who sits with you in this room [speaking of Ronna Herman, channel for Archangel Michael, who is attending]. Our job is easy. It is to support the ones doing the work—*you*. You may think to yourself, *Who, me? I seem so small and insignificant in this grand plan of Earth.* And we say that this is the reason we call you the Warriors of Light!

What we are going to discuss during this communication is the difference between dark and light. You may remember that it was two years ago when we brought you a message regarding the dark side. Much has changed since then. We are now free to give you a more complete message—one that is far less cryptic, and one where the truth will resound and be accepted and understood by many who are vibrating at such a high level. Just two years ago in the same place, this was not so.

Last year we sat in this energy and discussed Human biology (published in Kryon Book Six). We revealed things that we could not reveal before. So it is again that this entourage and this energy comes before you in a way that is special and unique and more powerful than ever before. Oh, dear ones, this is a time hearing (and reading) these words where you can have a change in your very cellular level. There are some of you who have come to this event (or who are reading this publication) with one thing in mind—and that is the solution to a problem. We're going to tell you about that in a moment.

There is core information to give you—some of which is a review, and some of which is brand new. We wish to examine darkness and light, positive and negative, the balance of what it is and what it is not, and what it means to you as a Human Being. The ability of understanding that is here is greater now than it has ever been before, and it will remain this way! For I am here to tell you that the critical mass of enlightenment here has been reached. We have told you that you few are the ones to make astounding changes for the many (speaking of planetary lightworkers). And it's not by standing on the hill and yelling out what you believe. It's by walking the path and showing others that you can have peace on this planet while living your truth!

Oh, dear ones, there will come a day, if it has not already happened to you, that by simply walking the path you will attract others. For they will ask "*What is it with you?*" They have felt a difference. "*Tell me everything about it*," they may say. And they will see in you the Golden Angel that walks that practical life upon this planet—the one who is slow to worry, slow to become upset. The one who has the patience and the wisdom of a saint. This can be you, and this will attract other Humans who will want to know what it is you have that they do not. This, dear ones, is the way others see God in you.

It is a new time here. It is a time when there is no catastrophe for the planet scheduled—as we have told you over and over. Instead, there is graduation, and we have given you the time frame of the potential of it. There will be remote viewers who go out beyond the year 2012, and they will say "*Woe is me! We're all going to die because we see nothing beyond that date that we recognize as humanity.*" What they see and report is that there is very little of the old energy left! There are potentials of energy from here to that date that would astound you—possibilities that you can do with this planet. Just a handful of Humans, of the numbers of the individual Human Beings in this room (and reading this)—each one vibrating at a high level—each one with the wingspan of 27 feet (some of you will understand what that means, and some of you will not), can bring miracles to this planet! And I say to you that indeed you are angels, every one, who are vibrating in this manner. I do not give you the following information lightly.

It is time for the teaching.

Darkness and Light

Let us start by giving you core information that has been given before, and then we will move on to a new teaching. First, we wish to define this subject. Then we wish to give you information about it. Finally, we are going to give you information on 12 aspects of it.

Many Human Beings do not understand what darkness and light is, and so again we tell you: The definition of the dark side is "energy without love." So many Human Beings are convinced that there are entities whose *job* it is to be dark! That is not so. There is no entity in the universe whose job it is to be dark. Again, there is no entity in the universe whose job it is to be dark.

Review

Darkness is a vibratory state. It is a state without love. Darkness is passive, while light is active. Darkness is simply an energy state without the active element of light. That's all it is. There's nothing more to revolve around it—no drama and no fear. The fear that you have regarding it, perhaps, can be dismissed by knowing that it's simply a lower vibratory state—love being the highest.

There is a balance present, which is what we wish to speak of this afternoon. We've given you this information before in order to exemplify the difference between a *passive* dark and an *active* light. Remember that light vibrates higher and takes more energy. Therefore, it has an active element. Darkness does not—and takes less energy. It's also easier to sustain because of that. [See the story of the two rooms in Kryon Book Six, page 112.]

Now some of you might understand why *you* illuminate a room just by walking into or through it. People will know who you are—they will feel it. There are places you can go and just stand that will make a difference for the planet because you carry the *active* element of light. I have said this before in two channellings, and we say it again now: We want you to visualize this scenario because it is practical. It may allay some fears for those of you who fear the darkness. Any of you who call yourselves lightworkers could go and stand in the middle of what you consider the most evil pentagram symbol—with those standing around you in red robes, chanting their darkness—and the light of your essence will illuminate the room and change *them*! Fear not! For the light you carry is the **Light of God**! Believe it. That's the profound difference between dark and light. Darkness is simply the absence of light. Light is the presence of God, in *you*.

There are 12 elements we wish to discuss regarding this balance, in pairs. They are as follows: We wish to talk about the negativity and the possessiveness of the planet, what it has meant in the old energy, and what it means now. We wish to talk about the tests you have and the solutions. We wish to talk about death versus life. We wish to talk about darkness versus illumination. We wish to talk about hate versus love. We will talk about fear versus peace. These 12 items are given in six pairs. When you understand the differences between them, you will begin to understand the differences between the old and new energy on your planet. You will also begin to understand the absolute power you have over the old.

The Balance of Humanity—Negative and Positive

Let us first speak of the negativity and the positivity of the Planet Earth—dark and light, if you wish—the things that seem to be positive—the things that seem to be negative on the planet and for humanity. Here is startling information about your New Age: The paradigm is shifting regarding the way the balance of dark and light works. As we have said before, one of the things that you who are vibrating higher are feeling is an uncomfortable countenance. Everything seems fine, but you are waiting "for the other shoe to drop." You are experiencing the new cellular *balance*. Get used to it.

In the past, there had to be a balance. It should be no mystery that the Master of Magnetics comes with a message about the balance of positive and negative. There must be a balance—always. It is the way of the Earth, and of the Universe. It is also the way of your cellular structure. One must always equal the other, or the energy of the one must at least be transmuted into something else that balances the whole. Even in death there is balance. This is the key to what has happened, which is now changing the way things work.

In the past, it was the *Human* energy on the planet that had to be balanced. All the dark and light balance was attributed to Humans, and it was the consciousness of humanity that provided the balance. So it always seemed that there was as much negativity as there might have been positive, or perhaps even the other way around. But it was humanity that was taking the brunt of the balancing act. Think about it. You have grown up always believing that if there is a winner, then there must be a loser. I am here to tell you that this was very two-dimensional old energy thinking!

This has now changed, dear ones. You have a new partner that you may not be aware of who walks with you in the new energy. Did you ever wonder where the transmuted karma goes when you give intent to drop it with the neutral implant/release? [see page 239] Did you wonder where all the potent energy of life lessons that you came in with went-lessons and situations that you were supposed to deal with? Where did that energy go when you gave intent to clear it? You see, there has to be a balance. I'm here to tell you that it did not go to another Human Being. As I said, you have always felt that for a Human to win, there had to be another Human Being who would lose. Every single one of your contests—and you can name them all—has this attribute, and again, it represents an old energy concept.

Imagine a contest with two winners. How could you have such a thing? It's possible now, and it's called the Planet Earth. I'll tell you where the transmuted energy went—where those old contracts went. I'll tell you what happens to a Human Being who decides to shed the old energy and move up in vibration. It takes a tremendous amount of energy—spiritual, cosmic energy—to accomplish such a thing And it's not just the entourage that's around you and your guides that gives it to you. It comes from another place, and we've been preparing for it for a very long time. Remember the Harmonic Convergence? This is where the measurement was taken that let us know you were ready. Remember the 11:11? This was *your* part in giving *us* permission to alter your DNA! Remember the 12:12? This was the sacred time where Humans were passed the torch or responsibility for the *balance*, and Earth became your partner!

There is no longer just humanity taking on these balancing energies. You now have an active light partner in **Gaia**. Start to recognize what is happening. Did you wonder why Earth is changing so? Why now? Why only in the last few years? Did you wonder why the acceleration of the seasons is upon you? Did you wonder why the storms of the century are coming every 15 years? Did you wonder why all the things are turning upside down regarding temperatures and seasons? It is because the energy of Human balance is being transmuted into the ground—transmuted into the energy that is Gaia—which has consciousness, and love for you—which is here and has always been in tremendous support of Humans.

When you realize that the very dirt of this planet is part of an entity, and you realize that the magnetics around it represents the cocoon that supports it, then you begin to understand part of the system that you're in. No longer does humanity have to take the brunt of the balance. It can't, because the critical mass has been reached where the active positive is beginning to outweigh the passive negative and because one lightworker is worth dozens of others without light. That is why the one Human with light and love can change dozens of others, and all this Human has to do is hold his light high—and the love shows!

Into the earth it goes, this transmuting of the old to the new, and the earth reacts (see "The Earth and You," chapter 4). That's what the earth changes are all about. You find yourself in the middle of something that may be fearful to you—wondering if the earth is becoming unstable around you. Dear ones, if you find yourself standing in an area where the earth is shaking, instead of fear, give it honor! Say out loud: "*I understand fully what is taking place. The earth is under construction. The earth moves because it is absorbing the old energy. It is our partner in the New Age, and it is taking on a role that we asked for!*" That's what's happening. Negative to positive. The balance is changing. Your Earth partner is in place.

Challenge and Solution

Here is a negative and a positive, seemingly a dark and a light that you call challenge and solution. We wish to review, ever so briefly, what happened not too many months ago in a beautiful area you call Banff, when we brought you an astounding message for humanity about "The Golden Tray" [the next channelling in this book].

As you will discover as you review that channelling, the answers to your most perplexing challenges are spiritually known in advance! Yet you sit there trying to figure them out. For you are learning, and the answers are not given to you in advance (any more than they were in school). But the solutions exist, even when you are in the midst of the test. In this message of "The Golden Tray," the concept is given to you of having solutions prepared in advance for the tests or challenges that you are now experiencing

Figuratively, the Golden Tray represents the new paradigm on your planet, where every single test that is in front of you has already been solved and is before you as if on a tray. The only thing you need to do is recognize that you created it, and pick it up off that tray. Doesn't it make sense in the balance of things, dear ones, that if you planned your tests, you also planned the solutions? Think of all the energy around the challenges, and all the fear and the worry. Now think of all the energy around the love that went into the prepared solutions! It's balance! These solutions were created and built in love before the tests were presented. How does it feel to know that the solutions were prepared at the same time as the lessons?

This knowledge should bring about a different kind of reaction in the enlightened Human. What do you do with problems? When you see a challenge coming or when you are presented with one that is a surprise, what is your reaction? Do you go into fear? Do you wring your hands in despair and say to God, "*Why me?*"

Old thought

The enlightened Human knows better. When an imbalance occurs, then a balance is needed. The solution to any challenge you may have isn't contained in the energy of old thought and worry! That reaction will keep you tied to the floor, and you will never be able to see past the introduction of the challenging energy. The first thing you can do with a challenge is to disarm it! When you receive it, celebrate! This gives the energy of wisdom and balance to the challenge, and begins to kindle the light to find the solution. Think of the solution as hiding. How do you find something that is hiding? Get out the light and search for it!

As we have said before, God does not take comfort in any Human Being wallowing in challenge and fear. The celebration is when the Human understands that there is balance in all things. Therefore, there is solution waiting for him to find.

The Human who is stuck in the "*woe is me*," is going to be tied to the old thoughts and energies, and will remain in challenge completely removed from the miracle of solution—from win-win—and from moving forward.

Death and Balance

Let's talk about Human life and death for a moment. What has changed from the old to the new is profound in this area. There is so much to share with you regarding something that is so fearful to you! Death as you Humans think of it is an old paradigm. There is no greater information we can give you that is more exciting than this. For there is no greater attribute that can accelerate this planet in the *new energy* than you living very long lives!

In the old days—the old paradigm—death was an exchange of energy, and it was quick. Your bodies, designed to last 950 years, were lasting only 60 and 70 years with your permission. Aging is something you designed! Chemistry was released in your body, acting on your DNA so that you would pass over quickly with short lives. And the reason was so you would come back with karmic overlays and have tests and dark/light energy challenges to work through—quick death and life—over and over. It was the engine of vibrational shift, and now it's gone. With permission, you have given yourselves (through the 11:11), a spiritual message for your very DNA, the code of life, and it said, "*We now have permission to survive much longer than before in order to facilitate a graduate Earth.*" Permission granted! The science of this is now being given to you slowly, all over the planet. We are here to tell you that if the potentials are reached that we see, that by the year 2012, Human life expectancy could double what it is now. Double! The new paradigm is this, dear ones: You are being asked to move to an area where death is only the death of the old energy—and the Human biology lives on and on! Let's see if your science will support it. Let's see if your society will fear it instead—keeping it from being implemented. It's very different than you might expect, and is dependent on revelations from the very fiber of your cellular structure. Secrets of life itself and of the aging process will be revealed.

The definition of ascension, as given to so many groups before this one, is: "The Human in the new energy, casting off his karma and contract, and moving into the next incarnation without Human death. Then, without an existing contract, creating one as he goes." This was the entire purpose of the story in the Kryon book *The Journey Home*. This is now yours for the taking, but some of you will choose not to take it. In all appropriateness, there are those of you who will not, and there are some of you who will try. Some years may have to go by before all is understood. But here is the general picture we are telling you: Not only do you have permission to remain, but the science and the energy and the knowledge will be given to support very long life. Moving to the next vibration—dropping your old karma—moving out of the old paradigm into the new, and living a very long time. This is profound information, generated by you, for you! This is information given because you gave permission to have it on the 11:11. Let *light* take on a whole new meaning! Let it change your balance. Let it change your power on Earth!

Actual Darkness and Illumination

Next is actual physical darkness and illumination and what it means to your cells. We wish to stay on the same subject of your Human biology. Soon your science is going to discover the workings of light in respect to what it means to the Human Being, biologically. Right now you are beginning to discover what makes aging take place, but there's still an elusive biological attribute that we will tell you about now. It has to do with the body clock.

The body keeps track of time. Did you know that? How else do you think it knows when to do certain types of things? Many of you in the audience (and reading this) have come into this energy this time as females. Did you ever wonder why it was that the body clock was related to a monthly cycle? That's a relationship with Gaia, is it not? Why should Human biology respond to the cycle of the moon? What is the process there? What does that tell you? The first thing it should tell you is that there is a relationship between the earth and the biology of the Human Being! The second thing it should tell you is that it's all base 12 (as discussed before in Kryon Book Three).

The earth responds to the physics of base 12. Its geometry is base 12, and so is your biology. The 12 strands of DNA, whose parts are in the groups of threes and fours, shout base 12 to you, and many of you already know of the sacredness of the shapes around the 12. It's all about the earth and *you*. The clocks in your cells, you see, keep track of your biology.

There are two things to keep track of. One, which we have discussed before, is magnetics. The body knows about magnetics! What do you think (what you call) "jet lag" is? When you take Human Beings and hurtle them through the grid, and ley lines pass through them quickly, the Human body reacts in a certain way. Did you know that if you go in one direction, you will have one reaction, and if you go in the other direction, you will have another? Did you know that one is depleting and one is invigorating? Start observing this. Your body reacts to the magnetics of the planet. We have told you this before-that magnetics are necessary to biology—and without them you would not be able to exist. The other, which is presented here in this discussion, is that your biology needs to count light and dark in conjunction with magnetic input. The counting mechanism is also involved with dark and light.

Let me give you something that perhaps you do not know, and we broach it for the first time here. Every cell of your body knows when it is day and when it is night. This has nothing to do with the sensors in your eyes. A sightless person has the same ability, for the cellular structure and the very blood that goes through your veins recognizes light and dark and attempts to count the days in concert with the magnetic attributes. Soon there will be evidence to show you what I am saying. The body clock is what you should look at next for life extension, for this clock can be addressed and changed. Look for the chronos portion of the DNA. The part that "counts" is critical in understanding the entire picture.

Hate and Love

Let us speak of hate and love. All Humans here are aware of hate and love. It may not shock or surprise some of you to know that the core energy of hate and love is similar. Let me tell you about hate. Hate is ignorance waiting for that anointed energy and wisdom of light to pass through it. That's what hate is. Go back to the definition of the dark side I gave you. If you remove light and love from any consciousness, anywhere, you will see the dark side manifest itself into doubts and fears. Darkness is simply the degree to which love is missing.

You all have heard of and seen Humans who seem to have no conscience whatsoever. They can seemingly do anything negative and not feel it. We are telling you that the core energy of hate and love are the same, and you are looking at a consciousness of ignorance without the element of love—waiting and potent with opportunity to be transmuted. Hate, therefore, becomes an energy waiting for change. It has a potential. It wants to change. Its vibration wants to go up. It does not enjoy itself in the hate state. It is miserable, just look at those who hate.

Love, on the other hand, is hate transmuted. Some of you have seen those who are convinced there is no God. These are the same ones who are convinced that there could be no good thing in the world. But then these same individuals often have some kind of experience that changes them overnight. You have seen hate scrubbed clean, and you watched the active element of light pop into their eyes. You get to see an individual who is changed forever. This is the meek one whom we have told you about—this one who synchronistically looked like they were hopeless. There will be a lot of "Ah-ha's" taking place in the new energy. There may be some of them sitting in this audience or reading these words. This is truly the miracle of the active part of love! Love transmutes hate and fear. When you shine the light into a dark place, the darkness is no more, and the transmutation is permanent! You can never "un-know" something. You cannot retreat into a state of unawareness once you understand how something works. The only way to do this is through denial, and that fosters unbalance and dis-ease.

Fear and Peace

Tonight we talk of fear and peace, which are seemingly at the opposite ends of the spectrum. The one who fears is in the dark. The one who fears is not ready to see the active element of light. The one who fears is the one who has not realized the self-worth of the grand one who sits inside their own heart. Like hate, fear is ignorant. But again, the ignorance is the ignorance of the golden one inside.

Oh, dear ones, when you come face to face with the Higher Self, you will never be the same again. When that golden one looks in your eyes and you see your face upon that angel, you will never be the same. Your self-worth will soar! The ones who have found this higher one are the ones who can wake up feeling peaceful, no matter what, for they understand that there is a piece of God right inside. The source, you see, is in here [Lee touches his thymus and his heart. Representing the inside of him].

How does it make you feel to know you are never alone? Never alone! Some of you don't believe that. You feel different. You indeed feel alone. And we say that you are experiencing a state of energy that is incomplete and longs to change—waiting for potential shift. Is there anyone who enjoys being in that state? I don't think you could sit in your chair here or be reading these words if you did. No. You want change!

Right now you are free to give intent for the change. Your body is reacting to truth and is in a state of transition. Fear and hate are temporary things that wish to be changed and are ready for a potential shift. Peace, on the other hand, is happy with itself, just like love, because it has pure intent and because it has the *active* energy of light. There is nothing like it, dear ones, to sit in that chair as a Human Being or to be reading these words and know that although the world may seem like chaos around you, you are peaceful with it all. The angel inside is the key. Your wisdom is the catalyst. Some have likened this to the ostrich in the sand—ignoring the problems. They don't understand that to have peace with chaos is a divine trait. It exemplifies your overview. It shows that you understand that there is balance in all things, and choose to balance your life with light.

The Parable of Mobie

Oh, there is one more thing, and now I am going to give you, my partner, the answer to a question you have had for a week. A word has been given that you have not understood, and you've shared it with no one, hoping the answer would be given. What does it mean? Why should it be given for you to ponder? The word is *passage*, and now I'm going to give you a parable about a Human called Mobie.

Mobie was a tribesman. He didn't know about the modern world, but Mobie was very smart. The tribe was buzzing with rumors about another civilization that had marvelous technologies—far beyond anything he could imagine. In a tribe where they barely used the wheel, Mobie was told that on the coast, there was an incredible city with people who looked different and had unbelievable things. They spoke a language that was different, and they acted differently, also.

Mobie also heard that there were stones and fabrics, common to the tribe, but that were valuable to that advanced town on the coast. Mobie was told, "If you take enough stones and fabrics, you can have anything you want!" Mobie had to see this for himself.

He made a decision to leave his tribe and find this higher civilization. Oh, he knew they were different and they spoke another language, but perhaps he could assimilate into it—so he went. Indeed, when he got to the town on the coast, it was inhabited by those who looked far different than he did, and he stuck out. They wondered where he was from, but they were indeed wise and welcomed him, for he brought valuable and rare stones and fabrics, and seemed to be rich with them.

So they accepted Mobie even though they did not understand his language. He did not understand theirs either. He lived there for a short time, realizing that there was even more yet to be discovered. He was told that on the other side of the vast ocean there was an even greater civilization! He was told that he could get there on a large boat that left often. So he said, "I'm going to go there."

Mobie was having no problem at all—even though he did not understand the language and perhaps never would. He had what it took to trade and get all that he needed, so he found the large boat—and what a boat it was! Mobie walked up the long ramp to that marvelous, huge liner, the size of a building! It was immense! But something was wrong when he arrived at the entrance. Those who boarded passengers would not let Mobie board. He offered his stones and his fabrics, the things that had gotten him passage into every shop and every store, but they shook their heads and would not let him pass.

He tried several times, then waited and watched others do it. Maybe he would understand if he saw what the officials wanted in order to allow him on board. It seemed easy. Those who boarded gave the official something and went on, but each time Mobie tried, no matter when he went, they shook their heads and pointed in a certain direction. He didn't understand. They tried to give him information, but he still couldn't understand. Obviously he needed something but did not have it.

There was a wise man who had watched this process on the dock, who finally helped Mobie. Although the man did not speak

Mobie's language either, he pointed out a small hut with some activity. Something was happening there. Business was taking place. Mobie was very smart. He understood that the man was trying to show him that the hut contained an answer he should seek.

So it was that Mobie examined the shack where the business was being done. He saw the exchange for something that he later learned was called a "ticket." So Mobie went to the shack and exchanged some of his gemstones and his fine garments and linens for a piece of paper. Mobie took that to the ramp—marched up—stood tall—and presented this little piece of paper to the ones who had shaken their heads so many time before while saying *no*. They smiled broadly and ushered Mobie onto the great ship. Mobie took his place in the first-class cabin, and the ship left for the new land.

Mobie had learned a great deal about this new culture. Even though he was very able and had goods that were highly valued, he still needed to exchange them for something specific that seemed small, but represented a placeholder for a great treasure, in order to gain passage. It became the final step that identified his intent to gain passage and make the trip.

Dear ones, you are going to discover that what worked in one energy won't seem to work in the other. Mobie needed a ticket for passage, and there are some of you who come into this New Age with the equipment that is enlightened and which has always worked before. This equipment represents certain energies that you have used, and ideas you have had along with specific powers, great meditations, and ways of doing things in the New Age. But now some of you are finding that none of these are giving you the results they used to. You are hitting a wall with them, and "passage" is being denied over and over. The results you used to get are not being achieved anymore.

I'll tell you where the ticket is: As Mobie discovered, he had to go to another place for the ticket, and I'll tell you what the place is called. It's a place you cannot hide from Spirit. It's called **pure intent, combined with *ownership* of self-worth**. It's that simple. You must go to that place that is different from any other place that you've been used to. With pure intent, you say to God, "*Show me what it is I need to know. I am ready with pure intent for passage. I AM, that I AM.*" Then be ready for that ticket with such a pure request!

No amount of old energy ceremony or ritual will get you passage. It's time to drop all the assumptions you had about "what works" to get you closer to God. Now it is *you* who are different, and your power that is the focus. Own your Golden Angel, and watch what happens! (This refers to claiming the Higher Self as real.)

It is not through your works that the rites of passage are given. It is not through anything that you have learned. It comes right from knowledge of the Golden Angel inside you! This is about intent and the assurance of your spiritual essence, and there is no more powerful thing in this universe at this moment than the power of Human consciousness and sacred intent! When you give it, you will be issued that ticket in a heartbeat, and you will waltz up that ramp and be shown into the first-class cabin. Then you are on your path, and we say that there is so much love in this process! It is brand new. There has been nothing like it on this planet until now. You find yourself sitting in an age with an energy that is more special than any before, and you have gifts that are astounding.

So, what made the difference? It was the knowledge that you deserve to be here. Those who fear the dark as evil are still in the dark! Those that shout "wo is me" when the problem comes, retreat into darkness on their own. No matter how spiritual they are, they have not discovered the "ticket." They have not discovered where the light is—the angel inside—the spark of divinity that is the Human Being.

Everyone who leaves this place today should have a ticket. It's because we love you! It's your ticket in a first-class cabin—and on the ticket it says, "Welcome home!" This is what it means to be in this New Age! This is why you're here reading these words!

Now, take a look at the fine print on the ticket. It has words like *healing*, *life extension*, *peace*, *love*, and *supreme and real happiness*—all obtainable right now by claiming the power inside you—by claiming the ticket you deserve.

So it is we come to another closing. It is the welling up of my partner that you see, which mirrors the feeling that we have for you. There is no grander time than when we sit and talk with the hearts of Human Beings! This is special! Recognize the feeling of *home* inside you. Feel protected! You are! We know what you've been through. We know what your contracts are. We know where the ticket is. It's being held by the golden one inside you...and it is yours for the taking.

And so it is.

Kryon

Humor

"Humor begets joy. You cannot have joy in your life without humor connected with it. Imagine a candle, and the wax of the candle is joy, and the wick of the candle is *you*. The candle stands there inactive. Nothing happens with the wax (the joy). It is suspended in a shaft that is going nowhere, but is poised and ready. Then the light and flame of **humor** is assigned to the wick (*you*). It will start to melt the joy and activate it. You can smell it, and the joy then becomes pliable. It is working, it gives off light, it is alive—because of the humor that is applied to it. Humor is the catalyst for joy. Joy begets peace and melts the Human heart. Do you understand what we're saying? Use this. Use it in all things!"

Kryon

From Kryon Book 6,

"Peace and Power in the New Age"

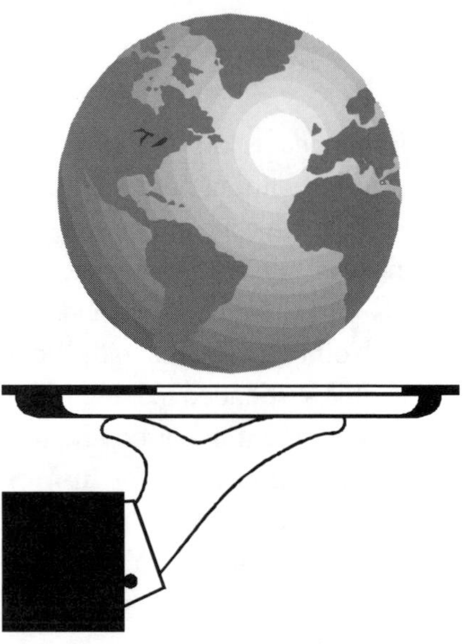

"How does it make you feel to know that the thing you're trying so desperately to co-create and figure out has already been accomplished? It is in the storehouse of a place that you are in and always have access to. It has already been solved! It sits on the golden tray, and the hand of the golden one that sits within you is holding the tray. "

Kryon

"The Golden Tray"

Channelled in
Banff, BC - Canada

The Kryon Writings, Inc.
PMB 422
1155 Camino Del Mar
Del Mar, California 92014
[www.kryonqtly.com]

"The Golden Tray"
Live Channelling
Banff, BC - Canada

This live channelling has been edited with additional words and thoughts to allow clarification and better understanding of the written word.

Greetings, dear ones. I am Kryon of magnetic service. Oh, my partner, it is a good thing to be back in this energy, is it not? For there has been much learned here. It is the intent of the love of Spirit at this time in this energy, to fill each and every chair with the love of God!

That's not going to be that difficult, because so many of you are ready for this. The subject this night is a practical one, and it is one about Humans and their reactions and interactions. And oh, dear ones, this is among Kryon's favorite subjects—how God and Humans work together. We allow a moment for our energy to press upon you from an entourage that has arrived with Kryon—to love you. The entourage is what we bring to enhance the intent of those who are here. For there are those sitting in the chairs at this time, intending change, intending information to be passed that would be helpful to them and to you. There is a great joke here and the joke is personal to each one of you. It is that each and every one knows this voice you are now hearing (or reading). For some of you are hearing or reading the English words and the voice of my partner, but you are feeling the energy of Spirit as we speak to your heart. The energy is from home.

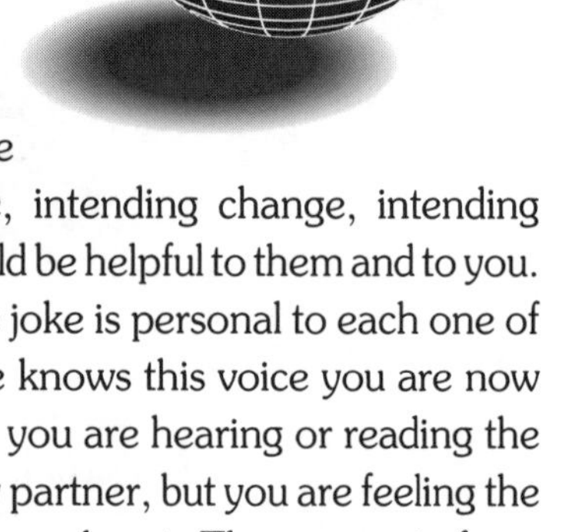

We say to you that we know everything you know—about you. The only thing that we do not know is what you're going to do next. For that, dear ones, is what this planet is all about—this planet of free choice—set up in advance with permission by you. Through eons of time, now is the payoff as you sit in the energy of the New Age and you listen to and read the words from a Human Being channelling the energy of divinity—an energy that shakes hands with the divine one that sits in your heart. Let the entourage that is here now walk between these seats and these aisles and do their work. Open your heart to what can be yours tonight! We do not come here to give you information, dear ones. We come here to pass life-changing energy.

The partnership we have developed with some of you is awesome. You have allowed us in, and now you know what it is like to create your own reality, don't you? Yet, still there are so many who doubt that such a thing could be—to walk hand-in-hand with your higher self, to claim to be a partner with the very "spark of God," to wake up in the morning not knowing what's going to happen or where your abundance is coming from, yet to have a smile and have peace in your heart that sings the song of love. That's the test, isn't it?

Again, we come to you apologizing that the new energy paradigm sometimes goes against the old Human nature. Some of you are finding that your needs are met, not in advance, but only at the last possible second. You who are experiencing this know a little bit about what it's like to be in the now. But that is the way God works—the answers given exactly when you need them, and usually not before. Is there any doubt that we know who you are? I speak to each heart now. You come here and you sit in the chair or read these words, and there is great honor from our side—honor for that entity inside you that has marvelous spinning colors, honor for that golden one inside each of you that has "wings" that can spread out to 27 feet! For the energy that each of you carries when you're not here is awesome! We know what your Merkabah looks like. We know of the colors you carry. We know of your spiritual lineage. We know where you've been, and we honor you! For the ones in this very room can change the energy of the planet. That's how much power is here.

If it were not for the duality, you would explode into a maze of colors and energy that would astound the universe. Everyone who ever lived on this planet is alive again in some form—did you know that? Some have passed over and have come back quickly, for they know this is the time that's going to make a difference. All are poised—looking and watching. There is energy being delivered from so many different sources. Oh, it's all about now. It's all about now. Humanity as a whole, at the cellular level, knows what this is all about.

Don't you think we know the feelings that are here, the questions, the unrest, the seeming unbalance, the problems? That's what we want to talk about tonight—the problems.

The Golden Chair

So it was, one year ago, that we sat in this very spot and in the energy of the mountains [Banff, Canada]. We spoke of the "golden chair." We opened a subject that we had never opened before regarding partnering with God so that we could expound upon it and have it carried from city to city all over the globe. Indeed, it has been transcribed and published, but it was initiated here where you now sit, for this was the place it happened originally, in front of those just like you. Some of you were there at that time and know of what I speak. We told you of the great golden one that sits on the chair in your heart. Inside there is something you call the "higher self." We've told you of the self-worth issue that you can grab hold of and claim. We invited you to metaphorically sit in the chair with that golden one to see who you were. We invited you to feel the love permeate every cell. We invited you to see the concept of the partnership with God that is available in this New Age. We invited the marriage to the higher self and we told you that it was the beginning step for many.

We told you that if you would do this, all things would start to be added, for the gifts and the jewels of Spirit that you need to move forward as a Human Being on this planet are special indeed, and they are different from any in the past. They have to be. There is **no** old energy tool that will serve you on a day-to-day existence on this planet as a Human Being as you walk into a high vibration. So, Human living and being "on the path" becomes a whole new paradigm—an entire new school, and the new gifts are given to you one by one. There are so many of you who do not understand what the gifts are. You sit in confusion, and yet in all love and honor, you have given intent to move forward—and intent is the catalyst for action!

Preparation for the Message

We would like to tell you of a concept this night that is going to be as radical and different as the golden chair was to you a year ago. We want you to understand that each and every one of you right now can claim that golden one before we hear more. I have an exercise for you, for it will help you in what's next. It is one that my partner has used many times on groups, but never in a channelling. We have told you many times, dear ones, that we are here to wash your feet. What is to follow is given in great love and honor for humanity. If you get nothing more this night than this, it will still be good—and that is to feel the love of God permeate your heart and feel your feet being washed—each one, by the tears of our joy that we supply for that purpose.

There are entities such as Kryon that would give so much to sit in front of you like this! It seems that in the perfect love of God, I drew the lot to be the one to help set the magnetic grid—to watch this grand time of yours and see what you've done on Earth—seeing hope, as well as the changes and the great love. Let me wash your feet in appreciation of your effort. Accept it, and know that you are honored.

Each one of you comes here with Human problems of living. There's a unique scenario with each person and this is as it should be, especially with those who find themselves searching in this New Age. There are upsets. Things are not always as they seem.

Suddenly some of you find yourself yanked away from something that was comfortable. Suddenly some of you find issues that never were there before: health, abundance, survival. Some of you have issues with family—biological and cosmic.

Here is the preparation exercise, and you will see how it plugs into what we're going to tell you. We wish you to see and visualize the problem that is at the forefront of your mind right now as you hear or read this. For some of you, there is more than one. And oh, we honor you for this. There is no greater love than that of a Human Being who is chosen to come to this planet and walk around in biology with the true higher self hidden from you—to see if you could find it—to experience the frailty of the flesh and the disappointment of the aging and your tests of humanism. That is why we love you so, if we haven't told you before. That is why you are deserving to have messages of enlightenment given in this manner. And that is why you are deserving to have energy passed into your life—absorbed into that golden chair—so that you could move forward, empowered with new gifts.

Visualization

We want you to visualize this problem that is in your life. Pull it out of its ugly place, and put it on your lap! Like a tiny ferocious animal, even though it might be ugly—black with fear—we want you to sit it right there in front of you—alive and filled with uncertainty. The reason we want you to do that is because you're going to have an opportunity to do something with it in a moment. For this night this ugly thing is either going to be solved or you're going to put it back where it was. You see, these things don't get cast away. They don't disappear. They *belong* to you. They're setups that you brought in. They're yours, with your name on them. You agreed to them. Pull them out, those unsolvable problems, and put them on your lap. Metaphorically and figuratively, they are going to sit there where only you can see them, for the next moment. They are going to hear the message, also.

Now we're going to tell you something: Before we can describe this new concept, we have to go into a scenario that is historic. We'd like to tell you what Humans normally do with the kinds of problems that are on your lap. We're going to discuss the *old energy* first, for it must be clear to you what the difference is between what used to be, and what is now.

In the old energy, there are five things. Humans did with problems of the kind that you bring here. You are not unique in the problem department, you know. As an enlightened individual, your problems are often similar to the ones that the others have, too. What makes the problems unique is that now *you* have them (not the others). Perhaps you find yourself as an enlightened individual. Just because you know how things work and who you are does not exempt you from some of these things. Let us describe for a moment what the old energy method is regarding the treatment of intense problems, and it's going to prove something to you—that real Human duality exists—as if you needed such proof!

Run

The first thing a Human Being will often do with an intense problem is run the other way. "*If I run far enough away, it won't be there when I get back*," some have said as they scamper here and there. You have seen it over and over. And so the running begins, and there are so many ways of running. There are ways to occupy your brain. There are actual physical moves. There's the process of ignoring the problem— "*Oh, it'll go away, it'll go away.*" But it remains, doesn't it? There it is, and it slowly gets worse. Sometimes it festers. Sometimes the energy of running actually intensifies it! You can't get away from it.

The old paradigm was first to flee. Now I ask you right now: Would such a thing be in a perfect spiritual nature? Why is it that fear and problems are so abhorrent to such an intelligent race? And the answer, dear ones, is a spiritual one, because these things on your lap have a spiritual energy! They are setups. Each time something occurs that is of a paramount nature—which creates fear and anxiety and interrupts your life—it's a setup. And the first thing the Human wants to do is get away from it! It's an odd thing to do, is it not, for a wise intelligent race? Instead, why don't you just face it and solve it? The answer is because there is a grand spiritual overlay here. There's a "piece of home" in every problem. There's a "piece of great love" in every problem. And so the first reaction is flight. "*I don't want to go there*," the Human says. Yet it's part of the contract. It's part of the duality. Sometimes it's a tough one to accept. Your duality creates the fear.

Least Resistance

When you flee, yet you realize that the problem remains, many find that the path of least resistance is the solution. "*Okay, I will act on this thing. I think I will do the thing that is the easiest*," the Human says, and here is a dichotomy. Many times that "least resistant" solution has nothing to do with the problem at all. It's a covering, so to speak—something to get it out of the way. "*What's the easiest thing I can do*," the Human Being asks, "*to rid myself of this? I'll deal with it, but what's the easiest way?*"

We're reminded of the parable of "Sarah and the Old Shoe," one that we have given to you before, which has nothing to do with a shoe at all. The old shoe is just a metaphor meaning that Human Beings tend to go to what is most comfortable (and the least trouble). Listen, dear ones: Many times what is most comfortable is in the old energy! The story of Sarah was easy: She prayed and prayed for the job of a lifetime—to be in her "sweet spot." All she wanted was this marvelous occupation—something that she could really do well. It was her passion, and she prayed, and she finally got it. The only thing was that she had to ride the subway train to get to it. Sarah had come into the world with an overlay of claustrophobia. She hated that train! Every time she got into it, she sweated, she had anxiety, she was fearful, and she could hardly wait for those few minutes to be over with until she could get out.

She had co-created, in a spiritual manner, the job of a lifetime, yet she had to deal with a karmic overlay that seemingly got in the way.

Finally, Sarah presented herself to God and said, "*This is not working, guides, golden angel, partner of mine—this is not working.*" The golden angel asked Sarah, "What would you like to do about it," and she said, "*Let's find another job.*" And the angel said, "The job is what you created and asked for. It's your passion—your gift. Why wouldn't you decide to change the overlay of claustrophobia instead?" And Sarah said, "*Because I've had claustrophobia for 50 years. I've only had the job three months!*"

Sarah went for the easiest solution. "*Find me a job that's next door*," she said. "*It's easier.*" Many of you know that this true story had a remarkable ending. Sarah indeed eventually decided, through intent, to clear the karmic attribute or her fear of small spaces—and keep the "perfect" job she had created. And she did. By the way, when she did, the Earth changed a bit, too. The Human often wants to take the avenue that is most likely to produce success the quickest, even if it does not create the solution.

Organize/Share

Another thing the Human Being does with problems in the old energy paradigm is what we call organize. There are Humans with problems in front of them who decide that if they share them with enough people, they will go away! So they organize themselves and their friends into "drama" groups. They call all of their friends, and they tell them all about their problems. They repeat their stories over and over and over, thinking that perhaps by doing so, someday their problems will go away. They feel that if they could just get more people involved, the issue might get diluted. They actually don't want suggestions or solutions; they really want to pass the issues to the group! It doesn't work that way. Involving others in this fashion shares the energy in an inappropriate way, since to do so is to turn your back on the responsibility issue that is actually at the basis of the problems. There is simply no one else who can take on and solve problems with your karmic name on it.

Worry

Oh, this next subject is one that some of you know very well! In the old energy sometimes the first thing that a Human Being wishes to do is create energy in the form of worry. We have spoken about this before. Worry is energy. Worry is the energy of the intellect without love. Did you know that? The intellect with love is a beautiful thing. The intellect without love creates worry and anxiety. Somehow, the Human thinks, the worry and the energy created with it diminishes the problem. Often, given the choice in the New Age of "peace or worry," Humans choose worry! It's back to the old shoe, isn't it? Indeed worry creates energy. Concentration on the problem often enhances and intensifies the it! We have spoken many times about the fork in the road coming up. It's easier, when you see a challenge looming in front of you, to sit down and worry about it, instead of walking up to it in order to solve the problem at close range. Many times the signpost of solution is only at the fork! You have to walk into the middle of the challenge in order to find the answer. It simply isn't posted on a sign before you get there. Worry is a common Human reaction, and it's spiritually understood because it's part of your *duality*. Think of all the things that you do instead of facing a problem directly. Is this the reaction of a logical, unbiased spiritual being? No. It's the reaction of a Human who has come into the planet with a bias—a duality that creates illogical reactions to the setups that you planned. Dear ones, this is why we have called what you do "work!"

Shut Down

When all else fails, instead of facing the problems in front of them, many Humans simply shut down. With the shutdown comes imbalance, and in this imbalance you invite health problems and disease. Many times instead of facing a problem in life, the person goes into a crisis of biology—a shutdown mode. Where is it in the wise Human brain where it says, "*It is better to leave the planet than to face the problem?*" We tell you where it is: It lives in Human duality! Is this not proof that there is something going on? What is "Human nature," anyway? A form of illogical behavior that appears comical—common to humanity? No. It's in the setup of duality—a spiritual attribute of a normal anointed soul on your planet. It's common to your quest.

With the problem on your lap, some of you have had one or more of these attributes presented to you that may sound familiar. Even those who call themselves "enlightened" and are vibrating at a high level will have the temptation to go to an old energy answer, until they catch themselves in it and move on to what will work. Why do we tell you about this? The reason is not only to show you the duality at work, but also to show you the beauty of what's coming, for all of these things in the old energy that you would call normal duality reactions are now able to be transmuted spiritually!

You as Human Beings, and we as Spirit, cooperating in a partnership, have control over these things in your life. We say it is time to eliminate all of them! There is no reason to flee and run, no reason to worry, no reason to try to find the avenue of least resistance, or to give up.

What then, does the New Age Human do with the problem of the kind you have in your lap? Let's examine that for a moment. The one who is totally enlightened, the one who knows who they are, the one who sits in the golden chair, the one who is vibrating at a high level, will do three things, which is the source of so many channellings that we have communicated. The New Age Human has an entirely different paradigm.

(1) The first thing New Age Humans will do is analyze metaphorically why the problem exists. This is greatly honored, for this is the key to what's next. They will look at their problem and say, "*Why has this been brought to me? What does it mean?*" They will meditate in front of Spirit, and without telling Spirit anything at all, they will ask the question, "*What do I need to know about this?*" Then they will ask, not for the solution, but for peace over it. This is very wise, very wise. First must come balance and peace. Next, revelation and complete solution. Peace over worry is absolutely necessary for co-creation! There are so many of you here and reading this who fit into this category of Human Being. I'm speaking about the way you handle your problems.

(2) The second thing that this enlightened Human Being will do in the new paradigm is to take responsibility for the problem, regardless of how big it is or what has happened—regardless if it appeared to be an accident or not. They will say, "*At some level, I planned it. I'm responsible for it. I own it, and therefore I can solve it.*" It is not "something that has happened to them." It is not a "woe is me" experience. There's no victimization.

(3) The third thing they will do is an action item: They will begin the process of co-creating the solution. We have spoken of this many times, and we have given many channellings about co-creating, but there is something more to know. There is a concept we are going to present to you today that we have never presented before. It's a concept that may change the way you think as a New Age Human Being—a concept which is going to give you an "ah-hah," an experiential input of new data, something to think about—something to claim and something to visualize that is actual and real! And it's going make spiritual sense.

In order for me to broach this subject, I'm going to have to talk about interdimensional things. This is difficult, for I deal with Human Beings who are single-digit dimensional creatures, and Spirit deals in multiple dimensions. Some of the concepts are beyond your understanding while you are on Earth, due to your duality. Let me give you an example right now, one we have never spoken of before. It will probably be just as meaningless to you now as it will be in ten years, until your science realizes the truth of it. Here is a science fact: The gamma ray activity that you see coming to you from billions of light years away is next door! If you could create a highway that is like a ribbon—a two-dimensional highway—and travel for billions of years at the speed of light until you were at the actual source of the gamma ray activity, when you turned over that two-dimensional highway, you would see your own solar system! It would appear as though you had never left. How's that for cryptic? It's the way it works. It's an interdimensional concept. It's something that you cannot understand. Did you know that your incredible "expanding" universe is a closed system? Can you understand how there could be no beginning to it? Picture it. Your Human brain has difficulty understanding this, and yet indeed there was no beginning. The Spirit of God, which includes every single one of you, has simply "always been." It is a fixture in the universe that has always been, and will always be, and you are part of it—each and every one of you.

We speak of the *now*, and that is what we want to talk about. The concept of the now is not understandable within your linear time. We speak of real time as in a circle. The reality of time is in the now (which also creates a closed universe). The time that has been created for you is linear. Do you realize that there is not one Human Being who exists in the now? For as you sit there, it's either the future or the past. As your linear clock moves forward, it's either the linear past or the linear future. You're never allowed to stop and *be* where we are, in the now. In the now, which is an interdimensional concept, Kryon and God and all of the guides and angels are used to a situation where the past and the present and all the "potential things to come" exist all at once. Now this is critical for you: I am telling you that your *potentials exist now* in the inner-dimensional reality of God's plan. It's hard for you to see this storehouse of *now time* when you're constantly looking at the past and the future. Your train is on a track that is constantly traveling, and all you can see when you turn your head is where it's been and where it's going. We, however, see your train in a circle. It's far different, and difficult to explain clearly.

My partner, it is critical in this portion of the channelling that you be crystal clear, for the logic of this must land correctly on those who are listening. The reality of spiritual time is that all things exist together. Everything that you have the potential to do has already occurred, and this has nothing to do with predestination. As we have said before, you control your own train. But we're telling you that the potentials for your problems actually exist now.

I'm going to give you an example: Some of you have said that being on Earth is like a school. We have told you about lessons and experience, and that is why you're here. The problems that are in your laps, therefore, are the tests, are they not? Now I want you to go back to school for a minute. Go backwards in time when you were in school and were learning the things that Humans said that you had to learn. Let us pretend for a moment that the tests were on your desk, and you sat there ready to write the answers to them as best you could. Do you remember a time like that?

Listen to this: In that school where you used to be, in some drawer somewhere, in some file cabinet somewhere, on some instructor's desk someplace, were all the solutions to every single test you were taking. Do you agree? For you could not be given those tests in that school without having the solutions there also. They were there to be given to you to compare them to your learning process. So I am telling you that in your young academic years, the solutions to your tests had already been worked out and were there for you to look at, even as you sat at the desk taking the tests. The solutions were hiding from you, but they existed, didn't they?

Now come back with me for a moment, and let's speak about the problem in your lap. Let's talk about an interdimensional partner that you have. Let's talk about the drawers and the file cabinets of Spirit, because I'm here to give you an anointed concept called "The Golden Tray," and I present this to you in all love, just like I presented to you the one called "The Golden Chair."

On that golden tray, dear ones, are the solutions to every single problem on every lap in this room! And it exists now, and it's in the now. The problem has already been solved. It is not in the process of solution—it is done! How does it make you feel to know that the thing you're trying so desperately to co-create and figure out has already been accomplished? It is in the storehouse of a place that you are in and always have access to. Look at that ugly thing on your lap—the thing that's fearful. It has already been solved! It sits on the golden tray, and the hand of the golden one that sits in your lap is holding the tray. There's also an unspoken invitation here.

What are you going to do with this? If the solutions already exist, it must tell you something about the way things work, doesn't it? There is nothing too hard—there is no solution that is beyond your reach. Since it's there for the taking, let me give you some instructions about this new concept. We're telling you that rather than struggling through co-creation, you are able to reach out and take it—something that has already been there. Do you know why it's there, dear ones? Do you know the careful hands that prepared it? This is going to make logical sense to some of you, and to others it will not. There must be a balance in everything. The question was asked earlier by one who had just come in to the Kryon energy and discovered the feeling of home. He asked, "*Where does the karma go when it's cleared and disabled?*" That's a great question, for it shows an understanding of energy balance. I will tell you where it goes: It goes right into the Earth—and you wonder why the Earth moves! That's the alchemy we speak of. Where does the old energy consciousness go? It goes into the planet where it's transmuted to the energy of change. The planet shifts and changes, and it moves around, transmuting the old Human energy. It's a wise person who understands that energy is always there. When you change as Humans in this New Age, there is indeed a process that facilitates planetary change because of your spiritual actions. It's called balance.

When Hale Bopp came through, it delivered an amazing amount of energy to your planet—to the very dirt of the Earth so that these Human processes could be transmuted properly. It was needed energy, and we reported it at the time. Now you know where it came from—and why it was needed. The shifting of energy is complex, and when even one of you gives intent to move forward and drop the old ways, the old paradigm, and the old karma, the Earth absorbs it. Earth changes are part of the grand plan and part of the balance of the New Age. So it should be no shock to you that every single test in this room has already been solved. The balance of the tests are the solutions on the tray. They're in the now, just like your problems are. They're in your now potential—all ready for you. But there are some attributes you should know about, because this is not simple. Let me give you some of those.

The first is this: As you see and acknowledge the fact that the solution already exists even though you cannot see it, **visualize the solution**. See the tray, and visualize the solution. Now, this is important: Don't visualize what you think you need to create the solution. Let that be your partner's job (Spirit). Let us do that. If a Human is going to run a race in the morning and wants to be one of the few who finishes, but doesn't know how he is going to get through that exhausting hill or around that tight turn, he might pray to God to help him with the tight turn and the exhausting hill. We're here to say that, instead, he should simply be visualizing passing easily over the finish line. Let us figure out the exhausting hill and the tight turn. That's our job.

Let us review for a moment the parable that was given to you regarding "Henry and the Missing Bridge." Some of you will remember that this was a story about a man who was speeding toward a bridge that he knew was out. Spirit said to him, "Continue on, Henry. Things are not always as they seem, Henry. You will be taken care of, Henry." The missing bridge was a metaphor for what Human Beings cannot fathom or see in the future, which God has already taken care of.

That parable, dear ones, is really about the golden tray. For the solution to Henry's problem of the missing bridge had already been taken care of. If you read that parable again, for it has been published, you will realize something within this new concept of the golden tray. As Henry approached the area where the bridge was supposed to be, he opened his eyes and realized that it was still gone. His fear increased—it was the last moment! It took everything he had in him not to stop right there, yet Spirit said, "Henry, continue on, continue on." So Henry, in all his faith, continued on even faster than before, trusting God, and the partnership within. Just as he thought he was about to have his vehicle careen over the cliffs to a certain death in the valley below, he saw workmen on the road guiding him around to an area he had never seen before—an area completely out of sight that he had never, ever observed. And standing in full glory there was a beautiful new bridge! It was a bridge that was so big and so awesome that Henry realized that it had been under construction long before he came along. He crossed it in ecstasy, realizing the power of his partnership with God.

Dear ones, this is the key to the parable. There are solutions on that tray to problems you don't even have yet! By the time you get around to asking Spirit for the solutions, they've already been built. It's part of the balance. There must be solutions for the tests that you've agreed to—and there are.

Henry didn't visualize how his bridge dilemma was going to be solved. The thought of a miracle bridge popping before him was silly. The thought was beyond his Human reality. So instead, he simply visualized moving to the other side—the end result. The runner visualizes breaking the tape. Regarding your problem? Visualize it all taken care of, and then leave the details to us. But you do the energy visualization often!

The second attribute, therefore, is that "**things are not always as they seem**." The answers may come in very shocking and unusual ways. Sometimes the miraculous energy will astound you. Sometimes the answers seem complex. In retrospect you might say, "*Long ago if person A hadn't done this and person B hadn't done that, then my solution would never have been possible.*" There is something in you that realizes that person A made his move before you ever needed it. How complex this was, you might say. How elegant and perfect! Not only that, but within your solution, no matter how complex the interaction is with others, somehow everyone seems to win! Dear ones, that's the mark of a spiritual solution. Visualize, therefore, the solution as having been taken care of. It's on the tray.

The third attribute is **don't limit God**. You don't know what's on that tray, and we do. There are so many of you who are standing here asking for a bush when Spirit stands with a tray containing a whole forest on it! You don't expect it since you don't feel the self-worth of it. The solution to your little problem may contain the whole forest as a gift for you! Things that you don't even know about yet will be solved within the solution of the one problem you have on your lap—perfect within the simplicity of the physics and love of Spirit, and the complexities of your humanism. So let us do the work. That's the overview of your partner (Spirit), the one you're holding hands with. That's the golden one in the golden chair—the one who knows everything about your potentials, about your contract—called the golden angel or higher self. It has the energy of Spirit, yet it also has your name. Don't limit Spirit.

Here's the fourth one: **expect synchronicity**. Now this is critical, and we have mentioned this many times: The old paradigm, even in the New Age, was to have God do things for you. And, as the concept went, if you trusted God and gave of yourself, somehow it would all work out. Now we're telling you that the partnership that we have for you involves a situation that we discussed the last time we were at an altitude in the mountains [Breckinridge, CO]. In taking the hand of the golden one, you stand up and move forward with God. Gone are the days when things are handed to you and done for you, and all you do is sit and say "thank you." You're not going to be able to sit at home and have good things fall upon you anymore. It is the responsibility of the higher self within you that gives you the ability and the gift to stand up and make things happen. That is co-creation. Nothing is going to happen, dear ones, until you stand up and push on those doors of life. Make the calls that seemingly never did anything before, and watch the results. Get together with other Humans and find out what synchronistic things take place to allow your life to move forward.

In this room, dear ones, are those who will meet others for the first time, and there is much synchronicity here. It's the reason for the mix of Humans here. For each will have something for you, and you may have something for them. There are potentials for lifelong relationships sitting here—like a tray before you with answers, but they never would have occurred in this manner unless you had the intent to be here at this time—to make the trek to sit in the chair you're in. There are things here for you that only the family can bring you. There are so many ways that this occurs, dear ones. Synchronicity, defined by Humans means "things that happen out of the blue." Seemingly, it refers to accidents or coincidences that take place that you did not expect and that cause great change in your life. Synchronicity, dear ones, as Spirit defines it, means "elements prepared on the golden platter." They're part of the solution, you see. And they're there in all love to give to you, but you've got to stand up and take them. You must push on the doors, make the calls, and show intent.

Healers, this is what my partner was talking about when he said that the one who is least likely to make the change or be healed will often be the one who will make the difference to the planet! And you hold the catalyst in your hand for this. The client in your life whom you wanted to throw away—the irritant—the one you wish would never come back—the one who complains the most—that's the one who may receive the love of God! That's often the one who is going to make the change—who is going to have the resolve to write the books, to have the waiting unborn children, to make the planet different. It is the meek one that we spoke of years before who will end up with the reigns of the planet...in all love...with full understanding of the golden tray. It's all on that golden platter, you see. But the point is, you can't see it now. That's where faith comes in.

The last item is for you to **own the concept** that we have presented this night—to know that for every problem, no matter how large, there is a solution that has been created already—one that is available and grander than you can imagine. It exists with your name on it, and it's not your job to figure out the details. The concept of the golden platter will now be disseminated and given through the next year and published accordingly. Some of you leaving this place will have full understanding and will claim the solutions to those things that are on your lap. Some will not. So here is the question: What are you going do with that thing that's on your lap?

The first thing we want you to do is to have peace over it. No matter how ugly it looks, have peace over it and feel the love of God surging through your heart that says, "We know what you've been through! We know about the problem! We know about the solution, too, remember? Have peace. Love us enough to have peace." That's the first step. The second one is a hard one. We ask you to look at that ugly thing—that thing that's your problem and your lesson, that thing you don't know what to do about—and love it. It's a piece and a parcel of the contract that you agreed to come in with, and it's right on schedule. It's part of the love that we give to you that you agreed to have happen. It's part of the reason that we wash your feet! Because you agreed to have it there on your lap. We asked you a moment ago, "Who created the tray filled with solutions?" The answer is: **You did**. As you agreed to and planned the problems, so it is that at the cellular level you also agreed to and created the balance of the solutions. Therefore, the solutions have the same energy to them that your problems do—an agreement of discovery, like finding pearls that you hid as a child in a magic box outside your house. All these things belong to you.

The Question

Each and every one of you is going to get up in a moment. When you do, you will lose your laps. So, the problem that rests there must go somewhere. You have the freedom as Human Beings to put it right back where it was. You have full choice and permission to flee from it—find the least energetic solution to it, worry about it, create drama, even to shut down. All of those things are yours to do. You also have permission to look at it and see it for what it is—something very small in the cosmic theme of things, something that has a solution on a familiar platter of gold that you prepared a long time ago. It is often covered metaphorically with tears of entities like me—guides and angels and those on the Earth who love you so much that we are able to shout a victorious yell when you discover the balance.

If you think this concept is powerful, just wait until you find out how long you can live! You may look around the majestic mountains in this area, and some of you wonder how long will you will be allowed to be alive and see these beautiful things. What a question! Our answer would be that you can "stay as long as you want." Those are the kinds of gifts that you're being presented. Watch for them, for your science will bring them soon. You're on the leading edge of a vibrational shift that will allow Humans to stay here for a very long time, and we honor you, each one, for your participation in this great time.

My partner is welling up because of the love that is being delivered in this room. It is awesome, because some of you are accepting this concept for the first time. It's going to make a difference for the rest of your life. It has nothing to do with the channel or Kryon. It has to do with who you are.

Thank you, dear ones, for allowing this kind of energy to exist. Thank you for being part of the family—a family that we are very proud of—an eternal family that has made a difference in the universe.

And so it is.

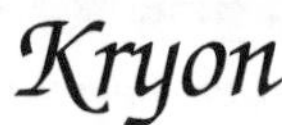

Kryon Book Six

Partnering with God

"If you liked the original Kryon series, you are going to love this book! - Probably the most practical Kryon book yet, all 400 pages of ***Partnering with God*** *are packed with the love of God for Humanity...a stirring read!"*

■ **The Leading Edge Review**

Books and tapes can be purchased in retail stores, or by phone
~ Credit cards welcome ~

1-800-352-6657

"Guides and Angels"

Channelled in Coal Creek Canyon, CO

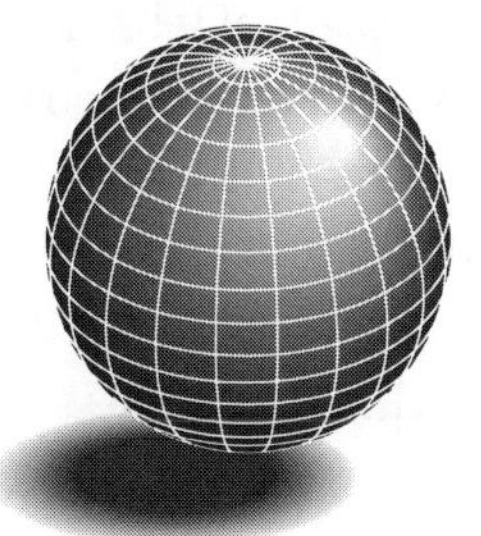

The Kryon Writings, Inc.

PMB 422
1155 Camino Del Mar
Del Mar, California 92014
[www.kryonqtly.com]

"Guides and Angels"
Live Channelling
Coal Creek Canyon, CO

This live channelling has been edited with additional words and thoughts to allow clarification and better understanding of the written word.

Greetings, dear ones, I am Kryon of Magnetic Service. As we have said so many times before, we say now that these next few moments will bring an entourage of loving entities flying through the crack in the veil to be with us—entities that are not frightening or scary, but who are family—each one. If you could see them and had the mind of God that you had before you arrived on this great planet, you would know them by name. They come here to walk between the chairs, to sit next to each Human and hug each of you. The little ones (the children in the room) that are here will feel the energy as well, and some of them may be excited due to it. For it is the feeling of "home," and they have just been there!

Some of you may realize that what is being felt is the feeling of home, and before this night is over, you will know that you have just been there, too, for all that is before you in this great land is temporary. It is, as my partner says, a setup for the "grand challenge" (covered in The Family Part V in this book).

Kryon comes with the love of the universe spilling over, knowing the names of each person here. There is no situation that is visiting you now that is unknown to us. You think, perhaps, as you go to sleep—alone—in your own mind, regardless of those who may be sleeping next to you, that perhaps you are the only one who knows what you know? You may think to yourself that the doubts that occur in your mind are yours alone? We say to you: There is no thought or dream of the Human Being that is not intimately known by those that surround you with the bubble of love as you walk through this planet.

Tonight's teaching is going to be regarding those who walk with you, and we are going to reveal for the first time, to this group and the readers through transcription, some of the mechanics of the energy of love that have not yet been revealed. Although some of it may seem academic to you, we tell you that this particular group has arrived to sit in these chairs (and read these words) in order to study the academia of Spirit. Their intent is to know more about the angel who sits inside you which you call your Higher Self.

There is great love here! Each of you has a shape that is unique within the colors that spin around it. A while ago, my partner shut his eyes during the channelling because he was distracted by the flashes of light that occurred within his mind, which were a residual of the meld that takes place from me to him. That's how we see you now. We do not see the genders that you are or the contracts that you have—we do not see any of those things. That is for another time. These visits that we have waited for—these visits that come all too seldom—allow us to pour through the veil and sit next to you. You see, it's because we want to be with you. There is no grander thing that is happening in this universe than what is happening here [on this planet]. The grandness and the sacredness of what must be on the other side of the veil does not surpass the potential that's happening here and now.

Long after this test is over—long after you and all the cells in your body have passed on and become simply dust on this planet, there will be those who tell about this time when the divine pieces of the universe that were grand indeed, decided to dress themselves in a Human form and purposefully become biologically weak, then come to the planet Earth in love to create something far grander for all of us. And the stories will be told (the best part is that you'll be there telling them) you see, for each of you is eternal. You'll come and go many times, but the energy that is *you* remains forever. And I say this to those who have lost loved ones, young and old [child begins to cry]—I told you so—[laughter], that the very energies that have been lost in the consciousness are here right now. They have the ability to do this [be here] because they are standing on the other side of the veil as well.

My partner [Lee] has always asked why it is that I have not come forth in this manner for him personally. I talk to him in his head, but as many times as he has tried, what you are hearing now does not occur for him personally. There is a reason for that, for this is about your intent and the power of the Human group that comes together and exchanges spiritual energy. It says, "*I want to sit in the chair and feel what it's like to be visited by the love of God.*" And we say to you, "You deserve to be here in the highest order." With planning that is astounding, there are no accidents that find you where you are (and reading this now). So it is, that the entourage of Kryon and Kryon himself comes to gawk at you, as the stars that you are to us. You see, we are the ones who have been expecting you this night.

The Balance of Spiritual Energy

We'd like to talk about energy transmission tonight. It sounds very boring! A mechanic of Spirit—a process of Spirit. We may reveal some things we have never broached before. We wish to speak about what happens to energy in the transmutation process from the old to the new. What happens with a miracle? Where does the energy go? What are the by-products? What are the mechanics involved in it? This knowledge will help you even in practical, everyday life. This information, finally, is able to be told to you in an energy that promotes such a thing from where we sit, to a group of people whose very desire is to vibrate at a higher level. There are very few of you [speaking of the room] who are here just to look around. Your intent creates an energy that postures itself with a possibility and potential for great information.

I'd like to tell you a little bit about your guides—something you didn't know before. Perhaps in the past channellings and in the writings and transcriptions, you remember that the parables were given about guides and Human beings. And you might remember in a parable that the guides were quiet. They existed, but there was very little pushing or prodding. Oh, they were there to hug the Human, but very little else was possible for the Human who was not giving pure spiritual intent. You may remember in some of the parables—and there have been many—that when the Human gave intent to find Spirit within, the guides became excited. The guides were activated. That's when their part began. They've always been there, dear ones...waiting for your action.

The Trinity (power of the three)

We're here to give you information about old spirituality and how it melds into the new. My partner has revealed to you the power of the "three." It has always been there. It is no mystery or accident or secret that the triangles that turn themselves in certain shapes to make other shapes have three corners. They are part of the energy of sacred geometry, and the power of the shape is often given to you in threes. When you look at the three of the divinity, even the religions of this continent give credibility to the power of the three. They call it the Trinity. We're here to explain, before we go into the teaching of energy, what that trinity actually represents.

The Father

The spiritual combination of the *three* is intuitive, and it does not only occur here. Look for the trinity in the other beliefs, for it is there. On your continent, you call it the Father, the Son, and the Holy Spirit. Let me tell you what the Father represents: The Father is the angel, the source, the parent, the one that is connected to home—that sits within each one of you. The Father is what is representative of the angel inside, the study of which you have just completed [*The Journey Home* workshop, a study of the book], the one whose face is your own, metaphorically. It is the piece of God that is within you.

The Son

The Son that is represented is of the lineage of the Father, and the Son is the Human Being that walks on the planet in duality.

The Master of Love (Jesus) referred to this over and over, and in his messages he said, "You can be just like me. I am the Son of God, and you have the power to be Sons of God." Look for it; it's there. The reference is clear. So the Son, metaphorically, is the Human Being (regardless of your gender), that is connected to the Father image, which is the one connected to the Source, which is the angel inside.

The Holy Spirit

Now, the revelation: In any belief, what you have called the Holy Spirit has never been one entity. No matter what spiritual system it is that you call for, they will explain that the Spirit is many. It always has an overview of "more than one." We're here to tell you that the Holy Spirit represents the guides (or angels) that are with you from birth. This is the trinity that you come in with—which is the divineness of the triangle within the triangle [speaking of the divine shape of the Merkabah]. I want you to notice something—something I don't want you to miss. As you walk from this place, *each* of *you* carries all three! Wherever you go, they're with you. It is not some illusive power in the sky. It does not come down only in groups. *You carry it with you.*

We've spoken of the power of a group, and now we're going to tell you why it's powerful. It is that which you call the "Spirit that is Holy" that represents the assemblage of the guides that create the power of the many instead of the one. So it is that your entourage, which perhaps you thought was here just to hug, hold, and love you, are now are being explained as the "catalyst of love."

Role of the Guides

Let me tell you about something that happens with the alchemy of energy. There must always be a balance in all energy, including the spiritual. I'm here as the magnetic master to tell you that there is always a balance. Even within the center of your very atomic structures, within the atoms, all physicists have wondered why it is that the nucleus is so small and the electron haze is so far away from it. You see, it doesn't make intuitive sense that the mass in the center would create such a physical situation of so much space. That's why we discussed the Cosmic Lattice (See Chapter Seven), the power that surges—that's always balanced all around you. It is no different, dear ones, as you walk on this planet with what you experience with your spirituality. For when one energy changes to another, there is a balance shift. When you transmute one energy to another, spiritually there is a by-product. We're going to tell you what it is in spiritual terms, but not in terms that are mechanical or physical.

Your guides are vessels, and they contain the by-product of energy that is generated by your intent. This energy is carried by the guides. For those of you who have given intent to drop your old karma and move onto a new path, you are about to ascend a ladder of vibrational shift that contains transmutation after transmutation, alchemy after alchemy. You're taking what *was*, and turning it into what *will be*. Every time you do that, there is a by-product of energy, created out of nothing, through your *intent*. It is so great, dear friends, that another guide is often added to you in the process! That's why the third one comes on-line, which we spoke of almost ten years ago.

Energy Creation

Now you know. The guides exist, among other reasons, to facilitate the energy you are creating seemingly out of nothing, which is all part of the balance of what happens when you make spiritual decisions. Let's talk about the first of three. It is only appropriate that we use three.

Intent

The first will not surprise anyone, for we are always speaking of it, and we're already there. *Intent* is the first. There is energy created with intent that transmutes karma. I don't think it's wasted on any of you to understand the energy behind the transmutation of karma. It is something profound, removed from you through intent, which transmutes into something else. We told you in other channellings what happens to it, for the potential of it has to go somewhere [for balance reasons]. The energy of potential karma represents an entire Human life potential! When you change it, what *was* the energy has to go somewhere in the transmutation process. As we've written, it goes to Gaia—to the very dirt of the earth, and the planet absorbs that energy. Therefore, it transmutes itself from a spiritual aspect of the Human Being to a spiritual container that you call Earth. There it is. The by-product of that alchemy is Earth change. That is why the earth moves as it does at this time, and that is why your oceans warm as they do. That is what is taking place, and we predicted that it would be so if you care to look. The speeding up of your planet's weather systems and geological attributes are a direct result of Humans taking their light.

Something else occurs when the intent of the Human to move forward is given. It creates a *new* energy. Seemingly out of nothing, there is another energy created—an energy that shakes hands with the Cosmic Lattice—an energy that is then stored by the guides of the individual that made the decision. This explains the *power* of intent, as we have discussed before. Pure intent draws from the Cosmic Lattice to create life change. In the process, this *new* energy is taken by the trinity within the Human, and the Human energy quotient is higher than before.

Other Humans (especially seers) suddenly are aware of your increased vibration and power. Your aura changes, and your light shines like never before! Did you ever wonder what it is that is "seen" when you carry your light? Let me tell you what it is. It's the fact that, metaphorically, your guides are carrying "vessels of *new* energy," and those vessels of energy represent the NEW energy that was created when you made the decision to move forward spiritually with your life. There's a reason why those guides carry that vessel. Before this time between us is finished, we're going to tell you why—and what the mechanics are around it.

What if a Human makes no spiritual decisions during a lifetime? We have told you before, dear ones, that there is no judgment about this. The Human is honored for the journey—for being part of the play. And when the curtain comes down, the cast party celebrates—even the one who seems to have been the villain in the play—or who even died in the play. But there's much more to it than that. Those who give spiritual intent during this New Empowered Age create energy out of nothing. That's alchemy! That's where the action and life change is. That's where the "activeness of light" we have discussed before, *is*. That's when things start happening to a Human that lets co-creation take place. That's how a Human creates a new path—one where they are in charge of their future in a way that was not possible before. That's one of the three—intent.

The Physical

Let's talk about the physical. Some of you believe that there are many Earths with many futures and many roads. It's an esoteric thought—that there could be simultaneous realities existing together. What of it, you might ask? You are not too far off. We have told other groups like this of the potentials that line up from the "snap-shots" of energy at a specific moment in your linear time. You see, these potentials of the planet are "recorded." It has to be this way, dear ones, because *we* are in the now. Your past and your future are all here *now*. The potential of this planet, therefore, is a snap-shot of *now*, and we can tell you what your future might be, based upon your decisions *now*, and the energy that is *now*. It's recorded, and it never goes away—never goes away. That's all part of the balance. This means that there's an interdimensional place where all those potentials are stored, like many simultaneous Earths—but only the potentials of measured energy at different linear times.

The physics of Earth is astounding. Your reality is changing, and your future continues to be a blank page. Almost monthly it is revised by what you're doing here. The miracles of the physical body and the physical planet are examples of transmutation. There is no magic—it is spiritual wisdom and regular physics that make these things happen. You continue to draw on the Cosmic Lattice, and continue to create NEW energy for the planet, which changes your future potentials.

The last time my partner [Lee] was here [Coal Creek, Colorado] he stood in front of you with an affliction he did not want to share. He had facilitation help by the ones he was led to, and it was an affliction that was physical and real. It was on its way to something bigger. He knew it, and he asked to have it removed, and he gave intent to have it removed. Even as he started the lessons the first time he was here, it was still with him. By the time he had finished the evening, the body had balanced itself. All semblances of that condition were gone, and he rejoiced in the fact that the consciousness of his intent had changed the physics in his body.

Let me tell you what happened. For in that tiny miracle where something real and painful seemed to have vanished, there was an alchemy, a transmutation, and the energy required for it was great. That energy transmuted from one kind of thing to another. His process healed himself and created a *new* spiritual energy at the same time that is stored by the guides. Part of the energy alchemy is still carried with him. The other part is stored in the earth, and I do not expect you to understand that at this time.

There was a potential that was generated in the *now* regarding what "could have been," and he carries that still. Part of his duality is his fear that it will return. So when he faces off with you and tells you of these things, know that he has experienced it himself. Now he realized that he experienced it in order for him to have the wisdom to impart the feelings of it to you. Much of what we give him is exactly for this purpose, for he had given permission for such a thing.

Oh, but there's more. A few weeks ago [February 98] your best scientists gave you information based upon their best computers that you would be hit by an asteroid not too many years hence.

Don't you find it odd that the same scientists with the same computers two days later came back and said "never mind, we made a mistake somehow, and it's not going to happen at all"? Dear ones, did you ever consider that in two days, perhaps you (the planet) had moved on to another "track" of potential? The energy potential of Earth that was there five weeks ago now lives in some dark place called "The Future That Used to Be." To some, this may sound like fantasy. To the wise, it is so.

The math spoke for itself. Orbital mechanics are absolute, and yet, through some mystery, only a few days later, the numbers were done again and the answer had changed [according to scientists, they were not done correctly in the first place, but they were released anyway]. We're here to tell you that this is an example of a miraculous transformation of energy, and it's caused by the *intent* of humanity, which we have called the critical mass. In the process of that alchemy, there was energy created that went from one place to another. It's still held in the planet, and it's still a potential, but the energy that was the by-product of the miracle is now held by the guides of every single Human who gave intent to change it—and everyone on the planet got to watch. This is not the first time you will see this kind of seeming "false alarm." *Intent* can change reality!

Emotional

Let me tell you about the third kind of alchemy—the most profound kind. You think the healing of the Human body and the balancing of the body is special? Let me tell you about Human emotion. This is the miracle of miracles, you see. This is the one that takes worry and anxiety, and through the alchemy of intent, transmutes it to peace. We have spoken about this over and over. Look at the energy it takes to create worry and anxiety—look at it. What happened to your body when you were in anxiety and worry? It changed—physiologically it changed. The cells—every single one—knew of the anxiety and the worry. You may have had weight loss, your skin may have changed—all of these things as a response to an emotion that you had. When you gave intent to vibrate at a higher level, through the knowledge and the preparation of what can be yours, you transmuted it into peace. There are some here that have done that very thing over and over—and there is so much love from Spirit sent to those who have learned how to do this!

I would like to ask you, "Do you know where the energy went?" Let me tell you this. There is just as much energy generated in a covert way creating peace for you as there was in the creation of anxiety and fear. But in the transference from the one area to the other, a new energy was created (which we call the "third" energy). It was spiritual—and the guides collected it like another color that spins into your Merkabah, for it was the color of victory. We have told you what happens when you walk through the bubbles of fear and face the tiger. Now you know what it is—the guides capture that golden ring that was generated by the victory. They put it into their vat (metaphorically). Some of you have taken sorrow and grief and transmuted it into peace as well, and those who sit in this room (and read these words) know of what I speak. They have said, "*It is miraculous that I know how I felt before, and I know how I feel now.*" The episode is still there, but the energy of the grief or fear is gone. The transmutation is complete, and the energy of the victory was passed to the guide and held for you. That's why they're here, dear ones—that's why they're here.

The Measurement

Now we're here to tell you what happens to those vats that the guides carry for you metaphorically. What happens represents the balance—the mechanics of spirituality and a bigger clue to how things work when the giant calipers of measurement metaphorically came down at the Harmonic Convergence to see how this globe was doing. Some of you will ask, "*What is it measuring? What does the phrase "the vibration of the planet" mean? What kind of measurement would that be? Is it too interdimensional for us to understand? What was being measured? Kryon, you have told us that another measurement is coming in 2012. What's going to be measured then? What is it?"*

Let me tell you what the measurement is. *It's the weight of the vats of the new energy held by the guides.* That's what's being measured. That's what we call the vibratory level of the planet, and there's a connection, dear ones, about how full those vats are, with what the dirt of the planet also has received and accepted in energy, because they're tied together. Lest you think you have nothing to do with the dirt of the planet, know that they're tied together. Therefore, the measurement is a correlation of what the guides carry and what the Earth has accepted—another difficult concept to explain.

So at the Harmonic Convergence in 1987 and then lastly at 2012, we measure what has taken place, and there's only one balanced way we can do so. In combination with the Earth, we're going to measure the Holy Spirit—the guides, and what they're carrying in those energy vats. Therefore, it is a ratio between the planet and the Humans—and the energy they have created. You wonder why we come to wash your feet with the tears of our joy? You wonder why we stand in line on the other side of the veil to greet you when my partner sits down and says, "Greetings, dear ones"? We have waited for this in love! Because, you see, we want to be here and sit at your feet. We know a great deal that is hiding from you. We know who you are and what you are doing!

With each one of you, there is a team of electrified, magnetic, polarized, beautiful cobalt-blue guides. They are smiling because they hold vats of new energy created from the alchemy of intent, every one of them. That's why we're here, washing your feet. Do you want to know where the real "sacred ground" is? It's here. That's where it is—right where you stand—right where you are reading this!

There is a spiritual house with many crates for you (The House of Gifts and Tools in the Kryon book *The Journey Home*). Some of you have sprung the lids of the crates and have taken out the gifts. Some have accepted the gift, but do not understand that you have to pry the lid off to use them! Action is required! Some of you in this room and reading these words have before you a puzzle, but you are living in trust day by day with the puzzle, and expecting the transmutation of energy by giving *intent*. We're here to tell you that you are elevated in the eyes of God for your trust. You're the ones, along with the others, we want to receive with our bowls of tears—washing your feet as if to say to you, "There's a gift here for you. Go forward and trust and understand the appropriateness of the challenge, and all will be clear in time."

Do you know what kind of energy it takes for you to trust in the unseen? To momentarily step out of your time-line and feel the *now* of spirit? It's astounding that you have gotten this far, for the hurdles of duality are great. Even now there will be those who do not understand, and who would rather be absorbed in the arms of the old energy duality rather than the new energy of the guides. This is your choice, and you are dearly loved due to the choice.

We know who you are—all of you—each of you. As my partner said earlier, Spirit does not exist in a vacuum. Each night as you go to sleep, we know your thoughts—we know of your dreams and your sorrows—and we're there. Part of the universe revolves around what happens here (Earth), and that is why this is the center of attention. That is why you see yourselves in such a monotheistic way. That is even why your scientists of old, in the very beginning, thought there was only one Earth and that all revolved around it. Well, it does!

That is the message for this time, available only because of the intent of the individuals in this room and those reading these words. This is not our favorite time as we metaphorically pick up our bowls and leave this place—seemingly to disappear through that crack that was open. But there's part of us that remains here always with you—perhaps in not such a present way—perhaps not in the way that you felt in this last brief period of time, but we're here. The energy of this channelling can only be sustained for a certain period of time. It has to do with energy balance; it has to do with my partner. It has to do with what you in this room can absorb. That's what governs the amount of time I'm here before you. And if you were ever to plot such things and know what those time parameters were, you would find that there is correlation and semblance of order with those numbers. Again, it's balance.

Perhaps you think it is trite that as we leave we say to you each one, "You are dearly loved," for you have heard it before. And even more trite, like Michael Thomas in the story you have studied this day (*The Journey Home* Kryon book), when we retreat from you, we are saying "Things are not always as they seem."

Then let trite things become profound...

And so it is.

Kryon

Kryon Book Three

Alchemy of The Human Spirit

"The Kryon channelled messages are growing to be as valuable as the Seth teachings"

■ **The Book Reader** - **San Francisco, California**

Books and tapes can be purchased in retail stores, or by phone
~ Credit cards welcome ~

1-800-352-6657

The Earth - Your Millennium Partner

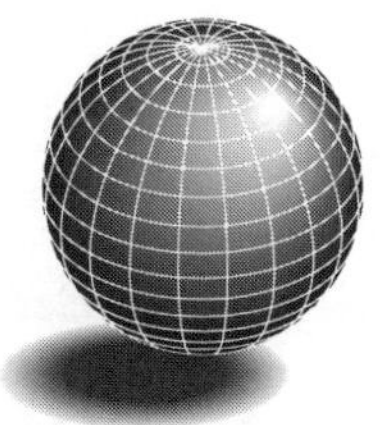

Chapter Four

Jan Tober's

Color and Sound Meditation

As presented in every Kryon seminar: Jan Tober guides us through the seven Chakra system using the enhancement of the ancient Tibetan singing bowls to help in the further decoding of our DNA and to help in the remembrance of the ageless God/Goddess and Golden Angel that we are.

On compact disc, avaiable in English and French • $14.00

This Jan Tober CD can only be purchased by phone
~ Credit cards welcome ~

1-800-352-6657

"The Earth and You"

**Channelled in
Sunnyvale, CA**

The Kryon Writings, Inc.

PMB 422
1155 Camino Del Mar
Del Mar, California 92014
[www.kryonqtly.com]

"The Earth and You"
Live Channelling
Sunnyvale, CA

This live channelling has been edited with additional words and thoughts to allow clarification and better understanding of the written word.

Greetings, dear ones, I am Kryon of magnetic service! Let it be known at this moment, dear ones, that this crack in the veil has been created by you and your intent in this place, and by those reading these words. There will be love flowing through the crack into this room, and more than that, there will be loving entities presented here to fill this room with an awesome power. Now humanity shakes hands with the other side of the veil, and that's what this is about. It is good to see you again, is it not?

The potential of the changes for the humanity in this room and those reading these words is awesome! In these next few moments, let the bridge be formed between intent and manifestation—between the intent to clear the karmic attributes that used to be yours, into the reality of the new incarnation that you have also planned for. Let the bridge be formed that will allow such a miracle, and let it be formed with the power that is in you and us together—which is the way of the New Age.

The entourage of Kryon comes with an emotion at this time, and it is the feeling of remembrance of *family*. We told you that we would explain this relationship between you and us, and simply put, the family reunites. You know me, and I know you. I know what your name is—and it's not the name you think. We, on the other side of this crack, are very, very familiar with what you've been through, and with where you are now in your growth.

As these moments continue, understand that this is precious time. This is the time when we've asked to wash your feet. At every Kryon channelling and every time that we've come to visit, with permission from the Humans in this room, we speak about the preciousness of the time where we can actually wash the feet of the humanity doing the work!

And so it is again that you get to experience the relationship that we have, you and I. And here it is again. It's *family*—and it's honor—and it's respect for those in this room and those reading this, who will take the time to sit and know more about themselves.

Let me tell you more about yourself.

Your duality tells you that there is a grandness of God, and also a smallness of Human Beings. It has you always looking upwards for Spirit. You think that you have made plans this day to come and sit in these chairs or read this? You think you have waited for this presentation, or for this energy to flood into this room? We can address you by name! We can invite the bridge to be complete. It is Kryon and the entourage that has known of your arrival at this state for some time. For the potential of you being here in these chairs or reading these words has been known for a very long time. Indeed, it is confusing to some of you here, to understand how we even know of those in your future who will read this—and we have been waiting for them as well. All is in the *now*, and what is your future today hearing this, is the present for those reading.

We've given you data in the past and information about how to co-create your reality. We've told you in the past how you can heal your bodies, no matter what condition you have. We have told you that your present state is not final. We are aware of the problems in this group, and of those reading this. Before this time is over this day, we wish to remind you that there is **no problem here that does not have a matching solution** by your design. In the balance of the divine, the Human forgets that in the planning stages not only were the problems and the challenges created for lessons, but the solutions as well. That is the divine balance for you to remember.

There is much to present, dear ones, about how you can affect your lives. This information is going to be new. We have selected this place at this time to allow for this information [San Francisco area]. Metaphorically, we're going to put a package on your lap right now. Even before the teaching message begins, this unopened package is one you will later be allowed to glimpse into when it's opened. It's not for you to keep—it's a vision—one that will disappear from your lap at the end of this energy—but a vision you collectively can manifest, if you wish.

The information that is going to be presented this day is intuitive. It's about humanity and the dirt of the earth. For some of you, this will be a reminder; for others it will be a revelation—and for all of you it will be information that is empowering. Never before in the history of humanity has this partnership with the planet been so real and so close! Is it any wonder that we love you so?

The Oneness of All Things

All things on this planet are made from the same elements that are common to the planet. Yet Human beings who walk here tend to feel that they are indeed apart from the dirt of the earth. They walk upon it—they see its grandeur, and wonder at its beauty. They also fear its power, but they feel that they are beings who are completely apart and separate from it.

We wish to remind you of something very special. The elements that are contained in your body also represent the elements that are contained on the planet. Like a closed environmental system, all that is here belongs to the earth—and especially the Human body. All of the things that went into the growth of the Human from that you call Mother was collected from the earth, ingested, and it allowed the mother to grow along with the child—and here you are! It is the dirt of the earth, therefore, that grew the nourishment that fed the mother and allowed you to exist.

As you know the cycle of life, you also know what happens at the end: The Human returns to the basic elements, does it not? The cycle is indeed complete. Still, Humans feel that they are apart. The item that tells them they are apart, intuitively, is what we wish to speak about. But before we do that, we wish to enhance the reminder that you are part of the elements of the actual planet.

We have spoken of the "consciousness of Gaia." So it is that we have spoken of the fact that humanity and the planet are seen as one unit. You cannot separate them—ever. That is the balance of it, and it will always remain in that fashion. Remember your history? The indigenous peoples of your land recognized the connection. They did more than recognize the connection, they enhanced it—through celebration, through honor, and through ceremony. Let this be a time for you to hear once more that ceremony is appropriate to again ground, link, and anchor you to dirt of this planet! It will only enhance what is to follow in your future—and what is to follow can be grand indeed. It has to do with that package on your lap that we will show you in a few moments.

The indigenous peoples, even of this very area and on this land, understood the need for celebration of the elements. If you will look upon their history, you will find the ceremony regarding the various elements of the earth. They applied those elements in their ceremony in a way that acknowledged the fact that Spirit was part of the ground! They acknowledged that they, as Humans, were also of the granite, even of the trees and other life. If you look further upon what they did, you'll see an amazing thing: Somehow, at some level, these indigenous people also recognized magnetics! Did you know that? For they honored the four directions of the compass—they drew lines on the rocks of the mountains where the ley lines were for the magnetic grid systems. Yes, they did! It's still there for you to see. For they had intuitive knowledge and followed it—on how the Earth was related to the Humans who walked upon it.

Finally, they honored the life that also was their sustenance. They saw the cycle that permitted the buffalo to be consumed for their own benefit and that of their kind, as well as the horse to carry their burden. They honored them in their ceremonies and in their drawings, and they considered them all a part of life along with the dirt of the earth. We remind you of this because part of your discovery and your enlightenment is a return to these basics—a return to the knowledge that the consciousness of the planet belongs to you, and that is the next subject.

The Human Consciousness of the Planet

If it has not been broached before, we wish to tell you now that there is something you should know about the consciousness of the planet. The separation that you feel between Human and planet is false. The planet is a system—a balance—and it works in a framework that supports humanity. It was created for you, and it waited for you to arrive so that you could help steer it into the new era. We're here to tell you that the mind of Gaia is also part of the consciousness of humanity.

We told you before what happens to spiritual energy that is transmuted with intent. It goes into the ground! [Chapter Three, "Guides and Angels] We have told you that it is shared with the earth and is part of the balanced spiritual system. We told you that much of the advancement in the cyclical weather patterns of what you are seeing now is the result of your intent. Ask your meteorologists and your scientists if there has ever been anything in the history of the strata that they study in geology that would explain what is taking place now. This cycle is not recognizable from past history because you have changed history! It is new. But you might say, "*Well, Kryon, something doesn't make sense here. The earth has been here a long time before Humans ever were. We seem to be like an afterthought.*" Let me explain some things:

There is an automatic self-balance that takes place on this planet that keeps it moving forward—that nourishes it. This is the balance in nature that you have been aware of only recently, and that you are trying to correct in many instances. You are beginning to recognize this balance as sacred and precious—and you are right. There are those who would question this "mind of the planet" scenario and ask, "*What about all those eons of time before Humans? Where was its 'mind' then?*" We'll tell you. This is the sacredness of it, so listen carefully. Like the meal for a Human that would take days and days of careful preparation—only to be consumed in only 15 minutes, the earth has been carefully prepared for you—very carefully. The balance has been created in a specific and unique way so that you would be safe and protected—so that you could live your lives with a peaceful, balanced atmosphere—so that you could live without turmoil on a planet made just for you.

When it was perfect and it was right—when the seed biology was given to you—you arrived on schedule—and we have discussed this before. So as you now take your power, which is the next step in the overall plan of you and Gaia, we wish to explain the miracle of this combination that most of you still deny. Some of these things are going to sound mysterious—in fact, strange and unbelievable. But there will come a time, dear ones, when science will provide answers that you first heard here from this chair, this day, about how you relate to the planet.

The automatic balancing system of the planet is very metaphoric to what happens in your body. There are systems in your body that seem to function without your thought. You have no consciousness control, you may say, over digestion, breathing, heart-beat, circulation, or the natural rejuvenation process of new cell division that is ongoing. Yet, there is a conscious mind at the top of it (your brain), and that particular conscious mind has been revealed to you through the yogis and the shamans for its ability to change everything that I've just said seems to happen automatically.

Therefore, it's with practice, experience, and the knowledge and revelation of the hidden power you have that allows for the control over these systems within your body, which you thought were automatic. So there is a centralization, is there not, of a consciousness that can affect these things for your benefit? You have seen it before. It is the reason, when you are peaceful in your heart, that it does not beat as fast. It is the reason, when you are angry and anxious and fearful, that your heart beats faster. This seemingly automatic organ responds to the consciousness of the central system. There is not that much difference between the collective consciousness of the Humans on the planet and the very dirt of the earth. We are going to give you some examples.

Here is information to disable a common fear. This information may give you a different perspective on what Humans perhaps fear most. Humans fear what they *cannot control*, and they instinctively fear death. Many times they link the two. Oh, there are those in this room and reading this who say, "*I do not fear dying. I am ready; I do not fear death.*" In all love, dear ones, we're going to tell you something: Your duality provides and dishes out great fear even when the spiritual part denies it! When you are at the death place of transition, you will know what I mean, for it is always there. That is one of the reasons we love you so, because this fear is designed by you to be exactly what it is—frightening and unknown—designed in this way so you do not stroll into the transition lightly. It is designed so that you will remain here!

Being terminated in an uncontrolled fashion by nature is perhaps one of the greatest fears of Humans. They see the earth as something unpredictable. Many Humans say, "*The power of nature is this, and it is that.*" They see this "nature" as apart from them, and sometimes very frightening. They never realize what the system really is or what it is attempting to create. On two fronts, we would like to explain your participation in the planet.

The Partnership—Physical

The first one is physical. The atmospheric system that you call weather is probably one of the most common things that you see every day. It's powerful and seemingly unpredictable, you might say. We're here to tell you that you have some control over this, dear ones! There are those of you who ask, "*Kryon, are you telling me that we can control the weather?*" No. Here's what I'm telling you: You can control the energy around *you*, and the weather will *respond* to it. That's what I'm telling you.

You do not directly and willingly control your heart-beat. The masters have shown you, however, that if your consciousness is altered, the heart will respond. It is the same with the physics of the planet, for the Earth recognizes the *intent* energy of the Human Being! It has to. It was created for you!

Here is another analogy: Let's say you are swimming in the ocean among giant waves and you are afraid. Suddenly you realize that by thought alone you might raise a platform of rock high enough so that you could be free from the threat of the elements. There you would stand with the waves crashing around you. Let me ask you this: Did you control the waves? No. They're still there. What have you done? You have only changed their effect on *you*. This is what we're talking about, and it's this consciousness principle that you have not been totally aware of.

We're going to give you an example. We're going to tell you how it's done in your own practical life. What we're telling you, dear ones, is that you can affect the energy around you, which will affect what the weather does around you. And when we say *you*, we mean the *collective you* (Humans together in collective thought). We are speaking of what a group of lightworkers and individuals can do to change an area of the planet where the weather is severe!

By way of your strong partnership with Gaia, you can create situations where weather will seem to "go around" where you are—like the rock in the waves. Responding to the energy that is created in a vortex of co-creation—of sacredness—the weather balance will remain, but it will go around those areas of consciousness that are created by the group. You see, Gaia knows who you are (I told you that this might seem unbelievable)! There are those among you, however, who have experienced this very thing.

The consciousness of the planet—much like the consciousness over your lives—is such that you can change certain attributes, but the system remains in place. You can heal and clear the energy of certain areas that need it—but the system remains in place. Therefore, there are certain places that will be healed and certain places that will not be affected, because of what you do in your lives both individually and collectively.

Let us talk about something germane to the area—the way the earth moves here [San Francisco area]. Ah, dear ones, you live in a place that shakes and you know it—and so does my partner [speaking of Lee, who lives in Southern California]. Let me tell you something: Some of you are drawn into areas that seem dangerous. There, you live out your lives. Some of you will be wondering why it is that you've been drawn to an area with a dangerous attribute. So it is that some of the metaphysical teachers and enlightened workers have been drawn to areas all up and down this coast that moves and shakes. There are faults in the ground that are poised to move, and are known to be actually moving in this area. They are part of the geology of the planet and the automatic balance that has always been here for you to see. Yet, here you are living! I'm going to tell you why; then you're going to understand what is taking place, and understand your place in it all. Then you're also going to understand the power generated by the consciousness of groups of lightworkers who know how to give *intent*.

You might feel that you are here in this place by accident, and that someday you will be able to escape the anxiety of the unknown ground movement. Did you ever think perhaps it's the opposite—that your presence here is what we call "the work"? There are lightworkers who have been moved through synchronicity and through love to sit right in these shaking spots! Here's what's going on, dear ones: When we talk about the physical Earth—when we talk about the thing that is feared more than anything else by Humans (that of being crushed by a boulder or a rock in the middle of the night, or to have the Earth shake in such a way that the family is threatened—or to have volcanic explosions in the mountains), I'm here to give you a revelation about it. And here it is: Just a room-full of people vibrating at a high level, which you call the ascension status, having given intent, can change what happens in your area. It can change something profound with potential into something small, just by the intent of the consciousness—because Gaia will respond. Gaia will respond! Gaia is part of you—like the heartbeat is part of you.

Here's how it works. There has to be what we call the "frontliners," and then there has to be a support group behind them. It doesn't matter if we are talking about weather, or if we're talking about a shaking Earth, or about a volcano, or impending floods. Let me tell you how it works: It's being done all the time! The frontliners are the lightworkers who have chosen to be at the point where it actually happens. These are the lightworkers who say "*I **own** my spirituality, and I **know** my piece of divinity, and therefore I know where I belong, so I'm going to **anchor** my area with my energy. I'm going to stay there and live there and call it my home. I'm going to send a shaft of light into the center of the earth to balance the planet. And I and other lightworkers, and frontliners are going to do the same.*" These are the "frontliners," the ones who are called to the areas to live right at the focus of where the changes are predicted—knowing full well that their consciousness is an anchor, but that they have support as well.

Let me tell you about that anchor: It has a chain. And that chain, figuratively, is connected to the thousands of lightworkers who are going to give this anchor power by giving it the energy of *intent*. Some of you have been doing this, and I'm telling you it works! It works! Can you change the weather? Oh, yes. In the area that is anchored—in the area that is being considered and being meditated upon—the weather will simply change there. See, Gaia responds to the energy of the Human and the Human group.

Have you ever heard my partner say that "consciousness changes physics"? It does. Consciousness changes matter—consciousness will change the planetary function and balance, and *you* are in charge. The planet was made for you! Doesn't it make sense that you would be able to do these things?

So it is that we have the frontliners and the support group. There are those who would ask, "*Kryon, can't we do the anchoring without a Human living there?*" The answer is no. It's *your* personal energy that makes it happen. You will know if you are called to be an anchor, but many are not. The mechanics of it, dear ones, are this: There *must* be *intent* of the frontline Human in the actual area for the chains to exist that attach to the support group. Let those chains then go outward to tens of thousands of you who can change the planet, for it's needed in the areas that we are speaking of in this environment [the West Coast of the United States].

The Partnership—Spiritual

Let us tell you the second phase of this, and it only makes sense that we would now reveal something else to you: The planet has a spiritual aspect. This cannot surprise you, for you must know by now that Earth responds to Human consciousness, and it always did. Here's what it responds to: It responds to being *loved*! And your indigenous people knew that.

How many of you can explain those who seem to be able to grow anything? They are in touch at a heart level, and the life in the dirt responds to them. They know they are connected to Gaia. You see, Gaia responds to *love*. It should not shock and surprise you that Gaia also responds to Human war, Human death, famine, injustice, and to the consciousness of fear and terror. It reacts to all things that change Human energy. While affecting Humanity, these high-energy events change the energy of the dirt as well! That's what Gaia responds to—*you*.

So what has this spiritual aspect of the planet got to do with anything, you might ask? What can you do with it? We're going to give you some examples of what you can change, and we're going to challenge you. We said that the earth responds to war, and the areas where war has occurred. There's more than that. As the consciousness of humanity responds spiritually to events and potentials that develop, you can change that potential with your spiritual consensus. Now, there are methods where you can clear the actual land of past energy, and we're going to tell you how that can happen—but beyond that, let me speak about the clearing of potential. This is an interdimensional concept and has to do with being in the *now*.

Any Human giving energy of thought and prayer toward this goal can join spiritually with the anchors in the area (even though they might not have understood the mechanics of it). Many times Humans seem to believe that their governments are in control of everything, and they are simply to sit back and hope things work out. They also believe their economies and quality of life are ruled by outside forces that are beyond their control. "*What can they do?*" they ask. I'm telling you that the consciousness of the group with intent can change all of that—all of that! There is nothing that you cannot accomplish—and if you noticed, some of your latest victories were done with world opinion, and not by the process of one government! World opinion is another term for collective Human intent.

Think of your past history. Compare it to the 1950s and '60s. What is missing? Through nothing more than intent, an entire group of Humans brought down an entire political structure that was extremely powerful. No government did it. You did it. No organized government has a chance to survive in the new energy without the participation and consent of its people. You are seeing that exact attribute right now as the former heads of old-energy governments are unseated by the people themselves. Watch, as this fact is repeated over and over through the years. The difference will be that unseated governments will now tend to have peace rather than simply foster another unstable leadership.

Let us talk about the potential of unrest that exists on your planet now. Let me give you information on where the spiritual focus can be for the greatest Earth help. Lightworkers, are you listening? Now that you know how to do it, do you really want to make a change in this planet? I'll tell you where to focus the love: Focus it at the heart, and that metaphoric heart at this moment (and for the next few years), is in that country that is small—far from here—and it is Israel. It's time to anchor the lightworkers there, and send out the chains. It's time for that conflict and spiritual puzzle to be solved. Doesn't it strike you odd that the largest potential for conflict on the Earth right now is about spirituality and ancient tribal claims? It is as we told you it would be when we spoke at your United Nations in 1995 [transcription published in Kryon Book Six, and on (www.kryon.com)].

Do you want to know the real potential for tension? It exists more than ever between religious beliefs on the planet. That's where it exists. Far beyond tribes, isn't it ironic that the tensions would be greatest between those who disagree about God? There's so much love from Spirit to *you*! There is so much uniformity in what you collectively believe—and there's so much universal truth! It's time to create understanding and realize these things! That is indeed the top meditation, is it not? For tolerance and peace?

Look at what you have done recently in this area. Here is still another example to look at regarding the power of Humans to create solutions in this new energy. In another place on this planet, there has been war and death for decades in a small country, and it has been about religious beliefs and tribal rights. The country is what you call Ireland. Right now there is an attempt like no other to finally solve the conflict, because of the consensus of Human beings on the planet, and in those areas that are saying, "*We're tired of the fighting. Let's make it work. Let's finally have peace here.*" What can *you* do to help them? Link to the "heart" of their intent! Be a piece of the whole that is giving energy for peace in that area! Own your power to do this.

There are lightworkers who are anchoring that land, sending out their chains to you—hooked to you, the support group. Listen to the ones who are on the front line—who know what they're doing. The test of the spirituality is there, for they *own* the fact that they are a piece of divinity anchored into the land, and that all will be well. That's the power you all have! Blessed indeed are those who have created this great possibility! Then realize that there will be no other time greater than this for potential strife, for the old and new energy are clashing like never before. The old energy will not go away easily. Your light will make the difference.

Clearing of the Old Lands

Let me tell you how land is cleared. First, there are the frontliners, and then there is the support group (surprised?). The land can be cleared, dear ones, by the *family* [speaking of lightworkers]. There is a certain portion of them who have to be *from* the land. This actually means that their origin (birth) is of the land they are on. You, as lightworkers in this area (USA) may send over your energy to support them and clear especially dark and soiled areas—filled with war and anxiety of the ages. You are, therefore, the support group for the ones from the dirt of the land, with the elements in their body that came from the soil. They are the ones who must start it and become the anchors.

We have waited until this time to tell my partner and his partner to be in these areas (Lee and Jan). They need to experience the energy personally for this information to be given to those frontliners. So, it is no error that finds certain people in certain places with certain enlightenment—to put down their shaft of light and say, "*This area is going to be cleared.*" Dear ones, this clearing is not difficult. Just as you clear a room of energy, simply and quickly, through the sage, indeed the land can be cleared as well. That is the task, is it not? Every square foot of the earth cleared. It is under way right now.

Coordinate with the frontliners of the areas, and specify times to meditate and send energy with identical *intent*. Visualize and "see" the land cleaned of the energy of war and strife. Visually pour love upon the dirt as the spiritual soap that Gaia needs to "breathe." It won't take long for the land to react to this grand outpouring of your effort. Don't be surprised if you feel the land loving you back!

The Grand Potential

Let me tell you about a potential that exists right now. Let's talk about the metaphoric packages on your lap. [Remember, they were given earlier in the message.] There's a visualization on your lap—one that you cannot keep on your lap—one that you may say is fleeting—a visualization of a potential of this planet. We will now open the package you received earlier. We have never presented this visualization to any group until now.

The opening of the package reveals a globe in front of you. It's small. As though you are looking down from space, you see this brilliant, glowing, beautiful jewel called planet Earth. It is the future Earth. You can't touch it. You can't go there. It floats before you as the potential of the *graduate* Earth, and it exists in the *now*. It's slowly manifesting in your time frame—slowly transmuting a potential into reality, and that is why we can show you the visualization.

We wish you to *feel* the energy around this, this visualization that's on your lap. You, from a place in space, from the entity that you are, looks down upon this graduate Earth. And this visualization can actually take place in not too many years. It is an Earth that is free of violence. It is an Earth that is balanced between Gaia and humanity. It is an Earth that understands that humanity is necessary to cooperate and trade with one another. It's a graduate Earth that is preparing a universal energy—an energy that says, "We are ready to meet the others"—an energy that says, "We are ready to have the time shift occur." It is an Earth that has the land cleared by the lightworkers. It is a planet where the Humans finally understood their place and their effect on the dirt. It is an Earth where the Humans have found peace.

How does it feel to know that this is a real possibility—as real as any other vision has ever been—and we're not going to take it away? No. We are going to ask that *you* take this vision with you. See? Remove it from your lap and place it in your *heart*! Believe it's possible! You're going to have to, you know. It's the only way to manifest it. You've got to *own* it. Feel the self-worth inside you. We've called that graduate Earth you are looking at, something that you've heard before—and there are those in this room and reading this who understand spiritual history, and who will know what the name means, for it is called the "New Jerusalem."

You changed your future in these past few months, did you know that? Through the love that you have for Humanity, and the understanding regarding the enlightenment and the power that you have at this time, many of you are beginning to understand what you are doing here. It's the balance of the physical and the spiritual and the knowledge of how to make it work that's going to make this visualization manifest into reality. And in the process, dear ones, don't be surprised if you feel connected to the planet in a new way. And in the process, don't be surprised if you find yourself with new passions, new eating patterns, and new sleeping patterns. There are those in this room and reading this who find themselves looking at a new situation in their lives that is so different from the way it was a few years ago! That's the *new* you, with *intent* to move forward with wisdom and understanding of the overview of your part on Earth. It's a rejuvenated spirit that you feel!

That's what happens when a Human Being stands before God and says, "*I recognize you now! You are my best friend. I know where Home is. I know where I AM. And the two concepts, that of God and Human, are melding together.*" And so that graduate Earth becomes the new home, and that's what this is all about.

We leave this place, dear ones, and we wish you to know and understand that a piece of home came to visit you today. Keep your visualization of the graduate Earth in your heart and mind. It has never been given in a meeting before like this—never. This is a visualization that is brand new, created within the last two years. Do not be depressed or alarmed over some of the things that will have to transpire before the clearing is done. Old energy transmutes to new with upheaval, then the healing comes. Do not be depressed over predictions of doom from the soothsayers. Not everything is as it seems.

Hold your light up high—and remember this time, when we came here for a brief moment in your life to reunite this side of the family with your side. Feel the love we have for you, because of what you are doing for all of us.

And so it is.

Kryon

"The crystalline grid structure of this planet is one you'll never see, any more than you will see the crystalline sheath around your DNA. It is interdimensional. It postures the planet's potential, and it also "talks" to the magnetic grid system. [It] contains the memory and potential of the planet! It contains the partnership remembrance of the fact that this [now] is the end of the test. As the planet shifts and moves, there is still an attribute of it that wants to push and pull the planet backwards and forwards—especially beginning this year [1999]. You are now feeling much of the tugging—the yin and the yang of these last throes of struggle."

Kryon

"The Crystalline Grid and Shadow Termination"

Channelled in St. Louis, MO

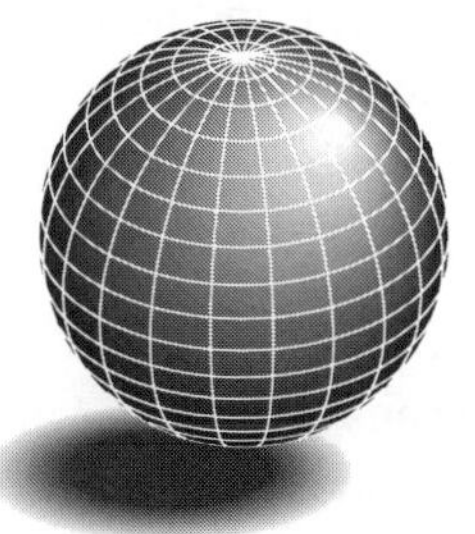

The Kryon Writings, Inc.

PMB 422
1155 Camino Del Mar
Del Mar, California 92014
[www.kryonqtly.com]

"The Crystalline Grid and Shadow Termination"
Live Channelling
St. Louis, MO

This live channelling has been edited with additional words and thoughts to allow clarification and better understanding of the written word.

Greetings, Dear Ones, I am Kryon of Magnetic Service. There is "family" pouring into this place, and this family is far larger than the number of those who are here—two, three, maybe even four of us for every one of you. We've been waiting around for the ones who we love, who we recognize and cherish. You'll feel us walk the aisles behind you, and you'll feel some of us eventually kneel—to wash your feet. Others may hug you. By appointment it is that you sit there, and we continue to inform you that we know individually of your lives. We know what it was that brought you here, and we know of the synchronicity involved. We speak to those who have just found out of this meeting days before this, yet find yourselves here. We speak to those who only weeks ago were drawn to the family's message, which now has been transcribed for over ten years. Indeed, timing is the key to your lives.

The "family" has expected you, you know. This is the way of it, and the way it has always been. It has only been in the last year or so where the energy allows such intimate contact between us—where you can feel the family as you do now. We tell you that this place had "appointment" written all over it. The chairs where you sit and the places where you reside here on the floor—even where you are reading this now—we knew of your coming. We know your spiritual name, and it's not necessarily the one you think it might be. Why should we know so much about you? It's because each and every one of you is family! You are never alone. You have an entourage with you who knows who you are—one who loves you wherever you go. Some of you have walked a very, very difficult path these last years. We're going to talk about that, dear ones. Some of you are walking a difficult path now, and all you do is seemingly wring your hands and say, "*Why me? Why now? This hurts*." We say to you, "Don't you think we know this?"

For those of you who have come for that reason, who understand this, let the hugs begin now! Let the foot washing begin now. Let the honor of this visit permeate the chairs. Feel the bubble of love energy around you, which presses upon you in various places on your body and says, "We are real. Just like you are." It's the family, and it's all of us together. The family is responsible for creating change on this planet. Imagine that! You are actually responsible for the Earth changes that you now sit within. That's what we want to discuss. There is new information at this time—information that some of you know all about at the cellular level. Some of you have to hear it, however, to really cement it in place.

There are those who have called these messages *the Millennium Channels*, and they're right. This is the information we specifically want you to have now. This is the information that is specific to the energy that is taking place right now. We speak now to family members, each one, who are going through a shift. You're in a struggle, and the struggle is not going to get any better in these next few months or years. There is a yin and a yang, but it is in the last throes of balance. There is a reason that we are going to try to explain to you, simply, why things are coming to a head now. First, we have to give you a tiny review, information my partner [Lee] has explained before, and some of which is transcribed. Not all of this information, however, has been truly understood by the Human part of the family.

The paradigm of existence on the planet—physically, mentally, and spiritually—is literally changing under your feet. We have told you that you're changing yourselves. We have told you that Earth is changing through your enlightenment and consciousness shift. We have given you information about daily life and daily living. We have given you validations regarding these things, but still many of you don't understand truly what this is all about. What you are experiencing at this moment, dear ones, is the end of a very long test—a test that you have created yourself. Most of those around you who have prophesied have given you the "end of the world" scenario. They have called the specific dates or date ranges over and over. The indigenous have, those who live now have, remote viewers have, and they're generally in consensus. We're talking about the Earth year of 2012.

The new message that is being brought to you in these years by the family, however, is that you have changed your future—that no longer is this test going to terminate you. All along, the termination was of your own making. It is what you decided for yourselves, as an appropriate end—a way to bring you home together. Instead, now we're seeing a vibration on the Earth that releases the secrets—a vibration that you did not expect to be in, based on potentials from many years. It is a vibrational energy that gives permission to go through the end of the test and work beyond it as Humans. So from now to 2012 **will not** be the termination of the planet. Instead, it's going to be the start of a new existence. Slow as it will be over these years, you will see year by year the potential changes we speak of. It is indeed a pivotal time for you. These shifting times take you into a difficult period (starting in 1999 through 2012). To the end of this year and slightly beyond, you are going to be dealing with a struggle between old and new energy, and we're not telling you anything that many of you don't already know or feel.

Textbooks of the Past

Perhaps you did not understand how profound you have changed things. Let me give you an example. Look in your spiritual textbooks—the ancient ones that describe the workings of spirituality. Go to the ones that were written as little as 50 years ago—the ones that helped set up the very nation that you sit in—the ones that had been called the "secrets of metaphysics." This book described the actual workings of the way things are—the spiritual workings of the way spiritual matters came to be. Some of the principles are revered, and some of them are looked upon as being absolutely the way it is.

Now, let me tell you what to do with that. Let me tell you what to do with what is in those books. Put them away, because they are no longer accurate!

"But Kryon, these messages describe the ways things work! They describe the structure of the universe. They describe Human Beings. They have layer upon layer of descriptions of entities and intelligences within our spiritual history. They tell us the way things work around us. Now you say, 'put them away'? Don't these messages apply any longer?"

Let me give you an example of what me mean, and we're going to do our best to fit the explanation into an analogy for you on this continent. We will speak of America for the first time. We've never talked about America before, or any other political system. This is because it is yours as Humans to create and run, and is only a temporary system to help facilitate your test on Earth. But my partner, Lee, can sit in this culture and speak about the system you have because it uses his knowledge, and a wisdom that takes place between his Higher Self and me. That's what you hear, by the way. The energy that is put forward is not my partner leaving his body so I can pop it. It's a precious meld—a partnership—it's also what *you* can do anytime you want. We'd like to talk about America. It suits the explanation example.

Those who founded this country and wrote your Constitution were great in completing their Earth mission. It's a country about choice, and it mirror-images the planet of free choice. It was also set up in sacredness, and was created with the honor of God in mind. If you will go to some of those historical places and read the words of these great men (and women, since gender is only relative to one lifetime) who put together this country, you will find the word *God* many times. I challenge you to read the words again, because they were channelled! Did you know that? That's why they've lasted as long as they have. The principles of free choice and honor for the individual family member are sacred ideas and exist within the mantle (the spiritual wisdom) of the Human Being. They are enlightened concepts.

The lineage of your young system is indeed great, and here is why we want to talk about this: Because you have set up a system that, with flexibility, has worked for hundreds of years. It is a system of checks and balances, and you have textbooks about the way the system works. You have a way, literally, of giving back to the system through what you call your taxes. You have a way of electing officials by choice. You have a group of men and women who are elected by choice, who sit in certain places and make decisions for you. There are many books that have been written for these hundreds of years about the way things work in your government, and also the sacred beginning books—the rules that you have called your "American Constitution."

Let us pretend for a moment. Let me take you 50 "pretend-years" out into the pretend future. Here is what you see in this fantasy: In 50 years, America is still here, and it is still cherished by those who are its citizens. It runs well. Let us say that there is still a great love of country. Ah, but look around. Things have changed in this pretend future. Let us say that the consciousness of the Humans in America, through the process of altering your Constitution, through the laws of the land, have put its citizens in a whole different paradigm of living. Let us say, for instance, that you no longer have national elections—or that there are far fewer elected officials. Let us say that, instead, there has been the development of technology and energies that would allow a polling of all Americans at once—perhaps even daily! Let us say that the old laborious process of law and policy making, or for elections to higher positions of government, is now instant! The consciousness of the citizens has shifted greatly, and they are very attuned to the country's changing needs. Let's say that happens.

Let us say in this pretend future that there has been tremendous reformation of even the way Americans give back their earnings to run the government. Let us pretend for a moment that it's efficient! [pause for laughter] Let us pretend for a moment that it bears no resemblance whatsoever to what you have today, because you have raised your consciousness. Let us say that this is what America looks like in 50 or more years. Is it the same America? Yes, indeed! The great country remains—the one of free choice—the one founded by channelled works—the one that works and is flexible in its process and its rules. It's a streamlined America, one that has changed itself through the process of its own core setup, and has given itself permission to evolve.

Now let's go get the American government textbook—perhaps the one that described in 1963 how it worked. What are you going to do with that? In 50 years, it is antiquated! The principles are the same, but the rules are different. The consciousness is different. The old book isn't valid anymore. What you do with it is put it away. Was it great? Absolutely. Did it describe the way things worked? Absolutely. Was it honored and revered for its sacredness? Absolutely, yet it is no longer valid since you have moved from the old ways.

Now this was an analogy. It's an example of what you are going through right now at a spiritual level. We are telling you this, dear ones: Not only have you changed the future of your Earth, you have changed the way it works currently as well. The placeholders left at the 12:12 gate. Individuals are planning, using their own power now. There's less organization needed, and less compartmentalization. You carry instruction sets of your divinity, each and every one of you, like a book that you carry inside that my partner has told you about. You are polled individually, instantly—daily! You continue to give permission for change. There is no central control of the family on Earth. Think about that! "*Who is in charge?*" you might ask. You are! Collectively. This is about family, and it's about time.

Therefore, so many of those "sacred metaphysical" books that you have clung to and you wonder about are now obsolete. You might look at them and ask, "*What about such and such? These were anointed—these were channelled.*" We're saying that what you are looking at is an old energy, and your energy now is new. That is how you have affected the very fabric of core spirituality on this planet! Things are not the way they used to be, and are changing day by day. Did you read about the lineage of spiritual government? Put it away. It's *you* now. Did you read about how things used to work? Put it away now. It's time to write the *new* textbook—the one that reflects what *is* happening, not what happened before.

Here is something very few of you will understand. What if you lived in a magical world—one with a time frame that didn't move in a linear fashion at all? What if you didn't date anything? What if contracts were always measured by the intend of the present? Strange, you say? Unworkable, you say? It's going to be more and more like that on Earth. What if, as you changed the way you think, your history books updated themselves with a different history? This example is the epitome of how things work in the "now."

Shadow Termination

We're going to tell you about something that many of you are experiencing. We've just gone through a review, and we have a name for something that is taking place on this planet. We have always told you of the potentials that used to be. Some of your greatest prophets have told you of an endtimes scenario that is filled with doom and gloom. We have just finished telling you, however, that you have a spiritual paradigm for the way things work that you can put on the shelf because it's outdated. The potential future has not only changed, but it remains unwritten, and this has all happened within the lifetime of most of you.

Now we're going to tell you something else, a fact that many of you have already suspected and are feeling. It is called "shadow termination." I'd like to speak about Human Beings—about the

DNA. We're going to get specific again because we want you to understand all about this "shadow termination" that is taking place. Dear ones, you can't take eons and eons of potential and change it at the last minute without feeling it. You cannot take a generation of Human Beings, billions of them, place them on the Earth, give them a cellular contract that says "Termination Termination Termination," without them feeling something at the appointed date! Even those in the "ascension" ranks feel something when the time comes when things were "supposed" to happen.

By your own wisdom, you have changed yourselves, and many of you have actually ascended past those potentials that would have removed you (by your own choice). But remember, we told you that entire humanity knows at the cellular level that the "end "is here. What do you think that fact will do to Humans? Do you see any profound alignment of the old against the new? Yes. It's called "Shadow Termination." At many, many, levels Earth resounds—those around you resound—*you* resound with what "could" have happened. Let me tell you about this.

Dear ones, there will come a day when the Human genome has been completely and totally mapped. When that day comes, science will revel in it, for they will be able to help *all of you* with what is being discovered. There will be the elimination of many diseases. There will be the examination of the genes, and many revelations to help extend your life—to keep you here longer. And this one event (the mapping of the genome) that will take place in the next few years, will compare to many of the great events of the past. It will be hailed as one of the greatest milestones regarding the control over Human health. This is all appropriate, and although not exactly a spiritual event, it is indeed one that is in the scheme of the new energy. Yet when it's completely done and the map is in front them, scientists will say that even within the billions of parts that make up this marvelous chemistry, there is still something missing. They will have exposed all the instruction sets for life. They will know how specific genealogy works. They will be shown the potentials from inheritance, from a chemical standpoint and a biological standpoint, but there's still something missing.

They will not have uncovered the "memory core," the item we spoke about four months ago. What you call the DNA, which we call the system of 12 strands, has a "sheath" that is **crystalline**. Although somewhat metaphoric (since the full explanation is a combination of science and Spirit), there are parts of this metaphor that are physically accurate as we describe this to you in a simple way.

This is the memory that "talks" to the instructions sets, and it talks to them about predispositions, contracts, and karmic overlays. It talks to them about how they were *designed* to work, and it talks to them about the divinity that they contain. It also tells the instruction sets how to work—and scientists won't find it. It's a core memory, and it is literally at the center of the spiritual information transferred to your cells about what you came to Earth for.

Do you know what's in that memory core? We have told you many times that you can never separate the physical from the spiritual. Your scientists have wanted to do that since the beginning. They actually pride themselves on the empiricism of their scientific method, and that it is completely separate from anything spiritual. The joke is that at the heart of all physics and biology is the spiritual plan of matter and life. It hides within the atomic structure, and also within the biology of each Human. There is something about it, however, that you should know. It is absolutely saturated with potential for termination!

I speak to Lemurians here, and I speak to those who resound to Earth, and the energy of potentials. Many of you don't spend much time "home," you know. All of you have been here many times, even the youngest in the room. Built into each of your cellular structures is a residue of termination. You may say, "*Well, Kryon, I gave intent to move past that, and now I'm in the light.*

Literally, I am different than before. Just like you said, I changed my future, so do I have this same termination memory?"

Yes, you do.

Dear ones, you have something the children do not. Regardless of your new intent or your new path, you still have a core memory that remembers why you came. It remembers the end of the test. It's a shadow of what could have been, and it has a clock that knows you are approaching that time! Now, let me tell you what this means.

From the political structure of life on the planet, to the purpose of those around you, to the Earth itself, there is a part of you that is still "tapping you on the shoulder," reminding you about the old termination schedule. Even if you have given intent for the ascension vibration, the memory of the old is still there. Let me ask you this, lightworker: When you gave permission to move onto a new path, did you suddenly forget who you were? Did your duality suddenly disappear? No. Instead, you were given wisdom and gifts to move beyond the old schedule, but its existence as a potential is still with you. Now, that's part of the duality, which we have discussed before. Therefore, it's appropriate. But here's what it does: It literally creates physical attributes within your lives.

This planet is going to have a tough time this year (1999). You want you to watch the actual planetary results of this core memory information as it pushes and pulls? The push says, "This is old energy talking, remember? We're going to terminate." The pull is, "No, this is a new Earth. This is a new paradigm, and we're not terminating at all. Instead, we're going to go into the future, and things are going to be far, far different. We have a new assignment, and the old plan is going to sail right past—the old energy plan of termination."

These opposing energies will push and pull one another constantly, and if you want to look at your politics or your world finance, you're gong to see it. Pockets of the old energy will constantly leap up to the forefront and seemingly grab away the opportunities of peace. Like some kind of a flailing dying monster, this is indeed real—and it's now! It is doing everything it can do, this core memory, to pull you backwards into the remembrance of what could have been. You might say it's a battle against dark and light, but it isn't. It isn't. Instead, it's a battle between old potential and new planning, and the old is not going to go easily.

Dear ones, all this pushing and pulling has to do with the structure you set up, in love, about this test you call Earth. It is "angels testing the vibration," and you are the angels! It all exists for a grand reason, which we have given you before in this book (Chapter Two, "The Meaning of Life"). Do you think what you are seeing on Earth between tribes in the world is a new development? Think again. We spoke of this very potential in 1989, in the first messages to you from Kryon. It's there for you to look at, and it is very specific about governments of old energy power in 1999! Find it, so you will understand that the changes you are seeing now are right on schedule. [See page 303].

Shadow termination is a real physical attribute, yet you are now asked to deal with the fact that although you know what intent does, and although you are receiving new science and understand what is taking place regarding the new energy at the cellular level, there is still a part of you that is yelling, "Termination!" How does this manifest itself? Take a look at those around you—not just Earth, but take a look at those around you. This is a time of closure. The loss of relatives and friends in unusual ways is beginning to be perceived. They are often those who don't understand the new energy potentials and who have decided that no matter what is happening on the planet, it's time to "go." So they do!

Some will tell you that they are going to leave, and despite everything, you may tell them, it will not have any effect. You might explain to them, "You're not even sick!" But then they will become sick in order to facilitate an excuse to leave. Then they will depart. That's the potential of what the core memory can do without the knowledge of the divinity of what's taking place. That's the profound power of the shadow termination memory. And, dear ones, it's honored. For these are the souls of family members that will turn around quickly and become the Indigo Children! Look back this year and last year. You're going to find a whole lot of people deciding to leave. They will leave in groups around the planet, and it will be honored and understood because this is the time of termination, or so they "remember." Again, do you remember us telling you about this ten years ago? Here it is, right now. There will be some of you who know people and friends who will go into the hospitals with minor afflictions, but when they come out, you will bury them. That's how strong it is.

You cannot force a different consciousness on any Human Being—no matter how much you tell someone that they don't "have to go." Unless they feel it and "own" it in their lives, they will not change. It's about choice, and about each Human's ability to decide for themselves. Do not think you have failed if you cannot convince a sick family member to recover and move back into health. As you celebrate their lives in a ceremony after their passing, honor the fact that they lived! Then honor the fact that almost before you continue with your life, they are back in a precious Indigo Child's body. Believe it! Death is a circle of life!

Let's talk about Earth. Let's present some information that you have not had yet about how this is being dealt with on the planet. We have told you that the planet is indeed alive, and you know that the indigenous knew it. What many saw as superstition is now becoming your truth. As we have said, Earth is your partner. This planet has consciousness. This planet is going through upheavals and change because you are, too. It has to! It is why the grids are shifting, since the planet shifts with you.

We have never before discussed with you the concept of an etheric crystalline grid structure, but now it's time. The crystalline grid structure of this planet is one you'll never see, any more than you will see the crystalline sheath around your DNA. It is astral, but beyond that, it is interdimensional. It postures the planet's potential, and it also "talks" to the magnetic grid system. And guess what is in that crystalline structure? That grid system that is crystalline contains the memory and potential of the planet! It contains the partnership remembrance of the fact that this is the end of the test. As in your own DNA, that memory also tells of "termination"! As the planet shifts and moves, there is still an attribute of it that wants to push and pull the planet backwards and forwards—especially beginning this year (1999). You are now feeling much of the tugging—the yin and the yang of these last throes of struggle.

Dear ones, starting with the new millennium change, you will be seeing a shift. This shift is almost like the core memory has been dismissed and the new memory can start to come in more fully. It is the end of the old and the beginning of the new. As you repaint the exterior of a large house, the weeks it takes you to do it are not pleasant to the eye of the beholder. Standing from afar, some might even wonder which paint color is the new and which is the old! Which one is going to win? As you begin to finish, however, the new color takes over until it is established, and the house takes on a new energy. Oh, your Earth shift won't happen instantly, any more than the project to repaint the house did. But you're going to see a gradual shift of Human consciousness away from the old "pulling back," and the struggle will be dramatic in the next few years as you approach 2012. Some may even stand back in wonderment, asking themselves which color is the new one. Which one will "win"?

I'd like to tell you how the crystalline grid anchors to the planet, and this is new information from this channel (although it has been given before to humanity). There are two anchors of the crystalline grid. These "anchors" are metaphoric to the way the crystalline grid communicates to the planet and responds to the dirt of the Earth and to the oceans. The first type of anchors are buried on the planet and are programmed crystalline structures that talk to the grids, and the programming is the knowledge of the ancients. Guess who they were? Many were Lemurians—those of you who participated in Atlantis and Lemuria before you were terminated. Before the termination, it was necessary that you program these anchors, and you did. These anchors contain information about the tests and about the timeline. The information speaks of the things that you're going through right now. They also contain science, history, and a full explanation of how the physical universe works. They even talk about potential termination, right about now.

Some of these anchors are being found and pulled out of the ground. Those who find them are astounded by their energy, and often will display them—reveling in their sacredness. Let me tell you, however, about an attribute of a "found" anchor: When one is found and pulled out of the ground, it ceases to work. It is no longer an anchor, but simply a historical object with energy. Because the energy is spiritual, it is very special. Yet Humans will find and remove them, not knowing that they are designed to remain in the dirt. Many are shaped like the anatomy of the Human case that surrounds the brain. This shape is not metaphoric, but actual. The only metaphor here is that intelligence and memory have many shapes, but the one you understand is the brain. Therefore, this "time capsule" is easily recognized for what it is. If you find one, dear lightworker, let it be. Honor what it is, and let it remain where it is. There are many more that exist than have been reported, so there is no danger of removing them all. There are also many that cannot be reached. However, the advice remains.

There is a second anchor system. It is not a backup system, for it contains the seeds of its own survival and is biological! The programmed crystalline structures that are buried are called "the absolute core of knowledge." But there is another system that also talks to the crystalline grid. This system contains "the variables" that modify the absolute core. Remember when we spoke of the American Constitution metaphor? There are several attributes of that channelled document. One has absolute structure describing the way things are designed, and the other is a description of how to change the rules as needed. Therefore, one is a core, and one is a modifier. This, then, allows for change. It takes both attributes to create a flexible system that honors the "choice of the Human." Therefore, there is facilitation for absolutes as well as change.

It is the same way within the crystalline structure that talks to the magnetic grid system. I know this is not understood by all of you, but we're going to tell you anyway: There is a living library "anchor" that is the partner to the absolute one. There is a living library system on the planet that is very much like the one that is buried, only it responds to the changing consciousness of humanity! Are you starting to get the picture?

The living library anchors—the ones that will talk to the crystalline grid—the ones that will facilitate change—the ones that will allow for the Earth to move from one age to another without termination—are the **mammals** of the ocean!

All the nations in the world some years ago got together to save those whales. It's the only mammal that has ever had that distinction on the planet. Did you know that? Why is it, do you suppose, that so many countries got together to make sure that this particular group of mammals did not go into extinction? At a cellular level, every single Human Being knows why. There will come a time when these libraries will "show themselves" and open up.

Speaking of whales and animals in general, there is more evidence of the magnetic shift that you can see everywhere in the life around you—not just in physics, but in the biological life around you. We ask you to look closely at the migration of these mammals. We also ask you to look at the migration of the birds in the sky, for all of them have magnetic sensors sensitive to the ley lines of the magnetics of the planet. It's how they "find" where to go when it's time to move. This magnetic sensor is the biological attribute that guides them from one place to another as they swim and fly the magnetic ley lines of the planet. That's why they don't get lost. By the way, some birds, renowned for their ability to "find" their way home, are very confused right now. Look for this as well. Are any of you aware of new patterns of bird migration? Are you seeing migratory birds in areas you never saw them before? Why is that? In addition, you may wonder why some of the mammals of the ocean seem to be beaching themselves on purpose—whole groups will simply run aground!

Dear ones, when the magnetics change, it doesn't alter the land mass. As it has shifted, those birds and mammals are simply following the ley lines as they always did. The direction and instructions to "go" are given to them through their core memories. With time, their inheritance (new generations that learn) will steer them away from the beaches. But for a while, there will still be groups that will simply follow the altered magnetics right into the new beaches that were never there before the grids shifted. When they are towed off the beaches, they will come right back. That's a profound core memory at work.

This is a dramatically changing Earth. Let me tell you more about this shadow that we call the "shadow termination." For a while, it has the potential to sap your energy even if you are a lightworker. You see, some of you are walking around right now with an old contract that said you weren't supposed to be here! Yet here you are. That's because sometime ago you gave intent to walk off that old path and take ascension (raising your vibration) status. Right now, this year, many of you are feeling sapped of energy—sapped of lifeforce. It's not going to last long, dear ones. Understand and recognize it, then celebrate what this is about! Listen: It's called "shadow termination" because it is no longer in your reality! It's only a shadow of what used to be. You're carrying an energy with a new lifeforce that was never originally designed for you. It was not part of the core memory sheath. You're rewriting the memory as you go! No wonder it feels odd. You are actually changing the very core engrams that talk to your DNA about life extension, and you wonder why you have no energy? Celebrate the rewrite. Erase the old, and program the new. Then start to feel energized as the new wins out over the old.

Some of you may have minor illnesses that will stretch on and on. They will lay you flat, and you will wonder what happened. It's part of your cellular structure, and it represents a piece of the "shadow." This was the time you were supposed to leave, remember? The test with humanity is supposed to be over, yet here you are. This shadow termination attribute will be most intense through this year (1999) and go partly into the next few years as well. Then it will start to fade out.

Dear ones, many of you are going to be feeling anxiety over this, and there are those of you who are not going to know what to do with it. At the cellular level, this sheath—this core sheath that talks to your DNA—is going to be confliction oriented. The bias of the yin and the yang on the planet, and within the political structure of countries on Earth, is for peace. All these things will come right down to your cells, and will push and pull, push and pull. The push and pull will ask: Should you be here? Perhaps you shouldn't be here? The real answer is: You deserve to be here!

Some will ask, "*Why is all this happening to me?*" Look at the closure around you! Some of you will have friends and family close down around you, or they will die. Some will just close down their affiliation with you. They are an old energy, and you're new energy—and they don't want your presence anymore. You know who I'm talking to, don't you? This is the year of closure, and you're walking right through it.

There's a family here that washes your feet and walks between these aisles, actively interested in you. There's a family here that shakes hands with the other family members that you can't see, but who surround you. This room and the one where you read is filled to capacity with entities who love you. It is anointed space around the chair where you are reading this! There is activity here that you can't even imagine. There are things being granted at this moment, through intent, that reflect why you came here or why you decided to pick up this book. You can walk from the place where you sit with the beginning of a healing energy and life change. Like the old history book, you can put it on the shelf. It's time to write the new book!

Through the understanding of the shadow termination, and by virtue of the fact that it has no power over you, you can stand from your chair different from how you sat down. Many of you will, because you've given intent to fully absorb the information we have brought you. Knowledge reveals truth. Action is indeed inevitable after the revelation of truth, and the action through your intent will cause you to transmute all the attributes of shadow termination, no matter how uncomfortable they are. Change is inside, dear ones. With understanding comes wisdom, and with wisdom comes solution.

The year of closure will not last forever. Get through these times, and you'll see that some of the things that may have seemed like a disaster to you will pass cleanly. Move through them and look for that sweet spot we have spoken about. Know that right now may be the fulcrum or the crux of the test. You are the frontliners of the ones changing right now, and that is why we call you "Warriors of the Light."

It is also why we call you "family."

And so it is.

Kryon

Kryon
Have You Seen!

The United Nations Channelling 1998

Chapter Five

"There has never been a greater time for you to implement a Council of Wisdom, a nonvoting council of indigenous Human Beings on this planet to reside in this building. And we are telling you that the consciousness of the building will eventually support this. The consciousness of the people will support it. The consciousness of the planet is pushing you toward it. It is the next logical step—and when you present it, present it to the public first. They will do the rest to help you implement it."

Kryon at the United Nations—1998

The United Nations Channelling

1998

Channelled in
New York, NY

The Kryon Writings, Inc.

PMB 422
1155 Camino Del Mar
Del Mar, California 92014
[www.kryonqtly.com]

The United Nations Channelling 1998

Live Channelling New York, NY

From the writer...

We look at this special event and feel that it really started in New Hampshire. The Bedford channelling on November 21, 1998, was profound. With over 300 attending, Kryon gave a message called "The Cosmic Lattice, Part II." It was a continuation of an explanation of non-Newtonian physics, which he calls the energy of the universe. It was presented in layman's terms of how it works—including its shape, size, how to access it, and some metaphors to allow it to be understood. This channelling really set the stage for the entire week, for facing all of us the next morning was a trip to Manhattan, then a Kryon lecture and channelling meeting each day for the next four days—culminating with the meeting at the United Nations on the 24th.

Many of you know that I love New York (Manhattan). If you know the full story, you may remember that my first trip to the Big Apple was to channel at the United Nations! I was afraid of the city then, only to "meet my contract" that year. I realized that my fear was a phantom. New York (Manhattan) holds the energy of many lifetimes for me. When I got there, I "knew" what was around every corner! It was actually familiar. It's a metaphysical joke for me, and I laugh about it every time I am there—and I go a couple times a year.

Jan and I had presented at the UN in 1995 and 1996, and this 1998 invitation was very much anticipated. We were excited to be back and were ready to "get formal" (something we seldom do, being from California), respecting the protocol at the United Nations meetings. I wore my black suit—the one I only wear for funerals, weddings, and the United Nations. I saw myself in the mirror and wondered who the undertaker was. Jan wore black, too. I guess it was our way of honoring the seriousness of the event. I apologized to my tie before I put it on, asking it to forgive me for wearing it only once a year—and hoping it wouldn't get even and strangle me in the middle of the meeting. I was tired from the week's schedule, but excitedly energized.

For those who don't know, the S.E.A.T. (known as the Enlightenment Society) is a chartered organization within the working area of the United Nations in New York City. Over the years it has become the place where delegates and guests of delegates meet and experience the knowledge and energy of what we are calling the New Age. Authors, channellers, lecturers, musicians, and spiritual leaders all have been called over the years to give their wisdom at these meetings. The public is not invited, and only those who work at the United Nations or hold membership in the society may attend.

Since the last time Jan and I were there, security had tightened considerably. Even knowing that, we asked the impossible: We tried to bring in 12 guests of our own, including Robert Coxon and all his electronic synthesizer gear! (Robert Coxon is a Canadian New Age recording artist.) We didn't know how it could happen, but we simply showed up at the appointed time at the visitors' entrance at the United Nations. There we sat in a group in the corner, waiting for a miracle. Time elapsed, and nothing happened. Then I told our folks that we would give Spirit five more minutes, or we would make other 3D plans to get in.

Jennifer Borchers is the president of the Enlightenment Society within the United Nations, and she met us in the lobby with our entourage. I know she gulped hard when she saw all of us, since protocol is king within the halls of that establishment, and we had a bunch of people and equipment (this is a bit different from most authors who are invited to speak). But Jennifer had done her homework and had made some arrangements I didn't know about. Just as I gave intent to wait only five more minutes, we got our miracle—the appearance of our "angel," Fernando—a United Nations security guard who is also a Sai Baba devotee, and originally responsible for helping get the Kryon information to the attention of the UN! Fernando simply waved at the FBI security station, and within a half hour or so, he got all of us into the "inner sanctum" of the building, including all of Robert Coxon's equipment! It was timed perfectly, and Robert was set up ready to go when we started the meeting.

You had to be there to understand how difficult this would have been without Fernando and Jennifer working with the light as they did! Our original UN host was also there, Zehra Boccia—holding the energy as she always did. No videos are allowed in the meeting—audiocassette recordings only. Equipment such as the kind Robert Coxon had usually takes a full week to inspect and approve! Here we had all this stuff, and it simply floated in through the front door! Naturally we all went through the sensitive metal detectors, "sniffers," and had our ID checked, but most of the tight scrutiny was waived (like taking things apart).

The guests we brought were mainly from the Kryon staff, plus some of the facilitators we carry with us on the road: Robert Coxon and his wife, Chenier (as mentioned); Linda Benyo and Geoff Hoppe (creators of the Kryon Magazine); Peggy and Steve Dubro (EMF balancing technique); Mark and Martine Vallé+ (French Canadian publishers of the Kryon books for the French language); Sarah Rosman (Kryon transcriber and recorder); and a few other personal friends and Kryon helpers including Bonnie Capelle, Pliny Porter, and Guitanjali.

Jan and I were familiar with the building. We had done this twice before—but this year it seemed more comfortable, and we were not nervous at all. All was in place at exactly 1:15 P.M. on Tuesday, November 24, in committee room B, not far from the general assembly, and where the Security Council was actually in session. Reporters were around, too, waiting for whatever might happen (which is common). It was a typical work day at the UN, and there was much activity in the hallways, with many delegates coming and going. Our room was filling up with delegates and UN workers (and our guests), and then right on time, the meeting began.

I started by giving the attendees a very short (15-minute) update on the Kryon work. I brought along the new HAARP documentary that was an outcropping of the 1995 and 1996 UN Kryon messages within that very building, and displayed the product (see page 288). I congratulated Paula Randol Smith within that energy for her efforts to manifest this very important mainstream TV program about HAARP. It all seemed so amazing to think of everything that has happened since our first visit in 1995 (Paula wasn't there, but her energy was)!

I mentioned several other things that were germane to both the Kryon work and the UN, and then my time was up for the lecture. Jan then did a 20-minute chakra balance and toning. Yep—they all toned! It was great to hear that kind of wonderful spiritual energy and listen to those voices fill the room within the venue of the United Nations. Jan did a great job consolidating her information and delivering it within the prescribed time. Robert Coxon (who not only set up, but did a full sound check in about ten minutes) was absolutely wonderful in the way he set the energy. Imagine having Canada's best-selling New Age musical artist playing behind both the meditation and the channelling! (Robert's latest work is "The Silent Path.") We both knew that this meeting was very tightly timed and that we had to be finished on schedule. Jan finished, and everything was ready for Kryon. Robert kept playing. I knew he was also channelling his music. The room was filled with a sacredness, and it seemed very appropriate for what was coming.

The power of the channelling that day was as great as anything I have ever experienced. It was also the shortest channelling on record! The information was very different this year as we are approaching the millennium. The flavor (as you will read below) was one of celebration.

Many of you have been to the Kryon seminars and know what the real Kryon message is: We have changed our future, and the consciousness of the planet is in transformation. The spiritual critical mass has been reached, and you can see it all around you. The overview proves it, although many can't really see the overview (since it isn't presented often on the news). Kryon has told us over and over that we have done something amazing. He often sits at our feet and just loves us. He regularly speaks about all the Humans—as angels pretending to be Human. He has even given us the message that our children are now coming in with the next evolution of spiritual tools that we didn't have! This message to the United Nations was, therefore, about congratulations and honor, but done in a very unusual way.

The room was ready. The delegates were poised and reverent. Everything became quiet, except for the anointed music of Robert Coxon continuing being played in the background.

Then Kryon began:

The United nations Channel (#3)

Greetings, dear ones, I am Kryon of Magnetic Service. Indeed, it is the voice of my partner [Lee] that you hear now, but the energy in this room provides the evidence that at this moment you are being visited. No, not by one entity, but by an entourage that flows into this space and wishes to walk between the chairs and the very aisles that are here—in a congratulatory and foot-washing mode. For this particular communication is going to be different than any before.

My partner, you said it felt like "home" here (the United Nations building). It is because this is your contract—this is what it always was—this is the area that we wish to fill with love in a grand way. Not just this room, dear ones, but an entourage that floods this entire building, this city, and even the place where you have decided to come and hear this message. This is a message that is going to be far different than you would imagine—far shorter, indeed, than any message we've had before. This one is especially for those in this room and for those in the building. But let it be known that this transcription is for all—the ears of those who are hearing and the eyes of those who are reading. It is for all on the planet.

This is not a time when you have come to revel in an energy because you are curious. This is about a reunion in the room, a reunion with an energy that was promised to you—an energy that was promised to you by appointment when you decided to come onto this planet again. We sit in front of angels, each one—designed as angels—on purpose as angels. We speak of all of those who sit in this assemblage pretending to be Human! For we know who you all really are [Kryon's continuing teaching that all of us are part of the angelic family]. We know of your courage. We know of your contract. We know what you've been through. We know of the infirmities in your body. We know of the shift you are going through, and we know all of these things because we are *family*. And this family wants to come before you now and do something that we've never done before.

This is the first time, dear ones, that this kind of message has ever been presented—and we do it quickly now. In the past we have promised you something: Spirit will never come before Human Beings and give a fear-based message. *Never*! Let it be known, if you ever come before any entity who says that they represent Spirit and you get a message dripping with fear and agenda, then it is not Spirit who sits before you!

Instead, what we do is come and celebrate new Human enablement, especially right now. There has never been a time like right now! This is of your making, and you should know it. You can walk from this place in a higher stature than when you came in, when you realize what you've done. I'm about to tell you in a way that is more graphic than ever before. This is not a fear message. You must understand the whole message before you stop listening or before you stop reading. Let this message be given in total, and never be quoted apart from its full intent. Those who would rip apart this message for their own purpose do not represent the new energy on the planet.

The Future

We're going to take you to a future Earth. This may be startling information, but we ask you to wait until the end of this message before you judge what is being given to you here.

We're going to paint a vivid picture of your future Earth, and it's going to be very disconcerting for you.

[Pause]

In this very land (the United States) there is water covering both coastlines— with major cities being under that water. There is disease—there is confusion—the stores are empty—there is a civil war here in this great land, and within it there is a smaller four-way race war. There is a removal of central control from all. There are police forces that are surrounding the cities, trying to keep order for their own area. The return to the "city state" is at hand, and they let no one in or out. There are state lines that are no longer state lines. It is chaos. There are submersible boats in the ocean carrying great weapons, which out of the integrity of their own commands, have sunk themselves—because they could not decide which port to land in. Each port has its own agenda. There is horror and despair in this country, in this land.

This is a future of Earth.

If you go higher in the land, you find the great country of Canada, which is divided completely in half and starting to arm itself. Two great cultures with differing languages are almost at war—unable to decide who is going to get the various parts of the land. The resources that are the most important reside mainly in one, and the other must share it to exist. As in the country below them, central control is all but lost. Culture and tribe awareness divide them.

This is a future of Earth.

We take you to just a few of the other continents to view what is happening: We find in the African continent that there is a full reversal of consciousness—a return to tribal warfare, just as it appeared many, many years ago. The place where civilization had its seeds is beginning to be the place where it will be buried.

At the southern pole, Larson's Ledge has broken off, sending an enormous tidal wave sweeping across the southern part of the great Australian continent, covering cities, killing millions, putting the country into chaos and grief.

The great dragon (China) is quiet. A quarter of Earth's population is quiet, but they are watching very carefully to find out where the power vacuum spots will be so that they can sweep in and establish their culture. Most of them have anticipated this, for it was in their prophecy—foreseen by their ancients.

This is a future of Earth.

Ah, but that is not the worst. We take you to what you call your Middle East. Listen carefully: There, dear ones, in the energy of the most Holy of Holies, the **beast** has arrived. And the beast, with its glowing eyes, has raised 40,000 feet tall and has planted its feet firmly on both sides of the ancient tribal lands—and it's there to rule for 4,000 years—representing half its life.

The metaphor of the beast, dear ones, in this context, is nuclear war—and it starts there—where Humans decided to destroy one another in the name of God.

This is a future of Earth.

I'm going to tell you what this is all about. We told you to listen to the entire message—this short message of today—for what is coming is profound! I'm going to give you the date of this future—the date of the future that we have just described to you.

[Pause]

The date when all this is to happen is October 1998!

"Kryon, you must have make a mistake! That date has already gone by. It's November 1998 now," some of you might say.

We know. Yes, the date has gone by. Dear ones, I just gave you the prophecy of Scripture. I just gave you the prophecy of the 400-year-old Nostradamus. I gave you the prophecy even of the New Age masters who had the visions of a "snapshot" of the Earth as it had been measured and foretold in 1962 [a spiritual measurement much like the 1987 Harmonic Convergence]. And what I gave you was *real*!

That was Earth's potential then, yet here you sit. None of it happened, you see. Not any of it happened! Not the catastrophes, not the race wars, not the nuclear wars. The Beast has been voided, and I sit in the very place that is responsible for so much of the consciousness shift. Listen to this, dear ones, listen: When the cook is in the kitchen, he has no concept of how relaxed and enjoyable the meal that is being consumed in the other room. [A metaphor for those at the United Nations who only participate in the strife and negativity and stress of the day-to-day existence, without being able to look at the overview of what they have done.]

Earth and all those upon it should be in massive celebration! And they should start right here by washing your feet! We speak of those who work here who deal with the children of the nations of the world—who deal with the deforestation issues. We talk to those who are responsible for disease control. It has worked! And yes, we address those who embrace peace over war, and who demand a planet with responsibility one for the other.

The consciousness of the planet is supporting what you're doing. This planet, which you think is filled with strife, is the kitchen (in the metaphor). Most of the planet sits back and enjoys a major shift, perhaps not even knowing it—an overview of a planet hurtling toward a new paradigm of coexistence instead of catastrophe and full war. Oh, there will be complications, and there will be strife, but look at the consciousness shift! Now the emphasis is about solving conflict and bringing permanent closure—instead of about "who is right" or "who deserves what." It's about responsibility for *all* Humans on Earth, and not just the good of the few in a certain area. The worldwide emphasis is on eventually creating a peaceful coexistence between *all* the tribes. It's about a planet coming together, finally, to move through a millennium that previously had a stigma on it of *termination*. Instead, I am sitting here telling you that as this millennium draws near, there is a spiritual potential now of graduation and wisdom, instead of that awfulness that I just told you about. The potential now is of the New Jerusalem— and it is in your hands!

Each of you came to the planet with full knowledge of the 1962 potential. Each of you also knew of the changes possible, and of the potential that the year 2000 would find far more peaceful news than the predicted catastrophe.

Look around! None of the prophecies are upon you! Even though there are still those who will try to force the old energy into the new consciousness, they will fail. They will "stick out" as old energy, and be rejected by the consensus of the planet.

There has never been a greater time for you to implement a Council of Wisdom, a nonvoting council of indigenous Human Beings on this planet to reside in this building. And we are telling you that the consciousness of the building will eventually support this. The consciousness of the people will support it. The consciousness of the planet is pushing you toward it. It is the next logical step—and when you present it, present it to the public first. They will do the rest to help you implement it.

This reunion is almost over [the meeting], and this family thathas come in here to wash your feet is doing so to say "Thank you." This family, which has come in to wash your feet, says "We're all going to go through a grand millennium shift now because of what you're doing here." Can it be any clearer? Can it be any clearer why we love you so? This is the message today, from this side of the veil to you.

Let the transcription go forward, so that all will know what took place here today. Let all know what it could have been, but what it is. None of the things as described have happened. None are scheduled, and none will be—not with the work you are doing.

So the entourage retreats. It has only been a few minutes, but it has been a powerful few minutes of love. Walk from this place and know who you are! Perhaps you thought you were a piece of a whole that nobody noticed? I'll tell you, the "family" noticed! You're never alone! When you go home tonight, look in the mirror. We challenge you to look at yourself directly in the eye and say the words out loud, "I AM THAT I AM." Because, indeed, that's who you are.

And so it is.

Kryon

From Lee:

Kryon finished at 2:15, and we had 15 minutes left for Q&A. We fielded a few questions, and then it was time to go. It all happened so fast! We were then led out of the committee room quickly (so that the next UN working group could come in), and we went to the UN cafeteria (all of us), where we socialized with many of the delegates who attended.

Again, my thanks to Jennifer Borchers for her work in getting us to the United Nations in '98. Most of you don't know that Jean Flores, the secretary of the Enlightenment society, was the one who invited us several months ago. When she suddenly died, Jennifer took the ball and got us there, and she was a great host.

I know that Jean is still with us in some way, and in that room on Tuesday we all felt her, plus so many who were watching and loving us, and holding our hands as Kryon also washed our feet.

The energy created at the United Nations that day was awesome. All felt it, and in subsequent meetings we had in Manhattan (including a meditation with the Enlightenment Society in a New York apartment), we discussed the fact that it was far different from anything before. Thanks to so many of you for your energy—we felt it with us that day!

Postscript: Kryon really doesn't make predictions, but he does give us potentials. Again I can't help but remember something he said in 1989 in Book One, *The End Times*, which now has profound meaning:

> "My process will take ten to twelve Earth years to accomplish . From now through the year 2002 will be the gradual change. Around the year 1999 you should know exactly of what I am speaking. Governments are run by men of power...not all of them are enlightened. Their inability to deal with the consciousness alteration could imbalance them, and the result could be chaos." [1]

I seldom speak of current events, since it tends to "date" a book. However, right now as I finish this Kryon book, we are embroiled in a struggle between old and new energy with a dictator [speaking of Kosovo]. It is not a war with country borders. It is a war between old and new consciousness, and a world struggle to find out how to best handle an old-energy governmental leader who has created chaos due to tribal issues and his ethnic-cleansing solutions. From the channelling in 1989, this is exactly what Kryon told us could happen in 1999. Here we are, ten years later, with it on our doorstep.

[1] *The End TImes* - Kryon Book 1; Lee Carroll, ISBN 0-9636304-2-3; 1993 (page 23).

NOTICE
THESE DOORS MUST BE KEPT CLOSED
DANGER
THIS AREA IS CLOSED OFF
CAUTION
THIS DOOR MUST BE KEPT CLOSED

Separation

Chapter Six

From Lee Carroll...

I guess I should have anticipated it. Kryon spoke of it, but I didn't understand. Now, the separations are beginning, and even those who claim to have love as the basis of their existence are starting to break into camps of "who they believe is evil" and who is not.

The following channelling only begins to open up an attribute both of Human nature and of a dramatic prediction—that of the fight between old and new energy even within the ranks of an awakening humanity. The old-energy spirituality actually wants structure and feels uncomfortable and threatened with the changes at hand. It fights to retain old concepts that say spirituality must have punishment as part of its core, that evil must exist to balance love, that Humans are worthless and must find a higher source to worship, thereby giving them strength, and that spiritual truth requires a hierarchy of organized men and women, buildings, texts, and a long lineage of "do's and don'ts" to live by.

The new-energy spirituality is indeed very different. It opens by stating that "we are God." It tells us that the only structure we need is inside, and that it's all there for the finding. It speaks of a plan where a fear-based existence grounded around eventual punishment is instead replaced by an awakening to self-responsibility—a responsibility that enhances wisdom and that creates morality from within. Replacing fear of punishment is the joy of creating Divine purpose. This new-energy philosophy also creates self-esteem and a joy-filled existence. It is self-regulated, without all the trappings of organization, buildings, rules, or priests. It honors the God within, and claims that the very essence of God is available there—all the "do's and don'ts"—and that all the spiritual strength is inside. It gives every Human the potential of a priest.

The chasm is great between these two ideas, and in the process of the push and pull between them, there is drama. Kryon told us that there would be those who would brand the new energy, evil...and this has indeed happened. I asked him, "*Kryon, what can I tell people about discernment at this time? How can they know truth from deception*?" He told me, "Look for the love. Follow it, for where love is, you will find truth."

I guess I should have anticipated it—the division. Many of you know that Kryon was branded as "the cosmic evil" by a prominent lightworker some years ago. This teacher also feels that the magnetic grid of the earth is evil. An evangelistic thrust of thousands of flyers proclaiming that particular fear-based opinion went all around the world, mainly to those about to attend Kryon workshops. You might ask, "*What was the end result of that drama*?" The end result? The attack continues to this day, but the lightworker who is responsible is now teaching the exact message of Kryon! "*We have changed our future—we can move into new consciousness—we are Divinity.*" Go figure. Why was it necessary? What was accomplished? It's part of what was expected. It's part of the intense struggle between old and new, as the following channelling will present.

Based on other channellings (fear-based), some have branded the New Age itself as being evil, and Kryon as Lucifer, the trickster. Supposed ancient entities are channelling that the New Age is a plot to capture souls. Some, believing this, have returned their books and asked me to convert to their new/old philosophy. They claim that Kryon has **tricked** us all. As proof, they bring me another channel!

My truth? Kryon is a very loving family member—a messenger who gives us this information: God (the family) will never bring you a fear-based message. Channelling with pure intent and love is sacred and empowering. Use it as information for your life. Apply only the things that you "resound with." Don't make it evangelistic. Don't force your truth on anyone else. Don't follow any entity (Human or otherwise) or join a cult in order to create enlightenment. **You** are enabled, enlightened, and loved by God because you are a piece of God. Never give away your power, since you are powerful on your own. Therefore, don't become a "follower." Control your own life using the incredible new spiritual tools that are being given to humanity right now. Discover the "God" within. Have peace. Live a profoundly interesting and healthy life by taking your own power. Help create peace on the planet by your own consciousness shift. We are all in a profound energy transition.

Kryon never asks us to join anything. There is no agenda in his words that tells Humans they "have to" do something. He honors our lives and our sufferings. He encourages us to find the hidden truths of God. He invites us to look around and discern all philosophies. He honors all religions in their "search for God." He sustains incredible love and has done so for over ten years. He is not exclusive, and invites any who wish to channel him to do so. He has never asked to be followed or worshipped.

He calls us "family," loves us as brothers and sisters, and washes our feet each time he comes to speak to us. His only real admonition? "Love one another!"

Some trick!

"Five Chasms of the New Age"

Channelled in Indianapolis, Indiana

The Kryon Writings, Inc.

PMB 422
1155 Camino Del Mar
Del Mar, California 92014
[www.kryonqtly.com]

"Five Chasms of the New Age"

Live Channelling
City, State

This live channelling has been edited with additional words and thoughts to allow clarification and better understanding of the written word.

Greetings, dear ones, I am Kryon of magnetic service. Oh, it is great, indeed, to hear the Human voice raised in this fashion (responding to the toning from the group in the large audience that immediately preceded the arrival of Kryon). Again we say to you that there is no greater honor than for the Human who gives intent to be in a place of self discovery such as you are.

As before, we are going to fill your space with an entourage that is going to bring love to you in a way you may not have felt before. Again we tell you that like a bubble of love—like a lid you would put on something simmering on your stove—we are going to encompass the energy and sequester it for you during the time we are together.

Again we tell you this, that whoever you are, you are loved just as much as the one next to you. You are loved as much as the one who accepts this experience and changes because of it. You are loved every bit as much as the one who walks from this place with life extension because they gave intent for the healing. There is no judgment in your journey, dear one. What you do with it is the test of energy balance you came for. How you handle the challenge is where the honor is, never a judgment! There will come a time when you and I will again know each other, for I am telling you that there is not one precious Human receiving this message who does not know me. I have seen you all and I know each name.

Let me tell you about those names as we fill your area with love, and as the vibration increases so that this message is well understood. The names that are yours are more than just sounds in the air. They are created from the energies within the Merkaba that you own. They are created out of sound and light and color—vibrations that you cannot even conceive of. And when they spin together they actually **sing** a name in my dimensionality that I "see" and know as *you*. The beauty of this would astound you. It is an interdimensional aspect of who you really are. I see you each as giant entities of love—part of the whole and aware at the cellular level of who you are.

Again I tell you that there will come a time when we will meet in the hall of honor, and during that time we will say to one another, "We remember that time when the veil cracked open slightly and when the love was allowed to pour in and flow into these aisles. The entourage of Kryon is the entourage of Lord Michael, and it is in the "now." This is the entourage that goes between the chairs of those receiving this message, and next to the one reading this. This is the entourage which hugs each guide/angel and who knows you intimately. Ah, dear ones, as we encircle you, we say to you that there is not one Human here or reading this who is not known to us! We tell you again that there is not one challenge in your life that is not known to us—whatever is surging through your life now, perhaps creating a situation that is causing you problems—we are aware of it. We give you an affirmation that has the seeds of truth like nothing else we have ever said: *There is nothing in your life that is unsolvable—nothing!*

Oh, dear ones, if you had any idea of the potential that exists for healing right now! We have told you this before, that figuratively we sit now before you with a bowl in our hands that is full with the tears of our joy—wishing to wash your feet. For that is how Spirit sees you. Before we start the teaching, we want you to be aware of how Spirit sees you. My partner alluded to potentials that exist on the planet (in a lecture session before the channelling). Just as there are potentials for the future of Humans on the planet, there are potentials for your future, individually. Before our time together is over, there will be an invitation (metaphorically) for you to reach out and grab the potential that you planned yourself! There exists a potential with your name on it, with the solution to every single challenge in your life. That fact is not some kind of accident, and it is not a "gift from God." It is also not anything that Kryon brings to you. Instead, it is something that you have brought to Earth, and it is part of why you are here.

The message of how this works is profound, and it is meant to be read at this minute—at this moment—as you hear it. You [the live audience] might ask, "*How could such a thing be?*" You'll know how it is when this live message is transcribed and *you* are reading it (like right now!). For to you, at this second, these audible words are in the now [speaking again to the live audience in the room]. There is no *time* with Spirit. For us, the experience of what you call time is circular. And right *now* there is the potential for the reader as well as the hearer, and it is happening all at once—all at once. We see things far differently than you do, and that is why we can look at the group assembled here and also see the one reading this. We can say to all of you, "Do you know who you are?" There are some of you who carry the seeds of planetary change, but before you facilitate the planet, you must change yourselves, and that is why there is so much love in this message.

We speak of *family* often. We have told my partner that we'll speak of it again now, and we get excited when we speak of this because there is a lineage with all of you receiving this message! The genealogy of Spirit is great. Take a good look at those who you feel you don't know, before you leave this room. Some of you have already connected, from distances that are great, with those who will play a part in your life from this moment on. It was *intent* that brought you here to sit in the chair or read this—by appointment! Spirit honors this by bringing others with the same intent, and together you will create an energy that will change your life—creating knowledge and energy. Oh, dear one, curb your impatience. You are receiving this for a reason, and I know whom I'm speaking to! I have expected your ears and eyes in this "now" time. Relax and know you are fine, and all is well.

I'm speaking to many *at this moment* who are wondering how everything is going to turn out in their lives, for they bring into this reality, problems that they cannot share with anyone—and some are profound. Some carry the potential energy of death itself. That is why we sit here and why we surge through the aisles in this place and sit upon the energy that you call your laps as you read this, and surround you with the love of God itself, and say these words to you: "There is no insurmountable problem here! Within the solutions, there is joy! In the solutions, there is healing and planetary shift! That is why we are excited about who is "here," sitting and reading.

There are facilitators receiving this message, who this very year will meet and greet Human Beings who don't seem to be on the path. These Humans will look at these dear ones for solutions and answers to what ails them. Somehow, someone somewhere, synchronicity brought them to stand in front of you, facilitator. And there will be a temptation for you to size them up and say, "*Here's one who will never, ever understand. Oh, I'll do my best, and I will love them in the process, but I know they will walk away untouched, and I will never see them again.*"

We are telling you to honor synchronicity! This is the one who has been brought to you by design. The process of planting the seeds of enlightenment has to begin in each Human somewhere—and now here they sit. They are attracted to your light, and the training will be your telling them how to take responsibility for their bodies. Get them used to verbalizing what they want, and for the first time ever they will experience this. Through their intent and your cooperation and knowledge, there can be healing. With that, dear ones, there will be a change of heart—and with that, dear ones, you will create an opening to create a lightworker that may have never awakened without you. This is how you change the planet!

How does that make you feel to know that perhaps your purpose is not entirely to heal—but to plant seeds? Some may come disguised in their duality and in their disbelief. Sometimes they are curt and have shallowness in the matters of Spirit. Watch for it. These will be the very ones who will be sent to you by design—your design. Lest you think that you are supposed to surround yourself only with those of like mind—lest you think that all that you wish to bring into your life are those who think and vibrate at a high level—it's time to think differently on these things. For walking into your lives, dear ones, will be those who have no idea of any of this, and they will look at you and you will recognize them from this time when I told you they would arrive. So it is that we begin the training of something that we have wanted to discuss for some time. This is something we brought to a smaller group not too long ago, but now it is to be repeated and enhanced, for we want it to be transcribed this night.

The Five Chasms of the New Age

We would like to communicate the five chasms of the New Age, and the New Age Human. You know, don't you, that you're going to have to come up with another term for "New Age." For the *New Age* has been here for a very long time and yet you simply have no concept of the *newness* that you carry. The *new*, New Age is what we speak of now. Perhaps a better name would be the *Now* Age? There is a potential for humanity that has never existed before. The seeds of that graduation is carried in those who are receiving this message, wanting to know more about who they are. If you could see the brilliance of the angel that sits inside, you would be astonished at the divinity that is present in the chair where you sit! All the things that come from this platform I am on would diminish, and the real glow and light would come from where you sit. That is why there is so much honor! You need to know what is going to take place, and this has to do with a Human Being who is vibrating high. This has to do with what you have called in the past *The Ascension Status*. This has to do with *you*. Should you choose to give intent for such a thing—to remain on this planet right now with the energy of that intent, it will be honored, dear ones, to the letter. And you can't be too surprised that your lives will change because of it. And in the change of life there will be challenge again, but this time it's a challenge that comes from a new contract—the one you are co-creating for yourself as you go. It has to do with the opening of a chasm of belief, understanding, and reaction between you and the ones who do not take the vibrational shift. Indeed, you will begin to see and experience a rift—and, in many cases, an unexpected one. There are five general categories that we wish to illuminate you with tonight.

Belief

The first and foremost one is that of belief. A dramatic difference will open up between those who believe as you do and those who do not. Some of you may say, "*Oh, I know where that's going to come from. We've always had trouble with certain ones who did not believe as we do. They are the ones with the buildings and the organizations. They are the ones who have been around a long time. They believe differently, and we have always seemed odd or even evil to them. This is where the problem will come from.*"

Dear ones, that's not where the fracture is going to come from. No. Some will call it an internal split, and I'm going to tell you where it's going to come from. The reason we encourage you to rename the New Age is because the split will come from within the New Age believers!

There will be those who will not agree with you that such a thing could be: That you, as Human Beings, could take on the power of the entire entity (Higher Self), which sits on the golden throne inside you. They will not agree that you have the power to take the Ascension Status. They will not agree that you can make your life span double in the amount of years in which they expect to live. And when you start doing it, dear ones, they and the others will brand you as something *different*, for they are in fear. They are not ready to awaken. All the things that they have studied in "their" New Age—whether it be through their psychic endeavors or through their energy work—is precious to them in the form they learned it. They will see what you are doing as a threat, dear ones, because suddenly you are able to do things for yourself that took them years to accomplish. What they did as facilitators of the old New Age is now being done individually by Humans taking on new power in the *Now* Age. You will be able to do things which, in the past, only they were able to do *for you*.

So we call the split, "the split of belief." My partner, you have already experienced this. At that time, we gave the feeling of that experience to you (that of being attacked by a seemingly well-intentioned lightworker) so that you could share what it is like, and to validate that the belief chasm is real. It was given so that you would be able to relate it to those who will come to you and ask, "*What do we do with our New Age friends who will no longer speak to us?*"

That's chasm one, and certain parts of your country will be profound in this area, and in others it will not even exist at all. Like in so many other spiritual attributes, there will be polarity and balance. We would not tell you such a thing without giving you the solution to it as well, and it is an easy solution. I want you to listen to the solution because the **solution** is the **same one** for every single chasm.

The solution goes like this: You are loved without measure, and that particular love that you have is your *light*, and you are to carry it high. You are not to ever let any other Human Being diminish it, even one particle. For it is real, and it will serve you well within the energy of its divinity. It is anointed, ordained, and it's yours. The changes in your life take place when you draw closer to that energy inside you that you call the "angel within." That *angel within* is frightening to many, for it contains new awesome power. These who resist your new energy and belief will see you as odd, different, and strange—that you could bring about such profound change within the energy around you. They will not recognize the change as part of the plan they have believed in. They will fear you and reject you. So the solution is to continue to carry the light as high as you can. Let nothing diminish it. Let not the doubter, even in your own camp, diminish the mantle of Spirit that you wear—the one that has become the I AM part of you. Practice saying, "*I AM a piece of the whole; therefore, I AM perfect in God's sight. No Human words or actions can change the I AM.*"

Family

The next chasm is family. Now we're not telling you anything that you don't already know about a chasm with family. But it will intensify, dear ones, and we're going to tell you why.

Can you imagine, right now, deciding to become a great artist? Perhaps you feel you have no artistic ability at all, but inside you want it so bad! So you take certain courses and classes. Because of new techniques, technology, and teaching revelations, suddenly you are able to paint—perhaps even as well as some very great artists! Sacred, indeed, is the energy of that talent. Imagine what you would do with such a talent. Colors would be no problem, for you would "see" them in advance and you would paint them skillfully using the new technology and training. There would be those around you who would praise you and your marvelous work, simply because you had decided to utilize the new gifts that allowed a hidden talent to be manifested.

Now let me ask you what you might do with that wonderful new talent. Would you make it a hobby? No. It would be your new passion! For in this newly discovered world, you would have results that would be astounding. It would fill your life with beauty—a creation of your own that would be your new life. In almost all of your waking hours, you would have a brush in your hand, creating masterpiece after masterpiece—because you had discovered that you could do it. You can do it!

Dear ones, this is the intensity and the purity of the *new,* New Age belief system. For when you begin your pure intent, spiritual passion will be created in your life that will change you forever. And when you start seeing the results of your intent and co-creative ability, you will not be able to put it down. And, like the ones who discovered that they could create masterpieces when they couldn't even draw before, you will have a change of passion. Suddenly the earth will have Humans with the overlay of a duality they came in with, transmuted and changed with the realization of the divinity that they have turned into. With that will come a passion for the spiritual quest. And the family we are talking about—the ones who agreed to come in with you as blood family—may retreat.

Whereas they may have thought of you as odd and strange before, you are "off the scale" now. For some of you there will be sorrow at this. But let me tell you about a section of the blood family that will react differently, and that's the children. For at the cellular level, they will see what you are doing; and at the cellular level, they will be exclaiming the words, "It's about time." So you will come into an alliance with the children, but at the same time, you will often alienate the others: the brothers and the sisters, the aunts, the uncles, the cousins, the fathers, and mothers. They do not resound with your new belief and are not ready to go along. That's the second one.

Relationships

The third one concerns certain kinds of relationships, and we speak now specifically of partnering. If you will recall in the tribes of your indigenous peoples, there was often in the tribe what was called a "medicine man," even though it wasn't always a man. This Human Being had an elevated status with the tribe because he or she could heal others. This person had potions and incantations, and they used energy—and they knew it. But there was an attribute about this medicine man that we wish you to look at. The attribute was that the medicine man always lived on the outskirts of the village. The medicine man was always alone, and that was because to vibrate at that level have that intuitive knowledge—to have that awareness and that energy—in those days it was almost impossible for that medicine man to find a partner who could exist with him or her. In addition, even with healing power, this individual was seen as different from the rest.

We are speaking about things now that we have spoken of before. It is going to be difficult, indeed, for those who decide to take the ascension status and to have a partnership that is matched and equal. Some have asked Kryon this: "*Is it possible for me to be unequally yoked with a partner (a believer and nonbeliever)? Oh, my partner loves me greatly, and he (or she) gives me space to do what I wish to do, and I love him and I wish to be with him. But is this okay?*"

As you decide to claim the Ascension status, the chasm will open even farther. There is the potential for fear on the partner's part, and it is a difficult challenge, indeed. Each case is different, but we have to tell you in all honesty that there will be some partners—very understanding now—who will not be able to endure the change. We would not tell you these things, dear ones, if they were not so. That is why we ask you to be careful what you intend and what you wish to have happen in your life.

Sometimes by holding your light, partner's actually see how you have changed into a better person, and they rejoice and renew their vows with you—even though staying at a "spiritual armslength," Many lightworkers have expected the worst, only to find that "*things are not always as they seem*," and the partner becomes a better partner in the process, transmuting fear with love! Each is different, but you must know that your change will affect the relationship.

Others that say, "*Like the medicine man, I have been alone for years. Is there really someone out there for me?*" We are here to tell you that there is! Because there are more and more of both genders that have decided finally to vibrate at a higher level, there is synchronicity available. Again, it's a solution you have designed. It's in places like this [the Kryon seminar] where you give intent to search internally for the Angel inside, where these kinds of synchronicities prevail. That is why we have said to you, "Don't pass up the opportunity to know who is here! Don't pass it up. Are you ready to meet *family* again? It's not just here. It's in all of the gatherings where, by *appointment*, you have decided to come and learn more about the angel inside. So, unlike the medicine man, get up and go! Find gatherings of others of like mind and manifest it.

Business

Number four is what you would call business. Vocations in your society are very spiritually interesting, and the interest is not for the reasons you think. By design, it's where you get to be thrown into a cauldron with people you would never have selected for family! That's where the "sand in the oyster" is planted. That's where most often the irritation goes on. Luckily, you don't have to go home with them—and we know you're so glad [laughter]. But let there be no mistake, dear ones, that it is no accident that within your vocations you are thrown in with those you never would have chosen to be with. Indeed, they are there by *appointment* in your life, just like you are there by *appointment* in theirs. Some have a black energy around them that creates problems for you. Know that when this occurs, at the cellular level you have an agreement to be agitated!

Even with this attribute of vocational interaction, things may not seem to be what they actually are, for the chasm at the workplace is actually going to start closing! Watch for this. Whereas the family will look at you and decide to distance themselves, quite often those at work will look at you, the *new* you, and decide they want to be your friend! This is due to the Human search—because they are starting to see that light that you carry, you see? They are starting to see a peaceful countenance within you. You are able to share problems with those at work that you would never tell those in your family. Some of them know you better than your family does! And when they start seeing solutions in your personal life, or your peacefulness within the situation of apparent chaos, they will start asking you, "why? How?" That's when you will get to share with them your specific brand of weirdness [more laughter] about responsibility for challenge, and an overview that does not allow for victimization—an active participant in all that happens "to" them.

The irony is that it's because they don't have to go home with you and don't have to *take* your burden, that they listen to you. For they can "put it away" or "take it" as they choose. Every single day as you begin to work next to them, over and over they will see the changes in your life. Many of them will secretly desire your company due to your balanced state, and I'm telling you that this is the place where synchronicity also really shines—not necessarily in partnership potential, but in the potential of you affecting and changing others by you carrying your light!

Here's another attribute of the Human vocation in your culture, from the standpoint of a Human giving intent for the Ascension status: Many of you have had a passion all your life for a certain vocation. You schooled yourself toward it as a child, and trained for it as an adult, and now you find yourselves doing it for a living. All seems fine—until now. Don't be shocked and surprised if someday you look around and say, "*What is this? I don't choose this any longer. It no longer means anything!*" And you walk away from it. Again, not all of you will experience this, but enough of you will that it will be considered a common attribute for those who have decided to give intent to follow a new spiritual path.

Human Biology

Number five is one of our specialties, and it's called Human biology. It's one of the things that we have spoken about over and over, and my partner has told you that your DNA is either changing or allowing you to change it. You have had evidence from even those who have presented this very day [in the seminar], who represent a mainstream of belief in medicine and research, and who are discovering what makes DNA work. As humanity, we have invited you to "discover" the nine elements that cause you to age and die early (before the 950-year life span that your bodies are designed for). Last year you found three of them (although you are not aware of the implications of one of them yet). Scientists and researchers, there is one other that we invite you to discover this very year if you choose. It's one of the nine that keeps you aging, and it is what we have called the body chronograph.

The body counts the days. The body counts the light and the dark, and the body coordinates it with the magnetism of where the earth is in the solar system. We are starting to give you some of the clues as to why the science of astrology works the way it does. Astrology has to do with magnetics. It has to do with the DNA and the cellular structure recognizing the magnetics of the solar system that you were born into. That is why that science works so well.

There is part of your body that counts the revolutions of the moon through magnetics. This cannot be that unusual to accept for those of you of a gender who have had biological changes in your body all of your lives with each moon cycle—and you wonder about your connection to Gaia? Oh, dear ones, it's always been there—but that's not what we want to tell you about the chasm in DNA.

Here it is. For the first time in humanity, there are going to be remedies that present themselves for your enjoyment and illumination that will work for you—and not for the others! Listen closely, for this will explain much that may happen in this area in your potential futures: Many Humans will be able to practice taking the same chemistry and the same procedures, but you will get different results from the rest! Depending upon the intent of the one receiving it, the very essence of the remedy will be altered. This is the natural extension of my partner's message to you that *consciousness changes physics*. For the first time, there will be experiments by scientists in which they will find that the scientific method does not work without the added energy of Human *intent*. [The scientific method works by creating tests that create common, repeatable reactions to experiments or actions. The results of the experiments then allow science to create a logical model around what the reactions should always be. This will be upset greatly with the introduction of the new energy of intent—an energy that must be allowed for, since it changes the physics of the experiment.]

Here is what the potential is of Human reaction, and the chasm around it: There will be a group of you who understands this fully and will start living longer lives because of your intent when you combine it with some of the new live essence substances. But there will be others who believe they know all about God and Spirit, and they will lift their hands to heaven in prayer asking God how such a thing could be—that you can do something they cannot. For they do not understand the mechanics of pure intent and will not listen to your simple, logical explanation of the new powers. They do not understand the mechanics of the new partnership with God. They are stuck in a paradigm of waiting for God to do something *to* them and *for* them, and it will not occur.

So there will be a rift that opens up between the ones who live longer lives and the ones that do not. That rift is going to brand you as evil. There will be those of you living with love in your hearts, with pure intent, with the Christed energy of the New Age master of love—with the white light sitting upon you—but who will be called "the work of the devil," and "a product of cosmic evil," a dichotomy of the highest order. All because you understand and have accepted *intent* within Human biology. For you will be living long lives filled with abundance and a joyful countenance—working with solutions and challenge—carrying your light very high. The others will never see it that way, and this, dear ones, is perhaps the greatest chasm of all. For it will span the other four of belief, family, partnerships, and yes, even business.

We say again to you that we would not bring these things to you if they were not so. It is time to let you know, as my partner says, "that is why you call it work"—lightworkers, each one. Part of the sorrow and the sadness of the challenges before you will be these chasms between those who will not simply come along and love you for who you are. They will cling, instead, to what they are told and to their doctrines instead of looking into your eyes and seeing the love that is there.

We wish to give you an exercise that is metaphoric. Good visualization is important here. There is a crate on your lap filled with gifts—the solutions to your challenges that you have right now are there. There are energy potentials for your future that are there. There is life change. Spirit knows who you are, and we are in the *now,* you know. We see what you can do, and, to us, the potentials using these solutions are as real as your reality of time is to you.

There is a crate on your lap with the solutions to your problems, and you created it. It has your name right on it. The invitation for those receiving this message is that you can open it very easily and watch that lid pop open. Spiritual solutions from home will flow out and glisten with their diamond light and their Godliness as they attach themselves to you. They are old and have been waiting for activation through intent. They represent a friendly energy—an energy that you have expected as a healing—that you asked for when you asked for instructions on what to do next.

Perhaps there will be those of you who will have trouble getting the lid open because you are still mired in the fear of the old New Age, you see. *Own* the catalyst that will make that lid pop open! I will give it to you in two words: *self-worth*! Know who you are! Never again are you a victim of what this planet has for you in everyday life. You never were, but the perception is strong through your duality. When you *own* the fact, just as the new children do, that *you belong here*—the lid will pop open. You will actually *own* the persona of being a spiritual creation on this planet. You will be able to hold your light and say, "*I AM a piece of the whole; therefore, I AM perfect in God's sight.*"

So the visualization is yours, and this is where Spirit is enabled to partner with you, or not. For you must own the self-worth that is truly yours. Can you start to understand who the Angel is "in there"—the one with your face and your name? Can you understand that the duality is almost, as you would call it, "a sham waiting for discovery"? Claiming your self-worth is when your life begins to change—when the joy factor starts to come in—when the peace will paste itself to you because you deserve it, regardless of any of the problems that you walk into.

Oh, dear ones, this has been a joyful time. This has been a time when we have hugged you with the energy of love from home. As we retreat from this space, we're aware that there will never be another time exactly like this—where the entities will come together exactly like this. It's unique. Unique—packed and filled with a love that comes from those on the other side of the veil, as well as from me.

So we pick up our bowls, the ones we have washed your feet with, and we stand to retreat from this place where you sit. Whereas you might think that you were honored this night by the presence of such entities from the other side, we have news for you: We are the ones who were waiting for you—to hear and to read. That's what we stood in line for. It's what we wanted to do with this time.

The energy of honor that disappears through that crack in veil as we depart should not be lost on you. You *are* dearly loved.

And so it is.

Kryon

A Postscript...

Anne K. Hudec graduated with a degree in Business Management. She has been combining her organizational skills with studies of multidimensional consciousness for the past 25 years. Transpersonal and Jungian psychology led to certification in NLP and TT, and now she is an E.M.F. practitioner. Anne has been giving workshops and delivering lectures on positive thinking in the United States, Canada, and Europe. Integrating the subtle energies and knowledge gained through intuition and experience is an ongoing process within her family, community, and wherever she goes. Anne K. Hudec was present at the channelling in Indiana that you just read. Do you ever wonder if these messages are applicable to real life? Who else is reacting to what has been presented? Is it real?

Anne has asked to address the Kryon readership.

I May Not Give You What You Think You Want

A Review of the Five Chasms of the New Age, One Year After Presentation

by Anne K. Hudec

"I will certainly give you what you need. Also, I will give it to you at exactly the right time. All you are required to do is recognize it for what it is. Even with that, I will assist. Trust me."

Have you had such thoughts? They are there, those reassuring words. Deep within, you hear them. They are like an echo of the call that you have heard all your life. There is no herald announcing a well-known master or angel or someone from some other star. It simply is, and it is yours. The call is real and serves us well, for it is ordained, anointed, and we are meant to understand the workings of Spirit within our hearts and minds. Our everyday thinking, our everyday words, are to carry the divinity that we are continuing to uncover.

Spiritual beings alight with wisdom and love in many a public forum and on many a written page. Within our own being, there is a response, and soon we know who it is that speaks to us.

Out of a parade of names and countenances, we wait for the resonance that speaks to our hearts and minds. When that teacher appears, we know. We are ready, for we have waited a long time.

Eight years ago, I was like many of you—on a personal quest with Spirit. Out of the pages of the Connecting Link Magazine, Kryon beckoned. I looked for the first book, but could not find it, so I wrote to Lee. He wrote back urging me to keep asking for it so the bookstores would get it in. That's the businessman speaking. However, he did offer to send it to me, for a price, if I was unsuccessful.

Like those of you who come to a seminar for the first time, I came to "check it out" with a friend. We drove to the first Kryon seminar that Terry and Jim Coddington hosted. There were not that many of us. It was at the St. Vincent Marten House, Indianapolis, Indiana. Jan and Lee were like "babes" at this. We laughed a lot, I remember. What I liked about all of this was the honesty, simplicity, and trust in what came through from Kryon. Over the years, this bonding to the universal message had grown. Kryon has helped us all grow in universal awareness.

Those first few seminars I attended were filled with curiosity. Like a child, I would sit there and allow the love of Spirit to wash over me and heal. Yes, it felt like home. Do you know that to this day I find it very difficult to let my Kryon material go out on loan? The books and the *Kryon Quarterly* are highly treasured. There are invisible ribbons attached to every book that leaves my home. After a few days, I keep reeling them in. Once I made the grandiose offer of lending three of the books out all at the same time, to a new contact. You see, we are like the woman in Scripture, who found a needle in a haystack and joyfully told all of her friends about the find. Well, after months passed, I requested my books back. My friend brought them back with great reluctance. I told her that if she liked them so much, she should buy her own. I later found out that she was saving her money to go on an African safari. We make choices. We are constantly making choices between the physical and spiritual life we live, never realizing that once you fulfill the spiritual, the pleasure is continual—not temporary and residing forever after in memory.

How many times have you heard from Kryon that we are all known by name? That we are all known in all our multifractal connections? That we all come together for a purpose? The right components are present for every channel given by Kryon for the very entities sitting in those chairs. We are responsible for the messages given and received. Oh, Spirit knows well in advance who will come to what seminar and read the message. You see, Spirit knows our weaknesses and strengths and projects upon the probable actions that we humans will make. Once we are present, the teaching is given.

On March 14, 1998, a channelling was delivered in Indianapolis that made us sit up. It was about the "Five Chasms of the New Age." What was different, at least for me, was that we were being asked to grow up and face the responsibilities that went along with the designation of what a "lightworker" is asked to deal with. As is customary for me, I started to take notes. I knew by now that sooner or later the channelling would come out in print. So a few notes would do for now. After a while, my friends and I stopped writing. We could not integrate what was being asked of us. This was not going to be easy. We were being challenged to go ahead and expect to find obstacles. When you talk about business and outside involvement, you say to yourself, "I'll deal with that when it arrives," but when it comes to family and personal belief structures, responses have a way of holding old hidden patterns of behavior. Is more change coming? Well, at that point, I stopped writing. It was too much. It must have been too much for Lee as well. His tape machine did not pick it up. They searched and found someone whose tape recorder had captured it all.

With great care, I picked up that gauntlet. You see, I had gone through the "implant" changes long before Kryon talked about them. I thought, <u>I am well into this transformation now</u>. <u>No turning back</u>. It is a spiritual passion in the very marrow of your bones. Also, I had confirmation by this time that I was smack in the middle of my contract. Only I was hoping for ease. There was no letting up here. More self-development required.

"We tell you again that there is not one challenge in your life that is not known to us." Okay, I had plenty of challenges, so it was nice to know that Kryon knew them, too. Certainly there was help offered here. "There is nothing in your life that is unsolvable-nothing!" Big inward sigh of relief. I listened more intently.

"There is no *time* with Spirit. For us, the experience of what you call time is circular. There are some of you who carry the seeds of planetary change. But before you facilitate the planet, you must change yourselves, and that is why there is so much love in this message." Some of you who have been with Kryon for a length of time know what that means. The heart strings of time get a workout here. The love energy seeps through you, and you are left crying like a wimp.

No sense in reminding yourself that we have been put on notice and have been told that love is a science.

These energies know their stuff, they know our magnificence and they know that with some coaching, we will do it. "Relax and know you are fine and all is well." Oh, sure! "There is a potential for humanity that has never existed before. The seeds (the potential, if we pick up the gauntlet) of that graduation are carried in those who are receiving this message, wanting to know more about who they are. If you could see the brilliance of the angel that sits inside, you would be astonished at the Divinity that is present in the chair where you sit!" If you and I allow it, the glow and light will come from wherever we are. Wow! Such enticement

When we give intent within the ascension status to take on the five chasms opening up before us, that intent will be honored to the letter. Kryon gave us the chasms in an overview. For each of us they would develop individually. We would not know what we faced until we found ourselves in the situations, but we were assured that in each case we would have the love that is our light.

Eager, cheerful spiritual seekers, were not so cheerful after this particular delivery. Should we wish to continue application of spiritual principles and decide to take the ascension status, our very beliefs, family, relationships, business, and human biology would be stressed. Pardon me. We were told that we would be faced with rifts. However, in the next breath of words came a promise of love and freedom from victimization. We were left to make our choices. Blessedly, we were given some time.

Have you heard the phrase "Misery loves company"? Well, I happen to be blessed with friends who have paths similar to mine. Over the years we have walked parallel paths, and when situations became too cumbersome, we would talk for hours and get clarity. When that did not work, we would go to "workshops" for new tools and information. Truly, this is a good thing, because it enabled us to be open and receptive. We were on a continual path of evolving. My friends and I did not talk about the five chasms for weeks. We did not want to look at them. Let's see what else we can busy ourselves with. There are plenty of other "worldly" activities to engage ourselves in. No, we did not want to talk about beliefs. We were already considered "far out" in our thinking. But you see, "far out" still did not feel like I had "made it." There was no turning back. We did not like the limited scope of thought out of which we had emerged.

There really was no other way but onward. I said yes to it all. Well, that is all that Spirit and the guides needed. The requirement was to step out of my comfort zone and stop running the show. I found myself in situations that I had never known to be a part of my imagination and vision. All of it was a tug of mind and heart. Thanks for Spirit and friends who had broad perception. I evaluated, took risks, evaluated again, and regrouped my resources. Throughout all of this, I was developing courage and trust—trust in the help that would come when I walked myself into a corner or wall of resistance.

I found my belief system present in all the chasms. This is what my decisions are based on. This is my action base. No wonder Kryon spoke of "belief " first. Unless I change some basic assumptions, I will continue to go around in circles. I wanted a spiral staircase. That meant that I would need to ascend to new belief structures. To do that, I would not only listen politely to advice, but incorporate it as well. There is internal knowledge, and there is external knowledge. There is heart and there is head. There is subjectivity and there is objectivity. There is spring. I met myself within. I extended my horizons. There is winter. I watched interactions in relationships. I saw how compatibility worked and how to release my guard. I spoke of secret longings that were not only my own. I had the company of many on the Kryon message board by this season. When I touched my heart of hearts, I felt my consciousness shift. To my surprise, I found the belief in myself grow as I released the old and embraced the *now*—the now that had "no judgment" and unconditional love as the springboard for my decision making. The solution to carry the light as high as we can proved to be correct.

Unconditional love is the transformative factor that has not been in our equations up till now. That is the part of the chasm message that was difficult to incorporate. That is what we are all asked to incorporate into every chasm that we encounter. Until now, we have had plenty of love based on conditions—conditions that we set up ourselves, or that others set up for us.

Robert Kegan, in his latest book, *In Over Our Heads*, points out that "what we take as subject and object are not necessarily fixed for us. They are not permanent. They can change. In fact, transforming our epistemologies, making what was subject into object so that we can 'have it' [Kryon's win/win] rather than 'be had' by it—this is the most powerful way I know to conceptualize the growth of the mind. It is a way of conceptualizing the growth of the mind that is as faithful to the self-psychology of the West as to the 'wisdom literature' of the East." This is all fine, you think, until you come Home with Kryon and have your heart swept up in unconditional love.

Many of us have studied psychology and the phenomenology of consciousness into nonordinary states. We have come to realize that no amount of LSD, holotropic breathing, hypnosis (or the inability to be hypnotized), shamanic experiences, rituals, rites of passage, or intense bodywork will disclose the moral, cultural, linguistic (NLP), and syntactical structures in which and through which subjective experiences arise. Growth always involves a process of differentiation of the emergence from one way of looking at life and oneself into another way of perceiving oneself. We are asked to let go of limiting concepts and see ourselves as co-creators with Spirit. This is news, indeed. What happens? When the subjective pole (us) undergoes differentiation through the de-embedding of the self from the organized structures of the past, it is a leap of faith and trust in Spirit, by which it is done. Do we know enough about co-creation with Spirit? Frankly, no. It is a "fly-by-your-seat" scenario. Standing outside of organized structures of the past, we are asked to love everything that we are served. This can be done only through a higher level of organizing structures. When we experience the love of Spirit via synchronistic events, we begin to learn more about higher levels of organizing structures within which our lives become embedded.

Do the chasms exist? Yes they do. Does shift happen? Yes it does. Are we responsible? Yes.

Once we agree to co-create with Spirit, we have all the assistance we require. We are never forced to do anything we do not want to do. Never. We have free choice in all we do. If we set intent, we will be guided to our destination. De-embedding ourselves from old structures does exact changes within all the chasms listed—there is no question about that. But, oh, the blessings gathered along the way enable us to grow in mysterious ways. How can it be any other way since everything really happens only in the now, and all we need do is fall in love with the Divine within us all.

Ann K. Hudec

Science

Chapter Seven

From Lee Carroll...

In previous books, this was the chapter where I presented scientific news that Kryon told us to "watch for." In Kryon Book Six, *Partnering with God*, we covered the gamma ray issue, the magnetic grid shift, faster-than-light physics, crop circles, healing principles, and other items that Kryon gave a "heads up" to in the past years. I have tried to show that many times Kryon gives us clues to subjects that we then find are relevant up to three years later, or that become the center of attention (as Kryon indicated they could).

I am not a scientist (not even close), so these science-oriented chapters are usually almost last in the Kryon books as my personal postscript. We never wish anyone to "hang their spiritual hat" on the physics and science that is presented along with the profound love energy in the Kryon work. I only present the science portion because I get excited when Kryon tells us that there are potentials for discovery—then it happens! It's my "man brain" acting up again, and I feel I would be remiss if I didn't share it with you.

With this book, the science chapter will be slightly different. Because Kryon channelled specific science these last two years, the main information will be within the energy transcriptions called "The Cosmic Lattice," instead of the kind of discussions presented in Kryon Book Six. Before we present the Kryon channelling, however, I wish to share one startling validation regarding nuclear waste. Then, after the transcriptions, I want you to see how "the Cosmic Lattice" energy information is being implemented by a new process that is really profound (the EMF balancing technique). This technique is so powerful that even private industry and NASA wanted to find out more. We wanted you to know about it, too.

Nuclear Waste

One of the most unusual potentials that Kryon gave us regarding our science was covered within an answer to a nuclear waste question in Kryon Book Two, *Don't Think Like a Human*, page 223, published in 1994. Kryon responded to the following question about nuclear waste.

From Kryon Book Two: Don't Think Like a Human

Question: *In previous writings, you said that our nuclear waste was one of the biggest dangers we currently have. The stuff seems indestructible, and it is volatile forever! What can we do about it?*

Answer: Your active atomic waste is indeed the largest danger you face. You have already seen how a vast portion of land can be poisoned for lifetimes simply by one atomic accident. Think of the tragedy of losing part of your country to such a condition—simply by ignoring items buried deep underground that are building to a critical point in their activity. Right now as you read this, you have a small city on your own American continent whose name begins with "H" that is prime for this condition. Disaster will indeed happen if you ignore it, since it is simple basic physics. You don't have to wait for a catastrophe before acting, however.

The real answer (for elimination) should be obvious. It must be neutralized. I spoke of this in earlier channellings, but now I will expand on it. There are many ways of neutralizing this waste, but the one that is currently within your technology is simple and available now. You should immediately turn to Earth biology! Look for the microorganisms you already know about that can devour these active substances, and make them harmless. Develop them using your science to increase their number and efficiency, and let them eat your waste!

You might ask why this is not being done now, since these organisms have already been discovered. Look to your world governments for the answers. Demand that the research be complete and that the process begin! Understand the Earth politics of why this has not been exposed fully to you or funded properly. An organism of this sort is small, easy to transport and grow, and doesn't care if it feeds on a weapon or a waste dump.

It's time for Earth's leaders to put away fear of technologies that might change the weapon balance. It is the irony of science that quite often new discoveries can be used for peace or war, and it is your enlightenment that determines which. Right now you are poised on some of the finest environmental tools ever developed—including the one I speak of to reduce your nuclear waste. You are also prime to receive a great deal of technology useful to increase your life spans, enhance disease control, and affect your health in general. Do not let the fear in the few hold back the good for the many.

***

Lee again: There are two main points here to look at that Kryon mentioned: (1) There is an organism that existed when this was channelled (1994) that science knew about, but that was not being recognized (or that was being sequestered). It could actually eat nuclear waste. (2) There is a town that we should start looking at beginning with "H" that is potent for nuclear waste trouble (subsequently identified as Hanford, Washington).

In Kryon Book Six, I reported the closest thing I could to what Kryon said to look for. We presented a science article that showed that certain special-bred plants were being used at the Chernobyl nuclear accident site in Russia to clean the water of cesium 137 and strontium 90 (potent radioactive stuff). It was biology, and I thought it was what Kryon was talking about. Although it fit the bill, I should have waited for the mother-lode—exactly what Kryon was talking about—a microorganism that could eat nuclear waste, which was already known.

On the facing page is an article from *Science News*, volume 154, page 376. [Metaphysically, the date of this publication is very fun: December 12, 1998—12:12]. Take a look at what has been discovered: a microorganism that eats nuclear waste—one that was know about from the 1950s, rediscovered in 1988, and only now being recognized for what it can do. Did you also notice the photo? It's the Hanford Nuclear Reservation.[1]

"Look for the micro organisms you already know about that can devour these active substances [nuclear waste], and make them harmless. Develop them using your science to increase their number and efficiency, and let them eat your waste!"

Kryon - 1994 - Kryon Book II

Meet the Superbug

Radiation-resistant bacteria may clean up the nation's worst waste sites

By JOHN TRAVIS

Hanford Nuclear Reservation in Richland, Wash., is one of many sites that contain radioactive waste. C. Anderson/Spokesman-Review

If a massive nuclear war ever blanketed the planet with radioactive fallout, cockroaches, despite all the jokes, would be goners. A bacterium known as *Deinococcus radiodurans* might survive, however. Its name, which means "strange berry that withstands radiation," indicates the reason that the microbe fascinates scientists. Labeled the world's toughest bacterium by *The Guinness Book of World Records*, *D. radiodurans* shrugs off doses of radiation many thousands of times stronger than those that would kill a person.

"I had difficulty believing anything like this could exist," says John R. Battista of Louisiana State University in Baton Rouge, recalling his introduction to the microbe in 1988.

Believe it or not, *D. radiodurans* does exist—and in some unusual places. Pinkish in color and giving off the smell of rotten cabbages, the bacteria were originally isolated in the 1950s from tins of meat that had spoiled despite supposedly sterilizing irradiation. Since then, they've showed up in elephant and llama feces, in irradiated haddock and duck, and in granite from Antarctica's Dry Valleys, the place on Earth thought to most closely resemble the surface of Mars.

Reviving the idea that comets seeded planets with the precursors of life, or even life itself, scientists have had fun speculating that only a radiation-tolerant bacterium such as *D. radiodurans* could survive interstellar journeys. "This is the kind of organism that could do something like that," muses Marvin Frazier, director of the Department of Energy's (DOE) Microbial Genome Program in Germantown, Md., which funded the just-completed effort to sequence all of *D. radiodurans'* genes.

In more earthly matters, investigators have crafted an explanation for why the bacterium evolved its immunity to radiation. They propose that it's the byproduct of skills needed to survive a lack of water. Scientists have also established that the microbe doesn't simply shield its DNA from the radiation. It instead has an unprecedented ability to repair genetic damage.

While the basic biology of *D. radiodurans* has proved fascinating, DOE's interest in the bacterium stems from a very practical issue. The agency hopes that the microbe, after appropriate genetic manipulation, might help detoxify the thousands of toxic-waste sites nationwide that include radioactive materials. Using microbes as a cleanup crew is a strategy known as bioremediation. A recent study, in which *D. radiodurans* was engineered to degrade an organic toxin common to such waste sites, offers encouraging results, says Frazier.

Scientists usually measure radiation in units called rads, and a dose of 500 to 1000 rads is lethal to the average person. In contrast, depending upon conditions for its growth, *D. radiodurans* thrives after exposures of up to 1.5 million rads. Cool or freeze the microbe, and it may survive 3.0 million rads.

Bacteria that form hard capsules called spores can withstand large amounts of radiation but not as much as can *D. radiodurans*, which doesn't form a spore. "It is supreme in its radiation resistance," says Michael J. Daly of the Uniformed Services University of the Health Sciences in Bethesda, Md.

Working with his colleague Kenneth W. Minton, Daly has for many years sought to explain how the bacterium's DNA-repair system accounts for its exceptional hardiness. "I was interested in DNA repair, so why not study it in an organism that does it better than anything else?" he asks.

Indeed, *D. radiodurans* faces quite a challenge when it is hit with millions of rads. Literally shattering the bacterium's genetic material into hundreds of fragments, the radiation creates complete breaks in the microbe's double-stranded molecules of DNA.

A double-strand break is the most difficult kind of DNA damage to repair. The well-studied bacterium *Escherichia coli*, for example, usually can't survive more than two or three double-strand breaks. Yet within a few hours, *D. radiodurans* begins to stitch its thoroughly fractured DNA together, and it eventually resurrects a genome free of mutations.

376 SCIENCE NEWS, VOL. 154 DECEMBER 12, 1998

[1] *Science News* Magazine; John Travis; "Meet the Superbug—Radiation-resistant bacteria may clean up the nation's worst waste sites"; Volume 154; Number 24; December 12, 1998, page 376; (ISSN 0036-8423); Published weekly by Science Service, Washington, DC.; [http://www.sciserv.org]

The organism is known as *Deinococcus radiodurans*. This name means "strange berry that withstands radiation." Is it new? No. But here is a quote from the article: "'I had difficulty believing anything like this could exist,' says John R. Battista of Louisiana State University in Baton Rouge. Scientists are impressed—newly impressed."

Here is something else that the article reported: This organism doesn't just shield itself from radioactivity, it has the ability to *repair genetic damage*! How about that, humanity? Interested? This bacteria can store its genetic code up to ten layers deep. Like rows of shark's teeth, when the top layer is destroyed or damaged by radiation, it simply moves the next layer up to take its place. It's being worked with and manipulated by Michael Daly, Kenneth Minton, and their associates from universities in Maryland and Minnesota. They are modifying the bug, attempting to make it even more powerful.

Another interesting portion of this article discusses the fact that if there ever was a microorganism that could withstand natural space travel, being transmitted from place to place via comets or asteroids—this is it! It's that strong—a real survivor.

The bottom line of this conservative science article? "Using microbes as a cleanup crew is a strategy known as bioremediation. A recent study, in which D. radiodurans was engineered to degrade an organic toxin common to such waste sites, offers encouraging results."

Here is a quote from another magazine, *Nature Biotechnology*, October 1998 (translated from the French language): "Deinococcus Version 98 [after being altered] can oxidize Toluene and eat it. Michael Daly and his team are hoping that this bacteria will soon be able to swallow and oxidize radioactive Toluene and Trichloroethylene. The *Deinococcus radiodurans* could then phagocytize dangerous radio-toxic products (such as Uranium) and consume them before they penetrate and pollute forever the ground where they are being disposed of."

Personally, I was thrilled to see in main-stream science magazines exactly what Kryon told us to look for, but there is far more here than meets the eye. The thought of safe, productive ways to clean the planet of nuclear waste is enthralling, but...how does *Deinococcus radiodurans* do it? This is rejuvenation at a very high level! Is there more here for us to learn? If a single-cell organism can do something like this, how about a multicelled organism called the Human Being?

I'm happy to be able to share this with the readership.

The Changing Consciousness of Science...

"In 1977 Nobel physicist Steven Weinberg of the University of Texas sounded a famous note of despair: the more the universe has become comprehensible through cosmology, he wrote, the more it seems pointless. But now the very science that 'killed' God is, in the eyes of believers, restoring faith. Physicists have stumbled on signs that the cosmos is custom-made for life and consciousness." [1]

[1] *Newsweek* magazine, Sharon Begley, "Science Finds God"; July 20, 1998; page 46; ISSN 0028-9604; published weekly by Newsweek, Inc., New York, NY.

America Online - keyword, Newsweek (archives)

[http://www.newsweek-special.com]

"The Cosmic Lattice" Parts One and Two

Each Channelled in New Hampshire, one year apart

The Kryon Writings, Inc.

PMB 422
1155 Camino Del Mar
Del Mar, California 92014
[www.kryonqtly.com]

"The Cosmic Lattice"
Live Channelling
New Hampshire

These live channellings, given one year apart have been edited with additional words and thoughts to allow clarification and better understanding of the written word. In addition, they have been combined together for ease of reading.

From the writer...

I am now approaching my 10th year of public channelling, and yet I am constantly surprised when Spirit decides that it is "time" to release new information. The following seems to be scientific information, but it is spiritual in the highest sense. It is the beginning of the revelation of how cosmic energy relates both to physics and to God. Those who have been facilitating with metaphysical energy work, and also those studying alternate energy, will find explanations here that will absolutely coincide with what they have been observing and learning for years.

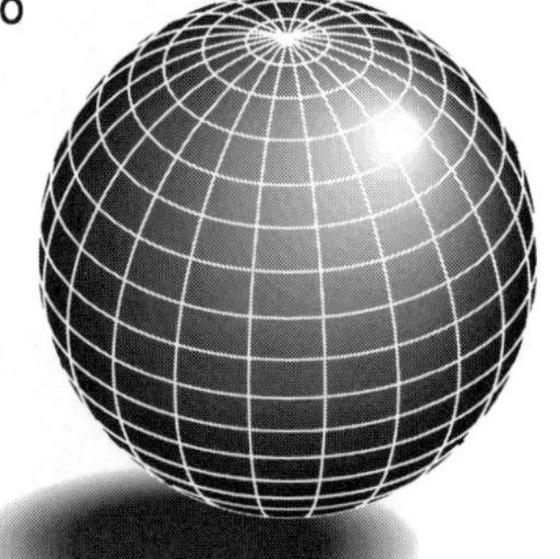

Greetings, dear ones, I am Kryon of magnetic service. Oh, it is good to be back in this energy before you. This night is going to be different from the last, for in this place there are going to be changed hearts, with permission. Some of you will see for the first time what the love of God truly is, and how it "shakes hands" with the spiritual part within you that is a piece of the whole. Tonight there will be revealed some profound principles that you are ready for, and the assemblage of Humans that is here is perfect to hear it.

Oh, family—oh, dear ones—we gather this night together, just the few of us, to feel the love of *home*. And we say to you that some will have a difficult time for a few moments understanding that the voice you are hearing (and reading) is no longer the consciousness of my partner who has spoken to you for these many hours (during the seminar). Oh no. For now you are hearing the voice and the consciousness of the one who loves you dearly—that being of the *God-essence* itself—the one who knows all about your life—the one who loves you more dearly than any in the universe—the one who knows your innermost secrets—the one who has no judgment around you. Oh, listen to this: Blessed are the Human Beings who will sacrifice themselves as entities of the universe and willingly come to this planet accepting the frailty of biology—hiding the magnificence of themselves, their Merkabahs, and their colors in order to stand with other Humans and try to remember who they really are. There is no greater love than this—that you would sacrifice yourselves to such a degree as to come here and make a change in the very fabric of the universe! You heard it right. For what you do here on this planet in the journey itself will change the way things work in a place that you have no conception of.

We use this time (pause) to wash your feet. It is the theme and the way of Kryon that between the teaching is the loving. So, again, we speak of things many of you have heard before—that figuratively we are here this night to reacquaint this energy with yours and to reach out our hands and take each Human foot one at a time, and wash it with our tears of joy. Walking the aisles of this assemblage right now, and for those reading this, are entities you know. Before this time of teaching is over, you will feel them as they encompass you and put their arms around you, as they tell you they love you. The spiritual entourage here is many times the number of Humans in this room, and as we continue this teaching session this night, we are going to tell you that this group will become even closer to you. There will be those of you who give permission at this time to go forward in your lives with pure intent and to understand what is being presented. Tonight's message may seem at first to be impersonal, but as we proceed, you will understand why it is being given at this time and what it means.

We're going to tell you some things that have never been told before. We are going to broach a subject, my partner, which is partially scientific and then later personal. Because of what is to come, I want you, my partner, to be very careful as you translate this. Go as slow as you need to, for this information is new. The transcribing process will be complete, and we can even see right *now* those who are reading this. It will be their "now," but it is in your future as you hear this. For this message will be profound in science, but like so many other science items we have brought to you, dear ones, whereas it may start off seeming universal, it becomes individual very soon—so stay with the message.

We are here to reveal for the first time, some of the ways things work that we have never told any group before. It is indeed appropriate that it be revealed in this place, for the consciousness here is one of love—one of desire for knowledge—one that is serious. I am speaking to lightworkers who are holding their light high! I am speaking to you, dear ones [reading and hearing this]. I know your heart and the purity of it. I know why you're here. This message is for you personally, as well as for the scientists—as well as for the metaphysicians all over the world. So it is that this message will go far. Let it begin.

The Cosmic Lattice

We wish to tell you this night of a specific kind of energy. We wish to tell you this night what some of you will think of as an object, but it is not—it is a phenomenon. It is something so common that it is around all of you, yet it is so mysterious that few know of it. It is the missing piece of energy that you have been looking for, for so long. It is the energy of love. It is the energy of Spirit. It is the energy of the universe, and we are speaking this night of something in English that we will call "the Cosmic Lattice." I will dole out this information carefully and slowly to my partner so that you will understand what it is and how it works.

Before this meeting is finished this night, you will understand how it applies to you.

It is very common in the teachings of Kryon that we start with the big and go down to the small so that you will understand the overview and how it affects the Human heart. The Cosmic Lattice, dear ones, is the ***common denominator of the unified energy source of the universe***. The common denominator—meaning that all things emanate from The Cosmic Lattice. It is difficult to define this all at once, so we will tell you its many attributes slowly this night. The Cosmic Lattice is everywhere. It is found throughout the universe. Everything that you can see and everything you cannot see contains the Lattice. From the smallest particles of your physics, and from the electron haze forward, the Cosmic Lattice is present. Those of you in physics will begin to understand and recognize this principle, and it will start to make sense to you.

The Size of the Lattice

Let us first begin with its size. This is only appropriate, even before we define how it works and what it is. The Cosmic Lattice is ***the largest energy you have ever conceived of***. It encompasses the entire universe and more. It is present everywhere. There is no place that you can conceive of—no matter what the dimension—that is without the Lattice. The Cosmic Lattice is perhaps what you could call the *consciousness of God,* and yet it is *physics,* and it is *energy,* and it contains conscious *love*. Therefore, what we are telling you is that it is pervasive everywhere and encompasses the entire universe, including all dimensions. Can you conceive of something so large? As far as you can see in the skies—as far as any astronomer can gather light over ours on a photographic plate—the Cosmic Lattice is already there. And yet it has one single consciousness all at the same time—always at the same time. Distance is nothing to the Cosmic Lattice, and this, my partner, is where things get difficult to explain.

Pretend for a moment that your hand was bigger than the universe itself, and as you outstretch your hand, all of the known matter that exists can fit within your palm in a small ball. You are, therefore, immense! You have the dimensions of God! Within that ball in your hand there are billions of stars, and within that ball there are distances that seem insurmountable and immense to those entities that live there. Within that ball, which is the universe, it would seem to take forever to get from one end to the other to an entity traveling within it, yet that ball rests easily in your single hand! The Cosmic Lattice is like this, for there is truly no distance that is insurmountable between your thumb and a finger, and the consciousness of your hand is singular. The cellular structure is of one, interlaced with a consciousness that reacts as one. And although within that ball that could be called the universe within your hand, there seems to be billions of light years of travel, and space and time to conquer, as you hold it in your hand, that is not so. Everything there—the billions of stars—is in your "now."

So you get an idea of the size of this energy, but you also get an idea of the *unification* of the Cosmic Lattice. The most distant part of this Lattice knows exactly what the part that is here in this room is doing. The part that is between the cells of your biology, which we have called love, knows what is happening 11 billion light years away! The Cosmic Lattice has no time, and we'll talk about that in a moment.

Shape - Order - Luminescence

The first attribute is the size, and the size is immense. It is the biggest energy known. It is the biggest energy that exists. Let us talk about its shape, and this, my partner, is even more difficult. It **is not a grid**. The Cosmic Lattice **has symmetry**, however, but it is not a grid. If its shape could be revealed to you, it would astound you, for it would give away something, and it would have to do with what you call Human time. There's evidence of the Cosmic Lattice already, and we're going to tell you how to look for this evidence. Your astronomers look from your Earth in a way that seems as though they had one eye closed. They have not really yet seen a stereoscopic view of what is around your planet that is clear. Instead, they look from Earth in a monocular way, with no depth perception of what is surrounding you. Therefore, you have not been able to see the *strings of darkness*. This is one of the attributes of the Cosmic Lattice that is there for you to see anytime you wish. The word *darkness* is interpreted here by my partner to mean "lack of light," as opposed to any spiritual meaning. It is as though you looked into the starry sky at night and saw that many of the star groupings had narrow "highways" of nothing between them but a clear pattern.

Some years ago we told you that your Big Bang—wasn't. We told you that it does not make sense to have a universe that explodes from one central creative point, not to be evenly dispersed. We told you to look for the clumping effect as evidence that there was no original point of explosion. Now there's more, and now we will tell you what that is. For there will come a time when you are able to put your "eyes" and your telescopes at very different and faraway places. One may even be on another planet, and together as they look at the universe in a stereoscopic way, like your two eyes look out upon the world, they will finally see the three-dimensional image before them. What they will see are the highways of seeming blackness between the clumps of star matter. Straight lines of darkness will be evident, giving the universe *direction*—giving it *symmetry*—allowing for a mystery to develop of how such a thing could be—like seeming highways with apparent nothingness between the clumps. Look for it. It is going to happen.

The Cosmic Lattice has no visible light, even though it is the essence of light. The Lattice energy is in a *null* balance, and we are going to tell you about that right now. For the energy is in a balanced state called the null balance, where the polarity of its most powerful attributes is balanced to zero. The null energy has fantastic power, but in its common resting state, it seems to be void due to the zero balance. It's when you unbalance the polarity that the power is released, you see. Your astronomers have looked at the universe and the cosmos, with their ways of measuring the energy there, and they look to the skies and they measure the whole energy. What they have noted, with some frustration, is that there is far less matter and light than there is measured energy! This is a known situation with your scientists. Ask your scientists why this should be, and they will postulate all manner of things, including the existence of "dark matter." Dear ones, what they are seeing is *void energy*. It is the Cosmic Lattice that they are measuring. The Cosmic Lattice energy is everywhere, and when I am done with this message, you will know what triggers it, and you'll know how it's used. You'll know how it reacts to other energy, and you'll know why it exists.

As mentioned, in a nulled form, this incredible active energy would appear to you to be at a zero measurement, yet this Lattice is potent at all points and in all areas. We have referred to it in the very small particles of the atom. When we talked about the distance of the nucleus to the electron haze, we were speaking of the Cosmic Lattice principle. When we gave you the working formula for the distance of the electron haze elements from the nucleus, we were speaking about the interaction of energy from the Cosmic Lattice. When we were talking about the gamma ray activity from 11 billion light years away, we were talking about The Cosmic Lattice. From the largest to the smallest, this energy source is immense, and it's quiet. It is only when it is called upon and destabilized in designed ways that it provides power. It is the common denominator and the stabilizer of all energy and matter everywhere—the Cosmic Lattice. And when the physics is known by Humans, all manner of things will open up for you—not just in communication, but unlimited power everywhere—*unlimited power*!

Time-Speed

Let me tell you about the Lattice energy. It responds to *time*. Here is something else for your scientists to look at: When you find an event in the universe that you know has timealtering potential, observe how its physical displayed energy bends. Everything in the universe seems to spin, does it not? According to the laws of physics, some particles spinning off should be at right angles to the spin. Some should be perpendicular to the spin. That's normal physics. Watch, however, for the ones that are neither! For those are the ones that line up with the symmetry of the Cosmic Lattice. They're the ones that "point" to the Lattice-patterned energy, and we're talking about events such as spewing black holes and other phenomena in the universe that seem to pour forth huge energy in a stream. Watch for those streams to point in a similar direction, but not necessarily to physically align themselves to the spin of the object creating them (as you might expect). Your scientists will ask, "*Why is such a thing existing*?" They eventually must postulate that there is another force that aligns this "pointing" —like a giant cosmic magnet. They are seeing the energy pointing and bending to the symmetry of the Cosmic Lattice.

You already know that time is relative. Your scientists have told you so, and we tell you that this particular fact is going to play a large part in knowing about the attributes of the Cosmic Lattice. Dear ones, spiritual things on this planet are related to the Lattice. The time frame that you are currently in is going to eventually change (as given in past channellings), but is related to the Cosmic Lattice. We have told you that the energy of this cosmic common denominator is related to time, and now we're telling you that time is also changing for *you*. What do you think that means? Let me tell you. It means that the Cosmic Lattice responds to Human consciousness! When my partner told you that consciousness changes physics [during the seminar prior to the channelling], that was an understatement. All things are possible with the intent of the Humans on this planet right now. For you have literal control of the Lattice, which is universal. Again, we tell you that the Lattice on the other side of the universe knows your name! We have told you that your consciousness has uplifted this planet into a vibration that is new. This consciousness has actually "pulled" upon the Lattice to enable the Earth to begin a time shift—one that will be relative to you, but obvious to others (off planet). What this means is that you may see or feel nothing unusual, but eventually look to certain attributes of the cosmos to appear to slow down. This will indicate that you are moving (or vibrating) in a different time frame. We have also given you the physics for this in the past. Now we are giving you the actual mechanical reason behind it, in that the Cosmic Lattice is doing the work. Your consciousness, therefore, has changed the physics of your own reality.

Oh, dear ones, listen to this carefully: You are already aware, many of you, of the communication between Humans that seems to surpass any speed known to man. Identical twins, twin flames, soul mates, one on one side of the Earth, the other on the other side, often have instant communications that have been reported and witnessed. Perhaps one twin is in an anxiety mode, and instantly the other one feels it! They might call each other and say, "*What happened a moment or two ago?*" They both realize they felt the same thing at the same exact time. What does that do to your physical idea of time? What does that say about the power of Human consciousness to transmute all distance and time? I'll tell you what makes it happen: It's the mechanics of the Cosmic Lattice. You are interconnected instantly and are using the Lattice. It is your Spiritual power source—and it's also using physics.

If we were able to take a Human right now and magically transport him to the other side of the known universe—incredibly far away—an unimaginable distance to you—we are here to say that the Lattice would allow for a common communication that is instant with him—no matter the distance! Long after this channelling is over, some of you are going to be putting together the pieces and the parts of this information, and you're going to realize why some of the things are the way they are in physics. The common denominator of this Lattice energy is without light only because it is null energy and null time.

We have spoken of *now* time, a multidimensional spot where Spirit is, and where all the things in the past and the potentials of the future are in one place—that is *now* time. The Cosmic Lattice is not in *now* time; it is in *null* time. *Null* time, dear ones, is time that equals zero, whereas *now* time has motion in a circle. The Cosmic Lattice is in a constantly balanced state, and in that balanced energy, it is potentially ready to receive input for release of energy, and that input, dear ones, is available to the Human consciousness. It "sees" all time as zero—never moving—even though many time frames exist within its energy. That is why, no matter what time frame is your reality, communication is instant between all entities that know of the Lattice. This is a difficult concept for you to understand, since you don't even yet believe that there are many time frames present as you look through your instruments at "impossible physics" being displayed in the cosmos (as stated before in previous channellings). Time is like the air you breathe. You watch incredible storms, with wind blowing many directions at many speeds, yet you breathe it gently and normally, even in the midst of a great storm. Therefore, the breathing air in your lungs is nominally at rest, even while the air around you is in turmoil. The Cosmic Lattice is like this.

The Cosmic Lattice, dear ones, is what allows the mechanics for co-creation, for synchronicity, for what we have called love. The Cosmic Lattice contains the mechanics that allow for miracles on the planet. It responds to physics—it responds to consciousness. So we begin to see the meld between what has been placed in the universe for you.

The Cosmic Lattice is not God! But, as we have said before, God (Spirit) uses naturally occurring physics for the mechanics of miracles. Some of you wish to separate physics from God. You say, "*Don't make science into God. Don't take away the magic!*" We say, "Your time is limited where you can think in this fashion. For when you eventually discover some of the physical mechanics of Spirit, it's not going to diminish the magnificence of it at all, for we have told you for eight years now that the elegance of God resides in the very cells of your body!" God absolutely uses the common physicalness of the energy around the cosmos for power—just like you are being invited to do. Understanding the physics of Spirit does not void out the love! Instead, it gives a beautiful symmetry and logic to all things, and these things will become clearer to you as you move into the vibration where you can also use the energy of the Lattice. The Lattice, therefore, is not God. It is one of the most powerful tools of Spirit that exists today, and contains much of what you have called unexplainable magic—the way of God. Does it shock you that Spirit uses the very physics it created to enable the way things work? Why create tools and then ignore them? No. This is a revelation to you of *how* Spirit works in the cosmos.

So we are telling you how it works. But that's not all, for the Cosmic Lattice is now responding to something it never did before on your planet. Energy is being created, and time is being altered—all through Human intent. There is no greater power in the universe than Human intent and love, and we have told you this fact repeatedly since Kryon arrived. This is the night we finally have to correlate and equate it with the physics of love!

Oh, dear ones, now do you understand that when you give intent it is not some mysterious energy that seems to fly into the ethers and somehow manifests something you want or need? Now can you see that it has symmetry and size and purpose and consciousness, and that there is a mechanical attribute of physics and love around it called Human intent? Now you begin to understand *why* New Age energy facilitators can do so much! They are "tapping in" to the Cosmic Lattice. There is no longer mystery regarding this; instead, it will someday be replaced with good solid science—God given and Universal.

I will not be the only channel to bring forth this principle. It will be known by many names and will be the source of tremendous power—actual physical power—that you can use for travel and energy—power that you can use for life sustenance. The resources of your planet that you have been using up to create power have a limit. There is no cleaner power anywhere than the Lattice. This is physics, and it is known even by the enlightened who travel from here to there within the cosmos—in fact, they often "ride" the Lattice strings.

Each one of you carries a light, dear ones, that is seen clearly by every entity in the universe. There are entities so far away that you cannot even conceive that they might know of your light. However, they know what is taking place here, and they are preparing for their changes because of what you are doing. They are sending you love, which is instant for what you have done. Your task on this planet is universal, and it has very little to do with Earth, did you know that? For what happens here will affect all of us, even Kryon.

Is it any wonder that we come and sit at your feet and love you so? Is it any wonder that we now marvel that the veil has lifted, and we can give you this information? We tell you that the physicists already know of part of the Lattice. The ones who are discovering that consciousness changes their experiments are the ones who know something's up. It's coming. Look for it. There is so much more we could say, and there will be a time for more information...but now we just want to sit at your feet and love you.

(pause)

And so it is.

Kryon

(end of part one)

"The Cosmic Lattice"
Part II
(One Year Later)

Greetings, dear ones! Last year at this time we presented, energy information that was new. We're going to do it again. For the next few moments, we will be talking about physics, energy, shapes, time, and mechanics. Within this process, don't be surprised when the information wraps itself back around, right to your biology and your Human heart. There is only one reason why we want to give you this: Spirit doesn't care about physics. Spirit cares that you understand how to stay here for as long as you can—in those bodies that sit in front of us—that are reading this—the ones you carry as angels pretending to be Humans. That's why, through the explanation and the transcriptions of this information, there will be knowledge developed, and it will dovetail with other knowledge that did not come from this stage, and it will verify itself.

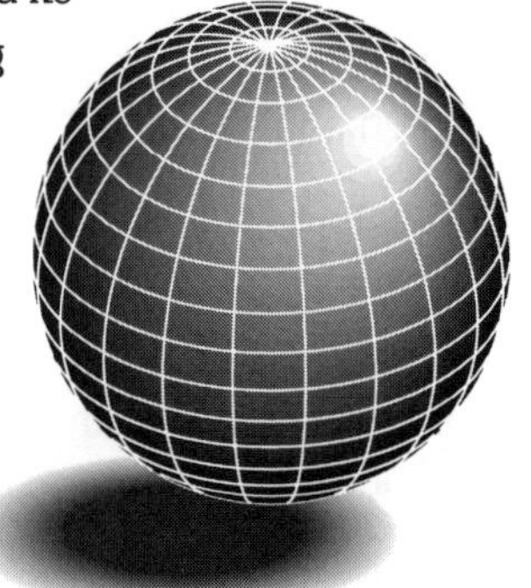

This information will eventually find its way into areas that potentially are going to keep you alive. For it's the only way your bodies, which are perfect in their potential, are going to find perfection in your reality. The day is gone for fast turnovers and quick lifetimes. There is no reason for you to continue that cycle. Are you paying attention? There is no reason. You have reached the end of the timeline. Now, here you sit—no accident that brings you to the chair to hear or read this, you know. It's almost like an appointment. Perhaps you only found out about this meeting yesterday? Really? You say you're here because somebody else brought you. Really? Welcome to the family, dear ones. Welcome to synchronicity! From this point forward, you can do anything you wish with this energy and this information. But even if you are in disbelief now, it doesn't matter to us. The welcome is still valid because we know who you are, and the love for you is as great as it is for the one next to you.

You're going to have to understand more about energy in order to facilitate life on the planet. You're going to have to understand more about energy to facilitate the biology on the planet. So, in the next few moments we're going to deliver a treatise that we will call "The Cosmic Lattice, Part II". It's no accident that the first Cosmic Lattice information was given in this energy as well (New Hampshire, November 1997). Precious, it is—an energy postured for this information. That is why it is given now.

This is the channelling designated to be transcribed; so therefore, I am talking right now to those reading this. I can say to you reading it, "We are in the *now*. You are not reading something that happened awhile ago. You are reading about an energy that can pour into your life right now, as sure as it also can for those hearing it with their ears. Although we do not see the future, we measure the potentials of your time line and we know who has picked up this book. We know who is looking at it right 'now' as certain as we know who is hearing this message."

We told you much about the Cosmic Lattice the last time we were together. We told you that the Lattice is an energy that pervades the universe and is consistent. We told you that it passes through all matter, and that it is available all the time. We told you that it is a physics staple of the way things work throughout all the universe that is visible. We told you that light is slow, compared to the communication of the Lattice, and that even though there is a mechanical attribute of the Lattice (which we are going to discuss), communication is almost instantaneous all through it. The speed of energy from one end of the universe to the other is almost instantaneous. (Actually, there are no *ends*.)

The cosmic energy event you see taking place 12 billion light years away did not happen 12 billion years ago. There is a communication attribute that indicates that it is happening now, to correspond with your millennium shift. It is not something that took place 12 billion light years ago. (see page 133)

We gave you elementary information of the shape of the Lattice. Now we're going to fill in the cracks in the information we gave you last time. We're going to tell you what the real shape of the Lattice is. We're going to tell you the construction of it, the best we can in terms that are nonscientific, which my partner can deliver. We're also going to give you several attributes of the Lattice, and we're going to tell you how to use it. Then we're going to tell you the real miracle, but the physics has to be shared first.

This information will tie together the science of the facilitators in this room, who have processes that would seem to be dichotomous [speaking of the physics of Dr. Todd Ovokaitys, and the energy work of Peggy Dubro of the EMF Balancing Technique, both in attendance]. Finally, you may understand how the Cosmic Lattice is indeed the very essence of the energy of healing.

Again, it may not surprise you that we go to the biggest of the big, before we get to the smallest of the small, in order to talk about Humans. In these moments that we speak about physics, we are also speaking of love. Some of you are going to feel the pressure of love during this time, and although you may not understand any of the science, you may feel the pressure, physically, and the washing—the pressing of the hugging, some on the head, and some on the shoulders. Some of you will feel the temperature shift, and you will feel the energy in this room as this new information is delivered in love. This time of discovery is given because you desire it and because you've earned it. That's why you sit in the chairs.

More on the Shape of the Lattice

The Cosmic Lattice is not a net. It is not singular. It is not one dimension. If it pervades the universe, as we have said, then it has to be everywhere, and indeed the Lattice is everywhere. We wish to reveal the shape: The actual shape of its cells are closed compartments. That should not shock or surprise you. It mimics your body. For now, we will call the cells "energy cells." They are in a honeycomb shape, and these shapes (the cells) each have 12 sides. Each energy cell of the Cosmic Lattice all around you remains unseen, but you will be able to eventually measure its energy. This Lattice is a structure, whose parts do not touch. Each one of these 12 sided honeycombed energy cells, which are everywhere, do not touch one another. Yet they exist side by side, as though they do touch. They even look like they do, but they do not, for there is something that holds them apart.

There is a mechanical physics attribute that is going on within the nucleus of the atom. This very same mechanical "law" that holds the Lattice cells apart is the same attribute that is responsible for unequally polarized pieces of atomic nuclear structure being held together. It's important that you understand that these Lattice cells never touch one another, and there is a reason why they do not. It is all part of the communication within the Lattice. Energy transfer within the Lattice also mimics physics at the smallest level—also being atomic structures that do not touch. It also mimics the most elegant part of your body—the part that is responsible for your thinking—for your memory, for your remembrance, and for your reactions—the Human brain. The synapse parts (the wiring) within that organ do not touch either. These are the ways of the physics attributes that transmit (or relay) energy. It is not new. Look for it, for it's everywhere. It is also the common structure of the Lattice.

Now we're going to give you some attributes of these cells, and we're going to ask you to follow along. Some of you, especially those who are science minded, will be entertained. The rest of you who are not interested in science may just sit—for we're just going to wash your feet.

Attributes

The Cosmic Lattice is balanced, but it is not quiet. The Lattice has astounding power. It has a flow of energy that I cannot explain to you, for there is no paradigm model for it yet in your thinking. Therefore, you would not easily understand. The Lattice has vents that we can best describe as necessary for the flow of energy. It balances the slight inequity of the polarity. The vents also have to do with time, which we will tell you more about in a moment. You will always find two vents together. One will be prominent, the other will be secondary. You might graphically and clearly see one, but you will have to look carefully to see its partner. There are always two. This is an axiom or physical rule of the Lattice energy, and of the universe.

The vents are usually at the center of the galaxies. The distance between the vents determines the spin direction of a galaxy, and the speed of matter around its center. It is a classic push-and-pull scenario, and matter responds to it. Now, here is something you will not understand at all: The vents are very necessary for the balance of your universal energy. The vents are also energy portals (drains, to you), and are where the front of the Lattice touches the back. The back of the lattice holds a universe whose vents are opposite. Note: This *is not* an alternate universe. It's also yours. Although this may bring you a paradox at the moment, those in your future, especially reading this transcription who have good scientific intuition, will discover the physics that will validate the meaning of this information.

Therefore, at the center of your own galaxy, there is a pair of vents, one of which you can see if you choose. The other one is hiding. But the vents always appear in pairs. This is dramatic; it is powerful; it is the Lattice balancing itself.

We're going to give you an attribute of the Cosmic Lattice and the energy within it, which is difficult to explain. We're going to discuss the mechanics of the speed of transmission of energy within the Lattice, and we are going to show you how the speed of the Lattice is stellar compared to the slow transmission of light.

The Speed of the Lattice

This discussion of speed has a metaphor, an analogy that exists on your own planet. Some of you are aware that if you were to take something physical and force it through the water in your ocean, it would be fairly slow-going. The water is thick, and it offers a medium that requires a great amount of energy to force something through it. Think of the fastest things in your oceans. They would be some of the fast fish, and even some of your mechanical devices [submarines]. But they and their speed pale in comparison to the speed of giant ocean waves created by the energy of an earthquake.

Many of you are aware that the speed of quake-generated waves in your ocean approaches the speed of sound itself! That's how fast it goes. Consider how much energy it would take to propel something the size of a mountain at the speed of sound, through your ocean. Many would say it could not be done, yet waves seem to do it easily.

The reason is that a wave is not the transportation of *matter* from one place to another (like a fish or a submarine or the matter in a mountain). The wave is the transportation of *energy* from one place to another. As you know, the molecules of water bump into one another. One bumps into another, and bumps into another, and the speed of the bumping transmission is very, very fast.

Although the metaphor has its limits as we compare the two, in essence, that is what takes place on the Lattice on a far, far grander scale. Light is the transportation of matter—photons in space. It might have a wavelike appearance, but its speed is limited due to its mass, and the speed is *relatively* slow. Similar to a fish or a mechanical device in the water, light is the transportation of matter through a substance. It's when the Lattice cells bump together that they create patterns (waves) due to their bumping, at a speed that is almost instantaneous through billions and billions of light years. Not only is light slow, but it must also penetrate through other matter—not just the emptiness of space. There is dust, gas, and magnetics—all of which block and bend it. The transmission of energy from the Lattice is clean, fast, and almost instantaneous throughout its vastness. That's because the energy medium is uniform and transmits with a system that easily recognizes what is being *passed* within (much like the wave does with water molecules). Now we have given you a mechanical attribute of how energy is transmitted in the real universe.

Energy Rules

There are three rules of physics for the universal Lattice, but none of them will respond to what you have called Newtonian physics or the relative physics of Einstein. For Newtonian and relative physics is mostly about the behavior of matter. The physics rules that I'm going to give you are about energy, and they are different—very, very different.

(1) The speed of energy moving through the Lattice is always the same. It never varies. It is a constant law of energy physics. It is the speed at which the Lattice cells bump together, and this creates waves of energy whose speed is always the same. That is the first one.

Here is the second, and it's tricky.

(2) It always takes the same amount of *time* for energy to traverse the internal distance of one Lattice cell. (An absolute time period to go from one side to the other, inside of a Lattice cell.) This *time* segment is always the same and never varies.

(3) The third axiom is this: The cells have a varying size. That is, there are areas in the universe where the energy cells of the Cosmic Lattice are large, and other areas where they are small.

"*Wait, Kryon*," you might say. "*You just got through saying that it takes a known amount of time to traverse the distance of a cell. If some are large and some are small, won't that make a difference in the* ***time*** *it takes? After all, you are changing the distance!*"

No, the time is always the same.

"*Then*," you might also say, "*something has to give. It doesn't make sense to take the exact same time to go a short distance or a long distance, if the speed has to be the same.*"

You're right. Here's where we challenge you to understand that the paradox of this is that the *time* elements, as measured, must change! Therefore, when you move into an area of space where the cells are smaller, you're going to receive a different measurement of time than when they're larger. This will explain to you what we have said in the past—why your astronomers see "impossible physics" through their telescopes—physics that cannot occur according to the assumed rules. They are looking at physics in a time frame that has smaller or larger cells than your own.

Therefore, the third axiom is the only variable one, and it is *time*. The units of time tend to change in relationship to the size of the Lattice cells.

Basic Physics of the Lattice

Now let us discuss the use of the Cosmic Lattice, physics-wise (not biologically). Dear ones, we previously told you that the Lattice null energy is balanced to zero. We told you that each cell has tremendous power, but it is balanced by another power along side it, which has opposite polarity. This "nulls" out the apparent potential so that it all appears invisible to you. The energy, therefore, appears to be zero.

It's when the Lattice is deliberately unbalanced that you really get to see the power. If you could only understand how to manipulate the null so you could unbalance it just slightly, the result would be tremendous free energy. Let us say again that one of the reasons this would be safe for you to accomplish is because none of the cells touch each other. You will not have a chain reaction, like you have in your nuclear matter science. So you can capture the energy of one, two, three, or as many cells as you wish, when you learn how to manipulate them.

Some have asked about the null—about the polarity. What kind of energies are there that would oppose each other so well? Let us give you an answer that might be difficult for you to understand at this time, but through discovery and with time, it will make sense. Opposite energy attributes that create the null are polarized energies. They are almost mirror images of one another that together create a quiet, zero null. This is part of the balance of the universe, and it is everywhere. It is also this way in light and matter. It is also true, however, that the "mirror image" of energy, light, and matter is not perfectly balanced. Due to the bias of your "kind" of universe (call it the "positive" one if you like), the "anti-energy," or mirror image of the positive is only slightly less powerful. It is this slight imbalance that creates the vents that we spoke of before. The vents are necessary to allow for the balance to be maintained. Otherwise, the major "null" posturing would not last long, and the Lattice would be constantly unbalanced. The vents, therefore, "drain" off the slight imbalance of the bias.

Cosmological Constant

The last physics attribute is one that we will only hint at. The Lattice is indeed the cosmic constant that has been looked for in science forever. There are those who have asked, "*What is the actual mechanical connection between the Cosmic Lattice and matter?*" Let's just say that it is the characteristic of this constant that "tunes the strings" of the music of matter. It sets the frequencies for the smallest parts, and those frequencies vary depending on where they are in the cosmos.

We would like you to eventually understand how to manipulate the Lattice so that you may pull on its energy. Understand that this can be done anywhere at any time—on Earth or in space. It is done completely and totally with magnetics—active magnetics. It is accomplished with the creation of carefully placed patterns of large magnetic fields, which must be active (created with energy, not naturally existing). When you discover how this works, you will also find that this particular process on the planet is not new, and that your experimenters have actually done it before.

During the times it was done before, no one understood what was happening. The process was far beyond your ability to control, and you didn't even know the principles—yet you tried it anyway. Now you have the ability to control the experiment and therefore create disciplined and sustained energy, seemingly out of nothing (the null). Like so many other physics processes, however, it is going to take a tremendous amount of energy in order to unbalance even one cell's null attribute. So you're going to have a vast amount of energy pumped into the experiment before you can see the results. Once you understand how to "prod" the null to unbalance itself, you will be rewarded with a steady flow of energy, far beyond what you put into it. This is accomplished, since you create your own tiny "vent." An unbalanced cell creates a situation where the other cells around it will try to "feed" energy to the one that is unbalanced. This creates a tap that will pull upon the Lattice indefinitely, as long as your work matches the properties that the Lattice expects to see. I know this sounds like science fiction, but eventually it can be *the* energy source for your planet.

Creating Physical Power from the Lattice

Here's how it works. Two magnetic fields together, postured in the correct way—a way that is very three-dimensional in your thinking process—will create a "designed magnetic field" that is very specific. It's one you have never seen, and it does not exist naturally. Start with trying many magnetics fields, postured against one another—of unequal force and pattern, and at right angles. Don't make any assumptions. Think freely. Done in the right fashion, these two fields will create a third pattern, which is unique and is the product of the original two. This third custom-created pattern is the one you what to deal with, and it is the one that has the potential of manipulating the lattice. One you have created it, you will know of its special qualities by how dramatically it changes the physics around it. It won't be subtle in its exposition, believe me. You will know when you have it.

Here is a word of caution: Keep this experiment away from your body! Keep the experiment in check with your scientific methods. Go slowly. Understand what you're seeing before you go to the next step. Do not expose yourself to any magnetic fields. Remotely conduct all energy experiments. Remember that magnetics also plays an important part within your body.

Here is another: Understand that if you unbalance the Lattice too grandly and too greatly, you will have a time displacement, for the process also involves the property of *time*. We don't mean that you have to wait for it. We mean that one of the actual physical players in the creative process of unbalancing the Lattice is the manipulation of the time frame of matter (a little known attribute of every particle of matter in the universe). This is not time travel, but time displacement. It is where you are actually addressing tiny parts of matter, and changing the time frame they are in. When the inequity of time frames meet one another (matter mixed up with differing time attributes), the result is a displacement of distance. Although there is no horrendous danger for the Earth within this time displacement, it can and will affect the local situation within the experiment. In other words, it can create a matter-distorting effect, completely stopping the experiment and actually dislocating the parts. We're not going to say any more about this at the moment, but the more astute scientific minds reading this will go to the next obvious step—and the answer is 'yes,' the Lattice is also the key to quick travel of large physical objects—even of very short distances.

Now it is time to talk about the miracle—to reveal why we're here. Some of you have gone through this scientific discussion while we washed your feet, only to wonder how it relates to your personal lives. Physics? Science? So where does the regular lightworker fit into this?

This is the part where those in this room working with the Lattice energy will more fully understand how the Human body responds to what they are doing, for the Lattice is truly available now for each person here. My partner has to be careful in this next statement, for it has to be very accurate.

The Lattice/Human Connection

The Cosmic Lattice communicates with Human biology through a series of magnetic resonant frequencies, which land upon a 12 segmented crystalline structure. We have not said the words "crystalline structure" for transcription before. We have not exposed this information before, and we do it now because the knowledge is critical, and the energy here will now allow us to tell you about it.

We're going to finally reveal the crystalline structure, which is around the coded structure that you call DNA. Remember that we define DNA differently than you do. Your word DNA actually got its name from the two strands, which are chemical, and which you can physically see. Our definition refers to the 12-stranded coding for the Human body, only two strands of which are chemical. The DNA—all the strands of it—are an encoding tool. The strands are instruction sets, and we have previously told you that some of them are magnetic. Some of them are also what you would call "spiritual." (But to us, they also have a physical property.) These strands contain all of the coding for your whole life, even those carried over from the life before this one. But there's more. The memory part of your life's system is separate from the encoding. It is the "stem," the crystalline structure. Many of you might ask, "Why would it be called *crystalline*? Will we find something that is crystal in there?"

The naming is metaphoric, yet there is real physics involved that is crystalline-like. In your crystal work, even at the basic level, you have realized that crystals do something special. Do you remember what that is? They hold energy. Therefore they retain energy-pattern memory. Now you're beginning to see how the computer of the Human body works. For the crystalline structure, which we would call the sheath around the encoding DNA, is the *memory* of your life force. It's the memory of every past life you've ever had. It's the Akashic record for you. It is the record of past and present contracts. It represents all of the things you have been through. That crystalline structure, therefore, is also spiritual. It is all that you are, memory-wise. There isn't one instruction set there, however. The instructions are within the 12 DNA strands, and the crystalline information is "wrapped" around the DNA package as the memory core—the stem—ready to pass needed information to the instruction sets. The crystalline structure also contains the perfect blueprint of a Human Being—also in memory.

Now, as you might be realizing, there is constant communication between the 12 DNA strands and the 12 segmented crystalline memory. Right now that communication isn't very good. On this Earth—on this planet—the communication between these vital parts in your body is less than 15 percent efficient. The biology, therefore, is not very "smart" in this area. There are wonderful healing and life-extending attributes within your cellular structure that will never show themselves without the efficient "remembering" from the crystalline sheath. The communication between the polarity of the encoding mechanism and the crystalline remembering-core is poor. This, dear ones, is a carefully constructed restriction that tempers your duality. It has been this way since the beginning, and is mainly responsible for the fact that you remember almost nothing about: (1) who you were, (2) why you are here, (3) the fact that you are eternal, (4) the spiritual test that you sit in, and (5) who your real family is. That's not all. In addition to all these spiritual items, there is the unfacilitated biology! This poor communication, which was carefully postured for you (by you), also: (1) doesn't remember how to regenerate efficiently, (2) is wide open to attack from common earthly disease because part of it does not remember how to totally work, and (3) lives a short life because parts of it that are actually there stop working during life, or are thwarted chemically.

What do you suppose "talks" to the crystalline memory? What do you think helps posture that balance of duality that keeps things inefficient? The magnetic grid system of the Earth!

We wouldn't be here to move the magnetic grid unless you had asked for it—unless the 1987 measurement had shown the potential of great change, dear ones. Family, I'm talking to you!

It is the communication between those two elements in the body that is the core of how close you can get to your Higher Self! Full remembrance at 100 % from the encoding of your biology would create an instant ascension status. You would walk around carrying your full potential—and that is an awesome thought.

There are those on this planet who are here in almost their full potential. Did you know that? They have to be here for the spiritual balance of the planet (as we have mentioned to you before). Some of them you know of, and we speak of the avatar energy that is represented by a few very special Humans living right now. Full communication of the principles we have been discussing allows for miracles! The creation of matter out of nothing—knowing how physics works, knowing how love works. It's a powerful combination, you know. Put them together and you can manifest anything; Full power over the physical, full power over your life span, full power over your own biology! Take a good look at what the avatars are able to do—that's who you all are!

Every single Human Being in the room and reading this has the potential for all knowledge. It resides in the crystalline—a 12 segmented crystalline structure that wraps itself around the encoding (DNA), and the encoding is just waiting for a better communication.

We told you many times during the "family" series of channellings that you were created equal and perfect and eternal. The only thing that keeps you from these things is the duality, and the poor efficiency of your current biology. All of it can be changed with better communication between the crystalline structure and the DNA. As the memory transmission is increased to the instruction sets, the body reacts—and by "the body," we mean the whole Human.

We want to tell you where that better communication is coming from. It's from the new position of the grid system of Earth. That is why we've moved it, and that is why our group came in 1989. Now you understand. Remember when we told you that no Human Being can exist outside of the magnetic grid of this

Earth? The magnetic grid of this Earth is what makes the communication possible that postures your duality and your very enlightenment. Without the magnetic grid, there is no communication. Someday your experiments in space will show this. The Human must have a magnetic complement to live in. Without it, over a period of months and years, the Human Being will die.

Elements on Earth come together for life, you know. Just look at your planet. Do you think you can just walk on it, live on it, and hope it behaves itself while you're here? It knows who you are, just as I do—just as the grid does. There is intelligence there. Therefore, the Earth is in cooperation with your very enlightenment. Just ask the indigenous people who came before you. At the core level of their spiritual beliefs lies the honor of the "dirt of the Earth." They *knew*.

There is more about the communication of the grids, and it involves still another crystalline structure. This will be given in a later communication.

Your DNA (the 12 strands) contains instruction sets for a 950-year life span of your body. Currently, much of this encoding isn't working. The encoding isn't working since it has no information from the memory core (crystalline structure). Within the core memory is information that will help the DNA chemistry "remember" how everything works.

Right now, your science is finally beginning to poke and prod your biology and to stimulate the DNA artificially. They are doing it with magnetics! This approach to health is a very real return to the mechanical processes within the "Temple of Rejuvenation," which we told you about some years ago. Magnetics, and the energy of the Cosmic Lattice, helps to posture your duality and your enlightenment. It also helps keep the balance of your crystalline memory, which is currently in a an inefficient mode—just as you designed it for your test on the planet.

Now things are changing.

There are those in this room (speaking of both Todd Ovokaitys and Peggy Dubro) who are slowly discovering the Lattice "tie-in" to cellular biology. One is discovering it through physics, and one is discovering it through the power of knowledge and intent. Both are working with magnetics at some level!

In both cases, what is changing is that the DNA is starting to remember! The efficiency of the communications is being enhanced and heretofore hidden parts and pieces of the biological and spiritual DNA are awakening. Remember what awakening is? It means that the knowledge is there—just asleep. The mechanics are there, just waiting for more efficient instructions.

Let me give you an example: Every cell of your body is designed for self-diagnostics. Every cell is designed to know whether it is correct or incorrectly in balance with the whole. Every cell is supposed to know that, but much of this information is hidden from it. The disease you call cancer easily fools this poorly functioning part of your cellular structure. If this part was working properly, cancer would not exist.

Part of the reawakening is the marriage, through magnetics, of the core memory and the encoding. When the rest of the instructions are known, which will allow for the cell's full intelligent knowledge using self-diagnostics, it will "recognize" itself to be out of balance and not reproduce. Only the healthy ones around it will be allowed to. In addition, it may actually commit "cell suicide" by itself! That's the full design. Look for it, for this is a well-known biological trait. Now it's time to enhance it. Think of it as a tremendous enhancement of your immune system—and that's just one attribute of the "whole Human" imprint.

Some of you reading and hearing this think we are only talking about science. NO! We are actually discussing self-healing—long life—and a whole new actively changing Human biological paradigm! For whether it is through intent of the Human consciousness, or whether it's physical facilitation through chemistry or physics, your DNA now has permission to change—and, dear ones, that's what the 11:11 was about! That's when you said yes to the very item we are discussing now.

Celebrate! Listen: When the communication between the crystalline structure and the DNA structure comes closer together, you can form bones where there were none before—there is creation of matter. You can have disease leave the body! The cells become more intelligent. You enhance the biology, and the miracle comes from within!

Healers, are you listening? Everything you are doing in your work ends up helping to bring these two biological attributes together within the cellular structure of the one that sits in front of you asking to be healed. Why do some get healed and some do not?

The answer is complex, but one of the main catalysts for miraculous healing is pure intent. The next time you're working with someone, make sure that the intent is there—make certain that they really understand what they are doing. When true permission is given and the intent is there, healing will occur. Some of the most magnificent healing you have on your planet right now is Human with Human, with no one touching anyone at all. It's profound. It has the properties of being miraculous—and it is the connection with the Lattice. This, therefore, is the explanation of where that energy comes from, because the Lattice is what is actually supplying all the magnetics. When you finally understand where magnetic fields come from, you will know of what I speak. They are an attribute of matter and the Lattice.

Some of you remember the story of Michael Thomas, and the channelling of the story, *The Journey Home* (Kryon Book Five). You might remember that Michael was told that he would meet the finest and grandest angel of them all in the final house of his journey—and he did. In that Seventh House, the grand angel was revealed to him, and it was gold, and it had his face! As Michael Thomas sat with that angel, he could barely breathe because of the Divinity that was around him. Realizing that the biology and

Divinity don't mix, he was having a hard time—on his knees. Michael was granted, at that time, a physical dispensation around him so that he could exist while he looked at the grand one that was his Higher Self.

When the great golden one was finished giving Michael Thomas information, he told Michael that there was to be no more teaching. They both had reached a time similar to what we have reached together right now. There's no more teaching in this message. Instead, all there is right now is love.

In *The Journey Home* story, the great gold angel asked Michael Thomas to turn around and sit upon the staircase, which the angel had just descended. Michael Thomas did so, and the angel said, "Michael Thomas, this has nothing to do with teaching. The learning is over. What I'm about to do is just love you." As you might recall, the great grand one—the sacred family member—the Higher Self of the Human, took Michael Thomas's feet one at a time and washed them. Michael wept.

You see, this is the partnership between a Human Being and his sacred family. This is the partnership between Spirit and Human Being. This is the message of Kryon. All the physics that was discussed today can be given to science. The love is the real teaching! The family is here—a family who knows you. Messages are given to enhance your life. Processes and procedures are given all over the planet for you, because you're going to have to live a lot longer to accomplish your work. And what is your work, you might ask? It is to hold your light!

Want to know the difference between **you** right now, as we wash your feet, and the Indigo children we've spoken about? That crystalline structure we have discussed today is just a little closer to their encoding than yours is. Those children come in from the other side knowing that they are royalty. Those children come in with a spiritual evolution that you did not have, and that is why they seem to be such misfits in your society. They know things that you didn't know, and they feel it at the cellular level. Some of them are actually creating their own culture because you are not listening to them. You are not giving them credit for being evolved. You are not giving them honor. Oddly enough, you are treating them like children!

Right now it's a time of foot washing, is it not? Most of you know that these are the closing moments of the channelling, yet we continue to wash your feet. We've poured energy into this room and also to those of you reading this. It's sacred family energy from the entourage that has come from beyond the veil. It has been delivered from those who love you—who pass between these aisles and these chairs and who give you hugs—those at your feet right now.

As we arise and take those bowls of our tears of joy, we withdraw from this place. If we could say that such an emotion exists on this side of the veil, we would say that there's sadness in our retreat. For we are family, and we wish to stay here! If you allowed it, we would be here in this room, or where you sit, for days. That's how family feels about family!

Let this time of preciousness go on record as being a time of great reunion—a time when Humans and angels got together and recognized themselves as family, and loved one another for it. There will be a time when I see you again in the Hall of Honor.

When that time comes, I will refer to this day, and I will say, "Remember that time in the place you called New Hampshire? It was precious—precious."

And so it is.

The Changing Consciousness of Science...

Washington: The Associated Press:

"It's an ancient Chinese remedy that many U.S. doctors will find bizarre: heating the herb mugwort next to the little toe of a pregnant woman to help turn her baby out of the risky breech position just before birth. But when thousands of doctors this week open the Journal of the American Medical Association,[1] they'll find a scientific study that says the Chinese therapy really works and Western women should try it." [2]

(The Journal of the American Medical Association)

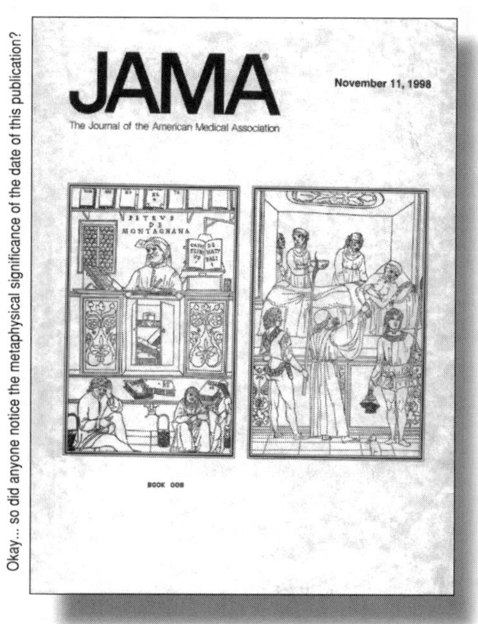

Okay... so did anyone notice the metaphysical significance of the date of this publication?

[1] *JAMA* magazine, November 11, 1998; ISSN 0098-7484; published weekly by the American Medical Association, Chicago, IL.

[http://www.ama-assn.org/jama]

[2] *Norwich Bulletin*, "Health Section"; The Associated Press; Wednesday, November 11, 1998;

The EMF Balancing Technique®

The Universal Calibration Lattice
Doorway to the Cosmic Lattice

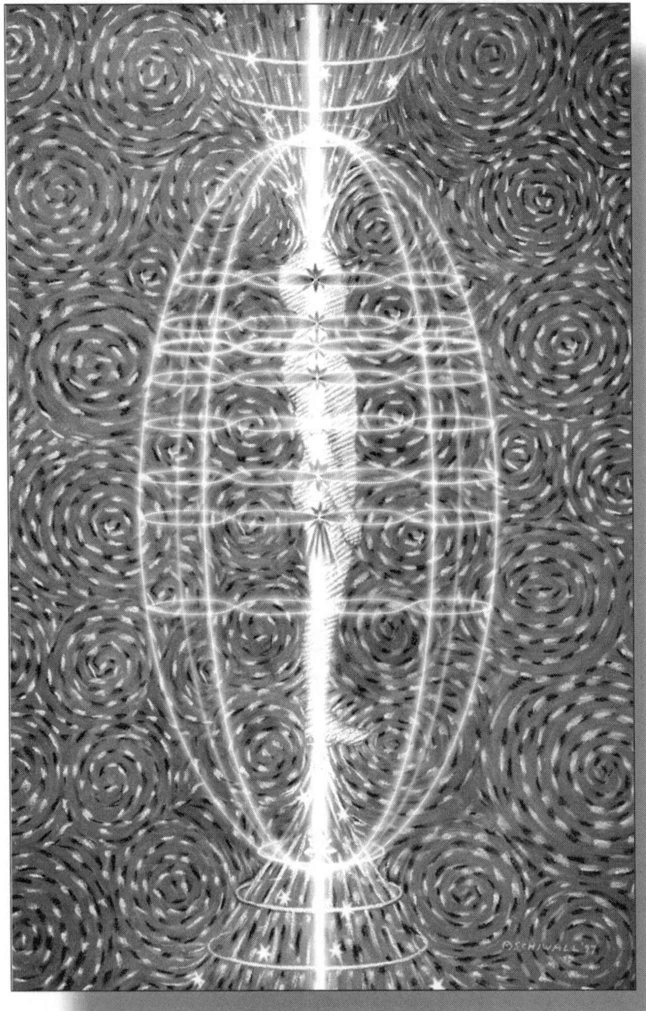

From Lee Carroll...

Peggy Phoenix Dubro channeled the information for the Universal Calibration Lattice, a system in our human energy anatomy that connects each of us to the Cosmic Lattice. Peggy also originated and developed the EMF Balancing Technique®. This is a new energy system which accelerates the integration of Spirit and biology, so that you can increase your health and co-create the miracle you are. The EMF Balancing Technique is also designed to work with the Universal Calibration Lattice to enhance and accelerate the evolutionary process. The technique utilizes the human-to-human effect upon the electromagnetic field, and is a simple, systematic procedure that anyone can learn. Channeled from Spirit, this procedure is a precious tool we may use now. This is the first of the new energy systems to which Kryon refers when he invites us to hold the full charge of our being. This is positive practical empowerment.

Peggy has worked with the lattice information for a decade, and has established herself as a leading authority on the nature and benefits of this gift of Spirit. Kryon says the Cosmic Lattice is the greatest tool we humans now have available to us (The New Hampshire channelling you just read). Tap into the energy of the Cosmic Lattice, through your own lattice, and enter into a state of cellular awareness that brings about new abilities. The latent abilities activated include clarity, profound peace, better health, and rejuvenation. People all over the world are waking up to their Divine Nature, and want to help others to remember.

The EMF Balancing Technique opens the door to the Universal Calibration Lattice in a gentle, powerful, nurturing way. As members of the Kryon International Seminar team, Peggy and Steve present life empowering workshops in the technique all around the world. The technique is a contemporary initiation into a new awareness of our electromagnetic nature. It provides information about our energy anatomy that permanently establishes a powerful connection to the Cosmic Lattice and allows us to use the new energy immediately. In effect, the EMF Technique rewires us for the new energy so that we can accept a greater charge of our being. Peggy has developed a unique understanding of the human energy field as fibers of light and energy. I now invite Peggy to tell you about her pioneering work with the UCL and the EMF Balancing Technique. Kryon calls the Universal Calibration Lattice the "doorway to the cosmic lattice." The EMF Balancing Technique is the energy work Kryon foretold.

The EMF Balancing Technique®
An Evolutionary Energy System of Love

It is a beautiful, sunny day in California. The room is bright and full of light. I watch twelve people in the room work with one another energetically. The golden strands within each one's energy field are being calibrated using a procedure called the EMF Balancing Technique. Today is the fourth day of the six-day training seminar for practitioners of this technique, and their movements already reflect grace and skill. Faces shine with the joy and recognition of Creator within as they work with the golden energy. Suddenly, the familiar warmth I know as Kryon begins to intensify in my heart. "Look at these people, these Dear ones," he says. "Only a few days ago, they were what you call strangers, now family-all." My eyes fill with tears of joy as I feel a wave of love wash through the room. When I mention to the participants what has just happened, they report feeling that energy of love. I tell them that in the last class someone was humming the tune "Getting to Know You," and we all laugh. This is Kryon's energy work in action.

Carrying Our Full Charge
Integrating Old and New Energy

Kryon urges us to be Self-enabled humans and encourages us to carry the full charge of our being. He says that we are already carrying more of our energy than ever before. The wonderful challenge each of us humans now faces is creating and maintaining a strong spirit capable of holding and using all of this energy! This can, at times, seem like an overwhelming task, but as Self-enabled human beings, we have earned many gifts to help us. The Universal Calibration Lattice (UCL) is one of those gifts. It allows us to make use of the unlimited energy of the Cosmic Lattice. Until now, the general path of the spiritual seeker has been vertical, that is, we have reached up to our Higher Self, or we have reached down to connect with the Earth. This movement was appropriate in the old, traditional energy. Now, in addition to the vertical movement, we are able to use a new horizontal energy movement to bring the energy into the here and now of everyday life. This empowers the co-creative process with Spirit as partner.

As you look at the illustration of the UCL you can see the horizontal fibers that connect the chakras to the long fibers of the Lattice. As you learn to strengthen these horizontal fibers, you increase your ability to co-create with God/Creator. This is the new spiritual path in the new energy, the result of all the work accomplished in changing the Earth's energy grids. We can now access the UCL to fully empower the co-creative process. This Lattice, when activated through awareness, energy exercises, and the wisdom of our emotions, is like an invisible armor that strengthens the being. As we come to realize that home is right where we are, we are being given an opportunity to build the framework with joy.

A Little Personal History
and a Big Meeting with Ahnya

Twenty-seven years ago, in my early twenties, I felt a deep desire to remember God/Creator. I was brought up in a religious environment; I attended Church, sang in the choir, and played the Christmas angel every year. I was passionate about God and reasoned that if God were my Father (I didn't know about Mother Goddess then), there must have been a time when I was a part of God. With all my heart, I wanted to remember God—not the judgmental, biblical God of old, but the God of *now*.

I didn't know then that my desire to know God in this lifetime, was also a desire to remember who I was. I knew nothing of meditation or mantras.

Nonetheless, I began to live and breathe this mantra: "I remember, I remember." And I did indeed remember. In an overwhelming burst of energy, I became "no beginning and no end." There was light everywhere. There was a rush of energy through every cell of my being, a feeling that I had stepped outside of time, and a love so profound and nonjudgmental that I knew God was a reality. Such love, such Light, and ... such confusion! It felt as though all the cells of my body were turned up to full power, and that power had lovingly overloaded my circuits. I later came to understand that all my chakras had been blown wide open.

There were no new-age magazines or resources to help me understand what had happened to me. For the next sixteen years, I studied anything that might help to explain the intense love energy I had experienced. That segment of my life I now refer to as "Confused by the Light." During this time I immersed myself in many different disciplines—Zen Buddhism, Shamanism(African, Brazilian, Native American), born-again Christianity, Siddha Yoga, even the martial arts (Tae Kwon Do, Tai Chi, and Kung Fu). I tried anything to get that wonderful energy active in my life. My studies yielded many fine spiritual truths: "the truth is within you and so are all the answers;" "we are magnificent beings and capable of Mastery." This gave me hope, but I had a hard time using these truths in my daily life, and they did not produce the intense love energy I so wanted to enjoy again. Despite the years of effort, my life, my work, and my home were a mess! I had touched the

Unlimited and continued to have profound visions, yet my daily life reflected powerlessness. My frustration deepened, but my love for God remained. I knew I had a "power pack," but how could I turn it on? This was a constant thought during my seeking. My heart filled over and over again as I gained understanding of ancient truths and the realization that we are all one. I also passionately wanted to hold the electrical charge of my truth. After years of seeking, in sincerity and exasperation, I asked, "If the answers are within me, then I want to know *exactly* where within me they are ... and HOW do I get to them?"

Finally, in the spring of 1988, I once again had the joyous experience of "no beginning and no end." This time, a magnificent, luminous female energy form was present. Her name is Ahnya. Kryon tells us there is no gender in the realm of Spirit. I have experienced Ahnya as a feminine energy, so, for convenience, I describe this Being as a she, though she is really an aspect of an entity that is a genderless whole. She is one of the Kryon teachers, a part of the entourage, complementing Kryon's planetary changes with the work we bring. Whenever I teach, Ahnya is present. I find myself in and out of channel because that meld is most comfortable for me at this time. Ahyna is present whenever and wherever an EMF Balancing Technique teacher presents the work, and whenever an EMF practitioner performs a session.

Ahnya and I merged as one being and I became infused with the energy pattern we would come to call the UCL. This was my first experience with channeling, and I received a tremendous amount of information in this one momentous event. When I first received the energy pattern of the UCL from Ahnya, I knew it was a gift, but I didn't know what for. The energy lay dormant for a year. Then, in 1989, with the arrival of Kryon, the Lattice became activated. My job (or contract, as I now understand it) was revealed: I was to interpret the Lattice, learn how to use it, and teach others to use it. Piece by piece the gifts of this Lattice were unveiled. I spent six years interpreting and mapping the Lattice that you see in the illustration, and developing the first four phases of the EMF Balancing Technique.

In 1989, I began to work out of my home, giving energy sessions following the patterns Ahnya had shown me. (I later likened it to tracing crop circle patterns through the human energy field.) I followed the patterns as they were given to me, but the results varied according to each person's need, or intent. There were sometimes physical healings, but these I viewed as side effects since my focus was to balance and activate this new system of the energy field I was touching. At the same time, my life began to change dramatically. While activating the Lattice within others, my own energy system became stronger, more capable of "holding the charge." I now had a place for all that universal energy to circulate. I realized I could hold my own power-I call this "Core Energy"-, and my partnership with Spirit came alive. For the first time, I started to feel at home right here on planet Earth.

Word spread of the positive results my clients were having in their lives and my private practice was begun. People reported feeling "different," and "lighter," and they noticed that their lives were more fulfilling. This did not always come easily, for there was work to be done, but the clients found they had more energy and stronger guidance to follow through on their Souls' next steps. By staying consistent and working with one person at a time, the reputation of the work grew. In the ensuing years, I taught in many public school adult-education programs and lectured at universities, new-age stores, whole-health expos, and mainstream businesses. I appeared on some small radio and television shows and was featured in a positive way by the local newspapers.

There was an exciting event along the way: in the summer of 1995 a respected Connecticut based research and development firm approached Stephen and me. The company specialized in government and military contracts (and produced J. Everett Koop's video health series). They wanted to collaborate with us to apply for a NASA grant to study the effects of using the EMF Balancing Technique to improve individual and team performance, and to strengthen the human health maintenance process for the astronauts. Our part of the experiment was to provide the training and exercises to test the effects of electromagnetic field energy balancing. In other words, we were to stimulate collective consciousness by integrating Spirit and Biology! We learned the timing wasn't right then, and were disappointed when the company did not get the NASA grant. Yet, we were very encouraged and still knew we were on the right track. One year later in the summer of 1996, Stephen and I finally read the words of Kryon. Like many, the recognition we experienced was profound. By the fall of 1996, we had met Kryon, Lee Carroll and Jan Tober. In February 1997, we formally became co-workers.

The Universal Calibration Lattice is the Energy Pattern of Self-Enablement

"What does the energy pattern of Self-enablement look like?" I asked Lee/Kryon this question when we were in Atlanta for a Kryon channeling. As I felt the familiar warmth in my heart that I know to be Kryon, Lee said, "I don't know what this answer means, but it is "crocheted." Yes, what a wonderful way to describe the Lattice I have been working with for the past ten years! Awareness of and understanding the energy pattern of Self-enablement is a crucial aspect of our evolution. Fibers of light and energy radiate horizontally from the chakras. These fibers form figure eight shaped loops that feed into long vertical fibers of energy that surround and permeate our energy anatomy. This is the framework that forms the UCL. I think of it this way. The physical anatomy has many systems within it e.g. muscular, skeletal, etc. The energy anatomy also contains systems. The basic pattern of this particular system—the Lattice—is universal, i.e.; it is fundamentally the same in each person. When light fibers are stretched in one part of the UCL, other fibers may respond in a different part. Like the Cosmic Lattice, the UCL is pliable and interconnected. Our personal energy lattice is a microcosm of the macrocosm! The UCL functions similarly to an electrical transformer, transferring energy from one circuit to another. This is why we refer to this process as the "rewiring for the new energy."

It allows us to receive and use the energy we are learning to release from the Cosmic Lattice through our intent.

The Role of Intent

Though the basic pattern of the UCL is the same for all of us, the calibration (meaning to gauge or strengthen) is uniquely personal. It is determined by the mathematical relationship between each person's vibrational frequency and the Cosmic Lattice. The calibration of the fibers of the energy anatomy is quite complex, and this is where the role of INTENT is so important. The basic intent of an EMF Balancing Technique energy session is to balance the human electromagnetic field, allowing the individual's energy to open as many circuits as possible to the Cosmic Lattice.

The movements are graceful and simple to perform. The person receiving the session may give intent for almost anything-from healing to Self-knowledge to simple stress reduction to the reconnection of their DNA. As the session progresses, a rewiring of the individual's energy field occurs, and a new order is created within the field, producing a stronger structure to receive energy from the Unlimited Source (the Cosmic Lattice). After the connections have been made, we often see a dramatic increase in the co-creating process of life. The determining factor is soul's growth. The process of balancing the electromagnetic field can lead to spontaneous release, even without insight, in a single heartbeat. With this strong foundation, we raise our own vibrational level, which in turn raises the Earth's vibrational level. This is how we can personally achieve what many think of as Ascension.

Kryon reminds us that the love we have given to Creator, the Masters (such as Jesus and Buddha), to our spiritual leaders, families, and to other relationships is a reflection of the love we have for ourselves. As we claim that love, Self-esteem grows. This love of our "higher Self" is vast, and the biology must be strong enough to hold it. That is why preparation is necessary! Holding that love in ourselves first, we become whole, or wholehearted.

We then share our love with others from a different perspective, one we may have never known before. Activation and exercise of the UCL is an integral part of the preparation to receive the energy of Self love and Self Worth as it rises like the Phoenix within us. This is a gift of Spirit as we move into grace. It had been some time in my own teaching since I had spoken of love. I felt, through the years, that the word was misused. Then I met Kryon and, oh, how my heart filled! The energy of the Earth is finally ready for the constant flow of love, and we are going to be able to handle it. We can do this graciously, lovingly, and joyfully using the UCL.

Strumming The Strands of The Universal Calibration Lattice—An Electrical Evolution

If you want to be really good at communicating with the Universe can develop this skill through practice. It's a lot like strumming a stringed instrument. Many of you already reach out and directly strum the strands of the Cosmic Lattice, creating vibration through meditation, energy work, or intent. By strumming the strands of the UCL first, you add your personal signature to the connection, and you give the Universe your return address! The outer strands of the UCL are part of your energy anatomy. As you look at them in the illustration, you may sense that they are alive and vibrant. When you learn how to use these strands of energy, you clarify and amplify your communication with the Cosmic Lattice. The resulting vibration within the Lattice can now respond directly and intimately to you. Touching the UCL through your personal connection makes for much more potent Self-empowerment. You are invited to participate in the cosmic scheme of things in a way that only the Masters have done previously. You are a master, you are soul. We invite you to unlock your own mastery.

We have been making great changes on the planet with all our "lightworker" efforts, and we've made great changes within ourselves. Our energy anatomy reflects these efforts as we move in the direction of holding as much light and energy as we can. Our hard work has contributed to the birth of this contemporary energy system, including the UCL. The mineral composition of your bones makes your skeleton an ideal conductor of electromagnetic energy. We are all electric-blue inside, whatever color our skin is. The "stuff" of which the UCL is composed is a part of your energy field and has begun to take shape. As I work with the energy patterns over and over, I realize that I have the awesome privilege of occupying a front-row seat to view the evolution of the light body. The information presented here about the UCL results from working with thousands of people, individually and in groups. (See illustration)

The Figure '8' Infinity Loops

Ahnya began to reveal to me the figure-eight fibers that radiate from the chakras and connect us to Core energy. These are the self-balancing loops of the UCL. They form the infinity symbol, representing the infinite connection between you and Creator. I observed these light fibers feeding information back into the human biology from the universe. When I saw the biology sending information back out through the figure-eight loops, I realized we had taken a sizable evolutionary leap with the activation of this part of the energy anatomy. Here is the means of bringing co-creation into the here and now. The returning wave of energy from the universe brings with it experiences that shape your future reality.

A short time after I first observed the figure-eight infinity loops, the long fibers that create the outer framework of the UCL formed. Twelve of these long strands constitute the outer layer of the Lattice. Recently, twelve more strands that run through the middle of the figure-eight loops have become activated. Working with intent and energy exercises, along with tracing templates through the field, helps the Lattice take its complete form. What a beautiful evolution this is! As you exercise the UCL, you strengthen your capacity to hold the new energy in your Biology. This in turn helps the UCL to reach its full formation. Even as you read these words and study the illustration; you are stimulating the energy of the

Lattice within your being. When we gain a basic understanding of how this "message system" works, we realize we truly are creators of our own reality. By sending out stronger, clearer messages in a loving, gracious way, we create a stronger, clearer reality. At the time of the 11:11, we accepted greater responsibility for ourselves.

Solaras' work involved accepting more of our own energy and, as a result, our personal records were released into our energy fields. Your history—your hereditary patterns, past-life records, and all the events you have experienced in this lifetime—are recorded within the long informational fibers located behind you. These records look like tiny disks of light; they hold the information in place electromagnetically. When an excess energy charge surrounds one of these disks, it will often manifest as a reality that repeats over and over in what we call present time. If that reality is one we desire, that's good. But too often our "energy history" creates a repetitive pattern that becomes an anchor of negativity that holds us back from forward growth. As we balance the energy charges within the long fibers behind us, our intent is to transmute the "energy history," or the "past," into a column of golden wisdom and support. We gently release the excess "negative" energy, now freed to be used in more beneficial ways as we co-create our reality in the NOW. We live in a time of opportunity for Karmic release in grace. These fibers are channels for the higher charge of energy we need to claim this personal state of grace.

Note in the illustration the column of pure light that runs straight down through the center of the body. Here, in your center, is found the unification of the chakra system in progress. This is the core energy, the open circuit of the UCL that connects us to Unlimited Source. The greater the flow of energy here, the greater the release of spiritual knowledge within. As Kryon told us in Lake Geneva, the wisdom of the ages is right inside of us. Spiritual intelligence is inherent in all of us; it is up to us to give the intent to use it. The marriage of Spirit and Biology is a reality, and the task at hand is the facilitation of that reality. A characteristic of this process is a feeling of profound peace, no matter what may be happening outside you. Remember Kryon's "Parable of the Tar Pit? [The Parables of Kryon, Lee Carroll, Hay House, Inc., 1996] "As you release the excess energy charges of the past and strengthen your core energy, the thick "tar" that slowed your progress washes away. You now move toward partnership with your Higher Self, and eventually to Ascension status. Here, in your core, you can begin to experience the eternal *now*.

The more present you are in the now, the greater the electrical charge you carry. The electrical charge of your history and the charge of your future potential all feed into the now. The power or "juice" needed for Ascension is in the unified now. The light strands in front of the human energy field comprise the field of potential possibilities. In linear time, we call this the future. Here, we place our hopes and dreams and wishes. We also place our fear-filled and worry-filled events in this portion of the UCL. The light disks contained in these long informational fibers function like transmitters, attracting "like" energy. The Universe does not make a judgment call—we have free will here. We are beings of infinite possibilities. Depending on how strong the transmission is, a potential reality may be manifested. Of course, when we focus on our hopes and wishes with positive thinking, we work toward eliminating our fear and worry. Thus, we strengthen our co-creative ability as we wash away the "tar", and "plant" our co-creating intent in the field of future possibilities. Now you may better understand the technical information about the UCL, what occurs as you co-create, and why we are told that what we place our attention on, we become.

Circular Time

As you study the illustration of the UCL once again, notice how the energy from behind (the past) connects and feeds information to the energy in the center (the present). This core energy connects and feeds information to the energy in the front (the future). The channels are open in both directions, so the future can feed into the present and even back to the past. Here, we begin to understand what it means to live in circular time. This connection of past, present, and future creates the eternal NOW. There really is no past, present, or future; there is only the NOW. This information is not new. I read (and loved) Ram Dass' book "Be Here Now" nearly twenty-five years ago. After all these years of study, I have returned to "be here now."

Yet, there is a difference: we can do this in a way never before available to us. This is because of the magnetic adjustments Kryon is making on the planet. Kryon encourages us to experience being in the NOW when he says, in channel, that "this information is for those of you who are hearing this in the now, and for those of you who will listen to this on tape in the now, or read these words in the now." In Portland, he reminded us that "the time is the same; the time frame is identical." As we learn how to live in the arena called circular time, we are indeed "carrying the greater charge of our being." The EMF Balancing Technique(teaches us a practical way to work in the NOW with this knowledge.

A Call to Universal Calibration

Kryon reveals to us that the Cosmic Lattice is one of the most powerful tools of Spirit that exists today. He urges physicists to study the energy of the Cosmic Lattice and promises great discoveries that will benefit humankind will be found there. Kryon also invites us to move into a vibrational frequency wherein we can personally use the energy of the Cosmic Lattice. In order to utilize more of its energy in our daily lives, we must strengthen and balance our own energy anatomy. The UCL is our personal interface with the Cosmic Lattice. This process of evolution will bring about, within our physical bodies, the complete expression of the golden energy beings we are. This energetic alignment sets the stage for a unique, interactive union with Creator. Calibration enables us to hold and express the increasing electrical charge made available to us by Kryon's work. We refer to this as the rewiring for the new energy. The electrical charge is the spiritual spark or power that is within all of us. The goal of the call to Universal Calibration is to consciously create a stronger union with the Infinite using our personal interface, the UCL. Coincidences (or synchronicities) are just the beginning! Some of you are now living the reality that home is right where you are. The feelings of aloneness are fading, as the veil of separation from Spirit becomes ever more transparent. This process intensified in the early 1990's and will continue to do so until the year 2012. Energy work is of utmost importance during this time!

Restoring The Electromagnetic Laws of love

Spiritual laws of love and Electromagnetism wait to be discovered and restored for our use in reconnecting with Spirit in co-creation and integrity. The UCL is alive and vibrates with love, and this must be respected. When interpreting the energy balancing information imparted to me by Ahnya, I was usually able to follow the energy patterns correctly. When I did not do a particular move the right way, Ahnya gently aligned me in a loving and patient manner. I felt as though my arms and hands were not my own as they were gently moved in the preferred sequence. I have since had several Guide changes, but initially there were three tall beings of golden light. They were always present and stood to my left. I lovingly called them the Three Wise Guys. One day, it came clear to me that it was time to name the work. Following strong guidance, I named this procedure "The EMF Balancing Technique" (with EMF meaning electromagnetic field). "What!" I said, "That's not catchy or flashy! How dull. Can't I call it "Stargate", or something else?" "No", they replied emphatically, and graciously explained that in the near future, people would become very aware of EMF and this name would have meaning to them. Remember, this information was received in 1989. We now know the electromagnetic field of the human body holds many keys to our evolution.

Golden Energy Patterns – Templates of Light

Along with the information Ahnya channeled to me I became aware of golden light radiating from within and all around us. I also saw many patterns of crystalline light. My experience of channeling these patterns was to "energetically become" them. This is not the place to describe that process, but to date I have "become" five of these patterns. They look like diamond -shaped templates of light and energy. I regard these templates as the tools that are the heart of the EMF Balancing Technique(. The templates are catalytic as the information is awakened, or clarified, within the UCL of each individual. The templates enable me to teach the energy balancing technique very quickly, and to make adjustments to the students' energy fields to allow them immediate access to the UCL.

The classes are presented with lecture, practice, and wordless communication: words to explain the theory; practicing the technique for hands-on experience; and channeling the light templates for wordless instruction. The instruction is very visual and easy to learn. There is much joy, and participants always comment on the sacred and loving feeling of the energy. These golden energy patterns are traced through the field in a repeating sequence of movements. This results in an energy repatterning, or tuning, of the energy with specific intents for activating and strengthening the UCL in a state of grace, without having to relive the pain of the original insult. Lesson learned = Wisdom gained. The work also facilitates understanding the dynamics of the human-to-human electromagnetic connection. The movements are graceful and Tai Chi-like as we work these patterns through the human energy field. The procedures are precise and very thorough. We work from the feet to the head, from the front to the back, and from the head back down again to the feet. We always complete this universal alignment with a strong connection to Earth. You don't need me to tell you how sacred and imperative it is that we honor our partnership with Earth!

The Four Phases of The EMF Balancing Technique—A Brief Overview

During an EMF Balancing Technique session, the calibration process occurs for everyone, whether or not one is conscious of it. Most people feel the energy moving through their bodies, but this is not necessary for a successful session. Each session begins: "From the Creator within me to the Creator within you, and the company we keep, let us begin." This serves as a mutual acknowledgment and honoring of inner wisdom. The EMF Balancing procedure contains within it four different energy patterns, or Phases, that are traced through the human energy field. These movements facilitate the calibration, which in turn strengthens the personal connection (or, as I sometimes call it, the "Ascension connection") to the Cosmic Lattice.

Each pattern has a specific intent.

Phase I: to balance the wisdom and the emotions (the mind and the heart). This first pattern results in stress reduction and a sense of freedom and well being. It is helpful, in the new energy, to contemplate what it may mean to think with the heart and feel with the mind. Learn to work with fibers of light and energy which compose a layer of the energy anatomy that interrelates with the chakra system. Balancing the wisdom and emotions is important. By wisdom, I am referring to mental qualities of reasoning, organizing and understanding.

Phase II: to focus on Self-direction and support. Here, we may gracefully and gently release emotional issues stored within our history without having to relive the painful events that gave rise to them. Our intent is to transform our history into a column of golden wisdom and support, a column of core energy that centers us in the now. This golden column supports the energetic posture of Self-enablement. No more negative energy anchors from our past to hold us back! The question is "How can I connect to the whole more efficiently?" This is why understanding the fibers, which I see as geometrically patterned discs of light containing information – hereditary, genetic, past-life, present life is important. Every minute detail is recorded. Kryon (8th May 1999) talked of the magnetic sheath to our DNA, which he said that scientists would not be able to find until they realize that there is "something missing." These are the magnetic codes of Creator.

Phase III: to intensify the core energy. This allows us to radiate the light we hold. Platinum energy is introduced, and a union takes place within the energy anatomy as the chakras align with the core energy. This alignment is necessary as we take a greater responsibility in the Universal scheme of things. Here we express our spiritual intelligence and experience peace, and the remembrance of I AM that I AM.

Phase IV: to focus on energetic accomplishment. We have a potential, to which we often refer as our future. In this Phase, we learn how to choose to tune specific energy receptors and transmitters within the UCL for the purpose of co-creating our lives with Spirit. We calibrate this part of the Lattice so that we may joyfully co-create our potential together. What a privilege it is to be in partnership with Creator!

In all the Phases, the pattern is followed in the same way it was originally received from Spirit, but the calibration is always in accord with each person's innate wisdom. Everyone is unique, so the results are always interesting and individual. I am still amazed at how personal the Universe is with each of us! The Cosmic Lattice is an intricate part of all of us, and we are all connected. Thus, Kryon calls us Family-all.

Mastery: The Posture of Balance

A major focus of the EMF Balancing work is the posture of balance in everyday life. This golden posture of balance is challenged repeatedly as we, our Earth, and the Universe continue to calibrate to the new structures of energetic reality that are in development. As you hold this posture, and gain the higher vibrations associated with it, you will find that conditions that are out of balance may simply fall away. Then you have what many people call healing. As you hold your individual sacred balance, you also contribute great peace and stability to the collective whole. This balance, then, is a key to the expression of grace.

Remember, we have been asked to practice mastery. To gain mastery is to hold the full charge of our being. Kryon asks us to do this and tells us we can do it gracefully. Some of us may do it comically, but we can do it. (Ahnya says it's okay to be a cosmic brat occasionally, as long as you do it with love and humor). Think for a moment about what living in mastery might mean to you: an always peaceful countenance, a joyful heart, complete lack of judgment of others, patience, humor, kindness, humility, quiet, grace, and so forth. Practicing mastery includes gaining the wisdom to know when to give and when to receive; it includes the discernment Kryon speaks of.

By gaining mastery over ourselves we help others achieve their mastery so that we can all hold the energy to reach Ascension. This is a loving process—we make our own lives happier and raise our vibration, helping others to raise theirs. One of our EMF Balancing Technique teachers said of this work: "To explain what can be expected from this system would be an impossible task, for when you begin to integrate Spirit and Biology, the outcome is never the same from one person to the next. But it always attains the highest good for each of us, our Earth, and our Universe."

The martial artist becomes a master as she learns the forms and practices the postures for strengthening the ability to direct energy. The concert violinist gives his life to the practice of the instrument. The Enlightened Human can practice mastery by living as if every moment matters, and by assuming responsibility for continued growth. Here is a spiritual strategy which, when combined with intent, and integrity, can be practiced to make your co-creative efforts much more potent. I teach it in every EMF Balancing Technique seminar. First, honor your history (the past) by expressing gratitude for the wisdom you have gained. Second, center in your core energy (the present), which aligns your connection to unlimited power. This leads to the third step: reach out, in balance, to potential reality (the future). Henceforth, you will co-create consistently and with greater clarity, whatever your intent. The more you practice living in the posture of a Self-enabled Human, the more Self-enabled you become. This isn't so very mystical, but it works!

A School with Wings

I have been teaching the EMF Balancing Technique for eight years. My years of experience have given me great confidence in the program and in the Beings of Light who attend every class with me. The one-day introductory seminar is for everyone; it provides helpful information about the UCL, as well as energy exercises to strengthen it and gives you practical tools you can use from day one. Those who choose to continue can learn the patterns of all four Phases of the technique, and can go on to become practitioners, and even teachers. The four-Phase practitioner certification and personal growth program requires three days for the basic training and another three days for the advanced. The training moves quickly because it provides each student a direct alignment with the new energy, and the instruction is concise. The movements are graceful and easy to learn. The energy is self-regulating and self-directing; it moves through the body according to the particular needs of the individual.

The EMF Balancing Technique seminars are energy events! Some people learn the technique for their own personal use, and perhaps for their relatives and friends. Some learn EMF as an additional modality to complement an existing practice. Still others learn the technique in order to begin a new career as an EMF Balancing Technique practitioner. For those who feel a strong alignment with this work, a certified teacher program is also available. Each teacher has successfully completed both the practitioner training and a six-day teacher-training program. A teacher is qualified to perform all four Phases of the technique, as well as to teach all four Phases to others.

Marrying Spirit and Biology Through the UCL

Kryon tells us that human consciousness has uplifted the Earth into a new vibration, that it has changed the physics of our own reality (New Hampshire channels you just read). Humanity has stepped forward to take responsibility and to work toward Ascension. Indeed, we have already reached critical mass. As we gain mastery of ourselves, we move in the direction of holding as much light and energy as we can. The UCL has taken form as a result of this work, done by Lightworkers everywhere. We are able to use a horizontal energy pattern to power the co-creative process; through this mechanism, we have brought co-creating energy into the here and now. We all have a part in this process of evolution even as we are the instruments of its achievement. Clearly, the gifts of the new age result from a true partnership between Spirit and us.

As we reach our full potential, physiological changes will occur. Our hormones will secrete differently. This will have a chemical reaction upon our brains and bodies, which, in turn, will prepare us for Ascension and to live in a new age and a new reality. Once the energy is coursing through our whole field—through the energy body—it will affect the physical body through these hormonal and chemical changes. Eventually, the body will be able to heal and regenerate itself over and over again with astonishing speed; hence, the lengthened lifespan Kryon has told us about. Moreover, our learning processes will change as we learn in dramatic new ways by knowing how to connect to the collective consciousness to obtain information.

The UCL begins in your heart at the very core of your soul/self. It strengthens your biology in a state of grace as a fully Self-enabled human being. This is where your personal connection to the collective All begins. Every one of us holds a piece of the collective truth within him/her self. On the road to spiritual success, when we help another human being move forward into full expression of his/her Divine potential, we help ourselves - so connected are we! As Kryon says, "Energy is being released and time is being altered—all through human intent. There is no greater power in the Universe than *Human Intent* and *love* (New Hampshire channel)." Kryon also reminds us how dearly loved we are by Spirit. Your personal connection to the Cosmic Lattice enables you masterfully to express the love, grow in the love, and *be* the limitless love of Spirit.

A Calibration Celebration

My husband, Stephen, is the other half of the EMF Balancing Technique work.

Stephen and I present our seminars all over the world. We activate the light templates, human-to-human. There are currently EMF Balancing Technique Teachers in seven countries: the United States, France, Canada, Australia, New Zealand, Great Britain, and Singapore. My Teacher/Partner, Ahnya, the Luminous Being from whom I received all of this information, is radiating love at this very moment. And she is in a posture of celebration. She reminds me to tell you something I take pleasure in telling my students: the long fibers of the Lattice that surround you often look like wings to me!

Namaste, Dear Family.

Peggy Dubro

Want to know more?

Web Site: [www.EMFBalancingTechnique.com]
Contact: Energy Extension, Inc. 624 Main Street, Suite 77
Norwich, CT 06360
E-mail: <energyinc@aol.com>.

(The full-color UCL meditation poster (page 374) and the Spiral Sweep Energy Exercise CD or tape, are also available.)

אתם בחרתם להיות **לוחמי האור**. אתם אלו האחראים לשינוי ויוצרים את ההבדל. כל השאר נמצאים כאן על מנת לתמוך בכם... אך אתם חייבים לעשות את העבודה. כל מבנה כדור הארץ שלכם, כל ההיסטוריה הארצית המתועדת שלכם, וכל אשר אתם רואים כבני אדם מתמקדים בכך. וזהי עבודה חיונית עבור היקום.

For a translation, see Kryon Book Two, “Dont Think Like a Human,” page 46

For The Jews

Chapter Eight

From Lee Carroll...

As I was finishing this book, I received an E-mail from an Israeli named Muli (nickname of Shmuel) asking for an interview with an Israeli magazine called *Haim Acherim* (Different Life). He was asking for specific messages to the Jewish people (and non-Jews) in Israel. Since Kryon has actively mentioned the Jews many times in channelling, and since the Kryon books are now in Hebrew, I wanted to do something that is long overdue, and that is to dedicate a special area of the book to the Jewish people, many of whom are my friends and Kryon supporters. What better way than to grant this interview?

Thank you, Muli, for giving me this opportunity to give this information directly to Israel.

Question: *Before everything, do you want to say something to the people in Israel? Who are you? Who is Kryon? Are you still two?*

Answer: My name is Lee Carroll, and I am a Southern California businessman and an audio engineer. I have a 27-year business (or did), that dealt with very practical and logical matters.

Kryon is the name of a very loving entity who presented himself to me in 1989 through a series of very startling events—ones that made me logically examine my spirituality. In 1989, I wrote the first Kryon book filled with wonderful news for the planet, and in 1993 it was published. The distance between '89 and '93 wasn't filled with efforts trying to get the book published—that was not a problem. Instead, I was learning "who I was." What was I doing starting this weird and spooky stuff? Was I really ready to be a channel?

Today, after over 350,000 books in print in eight languages, and three invited visits to the United Nations, I travel worldwide with the beautiful message that Kryon has supplied. My channelling is a "meld" with my Higher Self and with Kryon. This is the only way that is acceptable to me. The four-year period before releasing Kryon Book One (of eight) was spent learning to discern how to make the meld work and how to become comfortable with it. Perhaps if I hadn't been a man—or an engineer—this wouldn't have taken so long.

According to Kryon, there are eight other channels who have "contracts" to begin channelling Kryon (or publish) in their areas of the world. The areas are listed very specifically in Kryon Book One (1989), and mine is a contract that I have obviously accepted in my area (the North American continent). Anyone can channel Kryon. God (Spirit) is not proprietary, but the predispositions of nine of us on the planet have us presenting the first information in our unique cultures. According to what Kryon said, each of us would have the birth attributes of that culture.

Since my culture is obviously a Western one, you will find my message directing mostly to Christian sects, which is the predominant religious belief in America at the moment. There are many, many Jewish readers of the Kryon material, however, since the core spiritual message is for everyone. Although they may be Jewish Americans, and even born here, their "real" lineage is Jewish (just ask them). There is a very basic spiritual difference at birth between many Westerners and Europeans: In North America, we are not necessarily born into a lineage that includes a philosophy or belief system, as you are. Our birth heritage is a social cultural one. It carries with it no spiritual history as yours does. None of us are born Christians, for instance. Other cultures (such as yours) have you being born into a rich heritage of spiritual history, with impressive historical significance and protocol.

All of this is to say that I am profoundly aware of *who you are* as Jews, and Kryon speaks constantly of the Jewish heritage. I guess that's one of the reasons I looked forward to this interview.

Question: If you had to choose from all the material that came through you (co-creation, the implant, the new human, psychic material, intent, and so on), what is the most important point for my reader? Which points would you choose?

Answer: It is that we have changed Earth's future, steering it away from the certain doom and gloom predicted by multiple sources throughout the centuries. We have lifted ourselves into a status where we are being asked if we wish to live longer lives, and though physical and spiritual attributes of a changing planet, to actually change our Human spiritual evolution. We are also being told that a tremendous change of consciousness of humanity in general is potentially upon us. That's the core information from Kryon. The Middle East is often brought into this discussion as the focus of large change, and sometimes even given as validation of it.

Question: A few times Kryon has referred to the people of Israel as a special group. What does it really mean? Does the member of the group incarnate all lives as Jewish? Do they always come to Israel? I, myself, today in Israeli as a Jew, know about some Buddhist incarnations. What is the purpose and the function of this group? Does this group have any special mechanic?

Answer: Kryon speaks of the Jews constantly! Your question has many parts, and I can only tell you what Kryon has said: (1) The tribes have a tremendous spiritual significance on the planet. (2) They have been the targets of annihilation since recorded history, since at the spiritual level they are the *only* "pure" karmic group. At the cellular level, those in the old energy for eons have known that to rid Earth of the Jews is to become pure themselves. This struggle is through all recorded history. It is also responsible for the anti-Semitic attitudes—such as the way many might resent royalty. (This is an oversimplification and begs a greater discussion later.) Anthropologists tell us that the Jews are not a "race," but have all the attributes of one. (3) Kryon has said, "As go the Jews, so goes the world."

Kryon has told us that for whatever "spiritual accounting" reasons, the Jews are a pure karmic group (perhaps this means the first to develop Earth karma?). Anyway, they *must* exist on the planet for Earth to carry out its spiritual purpose. He continually says that it has something to do with "placeholding." (Another discussion.) He has also told us the following about Jewish reincarnation, which is specific to Jews: If you incarnate as a Jew, you stay in that group for many, many lifetimes. If and when you step out of the Jewish incarnate scenario, then you don't go back. You can come from any other group when you step in, but when you do,—you remain a long time (many incarnations). I think this has something to do with the "purity" of the group—they all knew each other through many, many lifetimes. Kryon has also said that because of the many Jewish incarnations, this group "knows how things work" more than any karmic group on Earth. This is a very real-world remark, given that we can actually see it. So many of the world's giant economic companies are run by Jewish men and women—almost like they have "been there, done that." By the way, many of us have been Jewish in past lives and never will be again. It's kind of like we "had our turn."

Two of the world's greatest avatars in history were Jews, and perhaps some more we don't even know about. It is no accident that Jesus Christ was a Jew. Look at the irony there! It was a Jew who is responsible for Christianity (and many other hybrid beliefs).

The Jews are a very special group, and they exist as a family all over the world (as you already know). They don't have to be in Israel, but most of them feel very connected to that land, wherever they are. Those Jews in Israel have a very special karmic attribute: They exist in a part of the world that will eventually decide the future history of humanity. I really honor and respect the Jewish role in the spiritual nature of who we all are within the spiritual family of humanity.

Question: *Now, speaking of the land (the place itself) of Israel, does it have any special qualities?*

Answer: Are you kidding? Three major religions of the world are all trying to worship in the same space! Your land is the eventual focus of world change, and I know you are feeling it. Most of you see and feel it daily. Am I wrong, or are many of you "waiting for the other shoe to drop?" (A Western phrase meaning that you expect more to happen and are anxious about it.)

Question: Kryon said that he is here for 11 years. So what will happen in the year 2002? Will you retire from Kryon work?

Answer: Kryon said that his entourage came in 1989 and is leaving in 2002. That was for facilitation of a grid shift (something that we have shown evidence of, by the way—see Kryon Book Six). Long ago Kryon revealed that he has been here in support of us from the beginning, and will indeed remain. He never left. It's his grid-changing group that will come and go. At first this was confusing, since he has often referred to himself as "The Kryon." I now realize that when he said this, it was in reference to his "group." Somehow he is tied to this group even after they leave. I will remain channelling Kryon as long as he wishes it to be.

Question: Speaking about karma, it seems that the people of this land have a heavy karma to clean. Is it true, and why?

Answer: This answer requires a big discussion, and one that cannot be answered in a few words to give the proper honor for the question. I can tell you that in any land that has a strong spiritual lineage like yours, the group karma is heavy. Look at what the tribes have been through! As for the land itself, look at how long it took to get it back. From a metaphysical standpoint, look at what the potentials are for forgiveness and clearing—literally from the beginning of your recorded history. I cannot think of a heavier burden of spiritual karma for any group on Earth, or for the land that you live on. Kryon has told me that it is only fitting that the "pure karmic" group be the one where the most change is expected of them.

Question: Kryon speaks a lot about love and the importance of it, but here in Israel our crazy daily lives are filled with mutual hatred and anger. It sometime sounds cynical to speak about love. What would you suggest to us? Maybe we need special help from the spirits?

Answer: I do not live in Israel, and cannot begin to imagine what it is like. However, I can tell you that if you could step away and see an overview with my perspective, something dramatic has happened to the consciousness of your area in the last 20 years. Whereas before, the leaders' "solutions" from both sides were about: (1) who was right and who was wrong and who "deserved" what land; (2) forcefully taking back what belonged to them; (3) a Holy war that would indeed bring about the destruction of Israel; (4) and getting "even."

Even with the hatred seemingly intact, take a look at what has happened. Somehow the consciousness of "solution" has changed. Now it's about: (1) how can real peace be achieved; (2) what is it the Jews have to trade that is precious for them to achieve a lasting balance in Israel; (3) when will the Middle East ever get two leaders together from both sides who can put this puzzle together; (4) and what can the Jews do for their grandchildren to have a less anxious and more stable life in Israel? I know some of these things to be true from my actual interviews with Jews in some of your most intense cities, such as Hebron. From my view, you have changed dramatically.

You may not realize it, but the difference from then to now is spectacular, and you think there has been no progress? Your "mutual hate and anger" now has a far different posturing than it did before. Some of you on both sides are beginning to realize that what you do now could be the beginning of a time when the grandchildren from both sides will only read about the "hate and anger" some day. That's the potential that you carry.

Again, I know that my view is an oversimplification, and perhaps even naive. But you are in the "thick" of it, with the fiercest anger of the "old energy" literally at your front door. I don't think there are many Westerners who really understand how difficult this must be. I greatly respect your perseverance through all of this. You must be very, very weary of it. I just want to tell you that when you step back, you'll find that there indeed has been change.

Remember Kryon's words at the 1995 United Nations meeting? He said, "Where the sands should have been running red with blood in the Middle East right now, instead there are two countries making water rights together." This was his "wink" that indicated that things were not going the way of the prophecies. Instead, a new path was being forged—very slowly.

Take a look at the second portion of the answer to this next question to get a realization of what it might take to finally temper that anger and hatred you speak about.

Question: What can Kryon tell us of the Traditional Exodus and the spirit of Moses?

Answer: Are you ready for something very different than you thought? Kryon gave a description of your Exodus in 1994 in Kryon Book Two, page 117. Most of you won't like it, for it has you leaving Egypt and crossing the "Red Sea" over a landbridge! That's quite a statement considering what the scriptures say about your Red Sea experience. All I can say about that is that you should read a book called *The Gold of Exodus* by Howard Blum. It tells of two men who spent ten years looking for the "real" Mt. Sinai. They say they found it in Saudi Arabia, along with Biblical relics that they expected to find—boundary stones and pillars set up by Moses—the altar (decorated with drawings of cows) used by Aaron for the worship of the Golden calf—just about everything except the pillars of cloud and fire. The fun part? They also found the land bridge, too! The book has photos of all of it.

This is an interesting view on where and how it took place, but hardy crucial to the Exodus itself. It's also not crucial to any metaphysical or New Age philosophy. It's just information that's interesting. I would love to know your comments about the book.

The most interesting thing that Kryon has given us regarding the Exodus experience is about the 40 years in the desert. Some historians have now estimated that the strength of the tribes combined could have been almost two million. That's a tremendous amount of people to lead in circles in the desert for 40 years! I asked Kryon why this was necessary. Obviously the desert wasn't that big. The answer also related to what is happening right now for you, and I believe it is also contained in scripture.

Kryon said, "Forty years was almost two generations back then. Most of those who had left Egypt would die out and be replaced almost completely by a new generation within that time. Therefore, no Jew would enter the "promised land" with the previous consciousness of slavery. Death was the only remedy to the elimination of hatred and the memory of a tribal identity that was enslaved. This is really profound stuff. Please note that Moses was not allowed to go there either!

Within your lineage, there are several major consciousness shifts that "stick out." The Exodus is probably one of the greatest, and it actually required generations to move about in circles until they had "cleared" the memory of who the Jews used to be. This is a very strong self-worth lesson. Another (to me) is the establishment of the Jewish State, Israel. The next shift is the beginning of compromise and slow release of hate in your area that will take you safely into the next millennium. Again, this will take a consciousness shift of the highest order, but this time without a 40-year march in the desert.

Regarding your current events, and for many of the same reasons, Kryon says that the leaders who eventually have the potential to find compromise and lead you into a lasting peace will both have to be born *after* the year of the founding of the State of Israel. Only one meets that criteria now—and he might not remain [he didn't]. This all has to do with requiring a consciousness of leadership that never knew a time when Israel wasn't a nation. You can't have a terrorist-turned-politician as one of them does (you know whom I speak of). It now makes sense to me. Watch for it.

Question: What is the "New Jerusalem"?

Answer: This is Kryon's description of the new potential of planet Earth with a consciousness that could slowly evolve starting about 2012. It literally means "Heaven on Earth," but metaphorically means "Peace on Earth." It starts right in your backyard as the name indicates.

Question: What should be the relationship between old religions (such as Judaism, Hinduism, and Islam) that are very orthodox be to the New Age theory? The New Age is much more open and talks of an individual freedoms instead of the old tradition system of thought.

Answer: Kryon just channelled on that very subject (Chapter One in this book). Again, it would fill the pages of this magazine, and it is oversimplified to try to answer in depth, but I will comment. Kryon says that we will never be without our divisions—both within our own beliefs, and with all the others. Therefore, the answer becomes understanding, tolerance, and a teaching that says, "Love one another." Enlightenment creates wisdom. Wisdom allows for tolerance—development of the feeling that the other guy deserves his ways of worship. Obviously, it has to go both ways, but when it does, there is nothing like it.

This also means change within old doctrinal teachings, especially the ones that say that, "the other guy has to go." The interesting thing we are seeing all over the world is that even some of the strongest old doctrines can change if the spiritual leaders lead the people out of them. From the Pope to the leader of Iran, it seems to be that spiritual leaders have the ability to change the attitudes of millions of devotees, and even change some of the most fundamental "rules" of their old systems. This means that these things are indeed in our hands, and that men and women of wisdom and enlightenment can make a difference. I guess what I am saying is that "old traditional systems of thought" are only as old as the leadership wants them to be.

Isn't it so that you also have divisions within old and new Jewish traditional thought? Spiritual change has to do with staying in tune with the newer vibrations of the planet, not just with becoming current with the fads of the time. Think of it as changing the spiritual rules to match the new spiritually enabled Humans!

I remember that in 1995, it was the president of the Enlightenment Society at the United Nations, Mohammad Ramadan, who invited us there. You can tell by his name what his beliefs might be. I wish you all could spend time with him. His wisdom and consciousness has transmuted old traditional thought. He is a grand lightworker, a friend to all humanity, but he still belongs to a grand spiritual heritage whose traditions he continues to respect and work with.

Again, mutuality is the key. Tolerance is the issue, and love is the catalyst. Can it ever happen? Many of you say no. They said the same thing in Ireland, and although hardly settled and still tentative, that agreement was initiated by both sides. The Ireland peace initiative is an absolutely classic religious war—something you may be familiar with.

Question: Working by myself with the energies of my land, I feel that the year 1999 is a very important one for this area. Energetically, we are at a junction and politically, we are now before our election. The peace process is stuck. Would you be so kind to ask Kryon what he has to say to the people of this land? Which messages can he give us in this crucial time?

Answer: In much of what I have said already, I have really addressed most of what you have asked. Yes...1999 is crucial. Yes, your area is the focus. Did you really ever think it was not? I also addressed the fact that you are sitting "in it," and I don't think you can easily see the overview that many of us have—that of very positive changes slowly occurring over time.

As to a message from Kryon for you? Kryon says:

Dear Ones, you are the crucible of the your potential (the holder of your future). Like those before you, you will be the focus of what historians will report about Earth eons from now. Another Exodus is upon you, but this is an exodus from 'the way things used to be' to 'the way things can be.' Enslaved by the chains of anger and hate, the potential is here for you to lift your land and your future beyond what you now see, to firmly establish the greatness of your lineage, and proceed with the expected part you were predisposed to play. You can become the wisdom keepers—the ones who made peace on Earth possible. You have the potential before you to change the karmic attributes of you and your former enemies. What is your intent? Do you think you can make a difference in what your former enemies feel about you? You can! Things are not always as they seem, especially in this new energy. The enemy has changed too, if you noticed. It's time to come 'out of the kitchen.' You have been cooking the meal so long that you forget what it's like to enjoy it. You are the key to much of what Earth is going to be like in the next 12 years. Celebrate your challenge, then look for the leadership that will give you what you deserve—a new consciousness Exodus to lasting peace in your land!

Kryon

Question: *Are you, Lee Carroll, not tired sometimes from Kryon matters and issues?*

Answer: Only when I face those who wish to argue and stir drama around "who is right." Indeed, I react to those who question my integrity. My belief is not evangelistic. I honor all searches for God, and so does God! I don't care if someone disagrees with me or does not believe Kryon is real. I just bless them and congratulate them on their individuality. Kryon tells me that we are all "family," working together to try and find the best way to create a peaceful Earth in the new energy. Some are "stuck" in the old energy, but they are still family. Some hate us, but they are still family. What good does it serve any Human Being to force his will on another? Then you are a conqueror. I'd rather be a peacemaker—who creates wisdom and tolerance. The other simply creates ego and a big stick. Which one do you think is the product of a spiritually evolved Human? I am a very peaceful man.

I do not tire from the love of God.

Question: *Do you have your own personal vision for your life?*

Answer: Yes. To create it day by day. To never decide in advance what God has for me. To never prejudge another Human simply because of what I have been told. To push my light to my foes so that their lives are not as dark.

According to 2nd Kings in scripture (our translation), Elijah told Elisha that he was going to ascend. Elisha wanted to take Elijah's "mantle" (actually, a double portion). This was Elisha's request to continue the great wise teachings of Elijah after he left. Elijah, in all his wisdom as an avatar, told Elisha that if he could see him ascend, then he could have his cloak. The rest is history, and we have a wonderful first-person account of Elijah's ascension. Also noted is that Elisha went on to do great teaching and had wonderful wisdom.

I look at this as my example. Like Elisha, I wish to take the "mantle" of my higher, ascended self and build upon its wisdom so that others will see *God* in me.

Submitted in Love,

Challenge

"Listen, dear ones: Challenges are issues given to you to solve—not to *endure*. God does not receive joy and pleasure from Human challenge that remains unsolved! Spirit does not delight, nor does the planet benefit from *family* members who elect to stay in challenge! Lack of closure and unresolved energy *never* benefits God! Perfect solutions found through the process of love and wisdom are what we all celebrate together!"

Kryon

Most-Asked Questions

Chapter Nine

Most-Asked Questions
Chapter Nine

From Lee Carroll...

Here it is again! The question and answer section of Kryon Book Six, *Partnering with God*, was the most popular new addition to the Kryon books...so we did it again. Many of these were published in our *Kryon Quarterly* Magazine in the last year or so. Some of the subjects are similar to the questions asked before, but with expanded answers. Again, some difficult questions regarding controversial subjects have also been included. Here is the list of categories that will be covered by Kryon in this chapter.

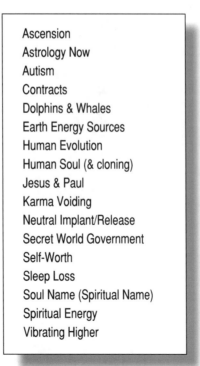

Ascension
Astrology Now
Autism
Contracts
Dolphins & Whales
Earth Energy Sources
Human Evolution
Human Soul (& cloning)
Jesus & Paul
Karma Voiding
Neutral Implant/Release
Secret World Government
Self-Worth
Sleep Loss
Soul Name (Spiritual Name)
Spiritual Energy
Vibrating Higher

Ascension

Question: *Dear Kryon, I feel drawn to the process of ascension. Does ascension affect the consciousness of our souls? Or are our souls already in the fullest state of consciousness of he source whom we call God? Is there one pathway to ascension, or are there a number of pathways?*

Answer: Let's define *soul* from our perspective. Your soul is that part of your humanism which is divine and eternal. It represents a part of your "Higher Self" (not all). The soul knows all and is perfect. It constantly shares information and is in an interactive state with entities around it, and with the "family" that is part of it on the other side of the veil. This is how current "planning sessions" are done—with the soul.

Within this definition, therefore, the answer to your question is that the soul is a partner in the Human process of ascension. Your vibrational shift is a *Human* one that is facilitated by your intent. Your soul is the part of divinity that is now allowed to give you the gifts, divine shapes, energies, and tools that it always had at-the-ready. The ascension process, therefore, is the integration of your 3D Human consciousness with the multidimensional soul that has your same name.

There is *one* door to ascension and many paths from the door. The door is **intent**, and the pathways are whatever steps you choose that will increase your awareness and your wisdom of the soul. The soul is really what we have called "the golden one," the "anointed Angel within."

Don't be mired in process, logistics, or what some might call the "absolute rules of ascension." Once you open the door, the personal path for you will be given, and it may be different from what you have been taught. Be wise in these things, and know that there are many ways that will lead you to your goal—not just one. Be wary of the Human who tells you otherwise—who may ask you to do it a certain way or suffer consequences. Fear is not involved with the ascension process. Just like your life is unique, so too is your learning path to a higher vibration. Some will soar past steps that used to be "required," and some may go very slowly through a uniform process that may seem arduous to others. It does not matter. Your intent to open the door is the key. Everything that follows is of your own making.

Claiming your Merkabah, moving into the fourth dimension, even co-creating a new *you*, is all done in ways that are unique for your process.

The common denominator for all of this is **intent**, and the Love of God realized in your life. Study it all, then move as you are led. Use discernment in your studies, and let no other person define for you what your sacredness should be. By your very intent, you claim the I AM! After claiming it, don't then give it away to another. Instead, let the others guide you into your own process—one that is perfect for you. Let them help you *balance*.

The intent to start the ascension status of enlightenment is an intent to break out of the mold of being in the "flock." The energy of the shepherd is therefore transmitted to **you**. Claim it!

Astrology Now

Question: Dear Kryon, In Book One, The End Times, you addressed "systems workers," those healers working with systems such as astrology—about realigning the planetary aspects two to three degrees to the right by 1992. It's now 1999. What advice do you have now about changing our systems? Has it moved more than three degrees to the right? What other aspects have changed? And how can we give our clients the most accurate information?

Answer: Again, we address the science of the magnetic systems. Do you understand that astrology is one of the oldest sciences on the planet? If we were to slightly change the way physics worked on the planet—say, the vibrational frequencies of the smallest parts, do you know what the results would be? It would change matter greatly. We would never be able to simply say to the scientists, "Move your physics a few degrees to the right!"

What you have before you is just the same. There is no way we can tell you all of the attributes that the magnetic shift has given to your science. We told you about shifts of three to five degrees. We told you that a "right-hand" shift was related to the actual movement. We originally gave you information that was accurate. Many of you, therefore, tried shifting your entire charts to the right, as though our magnetic work was also on a piece of paper. What do you think astrologers who use other planetary bodies as the "anchor" will do (Specifically the moon-anchored charts)?

In other words, there is far more to the right-hand shift than a chart adjustment. You are going to have to find this out for yourselves—just like you did in the beginning—but here is a hint. For those using the sun as the anchor (Western astrology), start experimenting with changing the *sizes* of the houses. Make your adjustments together equal a total of 4.5 degrees at the moment (through 1999). That is, all the changes together should equal 4.5 degrees. Which houses? Which ones do you think would change with an attribute of Humans on Earth receiving greater enlightenment? Which ones do you think might *have to* change to allow one sign to become another within certain borderline readings? Those of you who are very involved with astrology will have that answer. In fact, some of you regularly make this change anyway, since quite often the old method does not reflect the reality of who the individual actually is. In other words, many of you are already changing it correctly based on real-life experience in the new energy.

Here is another hint: You will find your greatest results by doing readings on the new children. The puzzle will be clearer to you by examining the energy of Humans who are coming in matching the new energy, instead of Humans who are undergoing changes within it.

The question is greatly honored. We do indeed want you to find the answer, but you must do it yourselves. Part of this is also to get you to work together—but then, you knew that, didn't you?

Autism

Question: Dear Kryon, In Kryon Book VI, Partnering with God, you talk about autistic children. Will you please reveal to me what is so special about autistic children?

Answer: I wish I could reveal all but I cannot due to what must remain your own discovery. An autistic child is a savant—a sage that is lurking in another dimension waiting for evolution to catch up. Those of you who have felt that the autistic child is far grander than appearances are correct. The biggest hint should be his relationship to the cetaceans and dolphins on Earth. Experiment with this! Find out what is happening! It will suit you to understand these special Humans and their connection to these other creatures.

The autistic Human is one who represents part of the next evolution of Humans. Their old mental tools are not incomplete, but rather, evolved, and therefore gone. The butterfly does not think like a worm, but the society of worms won't understand that. The autistic child is overloaded with unsorted crass input in a low-energy world. He expects elegant and refined energy communication and does not fit in with the current unevolved language that is given. If you had to exist in a land where everyone simultaneously shouted and motioned to you in groans and grunts that were not in the least understandable, you might begin to relate. The noise and confusion would become frustrating, and it would quickly overcome you. You would beg to be released! You would ask for things to be reduced to simplicity—for your own sanity!

This Human is not an anomaly or a defect. He is a glimpse of the future. By the way, all of these children respond best to love—the greatest universal communication.

Contracts

Question: Dear Kryon, I am a 50-year-old incarcerated woman. I am currently serving a 20-year sentence for a fatal accident that occurred while I was drunk. I don't recall much about what happened during the accident, but I know that I am now paying the *consequences. I began reading spiritual material while in prison, including one of the Kryon books. I have read about our spiritual contracts, but I am still struggling to understand how this works. Did I prearrange to "accidentally" kill this man? Did he agree to it beforehand? If so, does this mean we were both doing God's work? I am confused about how contracts work in such tragic instances. Please help me with this, as I struggle with it every day. I truly want to know how I can make amends.*

Answer: Thank you, dear one, for this profound question. Indeed, Human tragedy is most difficult to explain in terms of contract, but your intuition serves you correctly regarding your agreement with this man. His family might not agree, but they, as well as you, have a duality that is strong in this area—seemingly inappropriate death and victimization.

The two of you decided together to bring about a situation that would be a catalyst, or "gift," to those around you. In the process, you helped to facilitate (1) those around him, and (2) those around you. We have spoken before about the fact that often it takes going to the lowest Human ebb of life to create attributes with the potential of spiritual change. Not only do you find yourself at that bridge, but the potential was also given to the man who agreed with you to provide the gift.

Everyone around this situation of his death and your incarceration can do one of two things about it: (1) Dwell in the drama of the tragedy for your life—grieving and being constantly the victim, or (2) understand the "gift" of potential for change that has been willingly given, and celebrate the event by taking responsibility for part of the agreement. Then you can ask, "What now? What does it mean? What am I supposed to do with it?"

If you chose the first option, you have chosen to void out his life—making it meaningless and ignoring the energy of the experience— and the love that went into its facilitation for you.

Now, as far as *you* are concerned, no amends are necessary. It's time to see it for what it is, and time to start speaking to him every day and celebrating the fact that all went according to the potential you set up. By taking spiritual responsibility as well as moral responsibility, you now have to start looking around to find out why you are where you are. You agreed to it, now look around. Expect synchronicity in prison. Is there a place there where you can help hold your light? Were you brought there perhaps for this? What good thing can come from your time there? When all is done and you discover that good thing, realize that the man you "accidentally" killed knew very well of this potential, too. Mourn his loss appropriately, then celebrate the gift of his love that allowed him to go through with it!

Dolphins and Whales

Question: *Dear Kryon, I feel very connected to dolphins and whales. What is their relationship to Humans on this planet?*

Answer: Continuing with the discussion of the cetaceans and dolphins (from the autistic question above), you must know that the connection between them and Humans is profound. I cannot reveal what the connection is at this time, but if you remember, I have spoken of these creatures as the "library of the planet." In addition, I have told you that they are sacred and that they respond to magnetics. In addition, I have told you that they will be part of your future. Take all these hints, and project them to your own answer, using the discernment that you have been given. You will then understand.

All Humans know the answer at the cellular level, where the great secrets are all known about whom you really are and what you are doing here—and the potential of what is to come. Don't you find it interesting that regardless of culture or religion, the world as a whole has decided to save the whales? What other species has the world come together to save in this way? The answer is *none*!

Why? It's because these creatures are important placeholders of the energy and knowledge of what is to come, and at the cellular level, all Humans know it. I call the dolphins the "pilots." The whales I call the "library." Together they will lead you to knowledge in the future. It may sound strange, but it is so. Meanwhile, celebrate their existence, and "speak" to them often. They absolutely know who Humans are, and respond to you differently than any other creature on Earth.

Earth Energy Sources

Question: *Dear Kryon, Where should we (Humans) look to for new energy sources for our planet?*

Answer: Where they have always been. Start by considering the ones that are the oldest. Many of you feel that new energy sources always mean new technology. In a sense, you are correct. The best energy source you have is the heat inside the planet. Find new technology to get it efficiently! Stop *creating* heat! It's everywhere below you. The highest-tech power plants you currently have turn heat into steam. Now let the planet give you the heat, and turn it into steam. It really is there for you—without waste, without danger, without side effects.

Next, start capturing the incredible powers of the tides—the push-pull action that is *always* there. You have had the knowledge for a very long time about how to do this. Perhaps it was too low-tech?

Finally, when you are able to understand some of these basic energies of the planet and how they have been there all along to provide power for you, slowly move into capturing the main one. This process involves connecting to the Cosmic Lattice through knowledge on how to manipulate its vibration, and unbalance portions of it for your convenience. (See Chapter Seven, and the channellings on The Cosmic Lattice.)

Human Evolution

Question: *Dear Kryon, How does evolution fit in to our present Human condition? You made a statement that man as we know it began about 100,000 years ago, but there were different types* *of man starting about 300,000 years ago. (This is from memory, so I may not be quoting you correctly.)*

Answer: There has been life on your planet for a very long time, and several types of Human life as well. Some types even developed and became extinct. Other types evolved almost to what you see today. We told you that your actual race has a lineage of only about 100,000 years so that you would understand that although there might have been Humans before that, the kind with the adjusted lesson and seed biology (as given by those from the Seven Sisters) started about that time. Any study of humanity before that is a study of those unlike you.

You also should know that the Human Being on the planet right now is absolutely unique. Never in the history of the planet has a Human developed with the consciousness attributes that you carry at this moment. With time, there will be slight physical changes as well, with some enlarged detoxification organs, adding to the uniqueness of your time. Now, truly, is the demarcation point of a whole new Human Being!

The Human Soul (& Cloning)

Question: *Dear Kryon, I've been reading a lot about soul retrieval from other lightworkers. According to them, Human Beings often experience what is called "soul loss," meaning aspects of your soul must be retrieved and reintegrated with your soul for you to be able to move forward in the ascension process. Furthermore, they say you cannot do this by yourself—it takes a "specialist." Can you shed some light on what they are talking about?*

Answer: We have spoken many times of this in other words than you have asked with, but it will answer your question. The ascension process is working on capturing more and more of the divinity of the "angel within you." In that, you might then say that you are retrieving more of the divine soul and integrating (melding) with it. So the answer to the first part of your question is *yes*.

On your own, however, you have the ability to do this. You have earned it, and this has been the subject of our Human enablement channels, as well as the message of the master of love from over 2,000 years ago. Humans can now go to ascension status with intuitive steps and self-study.

However, there are several facilitating methods of energy work combined with knowledge that some will find helpful in the journey. Remember, Michael Thomas of *The Journey Home* was facilitated by no less than seven angels for his "fast track" to ascension status. There is, therefore, precedent in this, but it is important to understand that it is indeed possible by yourself. This is the main message of Spirit through the Kryon channel!

Question: *Dear Kryon, Would cloned Human Beings have souls as we do? Does cloning serve a higher purpose? If so, how?*

Answer: Dear ones, it is important for you to understand that Spirit does not exist in a vacuum! It was the energy of Spirit that provided the science for cloning, as well as for other enhancements in what you call the "normal" way Humans are "born" on this planet. Let me ask you this: When reproductive biology is "helped" with birth, does the child have a normal soul? What about the freezing of reproductive cells, then their use later? Does the resulting child have a normal soul?

The answer to all of this, plus the potential of cloning is *yes*! The entity that comes in with any of these Human incarnations, no matter what the technology, is totally aware of the circumstances around it and has actively chosen the challenge. Think of the challenge someday if you clone a Human Being! This soul will have stood in line for this—just like you did.

Jesus and Paul

Question: *Dear Kryon, In Book Six you said that the apostle Paul was a spiritual channel. Was he not, in fact, largely responsible for the distorted version of Jesus' teachings that eventually became orthodox Christianity? Indeed, it is my understanding that the other apostles considered Paul a heretic of the worst sort. Any additional comments about Paul?*

Question: In this life as a lightworker, I feel very close to Jesus. Sometimes I even feel like I lived a past life in the time of Jesus. However, I cannot relate to the story of Jesus as told in the Bible and as taught by today's churches. These versions seem so far from the truth! How accurate is the Biblical depiction of Jesus? Please help me to understand.

Answer: These questions are taken together, since they are caused by the same core issue of what truth is. In February 1999, we gave you a channelling about this important issue (see Chapter One, "The Integrity of God"). Here are some comments for you to consider, which were part of that message.

First, here are some questions that may expose some of your assumptions about what took place in history. Orthodox Christianity contains over 300 segmented boxes of those who feel God smiles only on them. Which one of those got the distorted view of Jesus' teaching? Which one is right? Which wars and carnage relating to believing the "right way" about Jesus do you think were sanctioned by Spirit (God)? Do you really think an abundant Human can't go to heaven? Do you think that the "truth" that priests had got changed a bit through the hundreds of years when they were also the heads of government? Would you give your most cherished religious doctrines to your American Congress to keep pure and change only when needed—for over 300 years? Yet that is what happened. Do you really think God *hates* Humans who carry heavy karmic attributes of gender identification into their lives? Do you think that an awesome, loving God, who created Humans in a spiritual image (family), would then kill them one by one—torturing them in hell forever because they didn't follow some rules—or *find* the truth through life—the children, too? That's who you are being told God is.

Now, you ask if you believe you have the accurate story? Obviously, something is not being translated—or got lost along the way.

I ask these things only as rhetorical questions that point out that this information you think you have does not accurately give you the big picture at all. Are you aware that Jesus was called "the wicked priest" by the other Jewish priests? If they thought Jesus was wicked, is it any wonder that some of the other followers of Jesus took issue with Paul's leadership? What other apostles received the kind of miracle that Paul did on the road to Damascus? Do you remember the difference between an apostle and a disciple? Do you think they might have been competing with each other? Does it remind you of any attributes of your own modern religious times?

I broach these things to give you the information that even while Jesus lived, and immediately afterwards, Humans were infighting over his immense power and what they thought he had said and done. Very few really "got it." There were many splits immediately—some leading to the lowest energy actions in the name of Spirit ever to be performed on the Earth.

To answer your question directly, no, you do not have the full story. To make things even more interesting, the full story (about Jesus' life) does indeed exist within the known sacred scrolls. Why then, you might ask, are there so many versions of what happened? So many different rules to follow? So many different ideas of exactly who and how to worship? The reason is that there are so many different Humans.

The scrolls are available, and potent. They contain information that would upset and unbalance the very core doctrines of those who believe they know all about Jesus. Why are the scholars somewhat hesitant to release them? How long does it really take to form opinions on the messages contained within them? So far, scholars have been at it over 40 years. Do any of you know what the real interpretations are—the ones kept at low profile? Some do, and they are having a difficult time with the issue of what to do with this kind of knowledge. Some wish they didn't know it. Some have released it and have been ridiculed.

Our instructions to you on this issue have not changed since we started giving you messages ten years ago. Regarding Jesus: He was an avatar and a shaman of great importance, and He gave spectacular information to humanity about Human empowerment. He ushered in a spiritual dispensation where humanity was slowly earning the chance to understand vibrational shift. He enabled Humans. He taught love. He showed Peter how to walk on the water, taught him how he could do it **by himself**, and Peter did! It was only when Peter doubted, that he took the hand of Jesus for help. Yet many of your priests of today interpret that to say, "Peter could not do it without Jesus." They forget what the real message was—that of empowerment. This is an example of how so much of what Jesus did was stretched to mean other things—things that usually didn't empower the individual Human, but the organization or priest instead. Is it any wonder why there were so many empowered priests? So many rules?

We told you ten years ago about religion: "Be still, and let *love* be your discernment." We have told you now many times that each of you has all the truth within you. You don't have to join anything or follow any Human to find it. We have asked you many times to set your highest priority regarding your religious differences to: *loving each other* within the scope of your divisions. We told you not to try to change the other, but only to love them. We asked you to invite wisdom into your life.

We told you early on that you will never eliminate the various doctrines or beliefs on Earth. They are not expected to come together into some vast melting pot. What you can expect, however, is wisdom—bringing the solution of tolerance—of understanding that Humans have the right to find God/Spirit in any way that is comfortable for them. Stop making all the other family members wrong. Stop trying to make them believe your way. Take care of your own spiritual matters, then allow the others, the rest of the family, to exist—just as you do—then celebrate them!

Dear one, do you relate to Jesus love? Indeed! So do we all! Do you relate to the love and wise spiritual teachings of Elijah? So do we all! How about the other great masters of many cultures? We celebrate and relate to the love! Love is love, and it will be found in many places all over the globe. Avatars are alive today and have vast spiritual power over matter and energy. It is a staple of the planet. Because they exist, does not mean they are against those who believe in Jesus! Understand that you are all together in your quests for enlightenment—now, **love one another**! Give space even to the ones you feel are very wrong about God. Let them find their own integrity and truth—then celebrate their life!

The basic truth is this: Love is the core of matter. Love is the key to future humanity's ability to change this Earth. Religion tells you a great deal about men, not God. Within each of the religious boxes, however, there are seeds of basic truth. You don't need religion to be enlightened—you need only to change yourself. Then if you wish to participate in religion, you can. Then if you wish to follow something, follow the **love**! The power is within the individual, not the organization—not within the many interpretations of what happened—not within the many rules made by men. Jesus' real message was about taking your power, and that you actually had the ability to do it.

The Jewish master, Jesus, was one of many masters through the ages. He is the one that represents the highest visibility within your culture, and that's why the subject is found so often in the pages of the Kryon material on the American continent. It is not the same for the other Kryon channels in the other cultures. Like so many other masters, Jesus enabled men and women with love. And like so many other masters, His message? **Love one another**! Then when you have been able to *own* that concept, go ahead and walk on the water.

Karma Voiding

Question: Dear Kryon, According to my understanding, our karma is voided by the implant. So what effect does our natal astrology have upon us from the point of taking the implant? Is our astrological chart no longer valid after we take the implant?

Answer: This is a review, but perhaps it is time, since the answers were given many years ago.

The implant does not void your astrological sign. That is your magnetic imprint, and is yours for your entire lifetime. What the intent for the implant/release does, is to void other astrological attributes that used to impact your sign.

We gave you the example of a fern. It is a plant, but specifically its imprint is as a fern. It loves warm places, indirect sunlight, and has a definite pattern of what it wants for sustenance (water schedule).

When the fern gives intent to change (the implant/release scenario), it will stay a fern. What will change are all the attributes around it that used to restrict it due to its "fern-ness." Although it will still love the shade, it can indeed exist in the sun. Although it will always enjoy a specific water schedule and will be predisposed toward it, it can move into the desert and survive. It never could before, and it remains a fern—alive and healthy.

Those of you who are of certain astrological signs know of your predispositions. You understand fully what the attributes are of the signs that were named and given to you by your astrological scientists. What you now have, however, is the ability to go beyond them and not be slowed down by previously known interactive magnetic planetary energies that would have done so.

Are there times when you were told *not to do this or that* due to your birth sign? That's what has now changed. Through your intent to receive the implantation of a new cellular awareness (the implant), you void many of the attributes of your astrological cycles. Therefore, many of the "do's and don'ts" that accompanied your sign are now a non-issue. Go ahead and try it. If you have been one who closely follows your astrological aspects, you are going to be surprised at what you are able to do—even at some of the worst times, as predicted by your sign.

This can't be a surprise to you, for moving off the path of your contract is all about spiritual freedom, co-creation, and the start of a new paradigm of life. With all of that will come a feeling of being a new "magnetic" person as well.

Neutral Implant/Release

Question: *Dear Kryon, How long a time do we have available to ask for the neutral implant? Is there a cutoff point or an optimal time to ask for it?*

Answer: Let's again remember what the implant actually is. During the last ten years, we have refined and exposed what the energy around this process is for a Human. Remember that it's just *you*, giving pure intent and permission to move forward to the next spiritual step.

You are being implanted with enablement to receive the gifts from within your own power source. It's opening a door for communication. It's giving notice that you are ready to move away from the old contract that you came in with. It's profound, but simple. Some have made it sinister and fearful. Some have thought that such a thing isn't possible, and that priests and leaders must administer and facilitate it. It's odd that they would acknowledge the 11:11 window of humanity's permission, but deny the ability of personal permission. Such are the assumptions of duality.

The answer to your question is this: Your guides sit very quietly with you for your entire life. As channelled before, they are activated by your intent to move forward into a new vibration (the implant/release). This is seen as a major action item by your spiritual helpers. They move fast when activated by your intent! Some of you have even complained about it.

Do you really think that they would give you a time limit? Do you think that you would not be heard? This is your family! Therefore, the optimal time to ask is while you are alive, and the cutoff point is at the point of death.

We really do love you, you know. You can give this intent anytime you wish. It has no rules around it other than you, having full integrity and great purity around the request.

Question: *Dear Kryon, I asked for the neutral implant/release several years ago, but continue to be tormented by a physical condition. Does this mean I haven't received the implant yet? What can I do?*

Answer: Requesting the implant/release is simply a Human's pure request to discover the divinity inside, and to start a process of vibrational shift—the realization that you are a piece of God. When you give this request with spiritual pure intent, it is given to you without you ever having to ask again.

Some do not realize the power that this spiritual attribute contains. Some use intent that is conditional. They say, "If I do this, then perhaps God will do that." They do not realize what pure intent is.

Pure intent is defined as what Abraham had in his arm when the dagger was on its way into the chest of his only son. Abraham loved God so much, that although he was miserable with the thought of what might happen, he trusted in the *love* of Spirit. He trusted in the fact that God is a partner and would never trick him. He was right—and instead of a death, there was a celebration on that mountain—a win-win situation.

What I am saying is that your request, and the subsequent granting of it, was not about your physical condition. That comes later—after you start celebrating your life, after you understand the Spiritual decision and all the ramifications of it, after you practice holding your light in joy even *with* the physical condition, after you show those around you the spectacular light of your inner being.

The implant/release is a lifelong application. It has as many gifts with it as there are Humans. When you stop wondering when the healing will occur, and start celebrating your existence itself, your biology will begin to change. For now, turn your focus away from the obvious, and start working with the real gift first. Then joy and peace—and yes, even healing, will be added to your life. Learn to "own" the self-worth of the angel that sits inside. Then these things you desire will fall into place.

Secret World Government

Question: *Dear Kryon, What are Kryon's thoughts and comments about the "secret world government"?*

Answer: This "secret government" of your planet has been discussed before in multiple channellings. Some of you have called it the "Illuminati." Whereas this conspiratorial and powerful energy was making some progress toward its goal of controlling the way things work on Earth (mainly through secret financial plans and Human control), they are now battling for their very existence and meeting a foe they never expected.

The foe that they are meeting head-on is called *truth*. This sword of truth is being carried by millions, as a result of technology and raised consciousness on the planet. In your Human communications, what used to be official and lengthy has suddenly become informal and instant. You have created a web of interlacing exposure, greetings, and information that is blasting light at the very foundation of this dark and secret group.

As we have told you before, "When everyone can talk instantly to everyone, there can be no secrets." There is no power that can stand against the truth. Take a look at what has happened even to the most powerful men and women on Earth, no matter what their wealth or political affiliation, when some spectacular truth has been exposed regarding their lives. They cannot hide! No amount of power or wealth can overcome the energy of truth (the sword). Knowledge (the shield) is the catalyst of the truth, and the wisdom to communicate it is what we have called the "mantle of God," or the armor.

As in the other question in this series, we told you that the light is *active*. Nothing can stand against the truth of it. The darkness retreats and shrieks in horror at being exposed. Ironically (due to its name), as this group is *illuminated*, it cannot work. The dark is reduced to gray, and their workings become known. Secrets cannot be maintained, and movement that heretofore was easy in the covert way this group operated is harder and harder to sustain.

This group is failing. That is the answer to your question. Still, there will be those who wish to frighten you into fear-based action. It's sensational information, and it is easy for a Human to get attention when he is carrying something that says, "*The sky is falling!*"

It is the "shadow within" that is attracted to this, and the "I told you so" intellect that will wish to motivate the Human to examine the dark. This is why Humans are attracted to the sensational. It is balanced and appropriate, but the **knowledge** of how it works creates the **truth**—and then the **wisdom** to discern it creates the **light**.

Self-Worth

Question: Dear Kryon, Why do we, as Humans, have difficulty loving ourselves? Isn't loving our total Self one of the most important tools for ascension?

Answer: Yes, therefore the test is working! Love of self and establishment of self-worth is something that Humans have to work at. It is all part of the hurdle that you face in finding the "God within." With the gradual buildup of the Indigo children, you have an entirely new attribute being given to Human consciousness. The children (as channelled before) arrive with a tremendous self-worth. Some even call them "head strong," not understanding exactly what the real attribute of this personality is. This is the beginning of Human types who will have far less trouble loving themselves than you have. Celebrate what you have done! Celebrate what you are becoming!

Sleep Loss

Question: Dear Kryon, Why is it that I can't go to sleep until late at night? I go bed at 2 a.m., but can't get to sleep until 4 a.m. I realize that I have very high vibes, but this late sleeping in the morning is very inconvenient (I have a part-time job). My health is good, and I have the energy to do whatever I like. I'm an 82-year-old lady who's not used to these late nights!

Answer: Bless you for your question. Start celebrating your new biology! Your energy will *not* be affected adversely. What you are seeing is a gift of vibrational shift. Let the information of your biological age let others know that this process is available for all Humans and not just the ones who feel they are of an age of apparent productivity! It is a Human change, and is not proprietary to any age group.

Change your schedule to fit your passion. What is it you would like to do with the new awake hours you have been given? Start changing your habits around your new energy. Find new things to pass the time that you feel help yourself and others. Change what you are "used to." Fit your new life into the gifts you are being given, and *do not* make old energy comparisons to the new attributes. Who you were is not whom you are becoming.

Celebrate! These changes are real, and are here because you have asked for them.

Soul Names

Question: *Dear Kryon, I would like to know my spiritual (or soul) name. How can I find what that name is?*

Answer: There is nothing you can do to *find* that name. I have two bits of information to give you regarding this subject:

(1) No person on Earth actually knows his real "soul name." Some of you might have been given information on the sound or spelling of a Human name that would be more favorable to your personal energy as you walk your path. This has to do with spiritual Human help. It is actually not your soul name at all.

Did you ever wonder why some are given this information and others are not? It's a Human assumption that perhaps those who were given the information were somehow better spiritually. This is not correct. Humans who are given special information about their names are those who are simply helped to change the energy of how they are known. It helps them to move forward on their path. Most do not need this information, so the ones who got it were actually given a tool to help them in a special situation. Most of you do not see it this way, however.

Know therefore, that the "spiritual names" that many of you have been intuitively given are gifts from Spirit to help you change your energy. Here is something else: These Human energy-helping name changes are not permanent! Be aware that those of you who get them might have another given to you later—to match your changing vibrations. This change, of all things, shows you that these names are not the ones you have on the other side (where there is no change).

(2) We have given this information before: Dear ones, don't spend time on attributes that do not match the energy of your task here. Do you walk around life anxious that you cannot see into the inner sanctum of your bodily functions? No. You celebrate their workings and understand that they are a vital part of *you*. Then you let them work. It is the same for the name you have on the other side of the veil. It would not make any sense to you if you knew it. It is not something you *say* into the air. It is an energy, a color, and a message all in one. It is interdimensional and has a strong light complement.

With that explanation, do you really want to spend time trying to find it? Go back and revisit the parable of "Jason and the Cave." [Kryon Book Four]. It is a snapshot of why we do not even begin to explain some things, including your soul name.

Spiritual Energy

Question: Dear Kryon, Whenever I link up with you in meditation, or whenever I read a Kryon book or magazine, I experience beautiful emotions—totally based in love—that can be overwhelming. I do not get these feelings with any other entity, guide, or channel. I know that there is something special, and I treasure it, but I do not know why it should be so intense. I feel there must be a reason. Am I here to assist the Kryon group in some way, or is what I experience simply par for the course for those of us fortunate enough to experience your magic?

Answer: Simply stated, you are finally feeling the essence of "home." My overlay is that of love, even though I am the mechanic. When you feel these things, you are absorbing a piece of the truth of who you are and where you came from, and there is a tremendous feeling of "remembrance." As for no other channel giving this? You haven't looked far enough, for Spirit will always bring you love-based information in this fashion if you allow it. Kryon is only one of many who carry the overlay of the seeds of home. There is part of you that will resonate with my message, since we all are from the same place—a place of great majesty and love—and one where you long to be.

As far as assisting me? You assist me when you hold your light up high for all to see. You assist me when you have tolerance for the intolerable. You assist me when you give *intent* for you Higher Self to talk to Spirit, and partner in a manner that heals your body. All these actions assist the whole, of which I am a part.

I am a piece of the great love energy that is life itself, and so are you! When you vibrate at a higher level, so do I! When you are filled with a welling-up of emotion over the feeling of home, you are feeling part of me. We are all allied, and the closer your vibration gets to my side of the veil, the more you will feel me.

We are family, you and I—and I speak to every pair of eyes that gives intent to read this transmission.

Vibrating Higher

Question: *Dear Kryon, You have talked before about the vibrational levels of our planet and ourselves. I would like to know what activities, behaviors, substances, and so on, help our vibrational levels. I would also like to know what hurts or hinders our vibrations. Thank you.*

Answer: The answer to this question may sound too simple.

- What hurts your vibrational growth are the following things:

1. Remaining in fear when you know the real truth of the way things work.
2. Worry!
3. Creating drama around things that are solvable without it.
4. Holding on to portions of your life that you know very well are of low vibration because you can't think of a way to exist without them.
5. Not trusting the angel/divinity within.
6. Having a wavering intent in spiritual matters.

- What *will* assist your **vibrational growth** are the following things:

1. Claiming the power of your inner guidance.
2. Lack of worry (peace) about the future, and an absolutely "knowing" that all is well.
3. Creating peaceful circumstances around areas that have potential for drama.
4. Casting away inappropriate energies in your life that at one time might have seemed "sacred," but which now you can indeed live without.
5. Spending time with Spirit meditating in a new way: (a) celebration of everything that is happening to you (no matter what), (b) visualization of melding to your higher self, (c) continually asking, "What is it you wish me to know?" instead of trying to "outguess" what might be the solution to problems at hand.
6. Realization of *self worth* to facilitate the creation of *pure intent*.

YOU ARE DEARLY LOVED!

Kryon

Chapter Ten

Kryon News

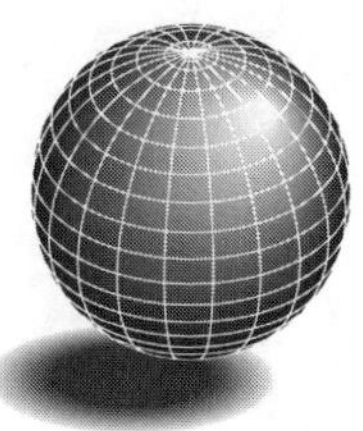

On The Internet!

[http://www.kryonqtly.com]

California Commercial site

Internet Address

http://www.kryon.com

This is the California Kryon web site. See the daily updated Kryon seminar schedule. See the latest channels (including all the United Nations transcriptions). See what Kryon products are available, and read the latest Kryon book reviews. Subscribe to the Kryon Quarterly Magazine. This is the Kryon "commercial" area. (Both Kryon sites are available from [www.kryonqtly.com].

On The Internet!

[http://www.kryonqtly.com]

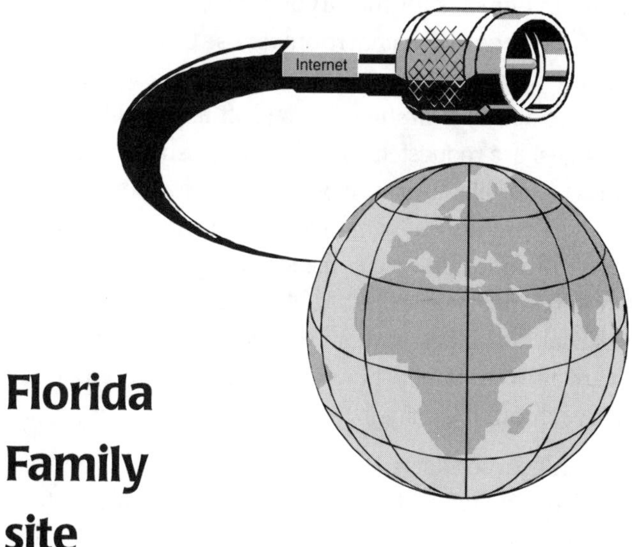

Florida Family site

Internet Address

http://www.kryon.org.

This is the Florida Kryon web site. Receive "marshmallow messages," personally chosen and sent to your EMAIL each day. Join in a chat room with others of like mind. Spend time on the message board. Find others in your area of the same consciousness. This is the Kryon "family" area - warm and toasty! (Both Kryon sites are available from [www.kryonqtly.com].

Kryon On-Line
by
Kryon WebMaster - Gary Liljegren

Many who read this book will be in a relatively comfortable setting, planning for their future and the future of their children and living in their "now." When the Kryon websites were designed, we set up our sites for the Kryon family worldwide. That included a message board and chat room for use by everyone, and now we are discovering the connectivity with all peoples. When messages are posted or *marshmallows* (Soft and uplifting daily EMAIL messages) are requested by people in Bosnia, Argentina, New Zealand, Colombia, Japan, Nova Scotia, Northern Ireland, York, and New York, we see what a diverse group we really are. We now have the opportunity to consider that some of the Kryon family are not in a relatively comfortable setting at this time as a result of political difficulties, natural disasters, or personal challenges. We are all in the family, however, and we can get together and support each other on-line!

If you haven't yet connected to Kryon on-line, you have a treat in store, as there are two websites that are linked in a variety of ways to supply information to the Kryon Family all over the earth and to interconnect the family with each other as we expand our knowledge and light. The two sites are [www.kryon.com] and [www.kryon.org] (see pages 436-437). The first page consists of New Age—channelled information from Kryon that is love-filled and empowering. It allows you to find out more about the Kryon related products, view portions of the books, subscribe to the national *Kryon Quarterly* Magazine, and read some of the latest, most powerful channellings.

The three United Nations messages from Kryon given in New York in 1995, 1996, and 1998 are also presented in full, as well as the latest Kryon seminar schedule. You may also find out which languages the Kryon books have been translated into and where to obtain them. In another area, links are provided to a variety of websites that complement the Kryon books and material.

There is a Jan Tober section that has a fascinating biography of Jan, a section on her art, a page about her available tapes and CDs (the "Color and Sound Meditation" is particularly nice), and information about her "Bubble Bowl Booklet." You can also order her products on-line.

The second site, [www.kryon.org] is the official Kryon Family Room. It is a comfy, relaxed place where you can interact with other members of the worldwide extended family. There is a chat room in which you will find people from a wide variety of ages and occupations who all have an interest in the Kryon energy. After dinner, and after helping the kids with their homework, you might sit down to your computer in the Midwest of the USA and introduce yourself to Ron or Aussie in the chat room and discover that they are typing on their keyboards in Australia, and it is "tomorrow" afternoon, according to their clocks!

Some of the family members use "screen names," and others use their natural first name, whichever is most comfortable. Usually we have no idea where someone lives unless that subject comes up. We had something unusual happen along those lines in the chat room one night. "Moonchild" was on her computer from work (daytime in Australia), and a new visitor with the name "Dolphin" came into the chat room. After some casual conversation, they realized that they were both in Australia! Then they found out that they were both in Canberra, and to everyone's surprise in the chat area, they learned that they were both working for the same agency, in the same office building, and on the same floor! They had said hello to each other as office workers but had never known they had a common interest in Kryon until they met in the Kryon chat room.

That was not Moonchild's only unusual event in the chat room (her real name is Jill). The following is Jill's actual story about twin souls reuniting in the Kryon chat room.

In mid September 1998, Jill attended her first Kryon seminar in Sydney, Australia, after having discovered Kryon earlier in the year. From the time of reading the first Kryon book, she had experienced an extraordinary sense of "coming home." Approximately four weeks after the Sydney seminar, in the Kryon chat room, she met "the most precious, wonderful, and special person ever to have come into my life."

From the first time they talked, Kenny and Jill experienced an incredibly strong and special connection, and neither of them could stop thinking of the other. Their Souls/Higher Selves had "recognized and remembered" one another. With lightning speed, the most incredibly beautiful, intense, and overwhelming love that either of them had ever experienced developed between them. Within days, they knew that they would be together forevermore. Nothing had ever been more real or right than this—it simply was meant to be. They are truly twin souls who have been waiting all their lives to find each other again.

Although they have exchanged photos, as yet they have not met in the physical sense. They live on opposite sides of the world—he in Massachusetts, and she in Canberra, Australia (over 10,000 miles apart). Prior to this happening, Jill would never have imagined it possible to fall in love with someone she had not met, and over the Internet at that. Now it seems the most natural and normal thing in the world.

Many interesting people can be found in the chat room and on the message board. You might be talking with "Aloha" and be surprised with a name like his that he is in Switzerland. You might be discussing crop circles with Amy and learn that she is a college student in Pennsylvania. You might also find an interest with someone whose circumstances are similar. There was a post in January from a person who was addressing her special situation. The following is her post:

"Kryon talks in Book Six about some people who, when you look at them and speak to them, tend to look at you blankly. I share my life, and I am honoured to do so, with

my youngest child, aged 21 years, who has Down's Syndrome. He does not have any verbal communication, but can use a computer with ease. He can also look into you and see all. He gets very stressed when he is around people who have negative thoughts, and this affects him for hours. I would love to know what other attributes my lovely man has. I would be very disappointed if I was missing something. Love is his main focus. I have a friend who is my age, whom he loves dearly and needs to spend a lot of time in her company. When I asked him the reason, thinking he should be with his peers, he typed "I love her for her light."

"Is this what it is, or am I missing something?"
Love, Kathy.

In the America On Line system where the Kryon on-line activity first occurred, and again in the *kryon.org* chat room, Lee Carroll has joined the Kryon family members in an activity called "Lee-Live." He types on his keyboard in California and interacts in real time with the others in the chat room. Geoff Hoppe in Colorado established the protocol for the "Lee Live" sessions on AOL, and it has been continued right into the existing websites. Using a speakerphone hookup during the last "Lee-Live" session, it was quite interesting to listen to Lee in California as he was typing on his keyboard like crazy—at the same time maintaining voice connection with me in Florida, where I was coordinating the chat room functions. Those who were in the chat room for the "Lee-Live" really appreciated the opportunity to interact with him directly.

What subjects are discussed during regular chat room times? When we first started the chat room, a common assumption was that Kryon would be discussed most of the time. Indeed, that happens, and particularly with someone newly arrived in the chat room. But much of the talk is about everyday activities—problems, asking for ideas, laughing, crying, and sharing a lot of love and caring. Sometimes the activity is light, and some days the participant list is long, with a lot of regulars from all parts of the world as well as many new people. Specific topics and guests are regularly arranged, and there is a *Chat room Schedule* page that shows the expected events in the coming weeks.

The Kryon Message Board is another area of heavy activity, and it continues to increase. When Geoff set up the AOL Kryon Folder some years ago, it became the busiest "folder" in the New Age area. It was typically running 500 posts in a month. Things have changed on the net since then, and as a comparison, the message board on *kryon.org* often increases by that same number in a two-day period of time. The love shared on the message board is hard to imagine until you read the posts and replies for a while and get the feeling of the caring and togetherness. Here is an example:

"Dear friends, thank you very, very much for your messages, which helped me get through one of the most difficult periods of my life. Specially, this last one is the best, and exactly what I have needed. Thank you again, Barbara from Slovenia."

The message board is an ideal location for meeting people. Often, family members begin sending E-mail to those with similar interests, and build strong friendships that continue and last.

The topics on the message board tend more to be "New Age" or Kryon-related. When questions are asked, it is amazing and beautiful how clearly the family responds. From Annie, Talet, Starsong, Bess, and many more, there are so many in the family who provide depth and insight in their posts. We have a collection of past postings in a number of areas where the topic seems to be of continuing interest. It is easy to check the past postings, then go to the current postings on the message board.

If you have questions while you are reading the Kryon books, the message board is the idea medium of exchange. Perhaps you live in rural Manitoba—you received a Kryon book called <u>The End Times</u> from your sister in Toronto, and you imagine that there is probably no one within 250 miles of you who thinks like you do. Surprise! Get on your computer and connect to the Kryon Message Board and the Kryon Family Chat room. It will seem like you have a house full of new friends who do think like you do—people who have answers to your questions, and people who want to share their love with you. It is a great feeling.

Another area that is increasing are the pages with pictures of seminars and other events. More and more, we are experiencing the coming together of the on-line people at the major events as well as the "At Home with Kryon" gatherings. People who have met on the website are now able to see each other in person. Pictures are taken and are incorporated into website pages so that all may enjoy and see what their on-line friends actually look like.

When a seminar occurs, within hours the posting begins reporting what happened. Those who were unable to attend because of distance or schedule can get in on the excitement. When all the shouting is done, we collect a number of the comments and put them in a "Past Postings" section for later review. The Past Postings area is also used for specific topics which frequently arise—something like a "Frequently Asked Questions" location.

Soon after *kryon.org* came up on the Internet, we started sending out "Marshmallow Messages (MM)" daily. These are messages of positive thought that are sent by e-mail only to the Kryon family worldwide. It is necessary to request them on our website; we don't register people without their knowledge. The MMs are daily reminders that we are loved. They are not very lengthy, but are usually quotes from well-known names of the last three millennia, as well as more recent New Age sources. Lee Carroll/Kryon is a regular contributor.

Although it seems like a few months ago, it was actually October, 1997 when the first 12 or 15 names from two or three countries were entered into the memory and the MMs started. Now we are sending daily messages to well over 2,000 of the Kryon family in approximately 90 countries!

Recently, requests have arrived from Israel, Denmark, Norway, Slovenia, Australia, New Zealand, Russia, Singapore, United Arab Emirates, India, Mexico, Germany, Guam, Hong Kong, Thailand, South Africa, and Switzerland—as well as a large number from the USA and Canada. International? This is certainly an illustration of the Kryon Family worldwide.

The name "marshmallow" was selected because it started with "m" and describes the messages that are light, fluffy, and bring knowing smiles from those receiving the messages, perhaps from pleasant childhood experiences. A surprise was in store because some in our worldwide family had never heard of a marshmallow. Elena, who is originally from Spain, needed to ask about it when she checked into the chat room from London. It's hard to describe a real marshmallow, isn't it? At the Orlando seminar in January, the *kryon.org* team offered samples from a bowl of white, puffy marshmallows. Elena had traveled from London to Orlando and tried a "real" marshmallow for the first time.

Another page of considerable interest is the Scientific Answers section. Some of the ways Kryon teaches are in technical areas, and many of the things channeled have a strong connection to the science community today. In many cases, topics channeled relate well to the leading edge of recent discoveries. The *kryon.org* website has a page devoted to these interrelated items ranging from Tesla to time.

The Kryon Family Room website also has a guestbook to sign, a "Quote of the Week," links to the family in their personal websites, and a Food Court that offers recipes for great tasting and nutritional foods. As we continue to find delightful additions of benefit to the family, they will be added to the website.

A number of times, people have posted on the website in their native language because they were not comfortable in English, yet they wanted to communicate with the family. If those posts are in any of five languages, French, Spanish, German, Portuguese, or Italian, there is no problem. There is a link on the message board that connects with a translation program on the Internet. It's address is [http://babelfish.altavista.digital.com]. A paragraph or two of information from anyone in those five languages mentioned can be translated to English or back again to the needed language. It is amazing how well it works.

A week ago, a new member of the Kryon family found the website and wrote an E-mail message to me: <gary@kryon.org>. Here is the message:

"Hallo Gary! Leider verstehe ich kein Englisch und kann die texte nicht lesen. Ich fühle mich auch so alleine in der Schweiz. Kannst du mir Adressen geben? Ich will meine Gefühle mit euch teilen."

Now, what would you do if you received an e-mail like that? Use the translation program! This is what appeared:

"Hello, Gary! Unfortunately, I do not understand English and can write the text to read. I feel also so alone in Switzerland. Can you give me addresses? I want to divide my feelings with you."

It isn't perfect, but one can certainly get the idea. A response was prepared in English, translated to German, and returned.

When people first find Kryon, it may seem lonely until others are found who share similar interests. Voilà: the Synchronicity section. This segment of the website is divided into four parts for the purpose of meeting others: (1) a special friend or potential partner, (2) others of like mind, (3) a Kryon "kids" section, and (4) one for those who may have a joint interest in starting a business with someone of similar thinking and background. The business area and those of like mind are set up geographically. The special friend/potential partner category and the Kryon Kids category are worldwide.

Who runs these websites? The Kryon office is in charge of the *kryon.com* site. It is the commercial part of the Kryon Writings, and is also responsible for the Seminar Schedule—a listing that is constantly revised personally by Lee Carroll.

I am the webmaster on the *kryon.org* site. I created the site and make the changes as time goes on, but I also have the help of 37 other "Angels of the Website," plus the 68 language volunteers who speak 28 different languages to assist the family. There is so much happening that it takes a team of volunteers to run the show. There are nine angels of the message board, nine angels of the chat room, and the rest are working in the other areas of the site. Starting in January 1999, you will be able to recognize these "angels" at Kryon events anywhere in the world by the gold and white "www.kryon.org" ribbons on their name tags. All the angels are listed on the *kryon.org* team page that is accessed from the first page of the website.

The *kryon.org* site also has another international flavor. There are two segments of the site, one in French and one in Spanish, which have been created by two website angels, Philippe Proix in France and Arturo Castro Gutierrez in Venezuela. They have translated the same website information into their respective languages. Both Philippe and Arturo have done an excellent job in their sites.

If you are a "newbie" (which means that maybe you bought your computer yesterday and are now connecting the cables), how do you find the websites? First, you will need an Internet Service Provider. Often they are in the phone book under "Internet." As soon as you have connected to the Internet, fill in the web address [www.kryon.com] or [www.kryon.org] in the line called "location" or "netsite." On America Online, use the "open line" just to the right of the "Find" button. Push the "enter" key and whoooosh—there it is: the Kryon logo. Whichever Kryon site you have landed on gives you a chance to visit the other one as well.

Now that you have connected on-line, we welcome you to the Kryon websites! Look around. There is a lot to see and do. We are pleased to share our love and light.

Gary Liljegren

Kryon WebMaster
<gary@kryon.org>

The French Connection

Many readers might not be aware of the popularity of Kryon in France. French is the only language which has translated all the Kryon books (Ariane Publishing). In mid-1999, Kryon presented before 3,000 people in one meeting in Amneville in northern France. The revenues from that one meeting completely funded the first and largest printing of this Kryon book . That means that the French supplied the energy for this English version, even before they got their own version!

We salute the French, and their spiritual work for Europe and the World.

Get together for a personal afternoon or evening with Kryon and Lee Carroll...in the comfort of a cozy living room or community center with a small group of dedicated lightworkers. It's called *"At Home with Kryon,"* the latest venue for joining in the Kryon energy. The special meeting starts with an introduction and discussion by Lee Carroll regarding timely New Age topics, then it continues with individual questions and answers from the group. Next comes a live Kryon channelling! Group size is limited to 50 or 60 people. Often lasting up to five hours, it's an event you won't forget!

To sponsor an *"At Home with Kryon"* event in your home, please contact the Kryon office at 858/792-2990 - fax 858/759-2499, or email <kryonmeet@aol.com>. For a list of upcoming *"At Home with Kryon"* locations, please see our web site at [http://www.kryonqtly.com].

The *Kryon Quarterly* Magazine brings you timely information about our transformation into the New Age with four information-packed issues per year. It's filled with the latest Kryon channels and parables, science and medical news, reader questions, astrology, inner child features, how-to information about working with your New Age tools, upcoming seminar schedules and much more. Stay tuned to the latest news about these changing times by subscribing to the *Kryon Quarterly*. Just $24 for four issues; $40 for eight issues. (*Australia and New Zealand - see below**)

TO ORDER THE *KRYON QUARTERLY*:

- PHONE (credit card orders only): Call toll free 1-800-945-1286
- FAX (credit card orders only): Complete this order and fax to: (303) 642-1696
- EMAIL (credit card orders only): EMAIL all information contained in form below to: <Kryonqtly@aol.com>
- MAIL Complete coupon below, include check, money order or credit card information to: *Kryon Quarterly*, PO Box 7392, Golden, CO 80403 - Make checks payable to *Kryon Quarterly*.

Name ______________________________

Address ______________________________

City ____________________ State __________ Zip __________

Computer email address (optional): ____________________

❑ Four issues $24* OR ❑ Eight issues $40.00* CO residents add 4.2%

*US dollars. Orders outside US, please add $10 *per year* for shipping.

Payment: ❑ Check/M.O. ❑ MasterCard ❑ VISA

Credit Card Number: ____________________

Expiration Date: ____________________

Signature: ____________________ Phone: __________

* For Australia and New Zealand, call direct: 800-44-3200 <crystals@senet.com.au>

Would you like to be on the Kryon mailing list?

This list is used to inform interested people of Kryon workshops coming to their areas, new Kryon releases, and Kryon news in general. We don't sell or distribute our lists to anyone.

If you would like to be included, please simply drop a post card to us that says "LIST," and include your clearly printed name and address.

The Kryon Writings, Inc.

PMB 422
1155 Camino Del Mar
Del Mar, California 92014

Index

Index

Index

The Human Being

"Blessed is the Angel, the divine being from the other side of the veil who chooses to come to Earth for the benefit of all. Blessed is this one who hides awesome grandness within the frailty of Human biology. Blessed is this one who then elects to work through the process of duality, which is imposed upon him with his full permission. Therefore, blessed is the Human Being who carries this divinity within him.

Therefore,

blessed are each of you!"

Kryon Live Channelled Audio Tapes

- **Ascension in The New Age** - ISBN 1-888053-01-1 • $10.00
  Carlsbad, California - "Kryon describes what ascension really is in the new age. It might surprise you!"
- **Nine Ways to Raise the Planet's Vibration** - ISBN 1-888053-00-3 • $10.00
  Seattle, Washington - "Raising the planet's vibration is the goal of humanity! Find out what Kryon has to say about it."
- **Gifts and Tools of The New Age** - ISBN 1-888053-03-8 • $10.00
  Casper, Wyoming - "A very powerful channel. Better put on your sword, shield and armor for this one."
- **Co-Creation in The New Age** - ISBN 1-888053-04-6 • $10.00
  Portland, Oregon - "Tired of being swept around in life? Find out about co-creating your own reality. It is our right in this new age!"
- **Seven Responsibilities of The New Age** - ISBN 1-888053-02-X • $10.00
  Indianapolis, Indiana - "Responsibility? For what? Find out what Spirit tells us we are now in charge of...and what to do with it."

Music and Meditation

- **Crystal Singer Music Meditation Tape** - ISBN 0-96363-4-1-5 • $10.00
  Enjoy two soaring 17 minute musical meditations featuring the beautiful singing voice of Jan Tober.
- **Guided Meditations Tape** - ISBN 1-388053-05-4 • $10.00
  Jan presents two guided meditations similar to those delivered at each Kryon seminar throughout the United States and Canada, with beautiful Celtic harp accompaniment by Mark Geisler. **Side One: "Finding Your Sweet Spot"** **Side Two: "Divine Love"**
- **Color & Sound Meditation CD** - ISBN 1-888053-06-2 • $15.00
  A complete color/sound workshop — an exercise to balance and harmonize the Chakras. Jan guides us through the seven Chakra system using the enhancement of the ancient Tibetan signing bowls. **Side One: 30-min meditation** **Side Two: 12-min meditation**
  Available in English or French! - please specify

Kryon Books On Tape

Published by **AUDIO LITERATURE** *Read by Lee Carroll*

- **The End Times** - ISBN 1-57453-168-9
- **Don't Think Like A Human** - ISBN 1-57453-169-7
- **Alchemy Of The Human Spirit** - ISBN 1-57453-170-0

Each audio book contains two cassettes, 3 hours, abridged - $17.95

- **"The Parables of Kryon"** - *Read by Lee Carroll*
  Published by **Hay House** *and scored with music!* ISBN 1-56170-454-7 - $16.95
- **"The Journey Home"** ***Unabridged!*** - *Read by Lee Carroll*
  Published by **Hay House** - *a six tape set!* ISBN 1-56170-453-9 - $30.00
  (seven hour listening experience)

Books and tapes can be purchased in retail stores, by phone or Email
Credit cards welcome ~ 1-800-352-6657 ~ <kryonbooks@aol.com>

Kryon Book One: "The End Times"

Published by **The Kryon Writings, Inc.** ISBN 0-9636304-2-3 (White Cover) $12.00

"This read is a can't-put-it-down-til-the-last-page experience"

New Age Retailer - Washington

Kryon Book Two: "Don't Think Like A Human"

Published by **The Kryon Writings, Inc.** ISBN 0-9636304-0-7 (Blue Cover) $12.00

"The simple manner in which the material is presented makes this a highly accessible work for newcomers to Metaphysics"

Connecting Link - Magazine, Michigan

Kryon Book Three: "The Alchemy of The Human Spirit"

Published by **The Kryon Writings, Inc.** ISBN 0-9636304-8-2 (Fuchsia Cover) $14.00

"The words of Kryon are loving, peaceful and reassuring. There is a lot of great news"

The Light Connection - San Diego

Kryon Book Four: "The Parables of Kryon"

Published by **Hay House** ISBN 1-56170-364-8 $17.00 (hard cover - with illustrations)

"For anyone who is ready for the next evolutionary step, this information from Kryon is invaluable. It is both self-healing and planetary healing...Kryon really lets us know that all is well and we have work to do"

Louise L. Hay - Best-Selling Author

Kryon Book Five: "The Journey Home"

Published by **Hay House** ISBN 1-56170-552-7 $11.95 (soft cover)

"Lee Carroll has given us a well written book that flows like a mighty river. And that river takes us to places like truth, hope, destiny, awareness, and home!"

Richard Fuller - Metaphysical Reviews

Kryon Book Six: "Partnering with God"

Published by **The Kryon Writings, Inc.** ISBN 1-888053-10-0 (Green Cover) $14.00

"If you liked the original Kryon series, you are going to love this book! - Probably the most practical Kryon book yet. All 400 pages are packed with the love of God for humanity...a stirring read."

New Age Retailer - Washington

Kryon Book Seven: "Letters From Home"

Published by **The Kryon Writings, Inc.** ISBN 1-888053-12-7 (Purple Cover) $14.00

Books and tapes can be purchased in retail stores, by phone or Email
Credit cards welcome ~ 1-800-352-6657 ~ <kryonbooks@aol.com>